The Best
AMERICAN
ESSAYS
1996

GUEST EDITORS OF
THE BEST AMERICAN ESSAYS

The Best AMERICAN ESSAYS 1996

Edited and with an Introduction
by GEOFFREY C. WARD

ROBERT ATWAN
Series Editor

HOUGHTON MIFFLIN COMPANY
BOSTON • NEW YORK 1996

For information about this and other Houghton Mifflin trade and reference books
and multimedia products, visit The Bookstore at Houghton Mifflin on the World
Wide Web at http://www.hmco.com/trade/.

ISSN 0888-3742
ISBN 0-395-71757-4
ISBN 0-395-71756-6 (pbk.)

Printed in the United States of America
QUM 10 9 8 7 6 5 4 3 2 1

Contents

Foreword

THIS VOLUME marks the tenth anniversary of *The Best American Essays.*

When I began the series in 1985, the world was a slightly different place. I communicated with authors and publishers mainly by letter and phone; now I often rely on fax and e-mail. A first-class postage stamp cost 22 cents; overnight delivery was used only in special circumstances. PC meant a personal computer and my only CD was a certificate of deposit. Looking back over my correspondence, I see that no publisher's stationery listed a fax number. Information that sometimes took weeks to obtain I now have in a matter of minutes. For this year's collection I reviewed more periodicals and screened more essays than I had ever anticipated.

The series just happened to be launched in the midst of a digital revolution that is still in process and that is shaping our lives in unpredictable ways. I can recall in the early eighties proudly showing a friend my newly set-up home office: an IBM PC sporting *two* 5¼-inch floppy drives and 128K of memory; an electric typewriter that could interface as a "letter-quality" printer; a 1200-baud modem, a compact copier, a phone with a built-in answering machine (but with a separate automatic dialer), and a fax machine on the same line that spewed out a continuous roll of waxy paper. My friend was impressed and termed it, I distinctly remember, "the office of the future." That future lasted about five minutes.

All I have left is my stalwart copier; everything else was tossed into a dumpster before I moved and is now contributing to the geological future of the New Jersey meadowlands. Though I no longer have any such illusions about being "wired," and though this collection itself is still the result of clunky technology, there's no doubt that the series will be relying increasingly on electronic media, as more and more periodicals set up websites and on-line services. It's difficult to imagine certain magazines becoming obsolete (what will replace their glossy touch, perfumed pages, and polymorphous sex appeal?), but many others may begin to find more readers on-line than off. Perhaps *screening* essays will soon be the perfect term.

But what of the essays themselves? Will they be shaped in some McLuhanesque way by the new technologies? Will cyberspace breed new essayists and new kinds of essays? Will original, literary prose works begin appearing in underground sites without benefit of agents, editors, publishers, and prestige periodicals? Will young, struggling writers find a quicker and less stressful way to break into print? As voice and video become increasingly common, will we be entering a new age of graphic/audio texts that will dramatically alter the reading habits of a future generation? In 2020, as one commentator wondered, will book publishers as a trade be as obsolete as blacksmiths?

Predictions of a bookless future have, of course, been commonplace for decades, and there's good reason to be skeptical about the announced "end" of anything, whether it be books, literature, or history itself. When Bill Gates wanted to evangelize on America's electronic future, he didn't go on-line but produced an old-fashioned thirty-dollar hardcover book with a first printing of 800,000 copies. The first thing my twelve-year-old son did when he got the book, however, was run the inserted "companion interactive CD-ROM" that contained the complete text, multimedia hyperlinks, video demonstrations, and an audio interview with Gates. Unbelievers continually say that nobody wants to read a book on a screen, and for that reason alone they consider books to be irreplaceable. But for my son's generation, books may routinely be read on screen, a cozy lightweight "papery" screen you can pop a CD into, carry anywhere, and comfortably curl up with and read in the dark. Why not? The practical advantages will be tremendous, and I'll be able to lift his backpack.

The issue really isn't about the future of books but of reading, and since people were reading long before the paginated book was developed some five hundred years ago, my guess is that they'll be reading long after it has been radically transformed. It is hardly a coincidence that the essay was invented not long after the book, for we owe to the physical feature of books the personal essay's idiosyncratic and circuitous manner. Montaigne equipped his home office with one of the earliest book-lined studies, where he loved to spend his time *browsing*. His mind too mercurial to concentrate wholeheartedly on any one volume, he would "leaf through now one book, now another, without order and without plan, by disconnected fragments." An idea took hold; he began to write just the way he read. His medium became his message, and the personal essay was born.

It will be exciting to see what new shapes the American essay will assume ten years from now, when we're well past the millennium and "twentieth century" will no longer be synonymous with "modern." I expect to be surprised. When I started the series I was more certain about what an essay is than I am now, after reading well over two thousand essays and discussing the genre with various guest editors who viewed and evaluated it from so many different critical perspectives. Elizabeth Hardwick bravely agreed to launch the series with the 1986 volume, and today I find especially appropriate the opening words of her introduction: "The essay?"

The Best American Essays features a selection of the year's outstanding essays, essays of literary achievement that show an awareness of craft and a forcefulness of thought. Hundreds of essays are gathered annually from a wide variety of national and regional publications. These essays are then screened and approximately one hundred are turned over to a distinguished guest editor, who may add a few personal discoveries and who makes the final selections.

To qualify for selection, the essays must be works of respectable literary quality, intended as fully developed, independent essays (not excerpts) on subjects of general interest (not specialized scholarship), originally written in English (or translated by the author) for publication in an American periodical during the calendar year. Periodicals that want to make sure their contributors will be considered each year should include the series on their complimentary subscription list (Robert Atwan, Series Editor, *The Best American Essays*, P.O. Box 220, Readville, MA 02137-9998).

For this tenth anniversary volume, I'd like to thank all of the fine writers who contributed — both as essayists and as guest editors — to making this series an annual literary event. Since the first volume, a number of people who appeared in these pages are no longer with us: Donald Barthelme, Harold Brodkey, Joseph Brodsky, Anatole Broyard, Anthony Burgess, Stanley Elkin, Robert Fitzgerald, Paul Horgan, Randy Shilts, and Lewis Thomas. They are sorely missed. I greatly appreciate the efforts of the Houghton Mifflin editorial and production staff — Janet Silver, Wendy Holt, Sandra Riley, Mindy Keskinen, and Larry Cooper — for their unflagging attention to the incessant details of an annual book. Having moved to the Boston area with my family in the midst of this year's editorial work, I was especially fortunate to find a spectacularly capable assistant, Matthew Howard, who helped me in innumerable ways and to whom I am deeply indebted.

It was a singular privilege to work with Geoffrey C. Ward, whose historical books, essays, and *American Heritage* columns I've admired for years. In assembling one of the most culturally diverse and "extroverted" volumes in the series, he deliberately calls attention to a side of the essay that's often overlooked: its outward reach to a world far larger than the Self.

R.A.

Introduction

SOME YEARS BACK, when one of my brother Andrew's funniest essays was anthologized in a college text on humor, it was accompanied by a series of earnest questions, aimed at explaining to students just what the author must have had in mind: "Since satire is meant to edify as well as amuse, what lessons does Andrew Ward mean to teach us?" "What are the stylistic clues that let us know he's trying to make us laugh?" "Just what is the *point* of his essay?" That sort of thing. Andy took the test — and failed.

I suspect I'll do no better trying to explain why I chose the essays that make up this volume. Jamaica Kincaid, last year's guest editor, put it as well as anyone has: her choices, she wrote, simply "pleased me, which is to say that I loved reading them and had that childish pleasure while reading them that everything else apart from reading was labor."

The pieces included here gave me precisely the same childish pleasure — and were chosen for just that reason. There is no discernible theme; subjects range from owls to Alice in Wonderland, Michelangelo to Michael Jackson, the joy of napping to the horror of very nearly being murdered by a madman. Nor is there any special length or distinctive style; the roster includes sprinters and marathoners, storytellers and ruminators, introspectives as well as extroverts.

In fact it's probably easier to say what these essays are not than what they are. To begin with, they were not written by cronies: of the twenty-two gifted men and women represented here, I'm embarrassed to admit that I'd never even heard of five before beginning to read their work, and still have met only four. There are no self-consciously showy writers among them, either: no one preens in these pages; substance is never sacrificed in the interest of strutting one's stuff. Nor do any of these writers feel called upon to complain about the alleged rigors of the writer's life. (The fact that perfect strangers are willing actually to pay to read what we rattle out has always seemed to me just short of miraculous; whining will surely queer the deal.)

Objectivity in editing is at least as rare as it is in any other field. My own memories, my own prejudices and enthusiasms, undoubtedly — if unconsciously — influenced at least some of my choices, and it seems only fair to state them for the record.

The shock of recognition is far greater if that recognition is literal, after all, and several of these essays evoke places familiar to me and mine. When my children come to visit us in Manhattan from their homes in Brooklyn, for example, they do so underground, aboard the same F train that whipped Ian Frazier back and forth between the boroughs; it was impossible, riding along with him, not to think that they may sometimes have been among his fellow passengers. My wife grew up in western New York, and its odd, blasted landscape — "fields of spiky grass, across outpourings of shale as steeply angled as stairs" — continues to haunt her just as it clearly haunts Joyce Carol Oates. I spent part of my own boyhood in New Delhi, and happen to have been there again in 1984 within a few weeks of the harrowing riots in which Amitav Ghosh manages to discover such unexpected and desperately needed hope.

Most of my own writing has been in the fields of history and biography, and it is perhaps inevitable that the past plays a large part in this collection: Jane Brox struggles to understand a nightmare through which her father lived more than seventy years ago; William Styron and Edward Hoagland vividly recall nightmares of their own; while Julie Baumgold hoards hundreds of telling details to evoke the many meanings of Elvis.

I've had my say elsewhere on the folly of presenting the past as if it were merely a more primitive version of the present, of trying to make over our ancestors into people precisely like ourselves. That may account in part for my special affection for the remark-

ably clear-eyed essay with which this book begins. In it, Joan Acocella single-handedly restores to the novelist Willa Cather something of the human complexity that two generations of academic
critics had stripped from her in order to further trendy agendas
that would have both appalled and bewildered Cather herself.

I never seem to tire of hearing that things are not as simple as
they seem, which may in part explain why so many surprises, large
and small, lurk in this collection. Gerald Early examines the literature of Afrocentrism, for example, and finds in its painful search
for identity a quintessentially American quest; William Cronon
dares us to reexamine the whole idea of wilderness; Gordon Grice
discovers in the black widow spider's exquisite web evidence *against*
the existence of a benevolent, designing God. And who could have
imagined that a few moments spent leafing through the sort of
glossy gift catalogues that appear in drifts on my dining room table
every morning when the mail comes would send Nicholson Baker
careening hilariously through the whole history of the printed
word?

It's time now for me to get out of the way and let all of these writers
— as well as their equally able but here unsung colleagues — speak
for themselves. I envy you the chance to read these pieces for the
first time, to discover for yourselves the familiar in the unfamiliar
— and to be surprised.

GEOFFREY C. WARD

JOAN ACOCELLA

Cather and the Academy

FROM THE NEW YORKER

NEAR THE END of her 1915 novel *The Song of the Lark,* Willa Cather serves up what is probably the most unsentimental betrothal scene in all Western fiction. Fred Ottenburg, who has been pursuing Thea Kronborg for many years, tells her he has pretty much given up on her. Thea, a great opera singer, says she doesn't blame him one bit:

> I don't see why anybody wants to marry an artist, anyhow. I remember Ray Kennedy [another suitor] used to say he didn't see how any woman could marry a gambler, for she would only be marrying what the game left. . . . Who marries who is a small matter, after all. But you've cared longer and more than anybody else, and I'd like to have somebody human to make a report to once in a while. If you're not interested, I'll do my best, anyhow.

She then excuses herself. Her car is waiting. She's singing Sieglinde on Friday, and she has to get her rest.

This scene is a kind of turning point in the history of literature. "Who marries who is a small matter, after all," Thea says. In the bulk of literature about women, who marries whom — or, at least, who goes to bed with whom — is not simply not a small matter; it is the subject. From Penelope and Dido on down to Anna Karenina, a woman might be a great soul — brave, intelligent, fine-minded — but only within the confines of a drama of marriage or adultery, only in relation to love. What if portrayals of men had been similarly restricted? This is a question that Virginia Woolf took up in *A Room of One's Own:*

Suppose . . . that men were only represented in literature as the
lovers of women, and were never the friends of men, soldiers, thinkers,
dreamers; how few parts in the plays of Shakespeare could be allotted
to them; how literature would suffer! We might perhaps have most of
Othello; and a good deal of Antony; but no Caesar, no Brutus, no
Hamlet, no Lear, no Jaques — literature would be incredibly impoverished, as indeed literature is impoverished beyond our counting by the
doors that have been shut upon women.

That was published in 1929. Fourteen years earlier, Cather had
quietly seceded from the tradition. *The Song of the Lark* contains
many passionate scenes — eagles shooting across the sky, sunrises
like earthquakes — but the passion is about Thea's work life, not
her love life. This book, to my knowledge, is the first really serious
female *Künstlerroman,* the first portrait-of-the-artist-as-a-young-wom-
an in which the woman's artistic development is the whole story,
with sex an incidental matter — as incidental, for example, as it
is in Joyce's *Portrait of the Artist as a Young Man,* which was published in the same year. Sex is so unimportant in Cather's novel
that it doesn't even merit a repudiation. In the end, Thea marries
Fred, but this is reported so casually that some readers actually
miss it.

Thea takes for herself a man's privilege: to have a sex — indeed,
to have sex (she slept with Fred years before the betrothal) — and
yet not to make this fact the boundary of her imagination. She is
able to do so because, basically, that is what her creator did. Not
only did Cather make her work her life; she decided she had the
right to, and therefore wasted no energy protesting against the
forces that might have stood in her way. She just opened the door
and walked through it. For this lordly action, she has been made
to pay, mostly by women.

Cather is traditionally regarded as the elegist of the pioneer period, the repository of what America thinks of as its early, true-grit
triumphs. She did write three novels — the so-called prairie trilogy,
all based on her childhood in Nebraska — that can be read that
way. In the 1913 *O Pioneers!,* a young Swedish immigrant, Alexandra Bergson, raises a blooming farm out of the barren Nebraska
plain. Then comes *The Song of the Lark,* in which Thea, another
Swede, stuck in another prairie town, dreams of becoming an artist

and actually makes it. In the beloved *My Ántonia* (1918), the struggle is more bitter and the rewards are fewer, but the heroine — a Czech girl this time — is still given what you could call a happy ending.

Those who see Cather as the bard of prairie gumption often forget, however, that she did not originally come from the prairie, and that her removal there was shattering to her. She was born on a sheep farm in the Shenandoah Valley in 1873, at the beginning of what was to be the flood tide of westward expansion. In the 1880s, more than a million people packed up their households and moved to the plains of America's Midwest. In 1883, the Cather family joined them. At age nine, Cather was "jerked away" (her words) from the snug comforts of Virginia's hills and valleys and dropped down onto the flat plain of Nebraska — "a country," she later recalled, "as bare as a piece of sheet iron." She seems to have felt stripped, skinned. "It was a kind of erasure of personality," she said. She soon came to love Nebraska, but she never forgot the trauma of her transplantation. We find it recalled at the beginning of *My Ántonia*, where Jim Burden, a ten-year-old boy, journeys by train from Virginia to Nebraska, just as Cather did. He is not only exiled but orphaned, and is going to live with his grandparents. The train finally arrives, and Jim is packed into the back of a cart, which then takes off across the plain:

> I tried to go to sleep, but the jolting made me bite my tongue. . . . Cautiously I slipped from under the buffalo hide, got up on my knees and peered over the side of the wagon. There seemed to be nothing to see; no fences, no creeks or trees, no hills or fields. If there was a road, I could not make it out in the faint starlight. There was nothing but land: not a country at all, but the material out of which countries are made. . . . I had the feeling that the world was left behind, that we had got over the edge of it, and were outside man's jurisdiction. I had never before looked up at the sky when there was not a familiar mountain ridge against it. But this was the complete dome of heaven, all there was of it. I did not believe that my dead father and mother were watching me from up there; they would still be looking for me at the sheepfold down by the creek, or along the white road that led to the mountain pastures. I had left even their spirits behind me. The wagon jolted on, carrying me I knew not whither. I don't think I was homesick. If we never arrived anywhere, it did not matter. Between that

earth and that sky I felt erased, blotted out. I did not say my prayers
that night: here, I felt, what would be would be.

To readers of the early-twentieth-century novel, this should be
a familiar scene: the human soul facing a great emptiness and
feeling that prayers will no longer be of use. Cather came by
it honestly, and it became the pattern of her imagination. The
two writers who probably influenced her most, Virgil and Henry
James, were both poets of exile, and almost all the major characters
in her novels are exiles — people trying to make their way in circumstances strange to them. Hence the inexpressible sadness of
Cather's work. Thea Kronborg becomes an artist, but in the process her life empties out. She is translated; she becomes only her
art.

The Nebraska plain seems to have turned Cather into a Platon-
ist. She saw human beings as permanently exiled from some realm
of happiness which they nevertheless remembered and kept in
view. Again and again in her work, she replays Plato's cave allegory.
She is always lighting things up — a tree, a plow — and then telling
us that the thing is unimportant, that only the light is real. The
most terrible instance is the scene in *O Pioneers!* where Alexandra's
brother Emil goes for the last time to meet Marie, the woman he
loves. They have sworn off each other (she is married), but Emil
weakens and goes back to Marie's orchard once more:

> Long fingers of light reached through the apple branches as through
> a net; the orchard was riddled and shot with gold; light was the reality,
> the trees were merely interferences that reflected and refracted light.
> Emil went softly down between the cherry trees.

He finds Marie and gathers her in his arms. A few minutes later,
her husband, spying them through a hedge, raises his .405 Winchester and fills them full of bullets.

Such things are not rare in Cather. A farmer who has lost his
hogs to cholera goes home quietly and strangles himself. A hobo
comes upon a group of people threshing in a field and, waving
gaily at them, throws himself into the threshing machine. These
events are described almost laconically — "The machine ain't
never worked right since," says a witness to the hobo's suicide —
so that their very clarity is baffling. And all the while that Cather
is describing life's terrors she never stops asserting its beauties: the

fingers of light, the orchard shot with gold. The dream is still there; we just can't have it. Jim Burden's arrival in Nebraska is recounted with the same lethal modesty. A child and, by extension, the rest of humanity are cast out into coldness, and the prose swells briefly to tell us this: "Between that earth and that sky . . ." But then it contracts again, Jim presumably falls asleep, and the wagon goes on bumping across the darkling plain.

Cather came from an ordinary country family. Her mother, Jennie, was a spirited, imperious woman who, when she thought it necessary, disciplined her children with a rawhide whip. The father, Charles, was the opposite — tenderhearted, unassertive. In Virginia, he made little leather shoes for his favorite sheepdog, so the dog wouldn't cut her feet on the rocks in the pasture. When he went to drive the sheep back into the fold at night, he often carried Willa, his first child, with him.

In Nebraska, the Cathers settled in the town of Red Cloud, named for the chief of the Sioux who had occupied the land there before the westward expansion. Charles set up a small farm-loans and insurance office, and the family — by then numbering nine and soon to increase — was packed into a seven-room rented house a few blocks away.

No money, no privacy, no great things around her, just a dusty prairie town (population about 1,200), a mother usually either sick or pregnant, and a pack of noisy little brothers and sisters: these might seem unpromising circumstances for the development of an artist, but in fact Red Cloud was a bonanza for Cather. She was one of those genius children — a showoff, an explosion, a pest. She dogged the footsteps of adults, particularly men. There was an old German piano teacher — one of the town drunks — who never got her to do her scales but sat for hours answering her questions about music. She befriended both the local doctors and rode with them, conversing about science, as they went on their rounds. (One of them let her administer the chloroform when he had to amputate a boy's leg.) But the most important of her friendships was with an Englishman named William Ducker, a clerk in the town's dry-goods store and a passionate reader of ancient literature. Starting around age thirteen, Cather studied Latin and Greek with Ducker. Together they read Virgil, Ovid, the

Iliad, and the odes of Anacreon, and they discussed the big questions: evolution, religion, good and evil. In her room at night
Cather devoured books on her own: Shakespeare, Byron, Tolstoy,
adventure novels, and the standard nineteenth-century classics —
Scott, Dickens, Thackeray, Poe, Hawthorne, Ruskin, Emerson, Carlyle.

Did she feel hampered by being a girl? In later years, she
brushed this question aside: "The fact that I was a girl never damaged my ambitions to be a pope or an emperor." But she had eyes.
She saw that the people she admired — the people who were cur-
ing the sick and reading Anacreon — were men. And so, at fourteen, Cather went to the barber and got a crew cut. She began
dressing like a man. She still wore skirts, but the rest of her cos-
tume was as masculine as she could make it: jackets, suspenders, a
derby. She took to signing her name "William Cather, Jr." or
"William Cather, M.D." In those days, girls kept albums in which
friends recorded their favorite color, what they would take to a
desert island, and so forth. The album of one of Cather's friends
survives, with an entry completed by William Cather, M.D., in
1888. Under the trait she most admired in women she wrote "flirting." The trait she most admired in men was "an original mind."
Her idea of perfect misery was doing needlework; her idea of
perfect happiness was "amputating limbs." If stranded on a desert
island, what she would most want was "pants and coat." Her ambition in life was "to be an M.D."

Of all the episodes in Cather's childhood, this so-called William
Cather period is the one that is the most exclaimed over today.
But what Cather did is not so remarkable. Her male impersonation
began and ended with adolescence, the period in which, at that
time, females were taught their proper place. How surprising is it
that a brilliant and ambitious girl should have rejected the lesson?
By this time, she may well have read *Daniel Deronda* and encountered Daniel's mother's words: "You may try — but you can never
imagine what it is to have a man's force of genius in you, and yet
to suffer the slavery of being a girl." In any case, she would certainly have read *Little Women,* where Jo, too, has her hair cut off
and, in the very first pages of the novel, declares, "I can't get over
my disappointment in not being a boy." Those were the days before
such sentiments placed one under suspicion of being a lesbian. Jo

just wants to have what she sees as fun and freedom, and so, presumably, did Cather.

Upon finishing high school, she again did something strange: she insisted on going to college. The family had no money, but she was desperate to go. The funds were borrowed, and Cather went off to Lincoln, home of the University of Nebraska. The following spring, for her English class, she wrote a theme on Thomas Carlyle which so impressed her teacher that, behind her back, he submitted it to Lincoln's foremost newspaper, the *Nebraska State Journal*. One day soon afterward, Cather found herself in print. The effect, she later said, was "hypnotic." She was no longer going to be a doctor; she was going to be a writer. Soon she became a regular columnist for the *State Journal*, writing mainly on theater. Between 1893 and 1896, during most of which time she was carrying a full load of courses at the university, she published nearly half a million words of criticism.

Between the publication of Cather's first essay and that of her first novel lies a gulf of twenty years: her apprenticeship. Many of her biographers try to get through it hurriedly, for it is unheroic material. She is no longer the marvelous child and not yet the marvelous novelist, but for a long time — too long a time, as with so many women artists — she was a drudge, with inky fingers and no money, and bored out of her mind. She graduated from college. She moved to Pittsburgh, then to New York. She published a book of poems and a book of stories, but mostly she worked for newspapers and magazines. She met the local-colorist writer Sarah Orne Jewett, then in her late fifties, to whom she confided her frustrations and showed her stories, many of them poor imitations of Henry James. Jewett told her to get serious — stop doing magazine work, stop copying James — and then died before she could help her any further.

These were hard years, but they contained an adventure — the development of Cather's ideas about art. She had a deep vein of primitivism: she believed in energy, in the fiery mysteries of the earth. Accordingly, she despised the more decadent aspects of the fin de siècle in which she lived: languor, daintiness, "charm." Yet she was of her time, and many of her principles were consistent with the wrecked romanticism of the French Symbolist poets. Like them, she viewed art as a religion. Like them, she felt that literature should focus not on reality but on "something else" — some ineffable emotional truth lying between the mind and the world — and should invoke it by subtle, indirect means. She began developing an austere, pared-down style, a kind of writing that would not so much express things as contain them. Years later, in "The Novel Démeublé," her best-known critical essay, she spelled out her guiding principle:

> Whatever is felt upon the page without being specifically named there — that, one might say, is created. It is the inexplicable presence of the thing not named, of the overtone divined by the ear but not heard by it, the verbal mood, the emotional aura of the fact or the thing or the deed, that gives high quality to the novel or the drama, as well as to poetry itself.

"The thing not named" — Mallarmé, in a famous statement, had pointed to the same ideal. "To name something is to destroy three-quarters of the pleasure of poetry," he wrote; the goal was to "evoke something little by little, in order to show a state of the soul." So Cather took the principles of a bunch of poets who sat around Paris drinking absinthe, and applied them to immigrant farmers battling horse colic on a Nebraska prairie. It is one of the stranger conjunctions in the history of literature, but, like other marriages of realism and Symbolism in the early twentieth century (Proust's, for example), it worked beautifully. In 1912, at the age of thirty-eight, Cather finally published her first novel, *Alexander's Bridge*. It was a dud — another Henry James imitation, a tale of adultery among the Boston smart set. She disliked it the minute it came out. But instead of losing heart she went back to her desk, switched gears entirely — from Boston to Nebraska, from imitation to autobiography — and, in a five-year lather of productivity (*O Pioneers!*, *The Song of the Lark*, *My Ántonia*), she found herself. And now she gained the attention of the critics.

Today's literary critics, in defense of their tendentiously political approach, often claim that the criticism of earlier periods was political, too, but in a hidden way. This was certainly true in Cather's case: again and again, she was extolled or condemned for her subject matter. In the 1910s, a rising group of young critics, led by H. L. Mencken, was calling for a new kind of fiction. These critics were tired of well-made plots about genteel Bostonians coping with suppressed emotions. They wanted novels about ordinary people — poor people, people outside the cities — experiencing "real" emotions and expressing them in plain American language. The naturalists, especially Dreiser, fit this bill; so, shortly afterward, would Sherwood Anderson and Sinclair Lewis. And so did Cather, with her farmers. She herself, in choosing this subject, probably had no political purpose in mind. She was simply writing about what she knew best. Nevertheless, it was the farmers who made her famous. Mencken, a notoriously disparaging critic, placed her in the front rank of American novelists. In *My Ántonia,* he wrote, she had taken a story of "poor peasants" and made of it "the eternal tragedy of man." Other critics took up her cause, and for the same reason — her broadening of subject matter. The beauty of her prose was also noticed, but that, too, was seen as a political virtue: her language was "authentic," not from Boston. Cather had unwittingly walked into a fight, and she was on the right side.

Not for long. Flushed by the success of her prairie novels, she decided to try a war novel. The First World War had just ended. Among the dead was a cousin of hers, and in her new book, *One of Ours* (1922), he became the model for Claude, a young farm boy who dreams of doing "something splendid" but can find no place for himself in the money-grubbing Midwest of the post-pioneer period. When the war breaks out, Claude enlists, and on the battlefields of France he discovers that in fact life is not all "cunning and prudence" — that "men could still die for an idea." Soon afterward, he does so.

One of Ours is a good novel and a bad novel in one. The first half, the Nebraska half, is superb. Nowhere else in Cather are the beauty of the world and its capacity to disappoint balanced with such mastery. The problems come in the second half: Claude's transformation from dismayed farm boy into valiant infantryman is too quick, unreal. And Cather seems never to have made up her mind about the war. Sometimes, as in Claude's dying-for-an-idea epiphany, she seems to believe in it; elsewhere, no. She vacillated.

For many critics, however, the problem was not that she vacillated but that she could even for a moment have viewed the First

World War in a heroic light. John Dos Passos's *Three Soldiers* was published in 1921, and E. E. Cummings's *The Enormous Room* in 1922, both of them vividly detailing the absurdity and butchery of the war. Then came *One of Ours*, with fresh-faced Claude dying for an idea. The critics immediately went on the attack. In *Vanity Fair* Edmund Wilson pronounced the book "a pretty flat failure," and he asked, "Can H. L. Mencken have been mistaken when he decided that Willa Cather was a great novelist?" Mencken himself turned on the book with fury, claiming that Cather's idea of war was basically that of "the standard model of lady novelist."

As for the middlebrow reviewers, many of them praised the book highly; they were glad to hear that the war was not what Dos Passos had said. Probably for the same reason, *One of Ours* became a bestseller and won the Pulitzer Prize — a reception that merely redoubled the scorn of the younger literati. In 1923, Ernest Hemingway wrote to Edmund Wilson:

> E. E. Cummings' *Enormous Room* was the best book published last year that I read. Somebody told me it was a flop. Then look at *One of Ours*. Prize, big sale, people taking it seriously. You were in the war weren't you? Wasn't that last scene in the lines wonderful? Do you know where it came from? The battle scene in *Birth of a Nation*. I identified episode after episode. Catherized. Poor woman she had to get her war experience somewhere.

The thing to notice is the condescension: "poor woman." Hemingway and Wilson were young at the time — Wilson twenty-eight, Hemingway twenty-four. But within a few years these two men would dominate the American literary vanguard — Hemingway in charge of fiction, Wilson in charge of criticism — and Cather would have no place in their world.

Cather was deeply wounded by the reviews of *One of Ours*, and they precipitated a crisis that had been building in her mind for several years. In *O Pioneers!* and *The Song of the Lark* she had written of victory, female victory: adolescent girls in dirt towns dreaming of doing something great and actually managing it — a subject not unrelated to her own life. Then she stopped believing in victory. Various theories have been advanced for this change of heart, but do we need a theory to explain why a person in her late forties might begin suspecting that the race is not to the swift? For a while, she tried to pretend otherwise. Hence the sentimental endings of *My Ántonia* and *One of Ours*. But then she stopped pretending. She accepted the loss, steered into it, and entered her great middle period, her tragic period.

It begins with the fragrant *A Lost Lady* (1923), in which a young man falls platonically in love with a beautiful woman who ultimately dashes his ideals. Next comes *The Professor's House* (1925), in which a man, in the *normal* course of things, loses everything he lived for, almost succeeds in killing himself, and then decides that he will simply live with nothing to live for. After this she writes *My Mortal Enemy* (1926), a slim, cold novella about the failure of romantic love. Finally, in 1927, Cather publishes *Death Comes for the Archbishop*, in which all these hard principles are still in force but are rendered benign by the religious faith of the protagonists, who are priests. Each of the four novels makes the same point: to desire something is to have as much of it as you will ever have. The mind dreams; life mocks the dream. (Or, in the best case, the dream is fulfilled — the archbishop builds his cathedral — and then the person is left with no dreams.) The only real life is in the imagination, in desire and memory. This is the same point that Proust was making, at around the same time. Cather makes it unflinchingly, and moves to the height of her powers. Of the four novels, *Death Comes for the Archbishop* is the most celebrated, and perhaps justly — it is a nearly perfect piece of writing. But *The Professor's House*, Cather's most profound book, has never received the praise it deserves, partly, I think, because it tells such a terrifying story, one that, as Doris Grumbach has written, "impresses the mature reader as dangerously threatening to his own self-possession."

When these books were published, however, none of them got the praise they deserved. By the mid-twenties, the literary terrain had shifted. Mencken and his cohort were no longer calling the shots. Wilson and his cohort were, and to them Cather was simply old-fashioned. What these people wanted was novels that would mirror their postwar disillusionment, the way *The Great Gatsby* and *The Sun Also Rises* did. They wanted experimentalism and subjectivity — James Joyce, Virginia Woolf. And they wouldn't have minded something about life in the city, about cars and gin and sex. Meanwhile, Cather kept on giving them stories about noble-minded people

living in small towns, often in the past. She did not examine her
characters' stream of consciousness or, for the most part, their
sexual activity. She examined their ideals, which she took seriously.
And she wrote about them in prose that looked decidedly nonex-
perimental — pure, classical, like something carved from white
marble.

A Lost Lady received some compliments from the younger reviewers, but their tone was often belittling. "A charming sketch,"
Wilson called this dark book. A few years later, lining up the current writers in an essay for *The New Republic,* he gave Cather just a
few brief mentions, one of which was "Willa Cather is a good
craftsman, but she is usually rather dull." Other critics admired
her more, but they tended to apologize for her, as if she were
some old-maid aunt who had suffered disappointments. In the *San
Francisco Examiner,* Tom Outland, the younger, second hero of
The Professor's House, was described as "a spinster school teacher's
dream of a Zane Grey cowboy."

Modern Cather critics often blame misogyny for these attacks,
but Cather's age was probably as important as her sex. The people
by and against whom she was being measured — Wilson, Hemingway, Fitzgerald, Dos Passos — were all more than twenty years
younger than she. She was old enough to be their mother. They
grew up in the twentieth century, she in the nineteenth. Cather
could never be mistaken for a nineteenth-century writer: her austere style is part of modernist classicism, her tragic vision part of
modernist pessimism. But the nobility of her characters and the
privacy she allows them are an inheritance from the nineteenth
century, and it did not go down well in the twenties, a decade
determined to throw off the past. Furthermore, Cather looked and
acted her age. She lived in Greenwich Village, but she had no contact with the partisans of Freud, Marx, and free verse who constituted Village bohemia in those days. Did they see her from their
cafés as she marched off every morning to do her grocery shopping at the Jefferson Market? Probably not. They wouldn't have
been up yet.

If she was condescended to in the twenties, in the thirties she
was attacked head on, for by then the literary scene had changed
again. The best young critics were mostly Marxists, or at least
convinced leftists, and to them Cather's tragic vision was a political

affront. She saw the wreck of the American dream: how could she analyze it as the operation of a timeless principle — something that must always occur — when it was clearly just a matter of modern economics? To quote *The New Republic*, she acted as if "mass production and technological unemployment and cyclical depressions and the struggle between the classes did not exist." Indeed, as others (Lionel Trilling, Clifton Fadiman) complained, she acted as if the *present* did not exist. Sensitive young men mooning around in nineteenth-century Nebraska, old priests riding their mules through nineteenth-century New Mexico: Were modern readers supposed to care about this? asked Granville Hicks in a 1933 essay. "Does it touch our lives?" No, Hicks said, it was simply "supine romanticism," harmless stuff that, as another critic put it, "could be read in schools and women's clubs."

If they despised her, why did they go on writing about her? Because she was so popular. Avant-gardes rarely waste any affection on artists whom the public prefers to them, and throughout the thirties, even though her work was becoming uneven, Cather remained one of America's best-loved writers. *Shadows on the Rock* (1931) was the most widely read novel in the United States in the year following its publication. *Lucy Gayheart*, the next book, was also a bestseller. Universities gave her honorary doctorates. *Time* put her on its cover. And the regular book reviewers generally praised her.

Others did more than praise her. The real shame of the left-wing assault on Cather in the thirties is not that it removed her from serious consideration by some of the best minds (Wilson, Trilling) but that it polarized the discussion of her work. The more she was senselessly attacked by the left, the more she was senselessly exalted by the right, and used as a stick to beat the left — actually, to beat anything that the right disliked. Experimental literature, for example. In the words of *Catholic World*, Cather's work was a rebuke to the "crude realism, Freudism, inchoate prose, shallow philosophy," and other vices that dominated modern fiction. Other Catholic magazines became her champions as well. To these journals, Cather, though an Episcopalian, was an honorary Catholic, and her books were Catholic books, radiating "a living light, like candles on an altar" *(Commonweal)*. With friends like these, it was not hard for Cather to find enemies.

Eventually she, too, entered the fray. In her politics, Cather *was* a conservative. She hated Roosevelt and the New Deal and big government. She also hated political art. (The artist's mission, she wrote, "is not to clean the Augean stables; he had better join the Salvation Army if he wants to do that.") Now she began to sound not just conservative but reactionary. When, in 1936, she published a collection of her literary essays, she entitled it *Not Under Forty*, meaning, as she explained in the preface, that people under forty should not bother to read it, because they wouldn't find anything interesting in it. She reiterated the point later in the book, in an essay on Sarah Orne Jewett:

> Imagine a young man, or woman, born in New York City, educated at a New York university, violently inoculated with Freud, hurried into journalism, knowing no more about New England country people (or country folk anywhere) than he has caught from motor trips or observed from summer hotels: what is there for him in "The Country of the Pointed Firs"?

As Cather saw it, Jewett's universe, and her own, had been cast into shadow; the world had been taken over by Freudians, journalists, body snatchers. This reply to her critics drew prompt rejoinders. In *The New Republic* Trilling summarized her views as merely a "defense of gentility."

Cather now withdrew from the public eye. She also restricted the public's view of her work. Paperback editions, Viking Portables, anthology requests, radio readings, movie deals, play deals — she refused them. At one point, Alfred A. Knopf, her publisher, got a six-figure offer from Hollywood for one of her books, but he didn't have the courage to mention it to her. In her will, too, she forbade the presentation of her work in any medium other than print. (It is only because her copyrights are now expiring that we have recently had TV movies of *O Pioneers!* and *My Ántonia*, both of them everything Cather might have feared.) She developed a mania for privacy. When she checked into a hospital — indeed, when she called a beauty parlor — she used a false name. When friends died, she asked the survivors to send her letters back, and she burned them. She also put a clause in her will barring anyone from quoting in print any of the letters that had escaped her incinerator.

Her old age, to all appearances, was wretched. In 1940 she

published one more novel, *Sapphira and the Slave Girl.* Then she developed chronic tendinitis in her right hand, and her productivity dwindled to almost nothing. She started a new novel, set in fourteenth-century Avignon. Entitled *Hard Punishments,* it was to be about two boys, one with his hands paralyzed, one with his tongue cut out — a reflection, no doubt, of how she saw herself at this time. Eventually she put the book aside. One day in 1947 she woke up from her afternoon nap, complained of a headache, and died of a cerebral hemorrhage. The obituary in *The Nation* described her as a minor novelist, "remote from the talents and problems of the past two anxious decades."

Cather, of course, was not the only writer harmed by the politicizing of criticism in the thirties. Faulkner was repeatedly bashed by the left. Joyce and Eliot were reproached for being too difficult and therefore of no use in the class struggle. Others besides Cather — Thornton Wilder, for one — suffered not only the abuse of the left but the deadly kiss of the right. What really suffered, however, was literary discussion, which was less and less about literature, and more and more about whose-side-are-you-on. Cather's is merely a representative case, and a sad one. She wrote twelve novels, most of them about the great subject of early-twentieth-century literature — the gulf between the mind and the world — and they were judged by her most energetic critics according to whether they embraced or opposed the struggle of industrial workers in the cities.

In the years following Cather's death, her admirers gathered up her abused corpse and took it back to their fort, while the rest of the critical establishment forgot about her. Important books were published on American literature, and her name did not appear in them. The monumental third edition of *The Literary History of the United States* (1963) devoted four of its fifteen hundred pages to her.

Still, there was a small community of scholars who went on writing about her. The first biographies came out — short, respectful, unpsychoanalytic studies. (One of these, E. K. Brown's 1953 *Willa Cather,* is still the best introduction to her, because of its excellent glosses on the novels. It is in print.) Other scholars did archival work, reprinting Cather's journalism and her early stories.

In 1955, a group of people in Red Cloud established the Willa Cather Pioneer Memorial foundation. As their exhibition space they chose the empty second floor of the Red Cloud movie house, where they assembled whatever relics they could find and installed them behind chicken wire. The Cather exhibit shared its space with the taxidermy collection of one of the board members.

The Cather criticism of the fifties and sixties was correspondingly taxidermic. These were years dominated by the New Criticism, which was concerned primarily with formal complexities in literature. But Cather's prose seemed to the New Critics to have no formal complexities, so they largely ignored her. Those people who wrote about her usually focused not on her style but on her content — her values, which they decided were transcendent, spiritual, and reassuring. Did the happy ending of *My Ántonia* seem a little desperate, patched together? Not at all. It was just fine for Ántonia, at the end of that sad book, to be baking *kolaches* in her cozy kitchen; she was a symbol of "calm and faithful endurance" (James E. Miller, Jr., *American Quarterly*, 1958), of "the value of human experience" (Terence Martin, *PMLA*, 1969). What about *The Professor's House,* in which Professor St. Peter, having failed to kill himself, decides that he will just "live without delight" — that is, live an empty life? Surely there was something discomforting here? No. *The Professor's House* was a book about the "Christian transcendence of desire," about death and rebirth. Actually, some critics did betray a worry about this book — a wish, perhaps, that it would go away. James Woodress, one of Cather's later biographers, described it as evidence of a midlife crisis. But after that bad spell, he claimed, she recovered splendidly, and moved on to "the rich affirmations of 'Death Comes for the Archbishop.'" Affirmation was the key word. That's what Cather was, and when she wasn't that, she wasn't really Cather.

Some good writings on Cather were published during the fifties and sixties, but they float like little barks of sanity on the great sea of piety that constituted Cather criticism in that period. Really, the situation was not unlike that of the thirties: Cather had been captured by the conservatives. The difference is that there was now no resistance to the "affirmative" line, for the Affirmatives were the only ones who paid attention to her. Her books were still assigned to high school students (no hard words, no sex scenes), and many ordinary people were still reading them for pleasure, but her work was rarely discussed in literary circles. Catherites, while lamenting this, marked it up to their author's uniqueness: literary discussion followed trends, and Cather fit no trend.

By the early seventies, however, the trend was staring them in the face. In 1973, a big conference was held in Lincoln, Nebraska, to mark the centennial of Cather's birth. Scholars got up and gave lectures on the usual things: Cather was universal, she was classical, she was affirmative. But, according to the proceedings, some unusual questions arose during the discussion periods. Ellen Moers, a Barnard professor, complained that in *My Ántonia* there was "a complexity we haven't even opened up — the whole feminine side of this book." At another point, when the Henry James scholar Leon Edel claimed that Cather "wrote intuitively," Blanche Gelfant, of Dartmouth, objected that this was what people always said about a woman writer — that "she really didn't know what she was doing but somehow this surged up in her." Edel protested that he thought "intuitive" was a good word. Why, he was on the record as saying that Faulkner was intuitive, too. The older Cather scholars seem to have been caught off guard. No one had seen it coming, but Cather now fit a trend — feminism.

An important job for feminist literary critics in the seventies and eighties was to assemble a "female canon," a list of books demonstrating that women were the equal of men as writers and therefore that their underrepresentation in the approved catalogue of classic literature was the result of politics, not biology. Cather was necessary to such a list. But the feminists didn't just need first-rate writers; they needed them to be feminists. Gertrude Stein's declaring the women's movement a bore, George Eliot's writing an essay called "Silly Novels by Lady Novelists": these things were an embarrassment. Cather's early prairie novels were everything a feminist could have asked for. They were about women, doing great things. But then came *My Ántonia,* in which the heroine did no great things; she merely endured. Furthermore, Ántonia had to suffer the indignity of having her story told by Jim — yet another case of men silencing women.

And that was just the beginning. For the rest of Cather's career, her main characters were sometimes women and sometimes men, sometimes good and sometimes evil. She seems no longer to have viewed the difference between male and female as crucial. Life was hard for everyone ("Even the wicked get worse than they deserve," one of her characters says), and the suffering had simply to be borne or, if possible, transcended through memory and art. The principles of life were changeless, and so the themes of art were, too. Hence Jim's description of Ántonia as something out of Virgil or ancient myth, something "universal and true." That, of course, is exactly what feminists did not want to hear. Universals, transcendence — these were the magic words by which women had been taught to accept a fate that in fact was not universal but assigned only to half of humanity, the female half. As for Ántonia, who stays home and stays poor while Jim goes to Harvard to study those Virgilian texts, the feminists saw her not as the embodiment of a changeless principle but as an oppressed woman.

It wasn't just Cather's fiction that fell short. Her life did, too. She was much closer to her father than to her mother, and in the list of other adults who nurtured her the men greatly outnumber the women. There was also the matter of the "William Cather period." Innocent readers might imagine that this is something feminists would sympathize with. It is not. "Male-identified" is a bad word in feminist circles. It means turning your back on women. And there was evidence that Cather did turn her back on women, or at least women writers. "It is a very grave question whether women have any place in poetry," she wrote in 1895. Female poets were so gushy — "emotional in the extreme, self-centered, self-absorbed." As for women novelists, all they could write about was love: "They have a sort of sex consciousness that is abominable." She attacked Kate Chopin's *The Awakening* on this score. How could Chopin have devoted her gifts to "so trite and sordid a theme" as adultery? All in all, women seemed to Cather to *use* art rather than to make it. "Has any woman ever really had the art instinct, the art necessity? Is it not with them a substitute . . . an escape valve for what has sought or is seeking another channel?" This is basically the same complaint that Virginia Woolf later made in *A Room of One's Own:* that women used writing as "self-expression" rather than as art. But Cather made it with uncommon ferocity: "If I see the announcement of a new book by a woman, I — well, I take one by a man instead. . . . I prefer to take no chances when I read."

Finally, in a time when feminist critics were trying to show that women inherited their literary tradition not from men but from women — literary "foremothers," often excluded from the established canon — it was not a pleasure for them to see Cather so clearly take her inspiration from male writers. Among modern authors, the ones who left the deepest imprint on her were Tolstoy, Flaubert, and Henry James. Only one woman writer was crucial to her — Sarah Orne Jewett — but, as Cather knew, Jewett was a minor writer. She was more a mentor than a model.

So Cather, having once looked as though she might advance feminist criticism, turned out to be another embarrassment. A number of feminists condemned her as such. Carolyn Heilbrun, in her 1979 book *Reinventing Womanhood,* claimed that most of Cather's novels demonstrated the "female urge toward the . . . denial of female destiny." Other feminist critics, however, were sorry to lose Cather. What if the wrongful attitudes that she expressed were not hers at all, they asked, but a reflection of the attitudes of *men,* the men in her novels? Jim Burden's intrusion into Ántonia's story, his acquiescence in her hard fate — what if these were acts of irony on Cather's part? Thus was born the unreliable-narrator school of Cather criticism. In a 1985 essay by Jean Schwind (University of Minnesota), the reader is warned not to trust Jim. He is genteel, sexist, and, indeed, racist and imperialist. Furthermore, he reads too much. His brain is crammed with Virgil, with "ideal 'forms'" and romantic conventions that have nothing to do with prairie realities, including Ántonia — and that is what Cather is trying to tell us. So, yes, Cather's fiction contains patriarchal attitudes, but only because she is decrying them; people just didn't notice before. This kind of reading has since been applied to other books of hers — Professor St. Peter is also a sexist pig — but it has proved a hard one to put over, for the traits that supposedly disqualify Cather's men as reliable witnesses were her traits as well. Romantic, elegiac, attached to ideal forms, besotted with Virgil — Cather was all these things, and believed in them, as her other writings show.

Clearly, a more subtle reading was needed, something that would both acknowledge Cather's endorsement of unfeminist values and yet show her in *conflict* with those values. According to some feminists, conflict was endemic to women's writing anyway, for women were torn between the wish to tell their own, female story and the need to write something acceptable to the male literary establishment. But Cather's prose didn't look torn. Plain and pure, it rose like a cliff wall in the face of the conflict-seekers, denying them access, insisting that it really did mean what it said. Some stick of dynamite was needed to blow the subject of Cather open. As the feminists soon realized, the thing they needed was already there. In a 1975 book called *Lesbian Images,* Jane Rule, a Canadian novelist and critic, had matter-of-factly stated that Cather was homosexual.

Was it true? Here, basically, is what we know of Cather's love life. In college, she developed a crush on an older girl, a brilliant student named Louise Pound. Some of Cather's letters to Pound survive, and they are certainly love-stricken. She tells Pound how beautiful she looked in her new Worth gown; she confesses her jealousy of Pound's other admirers; she moons and she pleads. That friendship ended while Cather was still in college, but later, when she was twenty-five and living in Pittsburgh, she met another woman, Isabelle McClung, then twenty-one, who was the daughter of a prominent judge. Cather was a journalist and a would-be artist; Isabelle was an arts lover and a would-be bohemian. They became fast friends, and two years later, reportedly over her parents' objections, Isabelle moved Cather into her family home. They may or may not have shared a bedroom — this is a subject of hot debate — but in any case they spent all their free time together, and Isabelle became the love of Cather's life. (Years later, Cather told a friend, "I think people often write books for just one person, and for me Isabelle was that person.") After five years at the McClungs', Cather was offered a job in New York, and she took it. She soon moved in with another woman — Edith Lewis, a fellow Nebraskan. But Lewis did not replace Isabelle in Cather's heart. Cather and Isabelle visited each other; they took trips together (without Lewis). Elizabeth Sergeant, another friend of Cather's, always noticed "Willa's shining face and quick stumbling rushes of talk and color" when Isabelle was around. This went on for ten years, until finally, in 1916, Isabelle decided to marry. Cather was devastated. Sergeant describes a walk in the park during which Cather told her the terrible news: "Her face — I saw how bleak it was, how vacant her eyes. All her natural exuberance drained away." The two women remained friends, and Cather periodically visited Isabelle and her husband. Meanwhile, for thirty-nine years — until the end of her life — Cather lived with Edith Lewis, who took care of all the practical details of their household. She fended off the callers; she helped correct the galleys. She did everything that "literary wives" used to do, and after Cather died she wrote a good book about her.

Most of these facts had been known for many years, but no special conclusions were drawn from them, or not in print. Then came gay liberation, and people began to argue that there was lesbianism not just in Cather's life but in her work. Her novels and stories are full of ravishing women, and she lingers over their charms. As for her men, they tend to be gentle, recessive types, not sexual. Or if they are sexual, they are evil. In her books, male-female passion generally doesn't work out: it rarely gets to first base, and the marriages are often unhappy. The woman is unavailable; the man broods and pines. According to a number of gay critics, what Cather's men feel is what she herself felt. This is her portrayal of lesbian love: silent, hopeless longing.

But the lesbian argument is not airtight. Crushes were common among college girls in Cather's time. And women in the nineteenth century had far more effusive, more physical relationships than women have today. They snuggled, held hands. In a 1911 story, "The Joy of Nelly Deane," Cather shows us two teenage girls happily drifting off to sleep in each other's arms as one of them talks about her marriage plans. Such female intimacies were not necessarily sexual, or, if they involved feelings that we now channel into sex, they were not defined as sexual. It was not until the end of the nineteenth century, with the Oscar Wilde trials and the writings of the early sexologists, such as Krafft-Ebing, that homosexuality became a subject of scandal and same-sex closeness came under suspicion. But by the end of the nineteenth century Cather was almost thirty years old; her attitudes were already formed.

She knew about the stigmatization of homosexuality — and endorsed it. Wilde, she wrote in 1895, deserved to be in prison. Verlaine was a "dirty old man" (though a first-rate poet). Of course, it is not rare for undeclared homosexuals to decry homosexuality, but if Cather had been a nervous closet lesbian, wouldn't she have been careful, in writing, not to say things that could be viewed as hints of homosexuality? She wasn't. In her art reviews of the 1890s she gushed over female beauty. In 1907 she published a love poem, "The Star Dial," based on Sappho. These facts, which are often cited as evidence of her homosexuality, are more logically interpretable as evidence that she was not homosexual, or not in her actions. Clearly, she felt she had nothing to hide. And this is true of her life as well as of her writing. When Isabelle McClung married, she grieved openly, telling her friends how heartbroken she was.

If I had to guess on the basis of the evidence, I would say that Cather was homosexual in her feelings and celibate in her actions. Nor does it necessarily follow that this left her with a permanent complex. Many of the important women writers of the nineteenth century were celibate. If Jane Austen and Emily Brontë managed without having sex, why not Cather?

Whatever Cather's sexual status, feminist critics seeking to rehabilitate her needed it to be one way. They had to show her in conflict; therefore, she had to be a thwarted homosexual. Meanwhile, the Affirmatives were still around and, together with members of Cather's family, they were doing what they could to stop these allegations. In 1980, Cather's niece Helen Southwick had an exchange of letters with Virginia Faulkner, an editor at the University of Nebraska Press. Faulkner sympathized with Southwick's outrage over these "gross and unsubstantiated implications and assertions" and warned her that some woman was at work on a psychosexual biography of Cather. She said she would try to get hold of the manuscript and, if its scholarship was defective, "blow it out of the water."

So a proof of Cather's lesbianism was needed, and, in the absence of any hard evidence, it had to be ingenious. The person who stepped forward to do the job was the woman who was writing the dreaded psychosexual biography, Sharon O'Brien, of Dickinson College. In a 1984 essay entitled "'The Thing Not Named': Willa Cather as a Lesbian Writer," O'Brien said that she would hold herself to a strict standard: to be called a lesbian, a woman had not only to show close ties with women but also to be "self-identified" as a lesbian. And one of Cather's letters to Louise Pound, O'Brien claimed, met that standard. Because of the stipulation in Cather's will, O'Brien could not quote the sentence in question, so she paraphrased it. The paraphrase read, "It was so unfair that feminine friendship should be unnatural, but she agreed with Miss De Pue (a classmate) that it was." There was the smoking gun: Cather viewed her feelings for Louise as unnatural; therefore she was a self-identified lesbian. And her lesbianism, O'Brien claimed, explained many things about her work — for example, her famous statement about "the thing not named" being the most important thing in any work of literature. This was a "startling phrase," O'Brien said, for it echoed the words used in evidence at Oscar Wilde's trial: "the Love that dare not speak its name." Clearly, those subtle truths that Cather felt could only be suggested, never enunciated, were just one thing — homosexuality. This was the "emotional source of her fiction," the basis of her work.

O'Brien's argument has since been widely accepted as proof of Cather's lesbianism. There are only two things wrong with it. First, Cather, in her letter to Pound, did not say she agreed with Miss De Pue that feminine friendship was unnatural. She said the opposite. Like O'Brien, I have signed an agreement with the Duke University library (where this letter is housed) promising not to quote Cather's words, but here is the tightest possible paraphrase: "It is clearly unjust that friendship between women should be unnatural, I concur with Miss De Pue to that extent." She knows that close female friendships are now viewed as unnatural; Miss De Pue has said that this is unfair; she agrees with De Pue. (If Cather had considered the possible consequences of her ban on quoting her letters, she might have thought twice about issuing it.) As for "the thing not named," this, as I said earlier, is more or less a restatement of a famous saying of Mallarmé's. If Cather didn't get it from him, she could have picked it up from any of a number of his contemporaries. Far from being a startling phrase, it was a commonplace of fin-de-siècle aesthetics.

No matter. The feminists now had what they needed. The surface of Cather's fiction could no longer be taken literally; it had to be read *through*. And what was underneath had to be a story about women. So Cather, who had thought to leave behind the subject of gender, was taken in hand and firmly led back to it. Having once been captured by the right, she was now captured by the left. In the process, she became as much a topic of discussion as she had formerly been a non-topic. Cather studies exploded.

The book that got the most attention was O'Brien's *Willa Cather:*

The Emerging Voice, which was published in 1987 and offered a new, integrated approach to Cather's insufficient feminism — the reconciliation model. In this scenario, Cather did let women down, but only early on, and only because she was in conflict over a woman — namely, her mother. O'Brien's argument is built on a theory that was put forth in the 1970s by the psychologist Nancy Chodorow: that girls, unlike boys, never truly separate from their mothers and therefore remain prone to conflicts over separation, alternately seeking fusion with the remembered mother and resisting engulfment by her. All her young life, O'Brien argues, Cather was torn by mother-fusion anxiety, which was exacerbated in her case by lesbianism. (Union with a woman would spell the dreaded engulfment.) Her male identification can thus be accounted for. Indeed, almost everything that Cather does in this nearly five-hundred-page book is a symbolic flight from or return to the mother. If she prefers George Eliot to the trashy romantic novelist Marie Corelli, that's because of the "conflicts of the mother-daughter bond." (Her mother was a Corelli fan.) If she forges a happy union with Isabelle McClung, that's because the relationship offers her "a satisfactory reenactment of the mother-daughter relationship."

But writing, according to O'Brien, was the crux of Cather's mother-fusion complex. Fleeing her mother, she identified fiction as a male endeavor and took male writers as her models. Therefore, in her early stories she could never express her true, female-identified self. It was only when she met Jewett, to whom O'Brien devotes a whole chapter, that Cather finally "received the gift of female literary inheritance." Inconveniently, what Cather then produced was *Alexander's Bridge,* a novel about a man written in the style of a man — Henry James. But O'Brien can explain this: Cather was still in conflict, and fighting her way out of it, as can be seen by the fact that Alexander, the engineer hero, is destroyed at the end of the book. The bridge he is building falls down, and he drowns with it. This is a "deconstruction of masculine aesthetics," a critique of the male need to dominate. (Bridge building is a domination of nature.) Having exorcised this last demon, Cather went on to write *O Pioneers!* — a book that, in its use of "home" material, signifies her return to the mother and celebrates her truly female art in the symbol of Alexandra's tilling of the soil. (Agriculture is not a domination of nature.)

And what of all the later novels, with their male heroes and their male narrators? O'Brien solves the problem by not analyzing those texts. Her book ends with *O Pioneers!* — the second of Cather's twelve novels. But here and there in her writings she comments on Cather's later novels, to the effect that they, too, are about the mother-daughter bond, though that subject may be "disguised." *The Professor's House,* with its account of the friendship between the Professor and his student Tom Outland, "could trouble a feminist reader," O'Brien writes. "Why would Willa Cather celebrate male bonding?" But these troubles vanish when we realize that the Professor's attachment to Tom is "only a mask for his deeper yearning to return to . . . the maternal presence."

Last year, in the *Times Book Review,* O'Brien published an essay on how she came to write her Cather biography. It was a product of her own life, she said. When she was young, she was plagued by feelings of powerlessness, the product of her domination not by men but by women:

> There is a certain kind of woman — powerful, self-involved, con-
> vinced of her own rightness and determined that her own views should
> prevail — who undermines my own sense of self more profoundly than
> the most patriarchal male.

She gives examples: her mother, the nuns in her school. These women "silenced" her, kept her from developing her own voice. When, as an adult, she conceived the project of writing a biography of Cather, the childhood drama was replayed. Here was this powerful woman, a famous novelist, "I, on the other hand, was an obscure academic." And Cather, like the women of O'Brien's childhood, was trying to silence her. Had she not burned her letters and prohibited quotation from any correspondence that surfaced later? But O'Brien could read the surviving letters, including the letters to Louise Pound, and when she discovered in them what she took to be evidence of Cather's lesbianism, she felt a "subtle power shift." If she were to write Cather's story as she now saw it, she would be "rewriting one of the silencing stories of my own life, my domination by women who tried to erase me." Still, she was worried, and Cather began to haunt her dreams. In one dream, Cather invited her to tea and said to her, "I want you to know that I am not gay." "What about the letters to Louise Pound?" O'Brien

replied. The dream ended there. (If it had continued, Cather
might have told O'Brien to take another look at the letter.)

After finishing the biography, O'Brien tells us, she wrote another
life of Cather, for high school students, as part of a Chelsea House
series called Lives of Notable Gay Men and Lesbians. In this book,
she says, she no longer had to take into account "scholarly (and
seemingly parental) readers" who might have intimidated her by
asking for evidence. She was free to dispense with documentation;
she could also omit "almost all the literary analysis." In other
words, she no longer had to prove her case. All she had to do was
state it. Not surprisingly, she found this "liberating." She was silenced no more.

O'Brien's reconciliation argument had a big influence. For many,
Cather's feminist credentials were restored. But, just as the unreliable-narrator reading had looked to some critics like a cover-up,
so did the reconciliation reading. The deconstructionists, with
their theory that all literary texts are unstable in meaning, were
among the unconvinced, and, together with practitioners of other
critical methods fashionable in the eighties, they came up with yet
another reading of Cather, the "conflict" reading. According to
this view, Cather was perpetually torn between her conditioned
deference to the patriarchy and her deep-down loyalty to feminism
and lesbianism — a psychic war that propelled all her work. Therefore, whatever she appeared to be saying, she was really saying the
opposite, or both. In a 1989 essay Eve Kosofsky Sedgwick, of Duke,
writes that *The Professor's House* might seem, on the surface, "het-
erosexist," but that its underlying rebellion against heterosexism
can be discovered by deconstructing the last sentence of the book
— specifically, one word in that sentence, "Berengaria," the name
of the ship on which the Professor's wife and daughter are sailing
home from Europe. Here is Sedgwick's deconstruction:

> *Berengaria,* ship of women: the {green} {aria}, the {eager} {brain}, the
> {bearing} and the {bairn}, the {raring} {engine}, the {bargain} {binge},
> the {ban} and {bar}, the {garage}, the {barrage} of {anger}, the {bare}
> {grin}, the {rage} to {err}, the {rare} {grab} for {being}, the {begin} and
> {rebegin} {again}.

This list of anagrams, which must have taken a while to work out,
supposedly reveals the maelstrom of lesbian energies churning

beneath the surface of *The Professor's House* — energies that Cather was venting when she gave the ship that strange name. Yes, Sedgwick says, the name has a historical meaning — Berengaria was the wife of Richard the Lionhearted — but otherwise it is a "nonsense word." She does not seem to know that it was the name of a real ship, a famous Cunard ocean liner on which Cather had returned from Europe immediately before beginning *The Professor's House.*

Conflict-interpreters, it should be added, do not look kindly on those who fail to see the conflict. In a 1986 essay Judith Fetterley (State University of New York, Albany) accused Jane Rule, the woman who outed Cather, of betraying lesbianism by claiming that *My Ántonia* was a "serene" book — that is, by refusing to acknowledge its burning lesbian subtext. "Homophobia can go no further," Fetterley declared. In other words, to deny that Cather's books are about homosexuality is gay-bashing.

Despite their differences, these political critics have one thing in common: an obsession with instinctual processes. No tree can grow, no river flow in Cather's landscapes without its being a penis or a menstrual period. Twenty years ago, Ellen Moers, in her book *Literary Women,* quoted a long description of a canyon from *The Song of the Lark* and called it "the most thoroughly elaborated female landscape in literature" — in other words, a crotch. This was not entirely far-fetched. Cather's description — the V-shaped gorge, the internal ridges, the fringe of foliage — does sound a little like a crotch, though it sounds a lot more like a canyon. For modern Cather critics, however, anything that is a little like a crotch *is* a crotch, and, in emulation of Moers's *trouvaille,* they have since taken us on a long crawl through the female reproductive anatomy. Most of Cather's main characters have been unmasked as homosexuals: Ántonia and Jim, the Professor and Tom Outland, and, of course, the two priests in *Death Comes for the Archbishop.* When these critics are not dwelling on sex, they are dwelling on the infantile, the "pre-Oedipal." They have little interest in ego processes: thinking, working. Indeed, they have little interest in writing. What Cather put down on the page is of almost no concern apart from what it supposedly reveals about her unconscious. The subject is not literature but biography, or inferred biography.

One senses in all this a certain vengeful glee. In part, it is directed at the Affirmatives; in part, at the New Critics, with their insistent formalism. But the vengeance is clearly aimed at Cather,

too. Other women writers uphold the feminists' description of
what it means for a woman to try to enter the patriarchal literary
tradition. Emily Dickinson cowering in her room, Harriet Beecher
Stowe writing with one hand while holding a baby with the other,
Kate Chopin hounded out of print for publishing indecencies:
these women tell the story that the feminists are trying to tell. But
Cather? If anything, she is a rebuke to feminists. All the things they
say a woman can't do — learn to write from men, create a life
centered on writing, with no intrusions — Cather did, and with
very little wear and tear. No booze, no abortions, no nervous
breakdowns. She jumped the gate, and therefore she makes the
gate look not so high after all.

Why should all this wild-eyed academic writing concern anyone
but academics? Because it filters down quickly to the public. Academics are the people who teach students. They are also the
people who write the introductions to new paperback editions of
Cather, the editions most likely to be bought by the general public.
Signet's *Song of the Lark* and Meridian's collection of Cather's
stories are both introduced by O'Brien, who, needless to say, offers
a feminist interpretation.

The new political readings of Cather are presumably being put
forth in the service of political causes. Will they help those causes?
Will it be useful if we argue that, while heterosexual men can write
about anything they want, women can write only about gender,
homosexuals only about sexuality? "Why would Willa Cather celebrate male bonding?" O'Brien asks. And why would Leo Tolstoy
celebrate a girl's experience at her first ball? Because they wanted
to write about life. A broad subject matter is something that a
woman writer in the early twentieth century might have sought
with special urgency, for it was precisely what was denied her. Such
a restriction, Cather decided, would not be placed on her. She
wrote novels showing that women could do something important
besides have sex. Then she wrote novels about history and exile
and the life of the mind in relation to the world — in other words,
all the things that women were not supposed to write about,
though today they do, partly because Cather did. If we now argue
that those subjects of hers were just covers, that what she was really
writing about was the very things she chose not to write about, sex

and gender, is this a vote for the rights of women and homosexuals? Or is it, however unwittingly, another attack on them?

Reading Cather criticism has taught me one thing. If it is not realistic to expect a nonpolitical criticism, one can still wish for and sometimes get a *sophisticated* criticism — one that, while indebted to a certain politics, can balance that concern with a sustained attention to what the artist is saying. In 1986, when other critics were accusing Cather of betraying lesbians and women and art by "masking" her homosexuality, Joanna Russ, a University of Washington professor, published an essay claiming that Cather's staying in the closet was actually good for her work, because it kept her from being confined to a narrow lesbian-novelist position. Russ, herself a lesbian novelist, wrote:

> It was possible for Cather, in masquerade, to speak more completely, more clearly, and less self-consciously than could, for example, Djuna Barnes in "Nightwood". . . . [She could] remain "normal," American, public, and *also* lesbian. Even now, any openly lesbian writer is almost forced to be a self-conscious rebel, a position congenial to some, but one that can be constricting nonetheless; such a role Cather simply did not take or need.

Cather's stance, Russ says, marks an early, innocent stage in the history of lesbian fiction:

> The innocence, of course, had to go. If the next stage can be called guilty self-consciousness, and the stage after that self-conscious rebellion, no matter what aesthetic advantages they offer (and I believe they offer many not available to Cather, honesty being one of them), they do not have the same advantages as Cather's masquerade; they cannot possibly create the aesthetic completeness and richness of Cather's work.

Aesthetic completeness and richness — strange words to encounter in modern Cather studies.

What can we call a critical position such as this? Modesty? Large-mindedness? I don't know, but without it we will soon have no history. What will today's gay critics do with Dante, who put the sodomites in Hell? What will the feminists do with George Eliot, who, feminist though she was, could not think of what to do with Dorothea Brooke except to push her into the arms of yet another man, or with Maggie Tulliver except drown her? As for Cather, what do the critics have left of her — of the profundity of her vision, of her originality, of her *ear,* probably the best in American fiction — once all these things have been ignored so that she can be turned into a feminist?

I should add that feminism is no longer the cutting edge of Cather criticism. Multiculturalism is, though most of the work in this area is being done by feminists. These critics, probably born, on the average, in 1950, attempt to cope with the amazing fact that Cather, born under Ulysses S. Grant, sometimes betrays views different from theirs about blacks, Mexicans, and American Indians. Now and then, someone notices that Cather's opinions were typical of her generation — indeed, that they were also expressed by good feminists of the time. Elizabeth Ammons (of Tufts), having called Cather a racist in her 1992 book *Conflicting Stories,* is forced to acknowledge that Kate Chopin, that feminist martyr, supplied the heroine of *The Awakening* with a small battalion of black people to clean her house and look after her children while she accomplished her awakening. But this, Ammons says, does not mean that Chopin silenced black culture in her book. For doesn't *The Awakening* have thirty-nine chapters, and isn't thirty-nine pretty close to forty, the number of weeks in the average pregnancy? Clearly, *The Awakening* is "structured as a pregnancy," and, since childbirth was an event attended to by black women, this means that the book "formally derives from black culture." So *The Awakening* is OK. Maybe someone can do the same kind of thing for *The Merchant of Venice* — reveal that it derives from Jewish culture. But maybe not. It was written by a man.

This is the new political critics' revenge on the "liberal humanism" of the fifties and sixties. It is terrible to imagine what the next generation's revenge on this generation will be. One is tempted to plead in advance for a little historical understanding — to point out, for example, that the cause of women, having been ignored for several thousand years, was urgently felt in our time, even to the point of such absurdities. But what historical understanding can these critics expect, who have shown none?

The parade of American literature goes by, float after float: realism, naturalism, psychological novel, social novel, political novel.

Cather belongs with none of them, which means either that she is left out or, if she is desperately needed, that she is forced at gunpoint to put on a paper hat and join a group in which she has no place. Hence her uneasy standing with the feminists. She is not one of them, and they know it. That's why they don't like her.

Who has liked her? Two groups, basically. Writers tend to be Cather fans. Rebecca West, Katherine Anne Porter, and Eudora Welty wrote loving essays about her. (Porter's is especially fine.) Sinclair Lewis called her "the greatest American novelist"; when he was awarded the Nobel Prize, in 1930, he said she should have got it instead. Fitzgerald admired her to the point of plagiarism, as he himself admitted. Faulkner considered her one of the foremost American novelists, and he, too, shows her influence. "We have nothing better than she is," Wallace Stevens wrote to a friend. Of course, as an author ill used by critics, she was easy to love; she didn't look like competition. (Lewis would not have said that his Nobel Prize should have gone to Hemingway.) But writers were also in a position to understand the rarity of her gift. All novelists, all poets want to imagine hugely and then find the perfect, discrete form that will both capture the thought and suggest what was uncapturable in it — glimpse its escaping wings. Few succeed; Cather was one who did.

The other group that has consistently admired Cather is the public. *Death Comes for the Archbishop* sells more than twenty thousand copies a year. Perhaps it is time for Cather to become a non-topic again, for the professional critics to give up and leave her books to those who care about them — her readers.

NICHOLSON BAKER

Books as Furniture

FROM THE NEW YORKER

ON THE COVER of a recent mail-order catalogue from a place
called The Company Store, a man and a woman in white pajamas
are posed in the middle of a pillow fight. But there isn't one
feather in the air, because The Company Store, of La Crosse,
Wisconsin, sells new pillows — not stale, corrupt, depopulated pillows from some earlier era of human insomnia but fresh, unasham-
edly swollen dream bags corpulent with clean, large-cluster white
goose down of a quality that only European white polar geese can
grow. The Company Store also sells things like new flannel blankets, new bed wedges, and new baffled-box comforters. They are
not in the business of selling beat-up editions of forgotten nine-
teenth- and early-twentieth-century books.

But in another way The Company Store is in fact a used-book
seller — or at least the people there are committed book propa-
gandists — since more than twenty old volumes appear in the
pages of the catalogue. On top of a pile of five folio-folded Wam-
sutta sheets in Bluette, Black Cherry, Ivory, Sunset, and Onyx,
there sits a worn oblong shape that looks to date from about 1880,
with a pair of wire-rimmed glasses resting on it — glasses that
might be used to read the pages they surmount. Sadly, it isn't quite
possible to make out the title on the book's spine. But the title in
another picture in this catalogue — a very small photograph on
page 66 — does, just barely, cross the threshold of decipherability.
The catalogue designer has reversed the negative, so that the
letters are backward, and the words they spell are partly covered
by a finger, but if you look closely you can still identify which book,

out of all the books that have ever been published, is lying open face down on a white-pajamaed thigh — the thigh, it seems, of the woman who was first seen pillow-fighting on the cover. Now she is alone, lost in a fiction-inspired reverie, leaning against a vertical pillow prop with low, stumpy arms that is helping her sit up in bed: one of those readers' pillows that my wife and her college friends used to call "husbands." The woman is in the middle of reading *The Wood-Carver of 'Lympus,* published in 1904 and written by someone named Mary E. Waller.

I went to a big library and took the elevator to the lowest level of the underground stacks, and found there a copy of *The Wood-Carver of 'Lympus* identical to the one in the picture. The novel is about an unsophisticated high-altitude apple farmer named Hughie, who lives in the Green Mountains of Vermont, on the fictional Mount Olympus — or Mount 'Lympus, as the locals call it. A falling log has left Hughie crippled in some serious and vaguely Hemingwayesque way, so Hughie, with marriage now out of the question, teaches himself woodcarving, aided from afar by cultured friends. They forward him trunkfuls of books and reproductions of European art: he reads Carlyle and George Sand and Browning and Bret Harte, and he stares attentively at a photograph of Michelangelo's *David;* and, little by little, under this mail-order tutelage and influence, Hughie succeeds in elevating himself from limping amateur whittler to Olympian panel artist and wainscoteur. One of his correspondents, Madeline, on her way through northern Italy, sends him a set of carved black-oak bookshelves. She writes him, "I like to imagine all those books you have been gathering and making yours on these special shelves."

I've been thinking about bookshelves myself lately, and imagining the shelves one might fill by searching through mail-order catalogues for the books they use as props (often searching at extremely close range: part of the delight comes in figuring out, with the aid of tiny clues and keyword computer searches, the identity of a book whose title at first seems totally illegible), and I've been thinking, too, about what our mail-order catalogues and our bookshelves, those two affiliated regions of cultural self-display, reveal about the sort of readers we are, or wish we were. We are not, clearly, whatever The Company Store would have us believe, casual bedtime consumers of the novels and travel books of Mary

E. Waller. *The Wood-Carver of 'Lympus* went through at least twenty-three printings after 1904, according to the copyright page — which would have made it a big book for Little, Brown — but my copy was last checked out on January 19, 1948, and was returned on January 20: too promptly, one suspects, to have been read. The model in the white pajamas and I could be the only two people who have read, or pretended to read, this work in several decades. And yet a very small image of it has been delivered by bulk-rate mail to thousands of households. In another picture in the catalogue, the pajama woman is asleep, embracing a seventy-two-inch-long body pillow: she is dreaming, needless to say, of disabled mountain men and the bookshelves full of Carlyle that taught them everything they know; *The Wood-Carver of 'Lympus* waits on her bedside table.

Nor is The Company Store alone among mail-order catalogues in giving prominence to the old or little-known work of literature. I counted thirty-six hand-me-down books, none with their original jackets on, in fifteen different settings, in the Crate & Barrel catalogue for the spring of '95. The books lie open on chairs, on hammocks, on the floor, as if whoever was reading them had left off briefly to check the status of an earth-toned lentil soup: on their pages rest studiously haphazard placeholders — a shell, a twist of ribbon, an apple, a daisy. The Crabtree & Evelyn catalogue for spring offers a pair of three-and-a-half-ounce containers of Southampton Rose Home Fragrance Spray, which is a kind of highbrow air freshener, for seventeen dollars; its dignity is enhanced, and its price defended, by its placement next to a fancily bound Italian biography of Queen Elizabeth from 1965, whose title, translated, is *Elizabeth I of England: The Virgin with the Iron Fist* — itself not such a bad name for an air freshener. On page 28 of the spring Tweeds catalogue, a woman wearing a nice cotton sweater holds open an unidentifiable clothbound book bearing visible, and quite beautiful, mildew stains. In one of the latest J. Crew catalogues, there is a literary interlude on page 33: a man in shorts and plaster-dusted work boots, sitting in a half-remodeled room — on break, apparently, from his labor of hammering and gentrifying — is looking something up in what close inspection reveals to be a *Guide Bleu* to Switzerland, probably from the forties, in French.

*

What is it with all these books? Isn't the Book supposed to be in decline — its authority eroding, its informational tax base fleeing to suburbs of impeccably edged and weeded silicon? Five minutes with the tasteful Pottery Barn catalogue of March 1995 may be somewhat reassuring. A closed universe of about fifty books circulates decoratively in its pages. The Pottery Barn catalogue's library may have been selected for the alpha-wave-inducing beige and blue-gray and dull red of its bindings, but the actual titles, which are nearly but not quite unreadable, sometimes betray reserves of emotion. In the tranquillity of a cool living room, a cream-colored book entitled *Tongues of Flame* appears, minus its jacket, on its shelf of the Trestle Bookcase, near the Malabar Chair. Then it shows up in some peaceful shots of iron end tables. Next, on the page that offers what the Pottery Barn's furniture-namers call a Library Bed — "a bed whose broad panels suggest the careful woodworking found in old English libraries" — a historical novel called *A Rose for Virtue* makes its quiet entrance, underneath a handsome ivory-toned telephone. Three pages later comes the big moment, the catalogue's clinch: for, lying at the foot of the Scroll Iron Bed, open face down on the cushion of the Scroll Iron Bench, as if it were being read, is a half-hidden volume that can be positively identified as *Tongues of Flame,* and leaning fondly, or even ardently, against it, at a slight angle, is *A Rose for Virtue.* Whether the rose's virtue survives this fleeting flammilingus, we are not told; it's enough to know that the two books, after their photographic vicissitudes, are together at last.

So I went to the library again, and checked out *Tongues of Flame.* It's a collection of short stories, by Mary Ward Brown, which was published by Dutton in 1986. (There is also a novel called *Tongues of Flame,* by Tim Parks, set in England, that came out in 1985, but the large pale-gold letters on the binding of the Dutton edition are unmistakable.) The title story is about a married woman who wants to help a stuttering drunk reform his life by taking him to church. Her program seems to work at first, but one evening the preacher delivers a sermon so potent it sends the alarmed man right back to the bottle; in a matter of hours, his clumsy cigarette-smoking has set fire to the church. "Save the Bible!" hollers one of the parishioners as the flames rise from the roof, and it is eventually saved. The author writes:

The wet pulpit, with the Bible still on it, had been brought out into the churchyard. Pews sat haphazardly about. Songbooks, Sunday School books, and Bible pictures for children were scattered on the grass.

Were it not for the color coordinating book lovers at Pottery Barn, I would never have read Mary Ward Brown's short story — and it's worth reading, more flavorful, perhaps, for having been found circuitously. Nor would I ever have troubled to determine which hymn it is that contains the simple but stirring phrase "tongues of flame." It's from "Father of Boundless Grace," by the prolific Charles Wesley (Methodist, brother of John Wesley, and inspirer of William Blake), and it was probably written sometime in the 1730s:

> A few from every land
> At first to *Salem* came,
> And saw the wonders of Thy hand,
> And saw the tongues of flame!

And if I hadn't read "Tongues of Flame," I might never have been reminded of the story of another, bigger book fire. It took place in London on Saturday, October 23, 1731, at two o'clock in the morning. What was to become the library of the British Museum — a set of about a thousand books and manuscripts, which included the collection of the old Royal Library, along with the fabulous accumulation of Robert Cotton — was shelved, far too casually, in a room in a house in Westminster, and was overseen (according to Edward Miller's *That Noble Cabinet*) by the son of the then aged classical scholar Richard Bentley. The room below the library caught fire; tongues of flame found their way up through the wainscoting and reached the backs of the bookcases — or book presses, as they were often called — and, as the conjoined libraries began to sigh and crackle, the Speaker of the House of Commons, who lived nearby and had hurried over when he heard the clamor, plucked warm and smoking bundles of ancient parchment off the shelves and tossed them out the window to save them. Like Chuck Yeager, smoke-smirched but ambulatory after his plane crash at the end of *The Right Stuff,* Dr. Bentley himself emerged from the conflagration with the Codex Alexandrinus, the priceless fifth-century manuscript of the Greek Bible, in his arms. He was dressed in his nightgown, but he had apparently taken a moment, in the

name of scholarly dignity, to slap on his wig. A hundred and
fourteen books were ruined or lost that night — some of them
"burnt to a Crust," many of them irreplaceable — and a number
of the ones that had been flung out the window to safety were
swept together into heaps of shuffled and water-damaged pages
and boxed away. Librarians didn't succeed in restoring order to
some of the surviving fragments until a century later.

And if I hadn't been reminded of that British Museum fire, I
wouldn't have been moved to reread the great book-fire scene in
Mervyn Peake's novel *Titus Groan*, published in 1946, which uses
some of the elements from the mythical prehistory of the British
Museum. Here's how Peake describes the passing of Lord Sepul-
chrave's library at Gormenghast:

> The room was lit up with a tongue of flame that sprang into the air
> among the books on the right of the unused door. It died almost at
> once, withdrawing itself like the tongue of an adder, but a moment later
> it shot forth again and climbed in a crimson spiral, curling from left to
> right as it licked its way across the gilded and studded spines of Sepul-
> chrave's volumes. This time it did not die away, but gripped the leather
> with its myriad flickering tentacles while the names of the books shone
> out in ephemeral glory. They were never forgotten by Fuchsia, those
> first few vivid titles that seemed to be advertising their own deaths.

Fuchsia and the others escape out the window, and the next
morning we view the library's desolate remains:

> The shelves that still stood were wrinkled charcoal, and the books
> were standing side by side upon them, black, grey, and ash-white, the
> corpses of thought.

Umberto Eco seems to have been inspired by this scene, right
down to its studded book spines, and inspired, too, by the story
of the British Museum fire, in writing the description of burning
books that ends his big book *The Name of the Rose*. "Now I saw
tongues of flame [*lingue di fiamma*] rise from the scriptorium,
which was also tenanted by books and cases," says Eco's narrator.
And then, revisiting the ruined abbey years later, he reports:

> Poking about in the rubble, I found at times scraps of parchments
> that had drifted down from the scriptorium and the library and had
> survived like treasures buried in the earth; I began to collect them, as
> if I were going to piece together the torn pages of a book. . . .

Along one stretch of wall I found a bookcase, still miraculously erect, having come through the fire I cannot say how. . . . At times I found pages where whole sentences were legible; more often, intact bindings, protected by what had once been metal studs. . . . Ghosts of books, apparently intact on the outside but consumed within.

How thoughtful of the Pottery Barn catalogue to send its consumers back on this short but fiery thematic mission, and at the same time to rescue Mary Ward Brown's *Tongues of Flame* from the prospect of absent-minded immolation — flinging it out the window, as it were, toward us, simply by photographing it. Bookstores and book reviews deal with new books, and even antiquarian-book sellers can only align old books on their silent shelves, where they wait for buyers. But the junk-mail catalogues — sent out by the hundreds of thousands to people who never asked for them but nonetheless look through them from time to time and puzzle over the versions of life they present — go further, extending to past books the courtesy of present inclusion, and surrounding printed fiction with life-size fictional rooms that resemble our own real rooms except that they are a good deal neater, costlier, and more literate.

We know that it's a lie. One of the larger pieces in the Pottery Barn catalogue is the Sierra Armoire, made of wormwood and machine-flagellated pine. The armoire, pictured with one of its double doors ajar, is stuffed with a miscellany of books whose bindings glimmer from its shadows: a textbook of pathology from before the Second World War, an original hardcover of Bellow's *Adventures of Augie March*, Paul Horgan's *Citizen of New Salem*, a bound German periodical from 1877, and also — so deeply shadowed that only its width and the faintest hint of a typeface give it away — *Tongues of Flame*. There isn't a self-help book or a current bestseller to be seen, because the men and women who live in the rooms of the mail-order catalogues never read bestsellers. In fact, they never read paperbacks. Next to the picture, the description says, "Long before there were closets to house clothing, linens and books, armoires did the job."

Well, this is true. Bookcases, or book cupboards, were called armaria as early as the first century, when some books were still published — that is, multiply copied — on rolls (*volumina*), and stored on their sides, with little tags hanging from their ends which bore their titles. Seneca, who died in the year 65, rather scornfully mentions book-bearing armoires inlaid with ivory in his essay "On Tranquillity of Mind." And in one of the earliest surviving pictures of a book armoire, found in a manuscript called the Codex Amiatinus, from the eighth century (but possibly copied from an earlier, now lost manuscript, the Codex Grandior), the books, large and bound in red, lie flat on the shelves, with the doors of the armarium open. The picture is reproduced in John Willis Clark's *The Care of Books,* a monumental history of the bookcase, first published in 1901. Professor Clark also quotes from the Customs of the Augustinian Order, which required that the armarium be "lined inside with wood, that the damp of the walls may not moisten or stain the books," and that it be "divided vertically as well as horizontally by sundry shelves on which the books may be ranged so as to be separated from one another; for fear they be packed so close as to injure each other or delay those who want them."

In English, the word "armarium" relaxed into "almery" or "aumbry," as in this sixteenth-century account of life at Durham Cathedral:

> And over against the carrells against the church wall did stande certaine great almeries of waynscott all full of bookes, wherein did lye as well the old auncyent written Doctors of the Church as other prophane authors with dyverse other holie mens wourks, so that every one dyd studye what Doctor pleased them best.

Eventually, armoires came to look more like modern bookshelves, shedding their cupboard doors, but thievery and misshelving led to the collateral invention of another deterrent: book chains. The books were flipped around, with their fore-edges rather than their bindings facing outward on the shelf; rings were clipped or riveted to their front covers; and these rings were linked to surprisingly thick, dangling, Jacob Marleyesque chains, some short, some several feet in length, whose other ends encircled iron rods that ran horizontally in front of a shelf or across the top of an angled lectern. Michelangelo designed a chained library. A bookcase historian named Burnett Hillman Streeter, who was a canon of Hereford Cathedral in the 1930s and a loving restorer of its chained library, reports that libraries at Cambridge remained on leash until the early part of the seventeenth century, while at Oxford the practice persisted until 1799. Samuel Johnson would have read chained books; and when Coleridge somewhere laments the impossibility of escaping the fetters of language — when he says, "Our chains rattle, even as we are complaining of them" — perhaps he has the memory of book chains specifically in mind.

So the Pottery Barn catalogue is invoking centuries of monastic and academic tradition when it observes that books were once stored in armoires, as were clothes and linens. But can its copywriter truly believe that anyone is now going to keep a book collection behind the closed pine doors of a $999 cupboard? No. Catalogue designers long ago learned for themselves and put into earnest practice the observation that one of Anthony Powell's characters made when he drunkenly pulled a glass-fronted bookcase down on himself while trying to retrieve a copy of *The Golden Treasury* in order to check a quotation: "As volume after volume descended on him, it was asserted he made the comment: 'Books do furnish a room.'" Catalogue designers know perfectly well that books, if we are fortunate enough to own any, should be out there somewhere, visible, shelved in motley ranks or heaped on tables as nodes of compacted linearity that arrest the casual eye and suggest wealths of patriarchal, or matriarchal, learnedness. Books entice catalogue browsers, readers and nonreaders alike, into furnishing alternative lives for themselves — lives in which they find they are finally able to perform that contortional yoga exercise whereof so many have spoken, and can "curl up with a good book."

What, then, will the Pottery Barn's armoire hold in practice? The catalogue copy quietly goes on to note that this piece of furniture is "roomy enough to hold a 20″-deep television or stereo equipment (holes must be drilled in back)." Now we see: it makes a nice decorative envelope for a TV — but it can't be pictured performing that primary and perfectly legitimate duty, because that would interfere with the catalogue browser's notion of him or herself. What will make the browser pause and possibly lift the phone is the promise, the illusion, that the armoire is magical, that the spirit of those beautiful shadowy books in the picture will persist after delivery, raising the moral tone of the TV — in other words, that the armoire's bookish past will give the TV a liberal education.

It's undeniable that books furnish a room, and it's nothing to be ashamed of. They require furniture, in the form of bookshelves, but they are themselves furniture as well. "No furniture so charming as books, even if you never open them, or read a single word" — so Sydney Smith, one of the founders of the *Edinburgh Review,* and a devoted Victorian reader, told his daughter as they had breakfast in his library. By chance, the book immediately to the right of *The Wood-Carver of 'Lympus* where I found it in the library was something called *Bits of Talk, in Verse and Prose, for Young Folks,* published in 1892, by Helen Jackson. She devotes a chapter to tips on making rooms pleasant to live in. She recommends sunlight first, and then color, especially the color red:

> In an autumn leaf, in a curtain, in a chair-cover, in a pin-cushion, in a vase, in the binding of a book, everywhere you put it, it makes a brilliant point and gives pleasure.

She goes on:

> Third on my list of essentials for making rooms cosey, cheerful, and beautiful, come — Books and Pictures. Here some persons will cry out: "But books and pictures cost a great deal of money." Yes, books do cost money, and so do pictures; but books accumulate rapidly in most houses where books are read at all; and if people really want books, it is astonishing how many they contrive to get together in a few years without pinching themselves very seriously in other directions.

Hunca Munca and Tom Thumb, the Two Bad Mice in Beatrix Potter, try their best to maneuver a dollhouse bookcase holding a faux *Encyclopædia Britannica,* bound in red, into their mouse hole, but it doesn't quite fit. At the age of eighty and between prime ministerships, William Gladstone became fascinated with the problems of book storage, and during a visit to All Souls College, Oxford, he "launched out on his theme one evening in the Common Room," in the words of one observer, "and illustrated his scheme of bookshelves by an elaborate use of knives, forks, glasses, and decanters." Gladstone was not entirely sure how England was going to shelve all the books it produced without its citizens' being, as he writes, "extruded some centuries hence into the surrounding waters by the exorbitant dimensions of their own libraries." But one thing Gladstone was sure of: bookcases should be plain. "It has been a fashion to make bookcases highly ornamental," he says. "Now books want for and in themselves no ornament at all. They are themselves the ornament."

Books are themselves the ornament. A tenth-century Arabic-speaking scholar learned the truth of this proposition as he was browsing in the book bazaar in Córdoba, Spain. Córdoba was a literary capital; it held what was then the largest library in the world. Our scholar (whose name I don't know) was looking for a particular manuscript that he hadn't yet been able to find for sale. Finally, to his inexpressible joy, he came across a copy, written in an unusually fine script. He bid for it eagerly. "But," he writes,

> always the auctioneer returned with a higher bid, until the price far exceeded the actual value. Then I asked the auctioneer to show me the competitor who offered so much. He introduced me to a gentleman in magnificent garments and when I addressed him as Doctor, telling him that I was willing to leave the book to him if he needed it badly, as it was pointless to drive the price up higher, he replied: I am neither a scholar nor do I know what the book is about; but I am in the process of installing a library, in order to distinguish myself among the notables of the city, and happen to have a vacant space which this book would fill.

Books fill vacant spaces better than other collectibles, because they represent a different order of plenitude — they occupy not only the morocco-bound spine span on the shelf but the ampler stretches, the camel caravans of thought-bearing time required to read them through. If you amass a private library of hundreds of thousands of volumes, as the great Caliph Hakim II of Córdoba did before he died, in the year 976, you can feel confident that you have secured a kind of implied immortality: you die owning in reserve all the hours and years it would take those who outlive you to read, not to mention copy over, the words each book contains — and that bank of shelved time is your afterlife. And if you will your books to a cathedral library, or to a university, with the firm injunction that the books you give be chained in perpetuity (a stipulation that a number of English and Italian library benefactors included in their wills), you can't truly die, or so you may

secretly believe: you can't sink to infernal sub-basement floors or
float off to some poorly lit limbo, because your beloved delegation
of volumes, the library that surrounded you in life, and suffered
with you, and *is* you, is not tethered firmly to the present; you will
live on, linked by iron and brass to the resonant strongbox of the
world's recorded thought. One testator of 1442 asked that his rare
books be chained in the library at Guildhall, so that, he says, "the
visitors and students thereof be the sooner admonished to pray for
my soul."

But no deterrent, including chains, is a guarantee of immortality. Books can burn, and they can suffer depredations under various kinds of zealotry, and they can simply get sold off for cash or
mutilated by misguided conservators. The particular manuscript
that the tenth-century Arabic scholar coveted and couldn't afford
(he doesn't tell us what book it was) was very probably a casualty
of several attendant centuries of civil war and turmoil in Spain. A
satisfyingly heavy blue tome from 1939, called *The Medieval Library*,
tells us that by the time Philip II of Spain was fitting out the library
of the Escorial, not a single Arabic manuscript, nothing from the
glory days of Córdoba, could be found anywhere in the kingdom.
("Fortunately, the capture of a Moroccan galley in which a considerable number of Arabic books and manuscripts was found relieved the royal librarian's embarrassment," writes S. K. Padover.)
In England, tens of thousands of manuscripts — works that would
have been dusted with foxtails by dynasties of whispering atten-
dants in the Vatican if they had been fortunate enough to escape
there — perished during the suppression of the monasteries in the
sixteenth century. They died slowly in some cases: used to polish
candlesticks and boots, to wrap pies, to press gloves flat, or to
repair broken windows. Manuscripts of Duns Scotus, who later
became Gerard Manley Hopkins's preferred scholastic philosopher, were nailed to the walls of outhouses and torn off page by
page, forced to become, as one proud library purger wrote, "a
comon servant to evere man."

All this distant adversity has one positive effect, however: the
books now on our shelves become more ornamental and more
precious — regardless of their intrinsic worth — by the charged,
Lindisfarnean absence of the books that could have influenced or
improved them, directly or at many removes, but can't because

they are lost. This explains why some of us, like eager high school science students doing a unit on fruit flies, are drawn to study up close the short-lived images in catalogues or magazines, in search of tiny, attractively arbitrary points of literary embarkation. These books happen to be the books we have now. They've made it — made the leap from library catalogue to mail-order catalogue. They're survivors. I haven't yet ordered one of the tall revolving-shelf bookcases that the Levenger company, that very successful maker of "Tools for Serious Readers," sells, but I did recently look up the multivolume *Biographical History of Massachusetts*, published in 1909, that Levenger has shelved for display in the revolving bookcase shown on the cover of its early summer catalogue. I found, in Volume II, the story of Henry Albert Baker (no relation), a nineteenth-century dentist and lecturer on oral deformities, who in 1872 discovered the principle of the pneumatic dental mallet, a device used for forcing wads of silver amalgam into excavated molars. Baker, in the words of his biographer,

> happened to have in his hands a tube such as boys use for bean-blowers. At the same time he had in his mouth a round piece of candy which dissolved rapidly. He playfully put one end of the tube between his lips and accidentally the candy slipped into the tube. He covered the lower end of the tube with his finger to prevent it from dropping. As soon as he felt it touch his finger he sucked the candy back and to his surprise it flew up the tube with such force that he thought he had fractured one of his front teeth. He lay awake nearly all the following night trying to evolve a plan to utilize the force so mysteriously concealed. The next morning he was at the machine-shop bright and early and within three days he had the pneumatic mallet complete.

What could be more worth knowing than this? We could do worse than accept the reading suggestions that fall unsolicited through our mail slots.

There is a surprising further development in the history of the book and the bookcase. Not only is the book the prop of commonest resort in the world of mail order; but objects that resemble books — non-book items that carry bookishly antiquarian detailing — are suddenly popular. The book as a middle-class totem is in fashion to a degree not seen since Joseph Addison in 1711 encountered a private library containing dummy books of "All the

Classick Authors in Wood," along with a silver snuffbox "made in the Shape of a little Book." ("I was wonderfully pleased with such a mixt kind of Furniture," he wrote.) Catalogues now offer book-patterned ties, book brooches, and settees covered in trompe-l'oeil-bookshelf fabric. Pier 1 recently advertised a round glass-topped table whose base is a fake stack of nine large leather-bound books. The latest Horchow Home collection includes, for $869, an entire coffee table made in the image of two immense faux books hewn from chunks of beechwood; the top one is pretending to be Volume I of an Italian edition of Homer. The catalogue for See's candies sells the Chocolate Classics, a book-shaped box of candy bars. The Paragon gift catalogue offers a fairly awful table clock with one fake gold-tooled book perched on top and two fake books underneath, bearing the legend, in gold script, "Times to Remember." Paragon also has an ex-libris frame for snapshots, in printed fabric, showing many shelves of black- and red-bound books — black and red being the colors, we remember, of the poor scholar's books in *The Canterbury Tales*. A catalogue called Ross-Simons Anticipations has a $300 mirror whose frame consists of several "shelves" of artificial old-style book spines, so that when you check your tie you'll be thronged with literary feelings.

And then there is the Eximious of London catalogue, which began appearing in American mail pouches several years ago. ("Eximious" is an archaic word meaning "distinguished" or "select.") It carries a four-volume set of book coasters (water-resistant), and a book pencil pot covered with precise replicas of Volume IV of an old edition of the collected works of Racine. I spoke with Cricket, of Customer Service, who told me that the Racine pencil pot was probably their best faux-book seller. And there is the so-called "scholarly magnifying glass with faux book-spine handle." The handle is a vividly lifelike mold taken from a book called *Ramsay's Poetical Works*. It's a provocative choice. Allan Ramsay wrote verse in what to an American ear is intolerable Scottish dialect, but he also has the distinction of having opened, in Edinburgh in 1725, the first circulating library — a place where, as in a modern video store, you rent what you can't afford to buy. Ramsay thus initiated the great change in the demography of readership which takes us from eighteenth-century Gothic chambers of sensationalism to the nineteenth-century coronation of the novel as the preeminent literary form, and, eventually, to the complete subordination of leather-bound books of poetry like Ramsay's own.

Finally, there is the Faux Book Cassette Holder. Several companies sell false fronts for cassettes, CDs, and videotapes, but this is the only one that made me want to read some Shakespeare. The product turns "an unsightly situation into a stunning bookshelf asset," Eximious says. "The mellow row of books looks exactly like a set of leather-bound antique volumes, because the resin mould was actually taken from such a set." What set is it? It's the Pickering's Christian Classics collection, published in the 1840s by the bibliophilic William Pickering, who had a thing for miniature books, or what librarians call "tinies." His tiny of several Latin poets drew the attention of Gladstone himself, who noted with approval that it weighed only "an ounce and a quarter." I couldn't put my hands on a copy of Saltmarsh's *Sparkles of Glory*, the eleventh volume in Pickering's row, or on Hill's *Pathway to Piety*, but I did read some of the ninth volume — Christopher Sutton's *Learn to Die*, a reprint of a work first published in 1600 in black-letter type. Those embarrassing multicassette pop-music anthologies you may have bought (or, rather, I may have bought) on impulse, by phone, while watching Court TV — the ones with titles like *Forever '8os*, or *The Awesome '8os*, or *Totally '8os* — can now reside, shielded from inquisitors, behind the binding of a book that contains morbidly helpful thoughts such as this:

> Seeing therefore, that on every side, wee have such urgent occasion, to passe the dayes of this wearysome Pilgrimage in trouble, and pensivenesse of minde, may wee not thinke them thrice blessed, who are now landed on the shoare of perfect Securitie, and delivered from the burden of so toilesome a labour: May wee not bee refreshed, in calling to minde, that this battaile will one day be at an ende, and wee freed from the thorowes of all these bitter calamities?

As for beauty, Sutton writes:

> Doe not some few fits of a feaver, marre all the fashion? The inconstancy of all worldly glory! All this stately and pageantlike pompe shall vanish away, and come to nothing, as if it never had bene.

Just the right note to strike in a cassette holder. As I read *Learn to Die*, I began wondering whether Christopher Sutton had been spending time at the Globe Theatre: variations on phrases and metaphors from Shakespeare's late plays, especially from soliloquies in *Hamlet*, kept cropping up. Even the opening words of the book — "That religion is somewhat out of joynt" — recall Hamlet's announcement that "the time is out of joint." So I got down a copy of *Hamlet*, and soon saw that I was mistaken. It wasn't that Christopher Sutton had been hearing Shakespeare; it was that Shakespeare had been reading Christopher Sutton: *Learn to Die* came out in 1600, while *Hamlet* wasn't produced until about 1602. And yet Sutton isn't listed in any study of Shakespeare's sources that I checked, or in the Arden *Hamlet*, or in the nineteenth-century variorum edition of *Hamlet* by Horace Howard Furness. Could the Eximious catalogue be giving us, for only $51.50 plus shipping, an admittedly minor but nonetheless significant and as yet undissertationed source for Hamlet's death-fraught inner sermons? Could a mail-order catalogue be sending us to graduate school?

It is a little disorienting, though — the wish to disguise one's cassettes or one's videotapes behind this extreme sort of leathery surrogacy. Better, truer, braver it would have been for Eximious to market a set of faux Penguin paperbacks, intermingled with a few faux Vintage Contemporaries. Our working notion of what books look like is on the verge of becoming frozen in a brownish fantasy phase that may estrange us from, and therefore weaken our resolve to read, the books we actually own. Hamlet, who was tolerant of bad puns, might have been tempted to point out that when a book turns faux it may cease to be a friend.

If we momentarily resist the gold-filigreed-leather archetype, we may discover that the essential generous miracle of the bound book — which is the result of its covert pagination (that is, its quality of appearing to have only two surfaces when closed but in fact fanning forth dozens or hundreds of surfaces when opened) — is, right now, undergoing more technical experimentation and refinement and playful exaggeration than at any other time in its history. The book, considered as a four-cornered piece of technology, bound on one side, is still surprisingly young. Signs of its youth are to be found, naturally, in the children's section of the bookstore, where a brilliant corps of paper engineers have lately made their mark. The children's section has third-generation pop-up books that arch and pose under the stress of page-turning like protégées of Isadora Duncan. There are lift-the-flap books, which carry subordinate pages on their pages, offering further surprises of surface area, and yet allow their flaps to be torn off without protest. (My son, who is one and a half, spends an hour each day reviewing his now flapless lift-the-flap books.) On these shelves you'll find letter-pouch books, like *The Jolly Postman,* and up-to-date variations on the old textural pat-the-bunny and feel-daddy's-scratchy-face theme; you will encounter rows of miniature, stiff-paged Chunky or Pudgy books, and the foam padded Super Chubby series from Simon & Schuster, and the patented double-wide House Books from Workman Publishing, all of which boldly make a virtue of the necessary thickness of the non-virtual page. Even *Goodnight Moon* is now a board book. And there are books here with neo-medieval tabs to hold them closed, and real wheels to roll on, and books that have a hole in every page and a squeaking pig in their heart. There are books that are really toy kits with pamphlets, like *Build Your Own Radio,* published by Running Press, which when opened reveals circuitry, not words; or the *Make Your Own Book* kit, with paper and binding glue; or consummations like *The Mystery of the Russian Ruby,* which includes its own Sherlock Holmesian hinged bookcase disguising a secret stairway and a disappearing high-heeled foot; or the folio-size construct that calls itself a book, and is published by St. Martin's, a reputed book publisher, but that upon opening burgeons into a 360-degree, two-story Victorian dollhouse. Upstairs, near the fireplace, there is a small lift-the-flap book cupboard holding six weighty, untitled volumes.

Several times lately, stirred by this foliated ferment in the children's section, or by the confident bibliophilia to be found in the bulk-mail catalogues, I have stood before my own six undistinguished bookcases and regarded the serried furniture they hold with a new level of interest and consideration. The best bookcase moment, I find, is when you reach up to get a paperback that happens to sit on one of the higher shelves, above your head. You single it out by putting a fingertip atop the block of its pages and pulling gently down, so that the book rocks forward and a triangle of cover design appears from between the paperbacks on either side. The book's emergence is steadied and slowed by the mild lateral pressure of its shelved peers, and, if you stop pulling just then, it will hang there by itself, at an angle, leaning out over the room like an admonishing piece of architectural detail; it will not fall. Finally the moment of equilibrium passes: the book's displaced center of gravity and the narrowing area it has available for adjacent friction conspire to release its weight to you, and it drops forward into your open hand. You catch the book that you chose to make fall. And, with any luck, you read it.

JULIE BAUMGOLD

Midnight in the Garden
of Good and Elvis

FROM ESQUIRE

HE FLEW. Belted into the blue velour King-size bed of the *Lisa Marie*, Elvis flew. With an ex–beauty queen, an alert young girl, strapped next to him, in a state somewhere between up and down, he flew between shows, ready to fall from the dark air onto the next stage in the next indoor stadium. He would arrive at intermission — he never liked to wait. He'd ask how the crowd was, always insecure. And he would always be nervous, so nervous his men got nervous with him. Maybe that is where his eternity finds him, with his men at his side, moving through the underground passages. The way was cleared until the end, and he would walk to something he loved, his studded pant legs flapping, his large, strained heart ready to burst, the sweat already beaded on his face. The flashbulbs started popping at the end as he went up the stairs, almost blind, hearing "Thus Spake Zarathustra" pounding. They escorted him right to the steps they had counted, and he walked up alone. "Have a good show," said the men. He was nervous then and through the first two songs, as he stepped from the dark into the streaming crisscross of lights that found him. He was never announced. He never needed to be.

Only a few like him would come along in a century and change the world. His mother could dance and his father could sing, and out of them came a magic son. Once magic people are recognized, no one can tell them no, and sometimes it kills them.

When he was forty-two years old and very fat, Elvis Presley went into his mirrored bathroom one morning, which was his night, and fell off the toilet, dead on the floor, his blue silk pajama bottoms crumpled at his feet. He died on his knees, bare-assed, his blue face smashed deep into the red shag on the day he was to start a sold-out tour. The toxicologist found Elavil, Aventyl, codeine, morphine, methaqualone, Valium, ethinamate, ethchlorvynol, amobarbital, Nembutal, Carbrital, Demerol, and Sinutab in his blood — some of them in ten times their lethal doses. That was how he consumed his drugs, cars, women, clothes, motorcycles, and planes — one was never enough to get Elvis up or down, to deaden his pain, interrupt his boredom, and bring him into the oblivion where he had found a new place to dwell.

Seeing these drug lists, the Elvis biographers — Albert Goldman (vilified) and Peter Guralnick (praised) — each had to seek out a drug expert to understand the effect of the disinhibitors, opiates, barbiturates, antidepressants, and euphorics that do not so much take the pain away as make you not care about it. The men, who lived it with him but never went as far, already understood, but none of them could quite explain. Surely Elvis had leftover pain from his mother's death, his wife's abandonment, from a freak colon that was two feet too long and twisted, glaucoma, a bad leg, and a heart that skipped beats and woke him with its pounding. It was hard for a vain man to get up fat every afternoon, and there was pain, too, from his men who betrayed him.

The bad death did not diminish his life. With Elvis, it is always better to hear the songs, watch the film clips and movies that fill the airwaves at tribute times. From the first performances, it was all there — the self-assurance, awareness, and charm of a natural. He had that weird sweetness that made everything all right and that young grin, as though embarrassed at being so loved. And yet he understood. The smile and different voice remained to the last swollen image, rambling, dripping sweat tears.

When he died, he was reading *The Scientific Search for the Face of Jesus*. He liked books about the promises of other worlds, alien existence, predestination, and the afterlife. He often read himself into a color or numerology number or a book like *The Impersonal Self*. Long ago, he had begun his paranormal life. He had become a beloved national ruin. He was famous first for moving loose, but now his moves were choreographed karate kicks, and his natural flashiness in clothes had become costumes and capes. His voice had lowered, but it was still beautiful, and a desperate love poured out of every song, even the most repeated.

At some point after his death in 1977, a form of twentieth-century religion began, and some of his fans became followers and then worshipers. The house became a shrine, the most visited grave in America, with candlelight vigils, annual birthday and death-day keening at the Graceland gates and in the Meditation Garden. Those who were close to him became either disciples, the nervous priests of the shrine, or Judases. Priscilla Presley, whom he met when she was fourteen and who went to live with him when she was sixteen, became the Virgin Mother, and her daughter, flesh of his flesh, almost became the Holy Child. Instead of remaining in Memphis, however, they absconded to Hollywood and left Elvis to a corporation. Dead, he could be whatever they wanted him to be.

Elvis the Saint, or at least the myth, is worshiped for the acts of goodness he did while on earth, for his generosity — the undeclared cash, random Cadillacs, and kindnesses he bestowed. Pieces of his life are enshrined and preserved as relics. A tear in his pool table remains unrepaired because that is the way it was just before he died. Only documented miracles are lacking to complete the process of sanctification, and there have been a few of those — the Make-a-Wish child here and there — as he has transmogrified from outcast to respected son of the South to radiant symbol.

David Leonard's TV documentary, *Why Elvis?*, was filled with people making Elvis/Jesus parallels. "Elvis clothed and fed the people and took care of them," one woman said. Annually, on his death day, the celebrants tour the sites of his life — Sun Records, Kang Rhee Karate Institute, Humes High, the Lauderdale Courts projects, and Libertyland and the Memphian theater (he took these over during the odd hours he walked) — which have become the stations of the cross.

All this saint talk bothers Jack Soden, the former Kansas City investment banker who runs Graceland and Elvis Presley Enterprises and wants to make Elvis a twenty-first-century profit center. It bothers the men who lived with him. It bothers the Memphians.

"Let's not take it all too seriously . . . the icon. The fans are so intense we make a joke about jelly doughnuts and they are pained by it," says Soden, who has hundreds of people working for Elvis eighteen years after his death. "There are an endless number of ways to see him. Little old ladies come through and say, 'He was so good to his mom.' And veterans come through and say, 'He cut his hair off and served in the army.'" They all have told on him now — the nurse, the cook, Priscilla, the stepbrothers, most of the guys.

The day he died is still marked by all sorts of carryings-on on Elvis Presley Boulevard as the pilgrims walk and weep, the wax tears dripping onto cardboard shields they have made for their candles. Some mourn the young Elvis and some the old ruined one, for his weakness was part of loving him. (Look what he did to himself for our sins.) Until his death, they did not quite know he was a drug addict. They only knew that, like them, he had grown heavy with middle age, for he was a star the same age as his fans, having started so young.

The dead Elvis became permanent sections of movies in video stores, whole walls of discs in music stores, more than 400 books, 150 registered impersonators, and as many artifacts as the merchandising brain could conceive. As the character Elvis, he entered plays and novels and movies. He was posthumous platinum, one hot eternal market. He was said to walk again after his death. Their blue Elvis. Original (or at least he amalgamated himself into an original). Different. First. There for each of them to save. His fans went around Krazy Gluing shut the covers of Albert Goldman's heretical book. It was one of the few times America loved someone like Monroe or Gable, who suggested, even in the middle of his sexiness, that he could laugh at himself.

Celebrity is modern myth, an attempt by studying the lives of famous others to find answers for ourselves. The pantheon changes but always is full of incarnate human gods, sacred marriages, taboos, kings killed when their strength fails, human scapegoats, expulsion of embodied evils. Supermodels, rock and TV stars, shaman-priests, and Elvis are examples of contagious magic, the myths created by many. Myths were explanations, and Elvis still explains how the lowly can rise, how the high can fall, how the magician can enchant, how the ritual can thrill and the man-god convince each he has come only for them.

Here in Memphis, at Graceland, in playlands and theme parks, Elvis is sold as an icon, Santa Elvis now, just an image, the voice on the records, hollow and echoing, for he was always strangely his own echo. Soden plans Elvis theme parks, Elvis casinos, and tasteful collectibles. "We're looking at concepts worldwide," he says. "There is a natural tie-in with Vegas. Asia is a big market. The Japanese like the American South."

Time and chance had allowed the image of the fat, addicted Elvis to be absorbed and the sightings of the Not-Dead Elvis to stop so that the thin young Elvis of the postage stamp could be reborn to be marketed and prevail. His sixtieth birthday last January was the time of the Elvis for eternity to be carried forward. The mythic Elvis had incorporated the heavyweight girdled into the jumpsuits. He was loved and forgiven, presented alongside the young rocker. He was a good actor, and even the windup Elvis of the late movies was full of joy and sex with his slurry voice, his big hands and feet, black glossy pompadour rising over his blue eyes and shadowing his pouty, naughty baby mouth. Another specter jumped forth — the black-leather Elvis of the 1968 comeback, a compromise. All coexisted, though the Elvis of the 1950s sells the best.

He was always out of his time, as the genius must be, for the genius is in the process of making his times. He was outside country, rock 'n' roll before it existed, then rock in the era of the Beatles, a drug addict when self-indulgence was not accepted as a medical problem and it was not all right to check into rehab, pre–public confession and pre–TV absolution.

In the beginning, he said to Hy Gardner, "It all happened so fast, I'm all mixed up." He thought he was invulnerable. He became his own hero. He could always get better. He fell for that old Southern line "Tomorrow is another day."

Near the end, Elvis talked to Red West, who was about to publish *Elvis: What Happened?*, and said, "I'm operating on but one cylinder . . . the fun ceased to exist. I couldn't pinpoint it. . . . I'd become an object, not a person. I felt terrible, alone . . . intensely alone at heart."

Memphis is a river city in cotton country, with a pyramid in the west built by an out-of-town character named Sidney Shlenker. It has Beale Street, where they play the blues in the night, and a hotel where they roll out a red carpet twice a day for five nervous ducks to walk through the lobby to their penthouse suite as trumpets play the "King Cotton" march. It is one of those Southern towns where no one is ever a stranger but everyone is a little bit strange.

Most everyone except the visitors to Graceland seems to have been born in America. There is not a great sense of irony or scorn here. Memphis chooses to forget the bad before and after a man's passing, which makes it a perfect tomb for this man who was bad mainly to himself.

It's a Southern habit not to talk about anything so unpleasant. Elvis of the South and his mother were surrounded by Southern denial: "If you can't say something nice . . ." Had Elvis lived in the North or stayed in the West, they would have been on to him in an instant — but the South is better at hiding things and forgiving.

Here are the cotton brokers of Front Street, where the Mississippi riverboats docked when Memphis was the world's largest cotton market. The Cotton Exchange is still in Memphis, but the Cotton Carnival had to change its name to just Carnival because of the secret societies, and of course they can't play "Dixie" anymore. They pretend to be hard-playing children, but the good ol' boys are sharp under their sleepy voices, and the women have former hard-won beauty-queen titles like Miss Catfish, Miss Okra, or Miss Boll Weevil.

Mud Island Museum is here, and the National Civil Rights Museum, where a woman named Jackie Smith has stood outside in protest every day since 1988. Cybill Shepherd has built herself a new little yellow castle on Chickasaw Bluff, because the natives always return. The silent Isaac Tigrett, who founded the Hard Rock Cafe and the House of Blues, came home. Bad Bob's Vapors Club has closed, but there is B. B. King's and a very large ghost who has big birthdays after his death. Those of a certain age, people who know the same songs, all remember Elvis. They appear, gray-haired, settled into their flesh, to reminisce with one voice for the cameras: He never put on airs, never forgot where he came from. A cabdriver says, "Elvis was a real saint. He always had something to give people — the winos, the men who shined shoes." Charles Chandler, who used to open his store after hours for Elvis to shop, remembers: "Sylvia waited on him when he was picking out fur coats for friends, and he told her to choose whatever she wanted, and she said, 'There's a marvelous lady in the alterations department, and all I want is for you to go upstairs and kiss her,' and he

did. . . . Bill Speer was the first person to photograph him. He had
the body of a child and the face of a man. The body was soft,
smooth, undeveloped, a beautiful young body, a child's body and
a beautiful face."

It was a startling face. It had a timeless, classical beauty, sensual
in a disturbing way for both men and women. It was open and
closed. The blue eyes were lidded, the nostrils flared, the lips full.
Walking through the starlight with his guys, even at the end, he
was the beauty of the group. As others have said — with just the
voice, without that shocking beauty, he would not have been Elvis.
The way he moved began it all — the shaking shoulders, the loose
legs, the swiveling on the balls of his white-socked feet as he
covered the stage in his own moonwalk, the twisting hips, the legs
collapsing out. With the lock of his hair flopping down, wrist
dangling, he fell to his knees, so the early photos show his pants
covered with the dust of the stage.

Just outside Memphis, across the state line on the two-lane Highway 51, is Tunica, Mississippi, the poorest county in the United
States. Nine major casinos have planted themselves here, dotted
like little white puffs through the cotton fields. Tunica sits and
sparkles hard and waits for *60 Minutes* or one of the other magazine shows to get around to it.

This area used to be called Sugar Ditch when Jesse Jackson came
here to point it out to the world and call for economic development. Some Memphians blame Tunica for sucking away their
dollars. Like Elvis, Tunica is something they used to laugh at until
it started making rich men into "mult-eye" millionaires. Splash
Casino opened in 1992 and briefly became the country's most
successful casino per square foot. The Southern Belle is closed for
now, and others will close soon. The only differences among those
that remain are the distractions hanging from the walls and ceilings of these fools' palaces.

The Hollywood Casino has many of the discards of fame. It has
the plane from *True Lies* and the biplane that crop-dusted Cary
Grant in *North by Northwest*. Merle Oberon's and Joan Crawford's
dresses have come to rest here on tiny dummies, and there are yet
more cycles, cars, and an Elvis jumpsuit. For big money, the Hollywood bought one of the Elvis TCB (Takin' Care of Business)
necklaces with the Captain Marvel lightning bolt.

SPECIAL SAUSAGE, GRITS, BISCUITS AND GRAVY, say the lights stitching up the marquee at the Hollywood. The casino hosts share a set of small offices off the casino floor. They are back living in the night, in Elvis time, where the day begins at twilight. One October night, on the weekend of the televised Tribute, three people connected to Elvis were there, in one office, as much in the background now as they were in the background of his fame. Here was George Klein, his high school friend. George introduced Elvis to lots of women, among them casino host Gail Stanton. Kim Hughes, the office manager, is the girlfriend of Richard Davis, now a security guard at the Sheraton but for many years an Elvis bodyguard and his stand-in for twenty-one movies. Many of the Elvis men are looking for the next thing to do, because for most of them Elvis was the thing they did best.

They were Elvis's lost brothers, and Graceland was always filled with friends and paid buddies as he, arrested in his teenage tastes, recreated the dream life of an only child, playing when and what he wanted and winning. He left them all behind to grow old.

"Richard had fun, but now it's over," says Kim Hughes. "Some of these people live their whole lives for Elvis." But some time later, Richard will contradict her: "It was like being a disciple. We were twelve guys when I started. . . . I still cry on him."

Elvis Presley is the big thing that happened in these lives. Gail Stanton's beauty took her into the high life with Hugh Hefner, and George Klein was a disc jockey with his own radio and television dance show, but Elvis was something else. In the Elvis years, all were sucked into the night, into the after-hours where Elvis lived, the big-time world of private planes that waited on whims and theaters that would open at 4 A.M. to show their movies — repeating reels if he wanted — and the great, increasingly sad adventure that was Elvis. They were near the one who was sought after. Now they are living ordinary lives with bills and sick parents, grandchildren, cars that don't start, looking at what things cost on menus. For some, all that's left are the cruise-ship lectures or the tape of an old *Geraldo* program they appeared on. That, and the interest that comes over most people's faces when it comes up in the conversation that they knew Elvis.

They handle life after Elvis differently. The Memphis mafia is full of rivalries and dissension. They were the ones who were there for the intimate duties and rituals of the levee and bedtimes. They were there to distract, to wind him up and down with the "medications." They were there to carry his Jog Joy flight suits onto the plane to fly to Denver for a tray of sandwiches, to ride with him on the snowmobiles, the motorcycles, and the powerboats and fight the childish mock battles he staged. They kept the girls from colliding and became expert at travel arrangements and booking suites. When he toured, they lined the windows with foil, laid out his kit. And, finally, the lost brothers were there to walk up the stairs with the packets of pills and hypodermics and trays of barbecued bologna and the strange, sweet foods the addict craves, to sit with him while he slept, sneak drugs to him when he was trying to get better in hospitals, and keep watch when Elvis was on the nod, unconscious, semiconscious, gone, gone, gone.

In the beginning, he tried to build this family filled with boys of similar Southern backgrounds and limited educations, who would play and ponder the universe with him. They didn't make much money, but around Elvis, everything was paid for. There was a time when they dressed alike in suits and shades and moved in packs of Cadillacs or horses, motorcycles through L.A. and Vegas, drugged with him and armed like him. Despite his spoiled tantrums, his rages and moods, they all loved him wildly and were ready to hurl themselves in front of "E." They all describe him as a Greek god — exactly those words. At last, he was popular and regarded, included as he never had been in high school. Even offstage, he was the center.

"We were driving around Bel Air and couldn't find his house, just walls and fences and shrubbery and stuff," Richard Davis remembers. "And he sent Lamar Fike in a Rolls-Royce to lead us up to the house . . . a big mausoleum-looking house with a chandelier and good-looking women everywhere, and our eyes were kind of big that night." Elvis, standing in a bathroom, hired Davis for sixty-five dollars a week. "In 1961, that was a lot of money. I'd been building highway, making sixty-five every two weeks."

They were with him when he was fidgety before the shows in the dressing room with his six-pack of Mountain Valley Spring Water and the shots of B_{12} and uppers. And he'd be pacing and twisting his ring, full of the fierce energy that built and built till he walked onto the stage and it exploded into the audience. They were there after the shows, when he was wound up, wanting to sing gospel, and they would find a positive thing to say right away and then later slowly introduce anything that had gone wrong. They handled the sweat-soaked scarves and pieces of himself he distributed, used their fists and big arms. They brought the cars around and beckoned the chosen into the circle of Elvis's light and stood around him to keep out the others.

This October night in Tunica, George Klein telephones Joe Esposito, who is on the way to Nashville to publicize his Elvis book, *Good Rockin' Tonight*. When Joe met Elvis, they were in the army and Elvis was wearing a maroon velour shirt with the collar up over his regulation army pants. Joe really never left, and became his road manager and best man at his wedding. Joe does not go to the Elvis conventions and wrote his book when there was a lull in his life three years ago. He is still trying to find something to do. "It's boring now," he says, "different on the road after Elvis." For him, for George, for Richard, Elvis was a hard escape.

"I was fascinated by him," says Joe. They had the same silly sense of humor. In *Good Rockin'*, he says Elvis had the stance of a black man and walked differently, "kind of hip and relaxed." He says Elvis hated people touching his food, liked to get people excited, "pulled out" when making love, living in the shah's house in Bel Air, didn't wear underwear much, and was visibly excited in the movie *Girls! Girls! Girls!* He called Priscilla his pet name for his mother, Sattnin, and she called him Nungin, meaning "young one," for he repeated his baby talk with the girls he liked the best. He says Elvis did not like to make love to someone who had had a child, including Priscilla. He confirms that Elvis liked to see videos of teenage girls wrestling in white cotton underpants.

Being with Elvis meant you talked about only what he wanted to talk about, for he was very spoiled by his mother, then by the world, and would do whatever he wanted to do. He would never admit he was wrong, just give the person a car. He was hard-headed and he had "a short fuse" due to his mood and 'lude swings.

"His whole family was very addictive," says Esposito. Elvis had one grandmother who took to her bed early on. He had an alcoholic mother whose medicine was moonshine. "And he was a hypochondriac. If there was a medicine, he would take as many as he could get. If one thing makes you feel good, two will make you feel better. We hoped that one day he would wake up and realize . . ."

No one said no. The drugs were prescribed, then overprescribed. Elvis charmed them from flattered doctors and awestruck local druggists, leaning over the counters, his skin glowing in the neon lights. It was Elvis Presley before them — that voice, those shaded eyes. After Priscilla left him, he was especially addicted to downers, which produced periods of motionless nirvana that grew longer and longer while he took his injuries up into the ether, prone in a sedative float, pleasantly deadened on soporifics, going over the hump between sleep and the high, into the rush, misty and safe. He could get away with anything, any amount. He was invulnerable. His mother had told him he was special.

He never could sleep. He could not stay asleep. He sleepwalked all his life.

"He didn't like the taste of alcohol, didn't drink beer," says Joe Esposito. "Sometimes had a screwdriver. But then he'd have ten, not one. He tasted peach brandy, liked it, and drank the whole bottle."

Later, George Klein says, "If confronted in a rough way, he'd throw you out of the house, and then what good could you be to him?" George had introduced Elvis to Dr. George Nichopoulos, who first treated Elvis's saddle sores and went on to tour with him as court physician. Klein married Dr. Nick's nurse, with Elvis as his best man. After Elvis's death, Dr. Nick was acquitted on drug charges — he supposedly replaced some of the drugs with placebos — but in the thirty-two months before Elvis died, he had prescribed nineteen thousand doses of drugs for him.

In Memphis, George Klein is the ambassador to the country that is Elvis. He goes on cruises and to fan-club conventions, "three-day deals" that bloom in chilly hotel lobbies set up with booths. He thinks of Elvis every day, and every day people tell him Elvis stories, which he writes on legal pads. He remembers how Dean Martin told Elvis not to act but to be himself, how Robert Mitchum offered Elvis a part in *Thunder Road,* and Streisand offered him the Kristofferson role in *A Star Is Born,* how Bobby Darin told him that Elvis could play one side of the street in Las Vegas and all the rest of them the other, and Elvis would still outdraw them all. When Elvis had his nose fixed, he made George have his fixed, too, and paid for it.

Klein met Elvis when Elvis was in the eighth grade, living in the projects. He was walked everywhere by his mother, his eyes on the ground. Gladys Presley hid behind trees to watch over him. They were in music class, where they studied Bach and how to put the clefs into staffs, when Elvis asked the teacher if he could bring in his guitar the last class before Christmas.

"Here he was, twelve years old, and he gets up. He was on the left and I was on the right, and I said, 'Wow.'" Elvis defined himself in high school by the way he dressed, which was different from other white boys, kind of dressy and fancy. He bought his clothes on Main and Beale streets and would wear pants with a white or pink stripe, sport coats, shirts with turned-up collars copied from James Dean and Marlon Brando, his long, greased hair endlessly stroked and sculpted into a pompadour and DA. He would see a sharp shirt and buy it on a layaway plan and work to make the money for it.

Klein was one of the guys retelling the old-time stories of touring in the car and trains, playing one town at eight and another at ten, as they sat at the gold-veined mirrored table at Graceland, throwing rolls at Elvis. They kept their mouths shut when they had something important to say, because the way to talk to Elvis was "one-on-one in privacy." They rented the roller rinks and amusement parks and movie theaters "because these were things we could not do when we were younger. . . . Every night was like Saturday night, like a dream come true, and I had this association with the biggest name in show business," says Klein.

Some nights, they went draggin' on Main Street in Elvis's white Lincoln Mark II, a limousine, or one of the Cadillacs. "He was red-hot, and the girls would hang around the house, and we'd come out the gate, and they'd follow us. They knew where we were going, and even if we lost them, they'd be there. . . . After the army, he could move more freely. The town went to sleep after the ten o'clock news. People who were cruising would want to shake hands, but it wasn't the hysteria of pulling off the license plates. Often, then, there were girls who wanted to party with us.

"After he left movies, some say he was feeling bad, but a great-looking eighteen-year-old would make you feel great," continues Klein, who got him many of the Miss Thises and Miss Thats, because he knew Elvis's type — "small, sincere, with a good figure, a Southern quality as opposed to the hard, showbiz quality." Kittenish girls like Priscilla. So Klein introduced him to Anita Wood, who was his girl for five years, then Linda Thompson (four years) and Ginger Alden, the last girl. At first, Elvis took care of them and they were small, and then they took care of him and they were large showgirls and beauty queens, though women with big feet frightened him. (This, together with his hair fetish and supposed fear of homosexuals, is interesting Freudian fodder.) Priscilla, Ginger, and Linda all looked something like his mother.

"I never saw anyone enjoy what he was doing as much as Elvis did," says Klein. "He liked touring and life on the road. He had finished with movies and was doing concerts. His manager, Colonel Parker, kept him to twelve- to twenty-thousand-seat buildings — which he could fill — by saying, 'Elvis, you know you like to play inside' and avoiding the fifty-thousand-seat stadiums."

Death and time are the great pardoners. Carl Perkins, the man who wrote "Blue Suede Shoes" and sang it first, walked through the gates at Graceland for Priscilla Presley's party before the October Tribute. In the dark, it took the TV crews a while to find Carl walking up the long driveway to the house on the hill. He said to them, "People like [Elvis] don't go away." Elvis used to walk down this hill at night to the gates, where there were always fifty or so fans, and he'd sign for them and pose. He never refused them until the time came when his life at Graceland turned indoors, upstairs, and further into the drug cocoons he had built for himself. Then, occasionally, the car would ooze down the driveway, the window would lower on E, his eyes always hidden by the tinted aviator glasses. The papers were passed in to him — he did not get out.

"Hi, cousin. Hey, man." Carl Perkins slaps palms with some of the musicians lined up outside Graceland, the house on the hill Elvis had been aiming at since they took away his first home, called a shotgun shack because if you shot a gun at one end, it would go right through the two rooms. His first big house was on Audubon, and when it started getting crowds, some of Elvis's rich neighbors called on him because of the traffic problem he was causing and offered to buy his house for above market price. Without pause, Elvis said he was prepared to buy all their houses.

The guests were lined up for tours of Graceland, and no one was giving them the rules about flashbulbs deteriorating the priceless artifacts, as the mansion's keepers do the 650,000 visitors who tour the house by day every year. It is a brilliant theme park modeled on Jack Soden's research and especially the tours of William Randolph Hearst's San Simeon. But what a sad house it is, its front promising a grandeur undelivered within. Graceland has become a National Historic House, a museum with scripted docents pointing to the green shag.

A wash of sadness comes over some of the Tribute musicians. They had been prepared to enjoy the famously bad taste arrested in the 1970s, but instead, Graceland is simply how a poor boy would try to live rich. Some visitors go through awed and weeping — an oxygen tank stands ready for the overcome in the corners — but not tonight. The rockers and country stars walk through the jungle room with its fake-fur lampshades, depressed at the outcome of this first rock-star fame. The small, low-ceilinged rooms are full of his problems. The heavily tented billiard room, the narrow, squeezed passages with carpet crawling up from the floor to the walls and ceiling, the dark, all say, Take me back into the womb, enclose me and hold me close. Back to where he lived with his twin, finally marrying the little girl he made look like his twin, as a narcissist would do. The set-for-eternity dining table resting on a stingy rectangle of marble, the smoky mirrors, the pictures of his father, slitty-eyed Vernon, the long sofas all behind ropes, say, Love me as tender as my ma, who kept her chickens in the back yard. Sit with me. And the girls did, mute in front of the television, laughing when he did, jostling close, eyeing each other for advantage, tense and jealous under their perfect, shiny smiles and good Southern posture.

Because Graceland is a shrine, the bullets that a bored Elvis and his armed guys fired from the main house into the smokehouse have been dug out of the walls and preserved in a dish behind Plexiglas. Graceland's wings now hold his collections of 11-D shoes and gold records and increasingly larger jumpsuits from the days when the collars had climbed to his ears and it was easier to sweat into the scarves without moving. Elvis's long-term girlfriends Linda and Ginger had each changed Graceland, but since his death, it has been restored to the cool blue-green days of Priscilla. It had been delivered from its last incarnation as a red-and-gold "whore-house" with Elvis up the red stairs, the chief prized whore on whose body the house ran. Elvis had grown to hate the red-and-gold Graceland and would always enter by the back and go up the back steps in his last years.

Priscilla Presley arrives, driven in one of Graceland's golf carts, now the forty-nine-year-old queen of the tent, a peerless ice beauty, standing frozen in a dignified black panne velvet dress, her hair the color of dark flames. She has the most remarkable mouth, an abnormally small, perfectly etched bow. Elvis was a good teacher, training her to be the cool survivor, the perfect flame-tender, bringing her first love from immortality through the centuries. I once asked Albert Goldman, whose sin was not understanding either Elvis's appeal or his misery, how Priscilla's mother and stepfather could have allowed her to go live with Elvis. He said she was a wild little girl. She was Elvis's pet to train into the virgin bride and photograph doing all kinds of things sixteen-year-old girls shouldn't do. There were videos and sexually explicit photos. They were both very young. They used to make giggling trips to the drugstore for film night after night. Elvis preserved his fantasies in a blue Samsonite suitcase, which the faithful Joe Esposito returned to Priscilla. "Tame by today's standards," he says.

When Elvis came back from the army, he coyly lied, "There was a little girl I was seeing quite often . . . but it was no big romance. . . . I have to be careful when I answer a question like that." He laughed then, because "underage" was dangerous territory, and they all knew it. He was the good son who got away with anything he wanted in the middle of the South, behind the gates of fame, which in those days Colonel Parker could keep tightly shut.

Esposito was in the room in Germany when Priscilla walked in wearing her sailor suit and white socks. She stood in the door. "We did not know she was fourteen — we thought she was sixteen, maybe." After a few dates, Elvis had it set in his mind he was going to marry her. And Joe believes, as Priscilla has said, that though she slept in his bed for six years, she was a virgin till they married.

"He taught me everything," Priscilla once said. "How to dress, how to walk, how to apply makeup and wear my hair, how to return love — his way. Over the years, he became my father, husband, and very nearly God." And then, one day in 1972, his song "I Was the One" came true, as songs have a habit of doing, and Priscilla, neglected and semi-duped by Elvis for years, went off with her karate instructor.

"Priscilla came in surrounded by lawyers and accountants and people trained to be worried, who told her to sell everything, but she refused. She never had anything but a long-term view," says Jack Soden.

Under a Harley strung with lights and flanked by pink wire flamingos, waiters are slicing pork loin and dishing out the sweet-potato fritters. Big country men like Dwight Yoakam walk right in while city folk like Iggy Pop, small and dark, slink in on the fringes of the tent and have to be propelled to Priscilla. Here are all the generations of rock and Elvis — some of the older ones with dyed hair or wigs. Everyone finds someone to impress them, and there are many strange convergences.

"He was a real good patient," says Elvis's nurse, Marian Cocke. "I'd give him some of the medicines, and he'd say, 'Oh, it tastes terrible. Do I have to?' And I'd say, 'Yes, unless you want to taste it twice.' I was like his old, comfortable shoe. He could relax around me. . . . He always called me Miss Cocke.

"He was working too hard, he had high blood pressure. He could not sleep. One night, he called me up at two A.M. and said, 'Would you sit with me?' Now, I am a toucher, and Elvis was a toucher, and I sat and I rubbed his hand and that was the last time I saw him," says Cocke, who now is appearing at Elvis memorial dinners, partying at Graceland along with Mrs. Jerry Lee Lewis, who's been married eleven years to the Killer. "Well," says Jerry Lee's wife, "I've been married before, and it's just the same. Breakfast, lunch, and dinner and washing the clothes."

Priscilla, hoping the Tribute will work, holds out her hands to show how they are shaking, and says, "We're trying to bring Elvis into the twenty-first century."

"I met Elvis," I tell her, and instantly she changes and says almost reverently, "Oh, he touched you."

"I find it hard to walk into that house," says one of the Jordanaires, Elvis's backup group. "I remember when his mama died and I walked in and he was sitting on that third step, crying his heart out. I'll never, never forget it. I can't look at that third step."

They all agree no one ever saw a man love his mother that much, and none had ever seen such wailing and grieving, such adoration, bringing people to the casket to see her "itty-bitty sooties" (feet, in Elvis language). To the disciples, it was a pure love. They don't believe his stepmother's new version — that Elvis slept in his mother's bed till he was sixteen or seventeen and was a "victim of abuse." After she died, he tried to recreate the maternal relationship with aunts and nurses and gentle girls who would indulge him.

Peter Guralnick's new biography, *Last Train to Memphis,* presents this portrait of Elvis as the sacred son with his own dishes no one could eat off and his own comic books no one could touch. Gladys didn't let him fly after an airplane he had chartered was forced to land in a cotton field. However, after she died, Elvis did everything and anything that would have displeased her, as though to punish her for leaving. No one stopped him ever again, and nothing mattered anymore. No one was there to forgive him, so he never again apologized.

"With his mother's death, he lost his belief," says Guralnick. "He felt he was here for a purpose and his success was for a purpose . . . and central was his ability to buy his parents a home, a material success to fulfill a destiny, a mystical belief that this was meant to happen. They had not had time to grow apart. He lost her uncritical and unstinting love."

The unbreakable rule of the current Graceland is that no one, no matter who, ever goes upstairs. Upstairs is sealed. On the balcony is the immense industrial-strength air conditioner that kept Elvis cooled as he sweated from his drugs into his silk pajamas. Upstairs is an office with a gadget-filled desk he ordered out of *Playboy.* Here, he used to sit listening to demos. Bedrooms were made into His and ever-changing Her dressing rooms. Lisa Marie's room has a round canopied bed.

In his black-and-red and heavily mirrored bedroom, behind the quilted black leatherette door, is his nine-by-nine-foot custom-made crimson bed. With the windows blacked out with tinfoil, a refrigerator in the closet filled with forbidden foods and vials of permitted drugs, a TV set at the end of the bed and two more in the ceiling, a screen showing views of the house and grounds, he lived the ultimate paranoid/fame situation — Elvis staring out, the fans staring in, hands gripping the gate, the whole house living his hours, waiting for and dreading the inevitable thud that they never did hear.

A new cast of guys lived in back, in little houses like trailers on a movie set. His life had turned into the first Elvis movie, the only one that ended sadly with his death. Downstairs, the immaculately kept *Imitation of Life* set — his Vegas-glamour, joy-boy suite reincarnated small-scale. Like a child, he liked these bright, glittery things — electric blues and yellows and the mirrors in which he could catch himself. Later, he would look away, impossibly far from the boy who used to comb his hair for forty-five minutes after he left the barber's chair. But he wound up living in two rooms just the way he had started life.

"It was always very silent," says Bill Ewbanks, the man who decorated the basement of Graceland in the Linda Thompson years and restored it. He used to have his appointments at eleven at night, and there would be Elvis, "stunning" with his "sexy, mischievous, little-boy look," beckoning everyone forward to take a chance and follow his dream. "There are a lot of spirits in that house."

The Tribute party was dying as a small group went to the graves. Many had been there that night to see the marker for Jesse, the stillborn twin who had been buried in a shoebox, Vernon, Gladys, and Elvis himself — "God saw that he needed some rest and called him home to be with Him."

Several days before Elvis died, he was talking to George Klein about the time George was in trouble and Elvis phoned President Carter on his behalf. He was heavy but not his heaviest. He had not been able to get thin for this tour. Most of the original lost brothers were gone. He felt old. "He was lonely and sad," says Richard Davis. "He wasn't lonely, he was bored," says Klein. "He had a short attention span." He couldn't talk to anyone around him, so he floated, watching the images. Turning forty had really bothered him, and he was already quite gray. Every couple of hours, whoever was on duty would feed him handfuls of the forty or so pills he took a day. He was keeping more to himself now, says Joe, not going down to the gates to be worshiped, though the fans were still there all day and night.

He was haunted by the 1977 book *Elvis: What Happened?*, by Red and Sonny West and Dave Hebler, his former friends and bodyguards. This was the book that portrayed him visiting mortuaries, shooting out TVs, ordering hits, hurling a broken pool cue into a girl's breast in a fit of anger, riding along with cops on drug busts in peculiar disguises. It told of his rages, tantrums, voyeurism, his face-lift and the lifts in his shoes. It showed him as a gun-toting paranoid demanding his cigar lit, his water poured. It was the first fully lit picture of his drug abuse. A lost, hopelessly generous Elvis staggers through this book, isolated like deluded royalty, lost in his belief that his hands can heal and his mind can move clouds and that there is life on other planets. He would not stop speaking about the book. Every night, he talked about what Lisa Marie would think, what it would mean to his fans. He never thought of denying it. And he had tried to make it untrue, tried hospital drug cures that did not work. No one refused him. He asked for hot dogs and kraut. "And I said OK," said his cook. So there he lay, surrounded but hopelessly unconnected, with no more challenges but to cure himself. Accept, go out onstage in a loose jacket instead of the jumpsuit, become another Elvis, which he was too exhausted to do.

After his early performances and the fame, the rest of his life had to be a performance and he had to be the Elvis he had created. Inside that Elvis was an ordinary man with an extraordinary talent, one of those different intelligences and a wild heart. With the fame came the guards and retinues and households to maintain. And that was the cycle — more work to meet the payroll of fame. The myth was that he wanted to stop and go fishing, see the daylight, be "ordinary," but Elvis wanted to work. He loved it even to the end, and what he did was never ordinary. He feared ordinary, having lived there, and then he was just too sick for the sun and the lights.

Albert Goldman had come to believe that Elvis killed himself. By the time Goldman decided this, *after* his book, he had been shut out. Joe Esposito was in the house that night, ready to leave with Elvis the next day on tour, and he and all the men dismiss the idea of suicide. "Elvis sounded fine," Esposito says. "He went to bed that day and said, 'Make sure you wake me up by four.' The previous night, he was not depressed. He was playing racquetball, playing the piano, singing." The last song he supposedly sang was "Blue Eyes Crying in the Rain." "Don't fall asleep," said the last girl. "I won't," said Elvis, or so the legend goes. "I know he wouldn't commit suicide sitting on a toilet. He had too much ego to have us find him that way," says Joe.

When Joe thinks of that moment, finding Elvis rigid, pulling up the pajama bottoms, much later going around the bedroom with shopping bags to remove all the needles and drugs, he tries to block it all out of his mind and think only of the good rockin'. Maybe Elvis knew Joe would clean up, as he always did.

"Your kisses lift me higher. . . . I feel my temperature rising. . . . *Ooooooooo,* I feel like I'm losing control. . . ." Elvis's "Burning Love" floats across the lawn. He sang it the last time he looked good, in Hawaii in 1973, in the white jumpsuit, the back leg shaking, the pant legs flapping, as the hands stretched out for swabs of his sweat.

The eternal flame shoots high into the blue Memphis night. Marian Cocke, the nurse, and her daughter are in front of the fountain in the Meditation Garden, where the floral tributes are heaped, the real with the fake, which stay until they begin to show the effects of the weather. Trashy flowers, wreaths of middle-aged heartbreak and eternally burning love for their Elvis, who fused the sacred and the profane.

"All for you," says the daughter to the bronze plaque.

"He wouldn't have liked those flowers. They ought to plant a few azaleas," says Miss Cocke. "When flowers came to his room in the hospital, he sent them away. . . . His aunt Delta and I used to come out here and clear the dead flowers away."

"I felt terribly alone," said Elvis.

THEY GO TO THE LAKE OF FIRE . . . REJECT THE GODLESS. HE IS BURNING IN THE LAKE. The rain whips back his sign, so the preacher man puts it down and glares at the crowd rushing into the Pyramid for Elvis: The Tribute. They have come from England, Montana, Japan, from towns of seven thousand on Starlite tours.

"You mean Elvis is in the lake of fire?" someone asks.

"Read your Bible," the preacher says, and the rain blows the crowds in past his big plastic-covered signboard full of Bible passages. Elvis, who was distantly Jewish and Cherokee, liked the Bible, too. He used it to support all kinds of theories. In its pages, he kept a police report of two people who had tried to invade Graceland during the days when he ducked at loud noises, collected law-enforcement badges, and walked onto the stage with a derringer in his boot.

This Pyramid rises up from the delta basin of the Mississippi as the pyramids of ancient Memphis did from the basin of the Nile. A statue of Rameses guards the King's giant tomb filled with his souvenir relics.

"You know it's gone, gone, gone," sing the Jordanaires, finger-popping away, stepping out in sync in front of the fake Graceland gates. On the monitors are the sad, serious young faces of Gladys and Vernon Presley. Depression faces — weary, poor, full of trouble and things they don't tell outsiders. They are white working folk with problems who don't necessarily find reason to smile when a camera is aimed at them. There's young Elvis with his poor-boy face and poor-boy clothes who knew what he wanted from the beginning, which was escape. Then Elvis the Pelvis, who called people "sir" and bought his parents a house and cars and got immortal and in trouble because his hips twirled, his legs shook, his lips curled into something between a nervous sneer and a smile.

"*Ooooooo, ahhhh, ahhhh,*" went the Jordanaires that afternoon as a group sang "Don't Be Cruel," and the producer told George Klein he wouldn't be introducing Michael Hutchence of INXS. "I'm disappointed, but I've been around," said George, knowing Elvis would not have liked this, but it never would have come to that, because the Colonel would have taken care of everything, as he always did.

When Elvis would get a stack of demos he'd listen, and when he did not like the song, he'd draw a cut line across his throat, and when he did, he'd touch the top of his head, which meant he'd want to hear it again. When he recorded, he wanted people in the studio so it would feel like a performance. He sang from instinct. He did not read music. He had started believing the songs, talking in lyrics, his final truths.

"Well, this time you gave him a mountain. . . . I'm so lonesome I could cry. . . . That means he's lost the will to live. . . . The silence of a falling star lights up a purple sky. . . . Now I'm numb, I've become unreal. . . . All my trials, Lord . . ."

"He was given an assignment by God, and he filled it to the last," says Estelle, one of the Sweet Inspirations, who sang behind him from 1969 to the end.

"Notice how his hand shakes when he reaches for the microphone in the 1968 comeback special," says David Leaf, who wrote this tribute. One day, when challenged, Elvis had gone walking on the L.A. streets in daylight and had not been recognized. It shook him. In his life, Elvis had to make many comebacks, returning from the army lost between eras, given B-side material, touring to smaller, older crowds with diminished expectations. He was a humble boy, a race-car-jailhouse-beachboy guitar stud. He was lost in the mid-sixties, when he knew he would not be James Dean, and lost musically, not recording. In the seventies, his two chins were sliced by the sideburns grown over his ears, the tumbling locks of hair were not deliberate, his face hot with cold sweat.

Priscilla opens the Tribute. This is the time in an Elvis show when the comedian would be on and the guys would be calming Elvis down, massaging his shoulders. He would be drumming his fingers on the table, jiggling his leg up and down and twisting the rings on his fingers, and the passageways under the Pyramid would have been throbbing and shaking for the dieted two hundred pounds of hyped energy, the firestorm that was Elvis Presley on his way to the stage.

But instead, here is Travis Tritt doing "Lawdy Miss Clawdy," Chris Isaak swooning into "Blue Moon." Almost none of them move. It is a kind of cosmic last laugh for Jerry Lee Lewis, Memphis's own surviving bad boy. One night, Jerry Lee grew tired of Elvis being called the King. "Shit, I'm coming over to settle this once and for all," said Jerry Lee, phoning up Elvis. OK, said Elvis, come on by. But by the time Jerry Lee got there, he found the gates shut. So Jerry Lee crashed into the gates a few times and the police found a pistol on his dashboard and that was more trouble for Jerry Lee. Now here he is, thumping away, without his old medicine — a bottle of Jack Daniel's unloaded from the trunk of his car and drained by the night's end. Tributes can be dangerous things, because sometimes all they prove is that it takes forty performers to not quite recall one Elvis.

In counterpoint to all the action on the stage is the attention focused on one particular Memphis-cop-rimmed skybox. In the immediate area, many people with binoculars are concentrated on the movement within the box as Michael Jackson and Lisa Marie Presley Jackson display themselves and vanish, peeping from the curtain. After opening the show, Priscilla has gone back to the box.

Michael hugs her and she gives what the Memphians in the next skybox called "the mother-in-law kiss."

In the Tigrett skybox, the gentry of the big houses and country club, who once snubbed Elvis, are here, curious but still not overwhelmed; though dead, Elvis is a big industry for their city. If you come to them with an introduction (extreme talent or fame needs none), they will take you in and drink and play all night till the breakfast parties. "Blues, booze, and barbecues," says Pat Tigrett. They are rather like the Eloi, creatures of the new South, of the sun, hiding their troubles. They drink and then they stop and coat their stomachs with a sack of Krystal burgers and drink some more. Inclusive, they want you to be happy and hug the people who serve them in an intimate, comfortable way. They want to show you the best time. Stay and play. . . . Did you like? . . . Come meet . . .

They have to peek at Michael, uniformed as yet another general in the army of the absurd, Lisa Marie with her father's face, Janet Jackson, then Priscilla. They distract from the stage — the accused child molester, Scientology cult members, former teen love slave, siblings with different skins, the unevolved daughter of the legend, the two extremely disciplined beauties, two lost permanent children. Lisa Marie intermarried in the city where Martin Luther King Jr. was gunned down. Two toy-loving child-men marrying at crucial career times, both once addicted to painkillers. Jackson puts his hand over his face and smiles a shy, overcome smile, hiding in public as Lisa stands in the doorway with her hand on her mother's shoulder.

"Keep moving, keep moving," the cop says. "You can look, but you have to keep moving."

Lisa Marie, who was nine when Elvis died, told *Life* in 1988: "He was always . . . shooting off firecrackers, driving golf carts and snowmobiles. He'd put me in a sled and scare me to death on that long, steep driveway that goes up to Graceland. He'd be picking me up and falling at the same time. . . ."

It is a different kind of show when acts tour now — maybe twenty-five trucks, planeloads of equipment. Elvis traveled light — a few risers, the instruments, the band. They got it all in one truck. No introduction, no encores. At the end, he had begun to sing goodbye songs. On his bad nights, he would fumble the words, miss notes, lecture and ramble, stretch out on the stage.

"Be careful stepping up," Joe would say in the last weeks when his largest jumpsuit had to be unzipped. He was nervous, his hand barely stroking the guitar. Still, they forgave him. Long ago, he had made a pact with them: "Take this heart I offer you and never set me free, / And then you'll be forever young and beautiful to me."

He always ended with "Can't Help Falling in Love." He was on one knee, arms up, a gesture with pinkie and thumb splayed out. In profile, like the first album cover. His arms were out, the heavy cape spread. "Thank you . . . thank you very much."

Then Elvis would stride off the stage, gone out of the lights. He would be blind again for a moment and hold on to Joe's shoulder, wet, his chest heaving as he went down the steps. He was moving now past faces that blurred and would jump into the car with his cornermen protecting his head and throwing the towel over his shoulders, and then Elvis would fly away, belted tight in his bed so he wouldn't sleepwalk into the sky, and the audience would sit and wait. In the first and last days, some of them cried. They sat and waited even after the house lights came up and the voice said he had left the building. They waited then, but he was long gone.

JANE BROX

Influenza 1918

FROM THE GEORGIA REVIEW

IN ORDINARY TIMES, the bankers, lawyers, and mill owners who
lived on Tower Hill opened their doors to a quiet broken only by
the jostle of a laden milk wagon, the first stirrings of a wind in the
elms, or the quavering notes of a sparrow. It was the height of
country; the air, sweet and clear. Looking east from their porches
they could survey miles of red-brick textile mills that banked the
canals and the sluggish Merrimack, as well as the broad central
plain mazed with tenements. To their west was a patchwork of small
dairy holdings giving over to the blue distance. But for the thirty-
one mornings of October 1918 those men adjusted gauze masks
over their mouths and noses as they set out for work in the
cold-tinged dawn, and they kept their eyes to the ground so as not
to see what they couldn't help but hear: the clatter of motorcars
and horse-drawn wagons over the paving stones, as day and night
without ceasing the ambulances ran up the hill bringing sufferers
from the heart of the city and the hearses carried them away.

It had started as a seemingly common thing — what the line-
storm season always brings, born on its wind and on our breath,
something that would run its course in the comfort of camphor
and bed rest. At first there had been no more than six or eight or
ten cases a day reported in the city, and such news hardly took up
a side column in the papers, which were full of soldiers' obituaries
and reports of a weakening Germany. As September wore on,
however, the death notices of victims of the flu began to outnumber the casualties of war. Finally it laid low so many the Lawrence
Board of Health set aside its usual work of granting permits to

keep roosters, charting the milk supply, and inspecting tenements. The flu took up all its talk — how it was to be treated, how contained, how to stay ahead of the dead. The sufferers needed fresh air and isolation, and their care had to be consolidated to make the most of the scarce nurses and orderlies. So the board took a page from other stricken cities and voted to construct a makeshift tent hospital on their highest, most open land that offered the best air, which was the leeward side of Tower Hill where a farm still spread across the slope.

Lawrence, Massachusetts, in 1918 was largely a city of immigrants who had come for work in the textile mills. Most had been in the city for only a short time and still spoke Polish, Arabic, French, Italian, German — forty-five different languages and dialects within the few square miles of the central district. They made worsteds and woolens; they were dyers, cutters, and weavers. They fixed the looms, rigged the warps, and felt along the yardage for slubs, working more than fifty hours a week, breathing in air white with cloth dust. At home they breathed in the smells of rubbish and night soil that drifted up from the alleyways between tenements. Where they lived was low-lying, so such smells, together with smoke and ash, hung in the air. Their heat was sparse. They were crowded into their rooms. The flu cut right through, spreading ahead of its own rumors, passing on a handshake and on the wind and with the lightest kiss. No spitting. No sharing food. Keep your hands clean. Avoid crowds. Walk everywhere. Sleep with your windows open.

They slept to the sound of rain — rain pouring from their gutterless roofs turning the alleyways into thick mud, rain on the wandering hens pecking at stones in the streets, rain on the silenced pigeons puffed and caged in their coops. At times it was hard, driven from the north like mare's hooves on their roofs, drowning the parsley and oregano set in enamel basins on the window ledges. Other times it fell soft and fine out of a pale gray sky, making circles fragile as wrists on the surfaces of the canals before being lost to the brown, frothy water there. And sometimes it was no more than a mist that settled in the low places, obscuring the bottoms of the stairwells and the barrels and the piles of sawdust, only to shift and reveal the same world as always. Then the rain would gather its strength again, seeming to rake their lives all that much harder. Scrap coal couldn't keep away its chill.

A doctor may as well have gone house to house down Common, Haverhill, and Jackson streets, so numerous were the cases. Often his knock would go unanswered, since it wasn't the family who had sought him out. More likely the sickness had been reported by their landlord or neighbor — afraid that the influenza would spread — so the doctor heard a sudden silence within and a face at the window disappearing into shadow. What kept the families from responding wasn't a lack of a common language so much as the fear that the doctor would tack a card to the door warning of the infection within, and the greater fear that their sick children would be ordered to the tent hospital. Once there, they wouldn't be seen again until they were dead or cured.

When the doctor finally gained entrance — at times with the help of the police — he could find whole families had been laid low, with the sick tending those who were sicker. They had sacks of camphor around their necks, or mustard spread on their chests, a cup of chamomile by the cot. Whiskey. Garlic and onions weighed in the air. Some sufferers lay in windowless rooms where the damp had kept in the smoke from a low coal fire, and what light there was wavered from a kerosene lamp. Almost always the disease had gone beyond a cough and aches and a runny nose. There was blood mixed in with their phlegm, and they couldn't move from their beds. In the worst cases their skin was tinted blue.

One doctor could see hundreds of cases a day, and in his haste to complete his records, he sometimes left out the ages of the victims and often the names. They come down now in the *Influenza Journal* distinguished only by their address or their nationality: *four Cases, 384 Common Street (downstairs).* Or: *Mother and Child. Baby Rossano. Father and Son. A Syrian fellow. Polish man.* When the rain finally let up and days of mist lifted to bring on clear dry air, the number of influenza cases still didn't slow. Every woman who gave birth, it seems, died. The elderly, schoolchildren, and infants, yes — but strangest of all was how it took the young and healthy who had never been sick in their lives. Just yesterday they had worked a full day.

The entrance to the tent hospital on Tower Hill was clotted with ambulances arriving with patients and standing ambulances awaiting their dispatch orders. Many were still horse drawn, and the mares stood uneasy in the confusion. The motorized cars idled and choked the air with gasoline, the tang of which overlay the warm, familiar smells of hay and animal sweat. Everyone wore gauze masks, and there was no talk but orders. *Don't back up. Bring that one over here.* Nurses checked the pulse and color of patients and listened to their lungs. *We need more masks. Find me a doctor. Help me with this one.* The gate was patrolled by a military guard to assure that only the sufferers and those who tended them went beyond. Waiting black hacks stood three deep.

Every day at 5 A.M. a soldier blew reveille. The quick, bright notes parted the confusion at the entrance and gleamed above the hospital grounds — a far call from a country those patients no longer came from. The general din at the gate may as well have been the sound of a market day in a port city, and they, drowsing on a ship that had pulled away. They didn't stir. It was no concern of theirs, each in his or her own tent, the tent flap open to the back of a neighboring tent. Tents were arranged in rows, in wards, and in precincts, making a grid of the old hayfield. Its crickets were silent. Its summer birds had flown. Electrical wires hung on make-shift poles, and you could hear them swaying in the storms. The soaked canvas flanks of the tents ballooned in a wind and settled back on their frames. Boardwalks had been laid down between the tents, and footfalls, softened by the drenched wood, came near and receded. The nuns' habits swished. What country was this? A cough. A groan. The stricken tossed in their fevers. Their muscles ached. One moment they had the sweats; the next, chills. In forty-five different languages and dialects they called for water and warmth.

Many were cared for in words they couldn't understand. The student nurses and sisters of Saint Jeanne d'Arc spoke both English and French, but to the Germans and Italians and Syrians their voices may just as well have been more soft rain. A face half covered with gauze leaned near their own. They were given water to drink. Cool cloths were placed on their brows. They were wrapped in blankets and wheeled outside for more air. Someone listened to their hearts and then to their bogged-down lungs. A spoonful of thick serum was lifted to their lips. Their toes and fingertips turned blue from a lack of oxygen. In many pneumonia set in.

It was the same suffering in each tent, in each ward, in each precinct of the hospital. And the same in the surrounding country, in all cities, in all the known nations of the world. It struck those already stricken with war in the military camps, the troop ships, the trenches, in the besieged villages along the Meuse, in the devastated plain called the Somme, in the Argonne woods. It struck those who knew nothing of the war — all the Eskimos in a remote outpost, villagers in China. Some died without having given it a name. Others called it "the grippe," the flu — influenza — meaning "under the influence of the stars," under Orion and the Southern Cross, under the Bear, the Pole Star, and the Pleiades.

When care failed in the Tower Hill hospital, the sisters of Saint Jeanne d'Arc closed the eyes of the dead, blessed the body in the language that they knew, blessed themselves, and closed the tent flap. The sisters on the next shift said a last prayer in front of each closed tent and turned to the living.

In the central city those who were spared became captive to a strange, altered music. All the sounds of their streets — voices and songs, teams hauling loads over paving stones, elm whips cracking the air and animals, bottles nudging one another in the back of a truck, the deliberate tread of the iceman on their stairs — all these were no longer heard. Or they weren't heard as usual. Survivors strained at the absence, as if they were listening for flowing water after a cold snap, water now trapped and nearly silenced by clear ice. Schools and movie houses had been ordered closed and bolted shut; public gatherings were curtailed. Workers, their numbers halved, walked down Essex Street to the mills in a slackened ribbon. Their tamped-down gossip touched only on who had been stricken, who had died in the night. They traded preventions and cures, some wearing masks, others with garlic hung around their necks. More pronounced than the usual smells of the fouled canals or lanolin or grease were the head-clearing scents of camphor and carbolic soap.

The flow of supply wagons slowed as well. There was no commerce in bolts of velvet, silk puffs, worsted suits, or pianos. Bakers who used to shape one hundred granary loaves a day — split and seeded and washed with a glaze of milk — took to preparing fifty or sixty unadorned loaves. In the corner groceries, scab spread on the early apple crop, grapes softened then soured, and pears turned overripe in their crates.

The absence filled with uncommon sounds. Children with no-where to go played in the streets and in the parks as if it were an-other kind of summer. They sang their jump-rope songs and called out sides in the letups between rains. The pharmacies swarmed with customers looking for Vaporub, germicide, and ice. And all the carpenters — whether they had formerly spent their days roughing out tenements or carving details into table legs — had turned to making pine boxes. Their sawing and the sound of bright nails driving into soft wood could be heard long into the night. Even so, coffins remained scarce and expensive.

The streets running up to Tower Hill rushed with ambulances, police cars, and fire engines. The alleyways and side streets were clogged with passing funerals. Meager corteges where everywhere — there, out of the corner of an eye, or coming straight on. In hopes of slowing the spread of the epidemic, the board of health had limited the size of the funerals to one carriage. They prohib-ited church services for the dead, and forbade anyone other than the immediate family to accompany the coffin. So, a black hack or a utility wagon with a loose knot of mourners following on foot behind was all. Some of the grieving were sick themselves, some barely recovered, and they had trouble keeping up if the hack driver was proceeding faster than he should — there were so many, had been so many, and someone else was waiting for his services. The processions appeared to be blown by a directionless wind down home streets past the millworks and across the bridge to the burial grounds on the outskirts of the city.

The mourners entered a place starred with freshly closed graves and open graves with piles of earth next to them — clay, sea-worn gravel, sodden sandy loam. The gravediggers kept on shoveling — they had long stopped looking up from their work. Even so, they couldn't stay ahead, and most of the coffins had to be escorted to the yard and left near the entrance along with others to await a later burial. Few of the processions were accompanied by ministers or priests. The parents or children or sisters of the deceased bowed their heads and said their own prayers. Perhaps they threw a handful of earth on the set-aside box. Maybe they lay a clutch of asters on the top. So plain and unsacred, it may just as well have been a death in the wilderness. Small. A winter spider crawling across an old white wall.

*

"We knew it was serious, but we didn't know how serious," my father says. The farm is less than five miles to the west of Lawrence, but by the time news reached here, it was muted and slowed — no more than a rumor on the sea winds biting in from Cape Ann. Their eastward view was open then, and they could see the leeward slope of Tower Hill, though it was far enough away to appear plainly blue. On the first of October 1918 they woke to see the flanks of those white canvas tents set in columns and rows across the hill. And that night the horizon was so crowded with lights that it must have seemed as if the heart of the city had grown closer.

As in the city, whole families on some farms were stricken, others spared. His family was spared — all he knew of the flu then was white chips of camphor in an old sock around his neck, and his mother whispering to his father in the evenings: "You'll bring it here. . . ." His aunt and uncle, who had a nearby farm, and his cousins all came down with it in turn. It had begun when his uncle, for all his old strength, just couldn't get up. His aunt cared for him, until the whole household was confined to their beds. No doctor came. My grandfather, after he had tended his own herd, saw to theirs — to their water and grain, as well as the milking. He drew water for the house and brought them bread. He'd light the fires and bring in a day's supply of wood. Even so, with the windows open the rooms felt as cold as quarried granite.

The last to contract it, the youngest boy, died. The parents, still weak, were slow to perform the offices of the strong. They washed the body and had to rest. It seemed to take most of a day to make a respectable, small pine coffin. They cleaned the front room, set the coffin in the bay window, and took their turns sitting beside it. Not even small things were the same. Not the rust-colored chrysanthemums blooming against the kitchen door. Not the lingering fragrance of thyme and mint in the yard.

And the large things to be done — the work that had waited all through their sickness — waited still and weighed heavier. It was late enough in the year so that the weeding didn't matter anymore. But carrots, potatoes, and cabbages had to be harvested and stored. Wood to be gotten in. The late apple tree was laden with fruit — Ben Davis apples would cling to the branches all winter if you let them. Enough work to fill their days for as long as they could foresee.

There are two small, walled-in graveyards in the middle of our farm. They seem odd and adrift now among our fields and woods, though in the early part of this century there had been a Protestant church adjoining them. It was pulled down for salvage sometime in the forties, and its granite steps are now my parents' doorstone. My father sits on one of the pews when he pulls off his work boots. He will be buried among those graves, just up the hill behind a white birch. But in those years only the names of the settlers — Richardson, Coburn, Clough — had been chiseled into the stones. It wasn't a place for recent immigrants to be buried, so his uncle's family walked behind the coffin to Lawrence and set their child beside all the recent victims in the city. The mounds of earth beside the open graves were composed of heavier and stonier soils than any they had cultivated in the arid land they had been born to. Impossible to return to that country now, though they said their words in Arabic before turning west out of the gate.

For another week after the funeral they could still see the tents, white in the new days, just like yesterday. Then at the end of October the epidemic broke, the fires were banked. The tent hospital was taken down in a driving rain, and the stricken were moved to winter quarters at the General Hospital. At night Tower Hill once again appeared darker than the night sky. Predictable quiet returned to the neighborhood of mill owners, bankers, lawyers. The schools opened again, then the theaters. The policemen and firemen took off their gauze masks. On the twelfth of November, even the Red Cross workers marched in the Victory Day parade. When the city looked up, they counted more dead of the flu than of the war.

The winter of 1918 was so cold that the water over the Lawrence dam froze and had to be dynamited. The following spring, the field where the tent hospital had stood was seeded in hay. It was mown three times that summer and winds swept the timothy and redtop. Here, after the child had become bone, a liturgy was said for him. A child whose life is no longer given a name or a length, so short it is remembered by the one fact of his death.

It is a summer evening, and my father sits on his porch, looking at our own horizon. The long simple line of the hill is gone. Pine and maple have grown up and buildings square off against the sky. Out of nowhere he mentions the lights of the tent hospital, as if he could still see them, strange and clear.

AUTHOR'S NOTE

I am indebted to the Immigrant City Archives Historical Society of Lawrence, Massachusetts, where I was able to consult the *Records of the Board of Health, January 1918–April 1931,* and the *Board of Health Influenza Journal,* 1918–1920. In addition, the Archives house recordings of oral histories. Listening to these voices was invaluable to my understanding of the atmosphere of the time. The recordings made of the recollections of Daniel Murphy and Sister Jeanne d'Arc were particularly helpful. I am also indebted to Alfred Crosby's *America's Forgotten Pandemic: The Influenza of 1918* (Cambridge: Cambridge University Press, 1989) and to two local newspapers, the *Lawrence Telegram* and the *Lawrence Sun American* (September–November 1918).

WILLIAM CRONON

The Trouble with Wilderness

FROM ENVIRONMENTAL HISTORY

THE TIME HAS come to rethink wilderness.

This will seem a heretical claim to many environmentalists, since the idea of wilderness has for decades been a fundamental tenet — indeed, a passion — of the environmental movement, especially in the United States. For many Americans wilderness stands as the last remaining place where civilization, that all too human disease, has not fully infected the earth. It is an island in the polluted sea of urban-industrial modernity, the one place we can turn for escape from our own too-muchness. Seen in this way, wilderness presents itself as the best antidote to our human selves, a refuge we must somehow recover if we hope to save the planet. As Henry David Thoreau once famously declared, "In Wildness is the preservation of the World."

But is it? The more one knows of its peculiar history, the more one realizes that wilderness is not quite what it seems. Far from being the one place on earth that stands apart from humanity, it is quite profoundly a human creation — indeed, the creation of very particular human cultures at very particular moments in human history. It is not a pristine sanctuary where the last remnant of an untouched, endangered, but still transcendent nature can for at least a little while longer be encountered without the contaminating taint of civilization. Instead, it is a product of that civilization, and could hardly be contaminated by the very stuff of which it is made. Wilderness hides its unnaturalness behind a mask that is all the more beguiling because it seems so natural. As we gaze into the mirror it holds up for us, we too easily imagine that what we behold is Nature when in fact we see the reflection of our own unexamined longings and desires. For this reason, we mistake ourselves when we suppose that wilderness can be the solution to our culture's problematic relationships with the nonhuman world, for wilderness is itself no small part of the problem.

To assert the unnaturalness of so natural a place will no doubt seem absurd or even perverse to many readers, so let me hasten to add that the nonhuman world we encounter in wilderness is far from being merely our own invention. I celebrate with others who love wilderness the beauty and power of the things it contains. Each of us who has spent time there can conjure images and sensations that seem all the more hauntingly real for having engraved themselves so indelibly on our memories. Such memories may be uniquely our own, but they are also familiar enough to be instantly recognizable to others. Remember this? The torrents of mist shoot out from the base of a great waterfall in the depths of a Sierra canyon, the tiny droplets cooling your face as you listen to the roar of the water and gaze up toward the sky through a rainbow that hovers just out of reach. Remember this too: looking out across a desert canyon in the evening air, the only sound a lone raven calling in the distance, the rock walls dropping away into a chasm so deep that its bottom all but vanishes as you squint into the amber light of the setting sun. And this: the moment beside the trail as you sit on a sandstone ledge, your boots damp with the morning dew while you take in the rich smell of the pines, and the small red fox — or maybe for you it was a raccoon or a coyote or a deer — that suddenly ambles across your path, stopping for a long moment to gaze in your direction with cautious indifference before continuing on its way. Remember the feelings of such moments, and you will know as well as I do that you were in the presence of something irreducibly nonhuman, something profoundly Other than yourself. Wilderness is made of that, too.

And yet: what brought each of us to the places where such memories became possible is entirely a cultural invention. Go back 250 years in American and European history, and you do not find nearly so many people wandering around remote corners of the planet looking for what today we would call "the wilderness experience." As late as the eighteenth century, the most common usage of the word "wilderness" in the English language referred to landscapes that generally carried adjectives far different from the ones they attract today. To be a wilderness then was to be "deserted," "savage," "desolate," "barren" — in short, a "waste," the word's nearest synonym. Its connotations were anything but positive, and the emotion one was most likely to feel in its presence was "bewilderment" — or terror.

Many of the word's strongest associations then were biblical, for it is used over and over again in the King James Version to refer to places on the margins of civilization where it is all too easy to lose oneself in moral confusion and despair. The wilderness was where Moses had wandered with his people for forty years, and where they had nearly abandoned their God to worship a golden idol. "For Pharaoh will say of the Children of Israel," we read in Exodus, "They are entangled in the land, the wilderness hath shut them in." The wilderness was where Christ had struggled with the devil and endured his temptations: "And immediately the Spirit driveth him into the wilderness. And he was there in the wilderness for forty days tempted of Satan; and was with the wild beasts; and the angels ministered unto him." The "delicious Paradise" of John Milton's Eden was surrounded by "a steep wilderness, whose hairy sides / Access denied" to all who sought entry. When Adam and Eve were driven from that garden, the world they entered was a wilderness that only their labor and pain could redeem. Wilderness, in short, was a place to which one came only against one's will, and always in fear and trembling. Whatever value it might have arose solely from the possibility that it might be "reclaimed" and turned toward human ends — planted as a garden, say, or a city upon a hill. In its raw state, it had little or nothing to offer civilized men and women.

But by the end of the nineteenth century, all this had changed. The wastelands that had once seemed worthless had for some people come to seem almost beyond price. That Thoreau in 1862 could declare wildness to be the preservation of the world suggests the sea change that was going on. Wilderness had once been the antithesis of all that was orderly and good — it had been the darkness, one might say, on the far side of the garden wall — and yet now it was frequently likened to Eden itself. When John Muir arrived in the Sierra Nevada in 1869, he would declare, "No description of Heaven that I have ever heard or read of seems half so fine." He was hardly alone in expressing such emotions. One by one, various corners of the American map came to be desig-

nated as sites whose wild beauty was so spectacular that a growing
number of citizens had to visit and see them for themselves.
Niagara Falls was the first to undergo this transformation, but it
was soon followed by the Catskills, the Adirondacks, Yosemite,
Yellowstone, and others. Yosemite was deeded by the U.S. government to the state of California in 1864 as the nation's first wildland
park, and Yellowstone became the first true national park in 1872.

By the first decade of the twentieth century, in the single most
famous episode in American conservation history, a national debate had exploded over whether the city of San Francisco should
be permitted to augment its water supply by damming the Tuolumne River in Hetch Hetchy valley, well within the boundaries of
Yosemite National Park. The dam was eventually built, but what
today seems no less significant is that so many people fought to
prevent its completion. Even as the fight was being lost, Hetch
Hetchy became the battle cry of an emerging movement to preserve wilderness. Fifty years earlier, such opposition would have
been unthinkable. Few would have questioned the merits of "reclaiming" a wasteland like this in order to put it to human use.
Now the defenders of Hetch Hetchy attracted widespread national
attention by portraying such an act not as improvement or progress but as desecration and vandalism. Lest one doubt that the old
biblical metaphors had been turned completely on their heads,
listen to John Muir attack the dam's defenders. "Their arguments,"
he wrote, "are curiously like those of the devil, devised for the
destruction of the first garden — so much of the very best Eden
fruit going to waste; so much of the best Tuolumne water and
Tuolumne scenery going to waste." For Muir and the growing
number of Americans who shared his views, Satan's home had become God's own temple.

The sources of this rather astonishing transformation were
many, but for the purposes of this essay they can be gathered under
two broad headings: the sublime and the frontier. Of the two,
sublime is the older and more pervasive cultural construct, being
one of the most important expressions of that broad transatlantic
movement we today label as romanticism; the frontier is more
peculiarly American, though it too had its European antecedents
and parallels. The two converged to remake wilderness in their
own image, freighting it with moral values and cultural symbols

that it carries to this day. Indeed, it is not too much to say that the modern environmental movement is itself a grandchild of romanticism and post-frontier ideology, which is why it is no accident that so much environmentalist discourse takes its bearings from the wilderness these intellectual movements helped create. Although wilderness may today seem to be just one environmental concern among many, it in fact serves as the foundation for a long list of other such concerns that on their face seem quite remote from it. That is why its influence is so pervasive and, potentially, so insidious.

To gain such remarkable influence, the concept of wilderness had to become loaded with some of the deepest core values of the culture that created and idealized it: it had to become sacred. This possibility had been present in wilderness even in the days when it had been a place of spiritual danger and moral temptation. If Satan was there, then so was Christ, who had found angels as well as wild beasts during his sojourn in the desert. In the wilderness the boundaries between human and nonhuman, between natural and supernatural, had always seemed less certain than elsewhere. This was why the early Christian saints and mystics had often emulated Christ's desert retreat as they sought to experience for themselves the visions and spiritual testing he had endured. One might meet devils and run the risk of losing one's soul in such a place, but one might also meet God. For some that possibility was worth almost any price.

By the eighteenth century this sense of the wilderness as a landscape where the supernatural lay just beneath the surface was expressed in the doctrine of the *sublime*, a word whose modern usage has been so watered down by commercial hype and tourist advertising that it retains only a dim echo of its former power. In the theories of Edmund Burke, Immanuel Kant, William Gilpin, and others, sublime landscapes were those rare places on earth where one had more chance than elsewhere to glimpse the face of God. Romantics had a clear notion of where one could be most sure of having this experience. Although God might, of course, choose to show himself anywhere, he would most often be found in those vast, powerful landscapes where one could not help feeling insignificant and being reminded of one's own mortality. Where were these sublime places? The eighteenth-century catalogue of their locations feels very familiar, for we still see and value landscapes as it taught us to do. God was on the mountaintop, in the chasm, in the waterfall, in the thundercloud, in the rainbow, in the sunset. One has only to think of the sites that Americans chose for their first national parks — Yellowstone, Yosemite, Grand Canyon, Rainier, Zion — to realize that virtually all of them fit one or more of these categories. Less sublime landscapes simply did not appear worthy of such protection; not until the 1940s, for instance, would the first swamp be honored, in Everglades National Park, and to this day there is no national park in the grasslands.

Among the best proofs that one had entered a sublime landscape was the emotion it evoked. For the early romantic writers and artists who first began to celebrate it, the sublime was far from being a pleasurable experience. The classic description is that of William Wordsworth as he recounted climbing the Alps and crossing the Simplon Pass in his autobiographical poem *The Prelude*. There, surrounded by crags and waterfalls, the poet felt himself literally to be in the presence of the divine — and experienced an emotion remarkably close to terror:

> The immeasurable height
> Of woods decaying, never to be decayed,
> The stationary blasts of waterfalls,
> And in the narrow rent at every turn
> Winds thwarting winds, bewildered and forlorn,
> The torrents shooting from the clear blue sky,
> The rocks that muttered close upon our ears,
> Black drizzling crags that spake by the way-side
> As if a voice were in them, the sick sight
> And giddy prospect of the raving stream,
> The unfettered clouds and region of the
> Heavens,
> Tumult and peace, the darkness and the light —
> Were all like workings of one mind, the features
> Of the same face, blossoms upon one tree;
> Characters of the great Apocalypse,
> The types and symbols of Eternity,
> Of first, and last, and midst, and without end.

This was no casual stroll in the mountains, no simple sojourn in the gentle lap of nonhuman nature. What Wordsworth described was nothing less than a religious experience, akin to that of the Old Testament prophets as they conversed with their wrathful God. The symbols he detected in this wilderness landscape were more supernatural than natural, and they inspired more awe and dismay than joy or pleasure. No mere mortal was meant to linger long in such a place, so it was with considerable relief that Wordsworth and his companion made their way back down from the peaks to the sheltering valleys.

Lest you suspect that this view of the sublime was limited to timid Europeans who lacked the American know-how for feeling at home in the wilderness, remember Henry David Thoreau's 1846 climb of Mount Katahdin, in Maine. Although Thoreau is regarded by many today as one of the great American celebrators of wilderness, his emotions about Katahdin were no less ambivalent than Wordsworth's about the Alps.

> It was vast, Titanic, and such as man never inhabits. Some part of the beholder, even some vital part, seems to escape through the loose grating of his ribs as he ascends. He is more lone than you can imagine. . . . Vast, Titanic, inhuman Nature has got him at disadvantage, caught him alone, and pilfers him of some of his divine faculty. She does not smile on him as in the plains. She seems to say sternly, why came ye here before your time? This ground is not prepared for you. Is it not enough that I smile in the valleys? I have never made this soil for thy feet, this air for thy breathing, these rocks for thy neighbors. I cannot pity nor fondle thee here, but forever relentlessly drive thee hence to where I *am* kind. Why seek me where I have not called thee, and then complain because you find me but a stepmother?

This is surely not the way a modern backpacker or nature lover would describe Maine's most famous mountain, but that is because Thoreau's description owes as much to Wordsworth and other romantic contemporaries as to the rocks and clouds of Katahdin itself. His words took the physical mountain on which he stood and transmuted it into an icon of the sublime: a symbol of God's presence on earth. The power and the glory of that icon were such that only a prophet might gaze on it for long. In effect, romantics like Thoreau joined Moses and the children of Israel in Exodus when "they looked toward the wilderness, and behold, the glory of the Lord appeared in the cloud."

But even as it came to embody the awesome power of the sublime, wilderness was also being tamed — not just by those who were building settlements in its midst but also by those who most celebrated its inhuman beauty. By the second half of the nineteenth century, the terrible awe that Wordsworth and Thoreau regarded as the appropriately pious stance to adopt in the presence of their mountaintop God was giving way to a much more comfortable, almost sentimental demeanor. As more and more tourists sought out the wilderness as a spectacle to be looked at and enjoyed for its great beauty, the sublime in effect became domesticated. The wilderness was still sacred, but the religious sentiments it evoked were more those of a pleasant parish church than those of a grand cathedral or a harsh desert retreat. The writer who best captures this late romantic sense of a domesticated sublime is undoubtedly John Muir, whose descriptions of Yosemite and the Sierra Nevada reflect none of the anxiety or terror one finds in earlier writers. Here he is, for instance, sketching on North Dome in Yosemite Valley:

> No pain here, no dull empty hours, no fear of the past, no fear of the future. These blessed mountains are so compactly filled with God's beauty, no petty personal hope or experience has room to be. Drinking this champagne water is pure pleasure, so is breathing the living air, and every movement of limbs is pleasure, while the body seems to feel beauty when exposed to it as it feels the campfire or sunshine, entering not by the eyes alone, but equally through all one's flesh like radiant heat, making a passionate ecstatic pleasure glow not explainable.

The emotions Muir describes in Yosemite could hardly be more different from Thoreau's on Katahdin or Wordsworth's on the Simplon Pass. Yet all three men are participating in the same cultural tradition and contributing to the same myth: the mountain as cathedral. The three may differ in the way they choose to express their piety — Wordsworth favoring an awe-filled bewilderment, Thoreau a stern loneliness, Muir a welcome ecstasy — but they agree completely about the church in which they prefer to worship. Muir's closing words on North Dome diverge from his older contemporaries only in mood, not in their ultimate content:

> Perched like a fly on this Yosemite dome, I gaze and sketch and bask, oftentimes settling down into dumb admiration without definite hope of ever learning much, yet with the longing, unresting effort that lies at the door of hope, humbly prostrate before the vast display of God's

power, and eager to offer self-denial and renunciation with eternal toil to learn any lesson in the divine manuscript.

Muir's "divine manuscript" and Wordsworth's "Characters of the great Apocalypse" were in fact pages from the same holy book. The sublime wilderness had ceased to be a place of satanic temptation and become instead a sacred temple, much as it continues to be for those who love it today.

But the romantic sublime was not the only cultural movement that helped transform wilderness into a sacred American icon during the nineteenth century. No less important was the powerful romantic attraction of primitivism, dating back at least to Rousseau — the belief that the best antidote to the ills of an overly refined and civilized modern world was a return to simpler, more primitive living. In the United States, this was embodied most strikingly in the national myth of the frontier. The historian Frederick Jackson Turner wrote in 1893 the classic academic statement of this myth, but it had been part of American cultural traditions for well over a century. As Turner described the process, easterners and European immigrants, in moving to the wild unsettled lands of the frontier, shed the trappings of civilization, rediscovered their primitive racial energies, reinvented direct democratic institutions, and thereby reinfused themselves with a vigor, an independence, and a creativity that were the source of American democracy and national character. Seen in this way, wild country became a place not just of religious redemption but of national renewal, the quintessential location for experiencing what it meant to be an American.

One of Turner's most provocative claims was that by the 1890s the frontier was passing away. Never again would "such gifts of free land offer themselves" to the American people. "The frontier has gone," he declared, "and with its going has closed the first period of American history." Built into the frontier myth from its very beginning was the notion that this crucible of American identity was temporary and would pass away. Those who have celebrated the frontier have almost always looked backward as they did so, mourning an older, simpler, truer world that is about to disappear forever. That world and all of its attractions, Turner said, depended on free land — on wilderness. Thus, in the myth of the vanishing frontier lay the seeds of wilderness preservation in the United

States, for if wild land had been so crucial in the making of the nation, then surely one must save its last remnants as monuments to the American past — and as an insurance policy to protect its future. It is no accident that the movement to set aside national parks and wilderness areas began to gain real momentum at precisely the time that laments about the passing frontier reached their peak. To protect wilderness was in a very real sense to protect the nation's most sacred myth of origin.

Among the core elements of the frontier myth was the powerful sense among certain groups of Americans that wilderness was the last bastion of rugged individualism. Turner tended to stress communitarian themes when writing frontier history, asserting that Americans in primitive conditions had been forced to band together with their neighbors to form communities and democratic institutions. For other writers, however, frontier democracy for communities was less compelling than frontier freedom for individuals. By fleeing to the outer margins of settled land and society — so the story ran — an individual could escape the confining strictures of civilized life. The mood among writers who celebrated frontier individualism was almost always nostalgic; they lamented not just a lost way of life but the passing of the heroic men who had embodied that life. Thus Owen Wister in the introduction to his classic 1902 novel *The Virginian* could write of "a vanished world" in which "the horseman, the cow-puncher, the last romantic figure upon our soil" rode only "in his historic yesterday" and would "never come again." For Wister, the cowboy was a man who gave his word and kept it ("Wall Street would have found him behind the times"), who did not talk lewdly to women ("Newport would have thought him old-fashioned"), who worked and played hard, and whose "ungoverned hours did not unman him." Theodore Roosevelt wrote with much the same nostalgic fervor about the "fine, manly qualities" of the "wild rough-rider of the plains." No one could be more heroically masculine, thought Roosevelt, or more at home in the western wilderness:

> There he passes his days, there he does his life-work, there, when he meets death, he faces it as he has faced many other evils, with quiet, uncomplaining fortitude. Brave, hospitable, hardy, and adventurous, he is the grim pioneer of our race; he prepares the way for the civilization from before whose face he must himself disappear. Hard and dangerous

though his existence is, it has yet a wild attraction that strongly draws to it his bold, free spirit.

This nostalgia for a passing frontier way of life inevitably implied ambivalence, if not downright hostility, toward modernity and all that it represented. If one saw the wild lands of the frontier as freer, truer, and more natural than other, more modern places, then one was also inclined to see the cities and factories of urban-industrial civilization as confining, false, and artificial. Owen Wister looked at the post-frontier "transition" that had followed "the horseman of the plains," and did not like what he saw: "a shapeless state, a condition of men and manners as unlovely as is that moment in the year when winter is gone and spring not come, and the face of Nature is ugly." In the eyes of writers who shared Wister's distaste for modernity, civilization contaminated its inhabitants and absorbed them into the faceless, collective, contemptible life of the crowd. For all of its troubles and dangers, and despite the fact that it must pass away, the frontier had been a better place. If civilization was to be redeemed, it would be by men like the Virginian who could retain their frontier virtues even as they made the transition to post-frontier life.

The mythic frontier individualist was almost always masculine in gender: here, in the wilderness, a man could be a real man, the rugged individual he was meant to be before civilization sapped his energy and threatened his masculinity. Wister's contemptuous remarks about Wall Street and Newport suggest what he and many others of his generation believed — that the comforts and seductions of civilized life were especially insidious for men, who all too easily became emasculated by the feminizing tendencies of civilization. More often than not, men who felt this way came, like Wister and Roosevelt, from elite class backgrounds. The curious result was that frontier nostalgia became an important vehicle for expressing a peculiarly bourgeois form of anti-modernism. The very men who most benefited from urban-industrial capitalism were among those who believed they must escape its debilitating effects. If the frontier was passing, then men who had the means to do so should preserve for themselves some remnant of its wild landscape so that they might enjoy the regeneration and renewal that came from sleeping under the stars, participating in blood sports, and living off the land. The frontier might be gone, but the frontier experience could still be had if only wilderness were preserved.

Thus the decades following the Civil War saw more and more of the nation's wealthiest citizens seeking out wilderness for themselves. The elite passion for wild land took many forms: enormous estates in the Adirondacks and elsewhere (disingenuously called "camps" despite their many servants and amenities), cattle ranches for would-be roughriders on the Great Plains, guided big-game hunting trips in the Rockies, and luxurious resort hotels wherever railroads pushed their way into sublime landscapes. Wilderness suddenly emerged as the landscape of choice for elite tourists, who brought with them strikingly urban ideas of the countryside through which they traveled. For them, wild land was not a site for productive labor and not a permanent home; rather, it was a place of recreation. One went to the wilderness not as a producer but as a consumer, hiring guides and other backcountry residents who could serve as romantic surrogates for the rough riders and hunters of the frontier, if one was willing to overlook their new status as employees and servants of the rich.

In just this way, wilderness came to embody the national frontier myth, standing for the wild freedom of America's past and seeming to represent a highly attractive natural alternative to the ugly artificiality of modern civilization. The irony, of course, was that in the process wilderness came to reflect the very civilization its devotees sought to escape. Ever since the nineteenth century, celebrating wilderness has been an activity mainly for well-to-do city folks. Country people generally know far too much about working the land to regard *un*worked land as their ideal. In contrast, elite urban tourists and wealthy sportsmen projected their leisure-time frontier fantasies onto the American landscape and so created wilderness in their own image.

There were other ironies as well. The movement to set aside national parks and wilderness areas followed hard on the heels of the final Indian wars, in which the prior human inhabitants of these areas were rounded up and moved onto reservations. The myth of the wilderness as "virgin," uninhabited land had always been especially cruel when seen from the perspective of the Indians who had once called that land home. Now they were forced to move elsewhere, with the result that tourists could safely enjoy the illusion that they were seeing their nation in its pristine, original state, in the new morning of God's own creation. Among the things that most marked the new national parks as reflecting a post-frontier consciousness was the relative absence of human violence within their boundaries. The actual frontier had often been a place of conflict, in which invaders and invaded fought for control of land and resources. Once set aside within the fixed and carefully policed boundaries of the modern bureaucratic state, the wilderness lost its savage image and became safe: a place more of reverie than of revulsion or fear. Meanwhile, its original inhabitants were kept out by dint of force, their earlier uses of the land redefined as inappropriate or even illegal. To this day, for instance, the Blackfeet continue to be accused of "poaching" on the lands of Glacier National Park that originally belonged to them and that were ceded by treaty only with the proviso that they be permitted to hunt there.

The removal of Indians to create an "uninhabited wilderness" — uninhabited as never before in the human history of the place — reminds us just how invented, just how constructed, the American wilderness really is. To return to my opening argument: there is nothing natural about the concept of wilderness. It is entirely a creation of the culture that holds it dear, a product of the very history it seeks to deny. Indeed, one of the most striking proofs of the cultural invention of wilderness is its thoroughgoing erasure of the history from which it sprang. In virtually all of its manifestations, wilderness represents a flight from history. Seen as the original garden, it is a place outside of time from which human beings had to be ejected before the fallen world of history could properly begin. Seen as the frontier, it is a savage world at the dawn of civilization, whose transformation represents the very beginning of the national historical epic. Seen as the bold landscape of frontier heroism, it is the place of youth and childhood, into which men escape by abandoning their pasts and entering a world of freedom where the constraints of civilization fade into memory. Seen as the sacred sublime, it is the home of a God who transcends history by standing as the One who remains untouched and unchanged by time's arrow. No matter what the angle from which we regard it, wilderness offers us the illusion that we can escape the cares and troubles of the world in which our past has ensnared us.

This escape from history is one reason why the language we use to talk about wilderness is often permeated with spiritual and religious values that reflect human ideals far more than the material world of physical nature. Wilderness fulfills the old romantic project of secularizing Judeo-Christian values so as to make a new cathedral not in some petty human building but in God's own creation, Nature itself. Many environmentalists who reject traditional notions of the godhead and who regard themselves as agnostics or even atheists nonetheless express feelings tantamount to religious awe when in the presence of wilderness — a fact that testifies to the success of the romantic project. Those who have no difficulty seeing God as the expression of our human dreams and desires nonetheless have trouble recognizing that in a secular age Nature can offer precisely the same sort of mirror.

Thus it is that wilderness serves as the unexamined foundation on which so many of the quasi-religious values of modern environmentalism rest. The critique of modernity that is one of environmentalism's most important contributions to the moral and political discourse of our time more often than not appeals, explicitly or implicitly, to wilderness as the standard against which to measure the failings of our human world. Wilderness is the natural unfallen antithesis of an unnatural civilization that has lost its soul. It is a place of freedom in which we can recover the true selves we have lost to the corrupting influences of our artificial lives. Most of all, it is the ultimate landscape of authenticity. Combining the sacred grandeur of the sublime with the primitive simplicity of the frontier, it is the place where we can see the world as it really is, and so know ourselves as we really are — or ought to be.

But the trouble with wilderness is that it quietly expresses and reproduces the very values its devotees seek to reject. The flight from history that is very nearly the core of wilderness represents the false hope of an escape from responsibility, the illusion that we can somehow wipe clean the slate of our past and return to the tabula rasa that supposedly existed before we began to leave our marks on the world. The dream of an unworked natural landscape is very much the fantasy of people who have never themselves had to work the land to make a living — urban folk for whom food comes from a supermarket or a restaurant instead of a field, and for whom the wooden houses in which they live and work apparently have no meaningful connection to the forests in which trees grow and die. Only people whose relation to the land was already alienated could hold up wilderness as a model for human life in nature, for the romantic ideology of wilderness leaves precisely nowhere for human beings actually to make their living from the land.

This, then, is the central paradox: wilderness embodies a dualistic vision in which the human is entirely outside the natural. If we allow ourselves to believe that nature, to be true, must also be wild, then our very presence in nature represents its fall. The place where we are is the place where nature is not. If this is so — if by definition wilderness leaves no place for human beings, save perhaps as contemplative sojourners enjoying their leisurely reverie in God's natural cathedral — then also by definition it can offer no solution to the environmental and other problems that confront us. To the extent that we celebrate wilderness as the measure with which we judge civilization, we reproduce the dualism that sets humanity and nature at opposite poles. We thereby leave ourselves little hope of discovering what an ethical, sustainable, *honorable* human place in nature might actually look like.

Worse: to the extent that we live in an urban-industrial civilization but at the same time pretend to ourselves that our *real* home is in the wilderness, to just that extent we give ourselves permission to evade responsibility for the lives we actually lead. We inhabit civilization while holding some part of ourselves — what we imagine to be the most precious part — aloof from its entanglements. We work our nine-to-five jobs in its institutions, we eat its food, we drive its cars (not least to reach the wilderness), we benefit from the intricate and all too invisible networks with which it shelters us, all the while pretending that these things are not an essential part of who we are. By imagining that our true home is in the wilderness, we forgive ourselves the homes we actually inhabit. In its flight from history, in its siren song of escape, in its reproduction of the dangerous dualism that sets human beings outside of nature — in all of these ways, wilderness poses a serious threat to responsible environmentalism at the end of the twentieth century.

By now I hope it is clear that my criticism in this essay is not directed at wild nature per se, or even at efforts to set aside large tracts of wild land, but rather at the specific habits of thinking that flow from this complex cultural construction called wilderness. It is not the things we label as wilderness that are the problem — for nonhuman nature and large tracts of the natural world *do* deserve protection — but rather what we ourselves mean when we use that label. Lest one doubt how pervasive these habits of thought really are in contemporary environmentalism, let me list some of the places where wilderness serves as the ideological underpinning for environmental concerns that might otherwise seem quite remote from it. Defenders of biological diversity, for instance, although sometimes appealing to more utilitarian concerns, often point to "untouched" ecosystems as the best and richest repositories of the undiscovered species we must certainly try to protect. Although at first blush an apparently more "scientific" concept than wilderness, biological diversity in fact invokes many of the same sacred values, which is why organizations like the Nature Conservancy have been so quick to employ it as an alternative to the seemingly fuzzier and more problematic concept of wilderness. There is a paradox here, of course. To the extent that biological diversity (indeed, even wilderness itself) is likely to survive in the future only by the most vigilant and self-conscious management of the ecosystems that sustain it, the ideology of wilderness is potentially in direct conflict with the very thing it encourages us to protect.

The most striking instances of this have revolved around "endangered species," which serve as vulnerable symbols of biological diversity while at the same time standing as surrogates for wilderness itself. The terms of the Endangered Species Act in the United States have often meant that those hoping to defend pristine wilderness have had to rely on a single endangered species like the spotted owl to gain legal standing for their case — thereby making the full power of sacred land inhere in a single numinous organism whose habitat then becomes the object of intense debate about appropriate management and use. The ease with which anti-environmental forces like the wise-use movement have attacked such single-species preservation efforts suggests the vulnerability of strategies like these.

Perhaps partly because our own conflicts over such places and organisms have become so messy, the convergence of wilderness values with concerns about biological diversity and endangered species has helped produce a deep fascination for remote ecosystems, where it is easier to imagine that nature might somehow be "left alone" to flourish by its own pristine devices. The classic example is the tropical rain forest, which since the 1970s has become the most powerful modern icon of unfallen, sacred land — a veritable Garden of Eden — for many Americans and Europeans. And yet protecting the rain forest in the eyes of First World environmentalists all too often means protecting it from the people who live there. Those who seek to preserve such "wilderness" from the activities of native peoples run the risk of reproducing the same tragedy — being forcibly removed from an ancient home — that befell American Indians. Third World countries face massive environmental problems and deep social conflicts, but these are not likely to be solved by a cultural myth that encourages us to "preserve" peopleless landscapes that have not existed in such places for millennia. At its worst, as environmentalists are beginning to realize, exporting American notions of wilderness in this way can become an unthinking and self-defeating form of cultural imperialism.

Perhaps the most suggestive example of the way that wilderness thinking can underpin other environmental concerns has emerged in the recent debate about "global change." In 1989 the journalist Bill McKibben published a book entitled *The End of Nature,* in which he argued that the prospect of global climate change as a result of unintentional human manipulation of the atmosphere means that nature as we once knew it no longer exists. Whereas earlier generations inhabited a natural world that remained more or less unaffected by their actions, our own generation is uniquely different. We and our children will henceforth live in a biosphere completely altered by our own activity, a planet in which the human and the natural can no longer be distinguished because the one has overwhelmed the other. In McKibben's view, nature has died, and we are responsible for killing it. "The planet," he declares, "is utterly different now."

But such a perspective is possible only if we accept the wilderness premise that nature, to be natural, must also be pristine — remote from humanity and untouched by our common past. In fact, everything we know about environmental history suggests that people have been manipulating the natural world on various scales for as long as we have a record of their passing. Moreover, we have unassailable evidence that many of the environmental changes we now face also occurred quite apart from human intervention at one time or another in the earth's past. The point is not that our current problems are trivial, or that our devastating effects on the earth's ecosystems should be accepted as inevitable or "natural." It is rather that we seem unlikely to make much progress in solving these problems if we hold up to ourselves as the mirror of nature a wilderness we ourselves cannot inhabit.

To do so is merely to take to a logical extreme the paradox that was built into wilderness from the beginning: if nature dies because we enter it, then the only way to save nature is to kill ourselves. The absurdity of this proposition flows from the underlying dualism it expresses. Not only does it ascribe greater power to humanity than we in fact possess — physical and biological nature will surely survive in some form or another long after we ourselves have gone the way of all flesh — but in the end it offers us little more than a self-defeating counsel of despair. The tautology gives us no way out: if wild nature is the only thing worth saving, and if our mere presence destroys it, then the sole solution to our own unnaturalness, the only way to protect sacred wilderness from profane humanity, would seem to be suicide. It is not a proposition that seems likely to produce very positive or practical results.

And yet radical environmentalists and deep ecologists all too frequently come close to accepting this premise as a first principle. When they express, for instance, the popular notion that our environmental problems began with the invention of agriculture, they push the human fall from natural grace so far back into the past that all of civilized history becomes a tale of ecological declension. Earth First! founder Dave Foreman captures the familiar parable succinctly when he writes:

> Before agriculture was midwifed in the Middle East, humans were in the wilderness. We had no concept of "wilderness" because everything was wilderness and *we were a part of it*. But with irrigation ditches, crop surpluses, and permanent villages, we became *apart from* the natural world. . . . Between the wilderness that created us and the civilization created by us grew an ever-widening rift.

In this view, the farm becomes the first and most important battlefield in the long war against wild nature, and all else follows in its wake. From such a starting place, it is hard not to reach the conclusion that the only way human beings can hope to live naturally on earth is to follow the hunter-gatherers back into a wilderness Eden and abandon virtually everything that civilization has given us. It may indeed turn out that civilization will end in ecological collapse or nuclear disaster, whereupon one might expect to find any human survivors returning to a way of life closer to that celebrated by Foreman and his followers. For most of us, though, such a debacle would be cause for regret, a sign that humanity had failed to fulfill its own promise and failed to honor its own highest values — including those of the deep ecologists.

In offering wilderness as the ultimate hunter-gatherer alternative to civilization, Foreman reproduces an extreme but still easily recognizable version of the myth of frontier primitivism. When he writes of his fellow Earth Firsters that "we believe we must return to being animal, to glorying in our sweat, hormones, tears, and blood" and that "we struggle against the modern compulsion to become dull, passionless androids," he is following in the footsteps of Owen Wister. Although his arguments give primacy to defending biodiversity and the autonomy of wild nature, his prose becomes most passionate when he speaks of preserving "the wilderness experience." His own ideal "Big Outside" bears an uncanny resemblance to that of the frontier myth: wide open spaces and virgin land with no trails, no signs, no facilities, no maps, no guides, no rescues, no modern equipment. Tellingly, it is a land where hardy travelers can support themselves by hunting with "primitive weapons (bow and arrow, atlatl, knife, sharp rock)." Foreman claims that "the primary value of wilderness is not as a proving ground for young Huck Finns and Annie Oakleys," but his heart is with Huck and Annie all the same. He admits that "preserving a quality wilderness experience for the human visitor, letting her or him flex Paleolithic muscles or seek visions, remains a tremendously important secondary purpose." Just so does Teddy Roosevelt's Rough Rider live on in the greener garb of a new age.

However much one may be attracted to such a vision, it entails problematic consequences. For one, it makes wilderness the locus for an epic struggle between malign civilization and benign nature, compared with which all other social, political, and moral concerns seem trivial. Foreman writes, "The preservation of wildness and native diversity is *the* most important issue. Issues directly affecting only humans pale in comparison." Presumably so do any environmental problems whose victims are mainly people, for such problems usually surface in landscapes that have already "fallen" and are no longer wild. This would seem to exclude from the radical environmentalist agenda problems of occupational health and safety in industrial settings, problems of toxic waste exposure on "unnatural" urban and agricultural sites, problems of poor children poisoned by lead exposure in the inner city, problems of famine and poverty and human suffering in the "overpopulated" places of the earth — problems, in short, of environmental justice. If we set too high a stock on wilderness, too many other corners of the earth become less than natural and too many other people become less than human, thereby giving us permission not to care much about their suffering or their fate.

It is no accident that these supposedly inconsequential environmental problems affect mainly poor people, for the long affiliation between wilderness and wealth means that the only poor people who count when wilderness is *the* issue are hunter-gatherers, who presumably do not consider themselves to be poor in the first place. The dualism at the heart of wilderness encourages its advocates to conceive of its protection as a crude conflict between the "human" and the "nonhuman" — or, more often, between those who value the nonhuman and those who do not. This in turn tempts one to ignore crucial differences *among* humans and the complex cultural and historical reasons why different peoples may feel very differently about the meaning of wilderness.

Why, for instance, is the "wilderness experience" so often conceived as a form of recreation best enjoyed by those whose class privileges give them the time and resources to leave their jobs behind and "get away from it all"? Why does the protection of wilderness so often seem to pit urban recreationists against rural people who actually earn their living from the land (excepting those who sell goods and services to the tourists themselves)? Why in the debates about pristine natural areas are "primitive" peoples idealized, even sentimentalized, until the moment they do something unprimitive, modern, and unnatural, and thereby fall from environmental grace? What are the consequences of a wilderness ideology that devalues productive labor and the very concrete knowledge that comes from working the land with one's own hands? All of these questions imply conflicts among different groups of people, conflicts that are obscured behind the deceptive clarity of "human" versus "nonhuman." If in answering these knotty questions we resort to so simplistic an opposition, we are almost certain to ignore the very subtleties and complexities we need to understand.

But the most troubling cultural baggage that accompanies the celebration of wilderness has less to do with remote rain forests and peoples than with the ways we think about ourselves — we American environmentalists who quite rightly worry about the future of the earth and the threats we pose to the natural world. Idealizing a distant wilderness too often means not idealizing the environment in which we live, the landscape that for better or worse we call home. Most of our most serious environmental problems start right here, at home, and if we are to solve those problems, we need an environmental ethic that will tell us as much about using nature as about not using it. The wilderness dualism tends to cast any use as *abuse*, and thereby denies us a middle ground in which responsible use and non-use might attain some kind of balanced, sustainable relationship. My own belief is that only by exploring this middle ground will we learn ways of imagining a better world for all of us: humans and nonhumans, rich people and poor, women and men, First Worlders and Third Worlders, white folks and people of color, consumers and producers — a world better for humanity in all of its diversity and for all the rest of nature too. The middle ground is where we actually live. It is where we — all of us, in our different places and ways — make our homes.

That is why, when I think of the times I myself have come closest to experiencing what I might call the sacred in nature, I often find myself remembering wild places much closer to home. I think, for instance, of a small pond near my house where water bubbles up from limestone springs to feed a series of pools that rarely freeze in winter and so play home to waterfowl that stay here for the protective warmth even on the coldest of winter days, gliding silently through steaming mists as the snow falls from gray February skies. I think of a November evening long ago when I found myself on a Wisconsin hilltop in rain and dense fog, only to have the setting sun break through the clouds to cast an otherworldly golden light on the misty farms and woodlands below, a scene so unexpected and joyous that I lingered past dusk so as not to miss any part of the gift that had come my way. And I think perhaps most especially of the blown-out, bankrupt farm in the sand country of central Wisconsin where Aldo Leopold and his family tried one of the first American experiments in ecological restoration, turning ravaged and infertile soil into carefully tended ground where the human and the nonhuman could exist side by side in relative harmony. What I celebrate about such places is not *just* their wildness, though that certainly is among their most important qualities; what I celebrate even more is that they remind us of the wildness in our own back yards, of the nature that is all around us if only we have eyes to see it.

Indeed, my principal objection to wilderness is that it may teach us to be submissive or even contemptuous of such humble places and experiences. Without our quite realizing it, wilderness tends to privilege some parts of nature at the expense of others. Most of us, I suspect, still follow the conventions of the romantic sublime in finding the mountaintop more glorious than the plains, the ancient forest nobler than the grasslands, the mighty canyon more inspiring than the humble marsh. Even John Muir, in arguing against those who sought to dam his beloved Hetch Hetchy valley in the Sierra Nevada, argued for alternative dam sites in the gentler valleys of the foothills — a preference that had nothing to do with nature and everything with the cultural traditions of the sublime. Just as problematically, our frontier traditions have encouraged Americans to define "true" wilderness as requiring very large tracts of roadless land — what Dave Foreman calls the Big Outside. Leaving aside the legitimate empirical question in conservation biology of how large a tract of land must be before a given species can reproduce on it, the emphasis on big wilderness reflects a romantic frontier belief that one hasn't really gotten away from civilization unless one can go for days at a time without encountering another human being. By teaching us to fetishize sublime places and wide open country, these peculiarly American ways of thinking about wilderness encourage us to adopt too high a standard for what counts as "natural." If it isn't hundreds of square miles big, if it doesn't give us God's-eye views or grand vistas, if it doesn't permit us the illusion that we are alone on the planet, then it really isn't natural. It's too small, too plain, or too crowded to be *authentically* wild.

In critiquing wilderness as I have done in this essay, I'm forced to confront my own deep ambivalence about its meaning for modern environmentalism. On the one hand, one of my own most important environmental ethics is that people should always be conscious that they are part of the natural world, inextricably tied to the ecological systems that sustain their lives. Any way of looking at nature that encourages us to believe we are separate from nature — as wilderness tends to do — is likely to reinforce environmentally irresponsible behavior. On the other hand, I also think it no less crucial for us to recognize and honor nonhuman nature as a world we did not create, a world with its own independent, nonhuman reasons for being as it is. The autonomy of nonhuman nature seems to me an indispensable corrective to human arrogance. Any way of looking at nature that helps us remember — as wilderness also tends to do — that the interests of people are not necessarily identical to those of every other creature or of the earth itself is likely to foster responsible behavior. To the extent that wilderness has served as an important vehicle for articulating deep moral values regarding our obligations and responsibilities to the nonhuman world, I would not want to jettison the contributions it has made to our culture's ways of thinking about nature.

If the core problem of wilderness is that it distances us too much from the very things it teaches us to value, then the question we must ask is what it can tell us about home, the place where we live. How can we take the positive values we associate with wilderness and bring them closer to home? I think the answer to this question will come by broadening our sense of the otherness that wilderness seeks to define and protect. In reminding us of the world we did not make, wilderness can teach profound feelings of humility and respect as we confront our fellow beings and the earth itself. Feelings like these argue for the importance of self-awareness and self-criticism as we exercise our own ability to transform the world around us, helping us set responsible limits to human mastery — which without such limits too easily becomes human hubris. Wilderness is the place where, symbolically at least, we try to withhold our power to dominate.

Wallace Stegner once wrote of

the special human mark, the special record of human passage, that distinguishes man from all other species. It is rare enough among men, impossible to any other form of life. *It is simply the deliberate and chosen refusal to make any marks at all.* . . . We are the most dangerous species of life on the planet, and every other species, even the earth itself, has cause to fear our power to exterminate. But we are also the only species which, when it chooses to do so, will go to great effort to save what it might destroy.

The myth of wilderness, which Stegner knowingly reproduces in these remarks, is that we can somehow leave nature untouched by our passage. By now it should be clear that this for the most part is an illusion. But Stegner's deeper message then becomes all the more compelling. If living in history means that we cannot help leaving marks on a fallen world, then the dilemma we face is to decide what kinds of marks we wish to leave. It is just here that our cultural traditions of wilderness remain so important. In the broadest sense, wilderness teaches us to ask whether the Other must always bend to our will, and, if not, under what circumstances it should be allowed to flourish without our intervention. This is surely a question worth asking about everything we do, and not just about the natural world.

When we visit a wilderness area, we find ourselves surrounded by plants and animals and physical landscapes whose otherness compels our attention. In forcing us to acknowledge that they are not of our making, that they have little or no need of our continued existence, they recall for us a creation far greater than our own. In the wilderness, we need no reminder that a tree has its own reasons for being, quite apart from us. The same is less true in the gardens we plant and tend ourselves: there it is far easier to forget the otherness of the tree. Indeed, one could almost measure wilderness by the extent to which our recognition of its otherness requires a conscious, willed act on our part. The romantic legacy means that wilderness is more a state of mind than a fact of nature, and the state of mind that today most defines wilderness is *wonder.* The striking power of the wild is that wonder in the face of it requires no act of will, but forces itself upon us — as an expression of the nonhuman world experienced through the lens of our cultural history — as proof that ours is not the only presence in the universe.

Wilderness gets us into trouble only if we imagine that this experience of wonder and otherness is limited to the remote corners of the planet, or that it somehow depends on pristine landscapes we ourselves do not inhabit. Nothing could be more misleading. The tree in the garden is in reality no less other, no less worthy of our wonder and respect, than the tree in an ancient forest that has never known an ax or a saw — even though the tree in the forest reflects a more intricate web of ecological relationships. The tree in the garden could easily have sprung from the same seed as the tree in the forest, and we can claim only its location and perhaps its form as our own. Both trees stand apart from us; both share our common world. The special power of the tree in the wilderness is to remind us of this fact. It can teach us to recognize the wildness we did not see in the tree we planted in our own back yard. By seeing the otherness in that which is most unfamiliar, we can learn to see it too in that which at first seemed merely ordinary. If wilderness can do this — if it can help us perceive and respect a nature we had forgotten to recognize as natural — then it will become part of the solution to our environmental dilemmas rather than part of the problem.

This will happen, however, only if we abandon the dualism that sees the tree in the garden as artificial — completely fallen and unnatural — and the tree in the wilderness as natural — completely pristine and wild. Both trees in some ultimate sense are wild; both in a practical sense now depend on our management and care. We are responsible for both, even though we can claim credit for neither. Our challenge is to stop thinking of such things according to a set of bipolar moral scales in which the human and the nonhuman, the unnatural and the natural, the fallen and the unfallen, serve as our conceptual map for understanding and valuing the world. Instead, we need to embrace the full continuum of a natural landscape that is also cultural, in which the city, the suburb, the pastoral, and the wild each has its proper place, which we permit ourselves to celebrate without needlessly denigrating the others. We need to honor the Other within and the Other next door as much as we do the exotic Other that lives far away — a lesson that applies as much to people as it does to (other) natural things. In particular, we need to discover a common middle ground in which all of these things, from the city to the wilderness, can somehow be encompassed in the word "home." Home, after all, is the place where finally we make our living. It is the place for which we take responsibility, the place we try to sustain so we can pass on what is best in it (and in ourselves) to our children.

The task of making a home in nature is what Wendell Berry has called "the forever unfinished lifework of our species." "The only thing we have to preserve nature with," he writes, "is culture; the only thing we have to preserve wildness with is domesticity." Calling a place home inevitably means that we will *use* the nature we find in it, for there can be no escape from manipulating and working and even killing some parts of nature to make our home. But if we acknowledge the autonomy and otherness of the things and creatures around us — an autonomy our culture has taught us to label with the word "wild" — then we will at least think carefully about the uses to which we put them, and even ask if we should use them at all. Just so can we still join Thoreau in declaring that "in Wildness is the preservation of the World," for *wild*ness (as opposed to wilderness) can be found anywhere: in the seemingly tame fields and woodlots of Massachusetts, in the cracks of a Manhattan sidewalk, even in the cells of our own bodies. As Gary Snyder has wisely said, "A person with a clear heart and open mind can experience the wilderness anywhere on earth. It is a quality of one's own consciousness. The planet is a wild place and always will be." To think ourselves capable of causing "the end of nature" is an act of great hubris, for it means forgetting the wildness that dwells everywhere within and around us.

Learning to honor the wild — learning to remember and acknowledge the autonomy of the Other — means striving for critical self-consciousness in all of our actions. It means that deep reflection and respect must accompany each act of use, and means too that we must always consider the possibility of non-use. It means looking at the part of nature we intend to turn toward our own ends and asking whether we can use it again and again and again — sustainably — without its being diminished in the process. It means never imagining that we can flee into a mythical wilderness to escape history and the obligation to take responsibility for our own actions that history inescapably entails. Most of all, it means practicing remembrance and gratitude, for thanksgiving is the simplest and most basic of ways for us to recollect the nature, the culture, and the history that have come together to make the world as we know it. If wildness can stop being (just) out there and start being (also) in here, if it can start being as humane as it is natural, then perhaps we can get on with the unending task of struggling to live rightly in the world — not just in the garden, not just in the wilderness, but in the home that encompasses them both.

STANLEY CROUCH

Hooked

FROM THE NEW REPUBLIC

IT USED TO BE that if one didn't hurry up and say something
about a show business event, the boat train was gone, splashing
egg in the face of the slowpoke commentator. Today's commercial
questions center around how long a product built to superstardom
can maintain a position at the top of the huckster's calculated
wave. Then those questions break down into how much print and
electronic media space it can attract. The final issue is whether or
not the product can become a marlin pulling the ship of public
gullibility on and on until — Lord have mercy on us! — it ends up
on the deck, not a real fish but a motorized piece of plastic
counterfeit sporting a serious price tag. Its falseness doesn't matter,
because so many of us, the hook actually in our own mouths, have
been trained to ceaselessly admire and drool over the special
effects of the marketplace. We resent anyone interrupting our
freedom to pay for being duped. We wear our hooks with pride.

That is why the Michael Jackson phenomenon helps us face what
has happened to our society as issues cut across all false fire walls
of race, class, gender, religion. At thirty-six, Jackson represents
both the hard facts of open opportunity and the swollen vision of
self-worth that have evolved in our narcissistic culture. A now
bone-colored big, big fish in the media, Jackson with every move
foams up cultural essences that are at the nub of our perpetually
embattled democratic grandeur and our equally persistent child-
ishness. He is an entertainer whom we have watched rise from an
itty-bitty cute kid to a man remade quite remarkably by modern
surgical techniques, all the while maintaining his emotional posi-

tion in the yellow submarine of adolescent sensibility. That is why his work, at its core, is a summation of the inflated failure that now dominates our popular arts, where the value of youth is hysterically championed at the expense of a mature sense of life. This exploits the insecurities of young people by telling them, over and over, that never growing up is the best defense against an oppressive world where fun isn't given its proper due. That kind of exploitation made Jackson the King of Pop.

Even so, none of this came about by natural means. It was all connected to the gold-rush entertainment possibilities of a country such as ours, where there are so many people that consistently hooking no more than 1 percent of the public wallet guarantees millions. That is exactly what went down. As a boy and part of the Jackson Five, he was pushed into the world of show business by his father Joe's ambition, which perfectly coincided with the slick Motown packaging of Berry Gordy and the high wind of teenage bad taste that accounts for so many blips on the sales screen. But Jackson eventually went further than anyone could have imagined.

He broke out of the Jackson Five and became a single, flipping and flopping his way into the air of international celebrity. Along the way, his looks changed. The tumbleweed afro of the past was replaced by a dark, gooey mop. His skin went from brown to beige to bone. The wide-angle nose went on a starvation diet that achieved ultra-slimness and an upward Peter Pan turn worthy of a self-willed Disney cartoon. Then the chin came clean with a cleft. The former child star was ready for another degree of prime time. As his videos and concert performances show, Jackson extended his stardom by adding to his repertoire all the basic trends of his idiom, white or black, and the slogans that pass for ideas. Always a mediocre singer given to progressively unimaginative phrasing and overstatement, Jackson delivers a shallow version of gospel, some maudlin rhythm and blues, uses the false bravado of hard rock inflection, postures as a love child reciting the pieties necessary for world peace, stoops to the vulgar gestures that are a priggish shorthand for lower-class rage, alludes to the spanking that paddles under the brand name of sadomasochism and executes a few leftover Jackson Five dance steps that serve as quicksilver interludes within a choreographed synthesis of cheerleading moves, navy signaling without flags and aerobic exercises. His album *Thriller* sold more than 40 million units worldwide, 24 million in the United States, which meant that 236 million Americans didn't buy it.

Michael Jackson became more than a whale of a success. He also developed into something of an entertainment blob, swallowing up whatever he came in contact with or whatever took him further into the mythology of pop aristocracy, where small but glimmering talents are elevated with a hysteria that bespeaks the swill of bad faith our culture has been guzzling since Woodstock. An eccentric jellyfish on the surface but truly a canny businessman, Jackson snatched up the Beatles catalogue when it was there for the buying, startling Paul McCartney and angering Ringo Starr. He was more on top than ever.

Then, after years of seeming a goody blue suede shoes, Jackson was sucked into a whirlpool of controversy by a child molestation scandal in which he was accused of slurping a twelve-year-old boy in unmentionable places. The response was dramatic: Jackson canceled a tour that was in progress, claiming addiction to painkillers. He disappeared. He reappeared. He went on television complaining that the police examined his weewee. He lost endorsements. He settled out of court for a large but unrevealed amount. Not one to stay outside the limelight, Jackson suddenly married a Lisa Marie who was the daughter of Elvis Presley, that Tarzan of rock 'n' roll, he who swung to ever-larger bank accounts on the vines of pop Negro rhythms and redneck sentimentality. It brought two entertainment kingdoms of swamp water together, Neverland flowing into Graceland.

At every point, the King of Pop was greatly helped by the arrival and evolution of promotional aids like *Entertainment Tonight*, MTV, VH-1, and channel E! These television shows and cable stations are dedicated to nothing but the marketing of products, few serious questions asked. Hype and genuflection are their trade. For the good ship of show business, pop stars, directors, choreographers and technicians are interviewed, promotional videos are shown, films of films being made, videos of the making of videos, all tagged by the glistening barnacles of a forced enthusiasm American entertainment used to lampoon at every chance.

Such things, along with the regular avenues of promotion, guarantee that we will have Michael Jackson and his latest recording, *HIStory*, pushed in our ears and faces for quite a while. In fact, Sony Entertainment has already spent $30 million on a promotional campaign planned to continue through two Christmas seasons.

Yet this kind of attention and success doesn't reduce the all-American tendencies to self-inflated melodrama and even more self-righteous bitching. While Jackson's millions allow him to build fantasy kingdoms, he also usurps the mantle of wealthy nut that Howard Hughes once wore with such unflagging madness. Like Hughes, Jackson also suffers from the distinct paranoia that those who must face legions of jealousy sometimes orchestrate into endless symphonies of plots and subplots, ranging from the press to the government. The alienation that comes with vast success builds upon the familiar theme of the poor little rich kid and becomes the basis for innumerable expressions of complaint.

This paranoia has not been missed, even in the world of rock criticism, where posterior-licking and fantasies of aesthetic value are assiduously taught. Though there was some understandable alarm expressed when Jackson's gargantuan poormouthing and his lyrics were examined in the double CD of *HIStory*, and while some rock critics even noted the fascist imagery of the video, what all of them missed was the problem at the very center of pop music, which is the function of its incantational rhythms.

Incantation always has two audience possibilities in our culture: one is the collective fused into a throbbing vitality through the repeating groove of a syncopated dance beat, the other is the transformation of individuals into a mindless mass of putty in the hands of a band or a central figure. The distinction is important, because the vital collective is the highest achievement of dance-oriented rhythm. Essential to that vitality is the expression of adult emotion. While blues might also have simple musical elements similar to those pop has derived from it, blues is fundamentally a music that fights self-pity and even holds it up to ridicule, the singer scorning all self-deceptive attempts at ducking responsibility for at least part of the bad state of affairs.

In jazz, for another example, the rhythmic phenomenon of swing is posed as an antidote to the sentimentality of the popular song, with the improvisation allowing for collective inventions that insert emotional irony and complexity into the music. The evolution of pop music is quite different because, far more often than not, the rhythm is used to *reinforce* the sentimentality of the material. Those pop rhythms now arrive in a form that has largely submitted to the mechanical, often using electronic programmed "drums" for static pulsations that never interact with the rest of the music, a supreme example of the very alienation it so successfully foments.

It is because of the subordination of everything to the beat that the lyrics so often go by, barely noticed. When they are noticed, especially when expressing the choked up, immature resentment of a demanding adult world, the words become either anthems of estrangement or bludgeons against some vision of corrupt and hypocritical authority. But, as with fascism, the authority of a mass "conspiracy" — of bankers, lawyers, politicians, educators, law enforcement and so on — is rejected through obeisance to a figure of gargantuan certitude. That is where the big beat of pop and the big idol of the rock star meet in the fascist garden of dance-oriented totalitarianism.

Michael Jackson has been evolving in this direction over the last few years, one video after another showing either the world or his opposition melting into mass chorus lines overwhelmed by his magical leadership. We see this most clearly in the video for "HIStory," where Jackson marches in front of legions of troops, children scream that they love him, and a huge statue of the King of Pop, one as ugly as any Hitler, Stalin, or Mao would have appreciated, is unveiled. We understand in clear terms the assertion that Hitler was the first rock star because of the way his rallies used technology to create hypnotic rituals of enormously magnified passion.

The Indian poet and philosopher Tagore once observed that the invention of the pen knife leaped past the centuries of evolution that resulted in the claw, but that we often find ourselves in a world where those with the pen-knife mentalities of adolescents command weapons of destruction that they aren't mature enough to handle. When we make embittered little boys into idols by genuflecting before a briny charisma that has negligible adult application, we shouldn't be surprised when they decide they should lead the world into a resurrection of an Eden, through which they will walk in the cool of the day, omnipotent as the jealous God of the Old Testament.

GERALD EARLY

Understanding Afrocentrism: Why Blacks Dream of a World Without Whites

FROM CIVILIZATION

> The White man will never admit his real references. He will steal
> everything you have and still call you those names.
> — Ishmael Reed, *Mumbo Jumbo* (1972)

> Furthermore, no one can be thoroughly educated until he learns as
> much about the Negro as he knows about other people.
> — Carter G. Woodson, *The Mis-Education of the Negro* (1933)

> [Alexander] Crummell's black nationalism was marked by certain
> inconsistencies, but they derived from the inconsistencies and hypocrisy
> of American racism, rather than from any intellectual shortcomings on
> his part. It was impossible to create an ideology that responded
> rationally to an irrational system.
> — Wilson Jeremiah Moses, *Alexander Crummell: A Study of Civilization and
> Discontent* (1989)

IN A SPAN of three weeks during the early spring semester of
1995, Angela Davis and bell hooks, two notable black leftist, feminist thinkers, visited the campus of Washington University in St.
Louis, invited by different student groups. They were generally well
received, indeed, enthusiastically so. But there was, for each of
them during these visits, something of a jarring note, both involving black students.

Professor Davis, entertaining questions during a panel session
after having spoken earlier on the subject of prison reform, was

asked by a black woman student what she had to offer black people as a solution to their problems. The student went on to explain that she did not consider herself an African American. She was simply an African, wishing to have nothing to do with being an American or with America itself. She wanted black people to separate themselves entirely from "Europeans," as she called white Americans, and wanted to know what Davis could suggest to further that aim.

Davis answered that she was not inclined to such stringent race separation. She was proud of being of African descent but wished to be around a variety of people, not just people like herself. Davis felt further that blacks should not isolate themselves but accept in partnership anyone who was sincerely interested in the cause of overthrowing capitalism, a standard and reasonable Marxist response to the "essentializing" of race in a way that would divert true political engagement "against the system." The student was visibly annoyed with the answer, which presumably smacked of "white" intellectualism.

Professor bell hooks, after her address on ending racism and sexism in America — love, I think, was the answer — was asked by a black woman student how feminism was relevant to black women. Hooks explained that feminism was not only for white women, that black women needed to read more feminist texts, even if some of them were racist. After all, Karl Marx was racist, but he did give the world a brilliant analysis of capitalism. She had said in her speech how disappointed she was that her black women students at City College of New York were not inclined to embrace feminism, rejecting it as something white. She felt that these black women were unduly influenced by black male rappers who bashed feminism. The answer did not persuade or please the student.

Later that day, I heard many black undergraduates dismiss hooks's talk as not addressing the needs of black people, as being too geared to the white feminists in the audience. Some were disturbed that hooks would feel that they formed their opinions on the basis of listening to rap records. None of this was said, necessarily, with hostility, but rather with regret and a shade of condescension that only the young can so keenly and innocently express when speaking about the foolishness of their elders.

I recall a fairly recent incident where a black student, a very bright young woman, asked if, when doing research, one had to acknowledge racist books. I told her that a certain amount of objectivity was part of the discipline of being a scholar. Anger at unjust or inaccurate statements and assessments was understandable, but personalizing everything often caused a kind of tunnel vision where crude self-affirmation seemed to be the only fit end of scholarship. She responded that she would refuse to acknowledge racist sources, that if the book was racist, then everything it said was tainted and should be disregarded.

The attitudes of these students have been shaped by Afrocentrism, an insistence by a growing number of black Americans on seeing the world from an "African-centered" perspective in response to the dominant "European-centered" perspective, to which they feel they have been subjected throughout their lives. Afrocentrism is many things and has many degrees of advocacy. It can range from the commercialism and pretense of the shallow holiday called Kwanza (no shallower, it should be said, than the commercialized celebration of Christmas) to the kente-cloth ads and nationalist talk that one finds in most black publications these days; from talk about racist European scholarship to a view that world culture is essentially African in origin and that Europeans are usurpers, thieves, and generally inferior. On the one hand, we have the recent cover story "Is Jesus Black?" in *Emerge,* an Afrocentric-tinged news magazine for the black middle class. The answer in this instance, of course, is clearly yes. (Obviously, this is grounds for competing claims between blacks and Jews; whatever can be said about Jesus' skin color or the religious movement that bears his name, there is no question that he was a Jew.) On the other hand, we have the first explicitly Afrocentric Hollywood western in Mario Van Peebles's 1993 film *Posse,* a jumbled multicultural critique of white fin-de-siècle imperialism and the myth of how the West was won.

No doubt, Afrocentrists specifically and black folk generally found it to be a signal victory that in the recent television dramatization of the love affair between Solomon and Sheba, Sheba was played by a black actress and Solomon by a swarthy Hispanic. In the 1959 Hollywood film version of *Solomon and Sheba,* directed by King Vidor — who, incidentally, made the first all-black Hollywood

film — Solomon was played by Yul Brynner and Sheba by Gina
Lollobrigida. It is safe to say that the real Solomon and the real
Sheba, if they ever existed, did not look remotely like any of the
actors who ever played them. But whom we want them to look like
is very important. The Afrocentrists will feel their triumph to be
complete when black actors portray Beethoven, Joseph Haydn,
Warren G. Harding, Alexander Hamilton, Hannibal, Abraham
Lincoln, Dwight Eisenhower, Cleopatra, Moses, Jesus Christ, and
Saint Augustine. Many African Americans are inclined to believe
that any noted white with ambiguous ancestry must be black. They
are also inclined to believe that any white with dark skin tones,
one who hangs around blacks or who "acts black" in some way is
truly black. At various times in my life, I have heard blacks argue
vehemently that Madonna, Phoebe Snow, Keith Jarrett, Mae West,
Ava Gardner, and Dorothy Parker were black, even though they
did not have a shred of evidence to support the claims. Blacks have
always been fascinated by "passing," by the possibility that some
whites are really black — "fooling old massa," so to speak.

Afrocentrism is an intellectual movement, a political view, a historically traceable evolution, a religious orthodoxy. It derives in
part from Negritude and Pan-Africanism, which stressed the culture and achievements of Africans. Both movements were started
by Africans, West Indians, and African Americans in response to
European colonialism and the worldwide oppression of African-
descended people. But Afrocentrism is also a direct offshoot of
earlier forms of black nationalism, in which blacks around the
world believed they had a special destiny to fulfill and a special
consciousness to redeem. More important, Afrocentrism is a mood
that has largely erupted in the past ten to fifteen years in response
to integration, or, perhaps more precisely, to the failure of integration. Many blacks who have succeeded in the white world tend to
feel most Afrocentric, although I think it would be a mistake to
see Afrocentrism purely as middle class, since significant numbers
of working-class blacks are attracted to some elements of it. The
bourgeois, "midcult" element of Afrocentrism, nonetheless, is very
strong. "Integrated" middle-class blacks see it as a demonstration
of their race loyalty and solidarity with their brothers and sisters
throughout the world, whether in American cities or on African

farms. (It is worth noting the economic clout of the black middle class, which can be seen in the growing number of black Hollywood films and filmmakers, in new black magazines ranging from *Body and Soul* to *The Source* to *Upscale*, and in the larger audience for black books. It is the market power of this class that has given Afrocentrism its force as a consumer ideology.)

So the middle-class black, having had more contact with whites and their institutions, is expected to speak for and to other blacks. Afrocentrism, like Negritude and Pan-Africanism, is meant to be an ideological glue to bring black people together, not just on the basis of color but as the expression of a cultural and spiritual will that crosses class and geographical lines. As W.E.B. Du Bois wrote in 1940: "Since the fifteenth century these ancestors of mine and their other descendants have had a common history; have suffered a common disaster and have one long memory. . . . The real essence of this kinship is its social heritage of slavery; the discrimination and insults; and this heritage binds together not simply the children of Africa, but extends through yellow Asia and into the South Seas. It is this unity that draws me to Africa."

Louis H. Farrakhan, the head of the Nation of Islam, is probably the most familiar figure associated with Afrocentrism. (Muhammad Ali introduced Islamic conversion to an even bigger public, suffering greatly for his religious and political beliefs and becoming the most noted and charismatic dissident of his era. Ali's prodigious athletic abilities and his genial temperament succeeded in endearing him to the American public despite his religion. He never became a member of Farrakhan's sect.) Farrakhan is a fiery preacher, prone to making extreme statements, with a militant flair and a racist edge, that have the conviction of truth among some blacks. He especially exploits the idea that he is a heroic black man at grave risk for daring to tell the truth about the white man. (Malcolm X used this device effectively, too.) He is also a master demagogue who exploits the paranoia of his audience. But then, as a friend once said to me, "What black person isn't justified in being at least half paranoid?"

Farrakhan has found three effective lines of entry among blacks, particularly young blacks, that draw on the Afrocentric impulse: First, that Islam is the true religion of black people. (This has led to a move among black Christian leaders to point out with great vehemence the African origins of Christianity, to make it, in effect, a black religion.) Second, that black people need business enterprise in their community in order to liberate themselves (an old belief among blacks, going back to at least the early part of the nineteenth century). And third, that Jews of European descent (whom he calls "false Jews") are not to be trusted, a charge that exploits the current tension between blacks and Jews — and that Farrakhan has used to move into the black civil rights establishment. All three positions enjoy remarkable support within the black middle class, a situation that has helped Farrakhan tap people's insecurities for his own purposes. The Nation of Islam may be famous for converting addicts and criminals, but above all, it wants, as all religions do, to win over the middle class, with its money, its respectability, and its organizational know-how.

Whatever might be said of Farrakhan's importance as a political figure in the black community or in the United States, he is a minor figure in the development of Afrocentrism. His position in the history of Afrocentrism is similar to that of, say, Rush Limbaugh in the development of American conservatism. He is, like Limbaugh, a figure the media can use to give a sellable face and voice to a unique temper among a group of people. For both Limbaugh and Farrakhan represent an intense sentimentality in American life, a yearning for a fantasized, idealized past of racial grandeur and simplicity. This sentimentality appeals powerfully to the black middle class, which yearns for a usable, untainted past. This partly explains why Farrakhan and the Muslims can often be found speaking to black college students.

In thinking about the connection between class and nationalistic feelings, it should be recalled that in Harriet Beecher Stowe's 1852 novel *Uncle Tom's Cabin*, the most light-complexioned blacks, the ones with the greatest skills, George, Eliza, and Cassy, return to Africa at the novel's end to retrieve their degraded patrimony. It might be said that this is purely Stowe's own perverse vision, since some of the fiercest advocates for returning to Africa have been Martin Delany, Alexander Crummell, and Marcus Garvey, all very dark men. Yet there is more than a little truth to the idea that class, caste, and race consciousness are closely interwoven. Nationalism of whatever sort has almost always been an affair of a disaffected middle class. And until the 1920s, the black middle class in America was disproportionately made up of light-skinned people.

The paradox of the bourgeois aspect of Afrocentrism is that it rejects cosmopolitanism as being "white" or "Eurocentric." Yet Afrocentrism has no other way of seeing cosmopolitanism except on the "Eurocentric" model, so it tries to make Africa for black Americans the equivalent of what Europe is for white Americans: the source of civilization. Indeed, by trying to argue that Africa is the source of Western civilization, the Afrocentric sees the African, symbolically, as the mother of white Europe (just as the black mother, the mammy, is the mythic progenitor of the white South, or so Langston Hughes seemed to believe, in his famous short story "Father and Son," which became his even more famous play *Mulatto*). The African becomes, in this view, the most deeply cultured person on the planet, which matches his status as the oldest person on the planet, with the longest and deepest genetic history. In short, Afrocentrism becomes another form of the American apologizing for being American to people he imagines are his cultural superiors. Afrocentrism tries to mask a quest for American filiopiety behind a façade of African ancestor and culture worship.

It would be easy, on one level, to dismiss Afrocentrism as an expression, in white workplaces and white colleges, of intimidated black folk who are desperately trying to find a space for themselves in what they feel to be alien, unsympathetic environments. Seen this way, Afrocentrism becomes an expression of the low self-esteem and inferiority that blacks feel most intensely when they are around whites; their response is to become more "black," estranged from the environment that they find so unaccepting of them. The greatest psychic burden of the African American is that he must not only think constantly about being different but about what his difference means. And it might be suggested that Afro-centrism does not solve this problem but merely reflects it in a different mirror. There is a certain amount of truth to this, especially at a time when affirmative action, which promotes group identification and group difference, tends to intensify black self-consciousness. And black people, through no fault of their own, are afflicted with a debilitating sense of self-consciousness when around whites. When whites are in the rare situation of being a minority in a sea of blacks, they often exhibit an abject self-consciousness as well, but the source of that self-consciousness is quite different. The white is used to traveling anywhere in the world and having his cultural inclinations accommodated. The black is neither used to this nor does he realistically expect it. The European exults in his culture, while the African is utterly degraded by his. That blacks should want to free themselves from the white gaze seems not merely normal but essential to the project of reconstructing themselves as a people on their own terms. And the history of blacks in the United States has been an ongoing project — tragic, pathetic, noble, heroic, misguided, sublime — of self-reconstruction.

> When it comes to black folk in America, the white man wants to say that if you have a $\frac{1}{32}$ portion of black blood, a mere drop of black blood, then you are black, no matter what your skin color. But when it comes to the ancient Egyptians, it doesn't matter if they have a drop of black blood — and we know that they had at least a $\frac{1}{32}$ portion of African blood. It doesn't matter how much African blood they have, they are still white. The white man wants to have his cake and eat it too. When it's convenient he wants you to be black, and when it's convenient he wants you to be white. Either you're a nigger, because he thinks you're nothing. Or you're white, if you have done anything he's bound to respect. The white man wants to control all the definitions of blackness.
> — A conversation with an Afrocentric friend

Afrocentrism, like a good many nationalistic ideologies, might be called the orthodoxy of the book, or, more precisely, the orthodoxy of the books. Afrocentrism is an attempt to wed knowledge and ideology. Movements like Afrocentrism, which feels both its mission and its authority hinge on the revelation of a denied and buried truth, promote a fervent scholasticism, a hermeneutical ardor among true believers for compilations of historical minutiae on the one hand, and for grand philosophical tracts on the other. The former might be best represented by George G. M. James's *Stolen Legacy,* published in 1954, the latter by Mustafa El-Amin's *Al-Islam, Christianity, and Freemasonry* and *Freemasonry, Ancient Egypt, and the Islamic Destiny.* These books were not written by professional historians or by college professors. The fact that several classic Afrocentric texts have been written by amateurs gives Afrocentrism its powerful populist appeal, its legitimacy as an expression of "truth" that white institutional forces hide or obscure. At the same time, this leaves it vulnerable to charges of being homemade, unprofessional, theoretically immature, and the like. It is one of the striking aspects of Afrocentrism that within the last twenty years it has developed a cadre of academics to speak for it, to professionalize it, to make it a considerable insurgency movement on the college campus.

There are several texts that might be considered the literary and intellectual cornerstones of the Afrocentrism movement. Molefi K. Asante, professor and chair of African American studies at Temple University in Philadelphia, is credited with inventing the name "Afrocentrism" or "Afrocentricity" (although currently the term "Africentrism" is on the rise in certain quarters, probably because there is a group of black folk who, for some reason, despise the prefix "Afro," as if the word "Africa" itself were created by the people of the continent rather than by Europeans). Asante's very short books, including *The Afrocentric Idea,* published in 1987, and *Afrocentricity: The Theory of Social Change,* published in 1980, are frequently the starting points for people seeking a basic explanation of this ideology. As defined by Asante, Afrocentrism seems to take the terms and values of Eurocentrism — intense individualism, crass greed, lack of spirituality, warlike inclinations, dominance and racism, dishonesty and hypocrisy — and color their opposites black, giving us a view of black people not terribly different from the romantic racism of Harriet Beecher Stowe and other whites like her in the nineteenth and twentieth centuries. I cannot recount the number of "race sensitivity" meetings I have attended where blacks begin to describe themselves (or those they perceive to be Africans) as more spiritual, more family-oriented, more community-oriented, more rhythmic, more natural, and less combative than whites. All of which is, of course, a crock of nonsense, largely the expression of wishes for qualities that blacks see as absent from their community life now. But, thanks to Asante, this has become the profile of the African in the Afrocentric vision.

Martin Bernal's massively researched two-volume *Black Athena* (published in 1987 and 1991) is a popular title in Afrocentric circles, in large measure because Bernal, a professor at Cornell, is one of the few white scholars to take Afrocentrism seriously — William Piersen, Robert Farris Thompson, and Andrew Hacker, in decidedly different ways, are others — and one of the few to write an academic treatise in its defense that forces whites to take it seriously too. (The irony that blacks still need whites, in some measure, to sell their ideas and themselves to other whites is not entirely lost on those who have thought about this.)

Black Athena supports three major contentions of the Afrocentrists: 1) ancient Egypt was a black civilization; 2) the Greeks derived a good deal, if not all, of their philosophy and religion from the Egyptians; 3) European historiography has tried strenuously and with clear political objectives to deny both. Bernal's book provoked a scathing attack by Mary R. Lefkowitz, a professor at Wellesley, who characterizes Afrocentrism as a perversion of the historiography of antiquity and a degradation of academic standards for political ends. Lefkowitz has also battled with Tony Martin, a cultural historian, barrister, and Marcus Garvey specialist, who began using and endorsing the Nation of Islam's anti-Semitic *The Secret Relationship Between Blacks and Jews* (Volume 1) in his classes on slavery at Wellesley. Martin responded in 1993 with his own account of the dispute, *The Jewish Onslaught: Despatches from the Wellesley Battlefront,* which elaborates his claims of Jewish racism and the hypocrisy of academic freedom.

Maulana Karenga, professor and chair of black studies at California State University at Long Beach, created the black philosophical code called the Kawaida, which was the inspiration for Kwanza and the seven principles (Nguzo Saba) that the holiday celebrates. The code contains a bit of Marxism to create a "theoretical" ambiance. Karenga is also author of the popular *Introduction to Black Studies,* used by many colleges in their introductory courses, despite its rather tendentious manner, which he tries to pass off as sharp-minded Marxism, and the fact that the book is weak on a good many aspects of African American life and culture.

Perhaps the most popular Afrocentric text is Chancellor Williams's *The Destruction of Black Civilization: Great Issues of a Race from 4500 B.C. to 2000 A.D.* (published in 1987), an account of his exhaustive research trips to Africa. Although not directly trained in the study of African history, Williams studied under William Leo Hansberry, a history professor at Howard University and probably the leading black American authority on Africa during the 1930s, 1940s, and 1950s. Hansberry did path-breaking work in an utterly neglected field, eventually becoming known as "the father of African studies" in the United States. (Scholars, until recently, did not think Africa had a "history." The continent, especially its sub-

Saharan regions, had an "anthropology" and an "archaeology," folkways to be discovered and remains to be unearthed, but never a record of institutions, traditions, political ideologies, and complex societies.) Williams also did research on African history at Oxford and at the University of London, where, because of colonialism, interest in the nature of African societies was far keener than in the United States. His book *The Re-Birth of African Civilization*, an account of his 1953–1957 research project investigating the nature of education in Europe and Africa, calls for Pan-African education of blacks in Africa and around the world. Williams concluded that "European" and "Eurocentric" education was antithetical, both politically and intellectually, to African interests, a common refrain in Afrocentrist thought.

Most Afrocentric scholars at universities today genuflect at the intellectual altar of Cheikh Anta Diop, a Senegalese humanist and scientist who began his research into African history in 1946, as the battle against European colonialism in Africa was beginning. Diop saw his mission as undermining European colonialism by destroying the Europeans' claim to a superior history. He was tenacious in demonstrating that Africa had a "real" history that showed that Africans were the product of civilizations and not of the jungle. This claim to history was a sign to the African that he was an equal player in the family of man, and was essential to any demand for independence.

For Diop, it was not enough to reconstruct African history; it was also necessary to depict a unified Africa, an idea that, whether myth or fact, was considered ideologically crucial by the Pan-African movement to overthrow European imperialism. Like every other oppressed people, the African could face the future only if he could hark back to some version of his past, preferably a past touched with greatness. This could be done only by running African history and civilization through Egypt, the only African civilization that impressed European intellectuals. As jazz and cultural critic Stanley Crouch suggested, Egypt is the only African civilization that has monuments, a physical legacy that indicates history as understood in European terms. Thus, for black people in Africa to be unified, for black people around the world to feel unified, ancient Egypt had to be a "black" civilization and serve as the origin of all blackness and, even more important, all whiteness. We know from scientific evidence that Africa is the place of origin for human life. If it is also true that Egypt is the oldest civilization from which Europeans borrowed freely (Bernal makes a persuasive argument for the influence of Egypt on European intellectuals through the nineteenth century), then Africans helped shape Western culture and were major actors in history, not bit players in the unfolding drama of European dominance.

Diop's doctoral dissertation, based on the idea that Egypt was African and that European civilization was largely built on Egyptian ideas, was rejected at the University of Paris in 1951. The story goes that he was able to defend his dissertation successfully only in 1960 when he was accompanied into the examination room by an army of historians, sociologists, and anthropologists who supported his views, or at least his right as a responsible scholar to express them. By then, with African independence in full swing, his ideas had a political currency in Africa as an expression of Pan-Africanism. And no one supported the idea of a unified Africa more than Egypt's then president, Gamal Abdel Nasser, probably the most powerful independent leader on the continent. Like Gandhi, Nasser called himself a black man, and he envisioned an Africa united in opposition to Israel and South Africa. It was a good moment for Diop to be saying what he was saying. At the 1956 Conference of Negro-African Writers and Artists in Paris, Diop was one of the most popular speakers, although black American James Baldwin was not much impressed with his thesis. (Admittedly, for Baldwin this was pretty new stuff.) For his part, Diop, a Marxist, thought the American delegation was blindly anti-Communist and naively committed to the integrationist policies of the civil rights movement.

Diop produced a number of volumes translated into English, some based on his dissertation. They include *The African Origin of Civilization: Myth or Reality; Civilization or Barbarism: An Authentic Anthropology;* and *The Cultural Unity of Negro Africa.* For Diop, everything turned on establishing that ancient Egypt was a black civilization: "The history of Black Africa will remain suspended in air and cannot be written correctly until African historians dare to connect it with the history of Egypt." Moreover, Diop felt that the African could not remove the chains of colonialism from his psyche until he had a fully reconstructed history — in other words, until he had a usable past. Diop was brilliant and clearly obsessed. His importance in the formation of African American intellectual history does not depend on whether his historical theories are correct. (Although there is considerable debate about ancient Egypt — not surprising, since there is no documentation of the claim in the language of the people who lived there at the time — it is now conceded by virtually everyone that the Egyptians were a mixed-race people.) Diop's work transcends questions of historical accuracy and enters the realm of "belief." Much of what Diop wrote may be true (he had vast amounts of evidence to support his claims), but, as a Marxist, he was not motivated simply by the quest for positivistic, objective "truth." He wanted to use the supposed objectivity of scientific research for political ends.

Diop brought together three important elements in understanding the origins of Afrocentrism: first, the tradition of professional, politically motivated historical research that buttresses the claims of untrained, amateur historians; second, the explicit connection between knowledge of one's "proper" history and one's psychological and spiritual well-being; third, the connection between "proper" knowledge of one's history and the realization of a political mission and purpose. If European history functioned as an ideological and political justification for Europe's place in the world and its hope for its future, why shouldn't African history function in the same manner? This is the reasoning of the Pan-Africanists and Afrocentrists who see "proper" history as the version that is most ideologically and politically useful to their group. Diop's research supports the idea of a conspiracy among white historians to discredit or ignore black civilization. Without a "proper" knowledge of African history, Diop argues, blacks will remain politically impotent and psychologically crippled. These ideas have become the uncritical dogma of Afrocentrism. By the time Diop died in 1986, he had been virtually canonized by an important set of black American scholars who identified themselves as Afrocentric.

Diop is useful for Afrocentrism today not only because of his monumental research but because he was an African, thus linking Afrocentrism to Africa itself and permitting the black American to kneel before the perfect intellect of the "purer" African. But Diop's ideas about ancient black civilization in Egypt and the importance of fuller knowledge of its history had been advanced earlier by several African American intellectuals, including W.E.B. Du Bois in his momentous book *Black Folk, Then and Now: An Essay in the History and Sociology of the Negro Race,* which appeared in 1939. Du Bois said he was inspired to write about the glories of the Negro past after hearing a lecture in 1906 at Atlanta University by the preeminent white anthropologist Franz Boas, debunker of racism and mentor of Zora Neale Hurston. Du Bois's work remains, despite the more richly researched efforts of Diop, Bernal, and St. Clair Drake in *Black Folk Here and There* (published in two volumes in 1987 and 1990), the best and most readable examination of the subject. Indeed, his work must be seen in a larger historical context, dating back to the founding of the American Negro Academy in 1897, when he and other black intellectuals tried to organize themselves for the purpose of producing scholarship that defended the race and promoted race consciousness. Yet Du Bois's book is not the central work of the Afrocentric movement by a black American writer.

That book would be Carter G. Woodson's *The Mis-Education of the Negro,* originally published in 1933. Woodson, a Harvard Ph.D. in history who launched both the Association for the Study of Negro Life and History (1915) and Negro History Week (1926), was as obsessed with the reconstruction of the Negro past as Diop or Du Bois. He churned out dozens of books on virtually every aspect of African and African American history. Some were wooden, opaque, or just plain sloppy, and several are unreadable (even in the opinion of his assistant, the late, brilliant black historian Lorenzo Greene), indicating the haste with which they were composed. Even so, Woodson was a serious and demanding scholar. Greene thought of him, at times, as having the pious devotion of a Franciscan friar and the crotchety temper of an eccentric intellectual consumed by his work.

The Mis-Education of the Negro, although written by a man who endorsed Booker T. Washington and the Tuskegee method, was generally critical of black education. Black people, Woodson argued, were not being educated in a way that would encourage them to press their own political and economic interests or make them a viable social group in the United States. They were, in fact, being educated against their own interests, largely because their education was controlled by whites who saw advantage in giving blacks an inferior education. Moreover, Woodson made the explicit connection between "improper" education, including a lack of knowledge about the black past, and the psychological degradation of the Negro, his internalized sense of inferiority. In short, a white-controlled education led to Uncle Tomism and black sellouts, to a defective Negro who suffered from false consciousness, or, more precisely, "white" consciousness. Some of this argument was restated in black sociologist E. Franklin Frazier's seminal 1957 work, *Black Bourgeoisie.* The black middle class was almost exclusively the target of this indictment — a fact that prompted that class to romanticize certain aspects of black lower-class life, particularly its antisocial and criminal elements, in an effort to demonstrate its solidarity with "authentic" black experience. This was true with the Black Panthers in the late 1960s and it continues with rap music today. Another consequence is that the black middle class insists on a degree of race loyalty that sometimes thwarts any critical inquiry that does not promote race unity.

Much of Woodson's argument resonates with blacks today because it seems to endorse the idea of Afrocentric schools and especially the idea that knowledge of a glorious African past would give black youngsters self-esteem, reduce violence and criminality in black neighborhoods, and lead to the spiritual and political uplift of black people. This is why history is actually a less important discipline to the rise of Afrocentrism than psychology. After all, the reconstruction of black history was always connected with the reconstruction of the black mind, a mind that existed before the coming of the white man — or at least a mind that could be free of the white man and his image of what black people were.

In some ways, the rise of Afrocentrism is related to the rise of "black psychology" as a discipline. The Association of Black Psychologists was organized in 1968, a time when a number of black professional offshoots were formed in political and ideological protest against the mainstream, white-dominated versions of their organizations. Somewhat later came the *Journal of Black Psychology,* given impetus by the initial assaults against black intelligence or pointed suggestions of black genetic inferiority by Richard Herrnstein, Arthur Jensen, and others in the early 1970s; this was also the time of the first wave of court challenges against affirmative action. The black psychology movement argued for new modes of treatment for black mental illness, the medical efficacy of using black history to repair a collectively damaged black psyche, and the destruction of "Eurocentrism" and the values it spawned — from the idealization of white standards of beauty to the scientific measurement of intelligence — as totally inimical to the political and psychological interests of black people. Rationality, order, individualism, dominance, sexual repression as well as sexual license, aggression, warmaking, moneymaking, capitalism itself — all soon became "white values."

That all of this happened during the era of Vietnam War protests, when white Western civilization was coming under withering intellectual attack from the radical left, is not without significance. Radical white intellectuals, who otherwise had no more use for a black epic history than a white one, found the black version useful as a weapon against "Eurocentrism," which, as a result of the Vietnam War, they held in utter contempt. In short, Jean-Paul Sartre and Susan Sontag were as instrumental, albeit indirectly, in the formation of Afrocentrism as, say, the Black Power movement of the late 1960s or the writings of African psychiatrist Frantz Fanon, whose *The Wretched of the Earth* became the revolutionary psychological profile of the oppressed black diaspora. Also occurring at this time was the movement on white college campuses to establish black studies programs, which provided a black intellectual wedge into the white academy. These programs, largely multidisciplinary, required an ideological purpose and mission to bind together the various disciplines, which is why many began to articulate some kind of Afrocentrism or, as it was called in the 1970s, "black aesthetic" — in other words, an ideological framework to give black studies a reason for being. When used to challenge the dominance of Western thought, Afrocentrism becomes part of a multicultural wave of complaint and resentment against the white man by a number of groups that feel they have been oppressed.

In an age of dysfunction and psychotherapy, no one can have greater claim to having been made dysfunctional by political oppression than the African American, who was literally a slave; and no one can have a greater need for recourse to psychotherapy in the form of Afrocentrism. But what made the black psychology movement possible was the rise of the Nation of Islam, particularly the rise of Malcolm X. The charismatic Muslim minister did two things. First, he forced the white mainstream press to take notice of black nationalism, Pan-Africanism, and the concept of African unity. Previously these ideas had been marginalized as ridiculous or even comic expressions of black nationalism, to be read by blacks in black barbershops and beauty salons as they thumbed through the Ripley's-Believe-It-or-Not-type work of the self-taught black historian J. A. Rogers (*One Hundred Amazing Facts about the Negro, Five Negro Presidents*, and the like). Malcolm X revitalized the ideas of Marcus Garvey, the great black nationalist leader of the 1910s and 1920s, whose Universal Negro Improvement Association became, for a time, one of the most popular black political groups in America. Malcolm, like Garvey, felt that the Negro still needed to be "improved," but unlike Garveyites, the Muslims did not offer costumes and parades but sober suits, puritanical religion, dietary discipline, and no-nonsense business practices. Malcolm himself was also, by his physical appearance alone, a figure who would not be dismissed as a buffoon, as Garvey often was by both blacks and whites. According to Malcolm's *Autobiography*, his father had been a Garveyite as well as a wife beater who favored his lighter-skinned children. Malcolm's Islamic-based black nationalism, his sexual abstinence, which lasted from his religious conversion until his marriage a decade later, and his triumph over his own preference for lighter-skinned blacks and whites were all meant to demonstrate vividly how he superseded his father as a nationalist and how the Nation of Islam had superseded Garveyism.

Malcolm enlisted a body of enforcers, the feared Fruit of Islam, grim-faced men who, one imagines, were supposed to personify the essence of an unbowed yet disciplined black manhood. In this way, he dramatically associated black nationalism with a new type of regenerated black male. It was said in the black community, and may still be, that no one bothers a Muslim for fear of retribution from the Fruit of Islam. Certainly, there was a point in the development of the Fruit of Islam and the Nation itself in the 1960s and early 1970s (Malcolm was assassinated in 1965) when both were closely associated with racketeering and gangster activity.

During this period, many East Coast mosques were among the most terrifying organizations in the black community.

Second, Malcolm, in his *Autobiography*, also managed to link the psychological redemption of the Negro with his reacquaintance with his history. The prison chapters of the *Autobiography* have become nearly mythic as a paradigm of black reawakening. Malcolm's religious conversion became, in a sense, the redemption of the black male and the rehabilitation of black masculinity itself. Lately, we have seen two major black male public figures who were incarcerated for serious crimes, Marion Barry and Mike Tyson, use the Malcolm paradigm to resuscitate their standing with the black public. The martyrdom of Malcolm gave this paradigm a blood-endorsed political heroism that has virtually foreclosed any serious criticism of either its origins or its meaning.

It is extraordinary to contemplate how highly regarded Malcolm X is in the black community today, especially in comparison with Martin Luther King. (When I wrote an article for *Harper's Magazine* that was critical of Malcolm X, I received three death threats.) Despite the fact that King's achievements were enormous — and that Malcolm left really nothing behind other than a book — King's association with integration, with nonviolence, even with Christianity has reduced him in the eyes of many blacks. When blacks in major cities, inspired by figures like Malcolm X and the romanticization of Africa that Malcolm's nationalism wrought, began to organize African-oriented celebrations, such as my aunts did in Philadelphia with the creation of the Yoruba-inspired Odunde festival in 1975, then Afrocentrism has succeeded not only in intellectual spheres but on the grassroots level as well. Its triumph as the legitimation of the black mind and the black aesthetic vision was complete.

Afrocentrism may eventually wane in the black community, but probably not very soon. Moreover, a certain type of nationalistic mood, a kind of racial preoccupation, will always exist among blacks. It always has, in varying degrees. Homesickness is strong among black Americans, although it is difficult to point to a homeland. What Afrocentrism reflects is the inability of a large number of black people to deal with the reality of being American and with the meaning of their American experience.

Stanley Crouch is right in pointing out that the Afrocentrist is

similar to the white Southerner after the Civil War. To black na-
tionalists, the lost war was the "war of liberation" led by black
"revolutionaries" in the late 1960s, which in their imagination was
modeled on the struggles against colonialism then taking place
around the world. (The enslavement of the Africans, of course,
was an earlier lost war, and it also weighs heavily on the Afrocentrist. He, like the white Southerner, hates the idea of belonging to
a defeated people.) This imaginative vision of a restored and
indomitable ethnicity is not to be taken lightly. In a culture as
driven by the idea of redemption and as corrupted by racism as
this one, race war is our Armageddon. It can be seen in works as
various as Thomas Jefferson's *Notes on the State of Virginia,* David
Walker's *Appeal to the Colored Citizens of the World,* Joseph Smith's
Book of Mormon, D. W. Griffith's *Birth of a Nation,* and Mario Van
Peebles's *Posse.*

Today, Afrocentrism is not a mature political movement but rather
a cultural style and a moral stance. There is a deep, almost lyrical
poignancy in the fantasy of the Afrocentrist, as there is in the white
Southerner's. What would I have been had I not lost the war? The
Afrocentrist is devoted to his ancestry and his blood, fixated on
the set of traditions that define his nobility, preoccupied with an
imagined lost way of life. What drives the Afrocentrist and the
white Southerner is not the expression of a group self-interest but
concern with pride and honor. One group's myth is built on the
surfeit of honor and pride, the other on the total absence of them.
    Like the white Southerner, the Afrocentrist is in revolt against
liberalism itself, against the idea of individual liberty. In a way, the
Afrocentrist is right to rage against it, because liberalism set free
the individual but did not encourage the development of a community within which the individual could flower. This is what the
Afrocentrist wishes to retrieve, a place for himself in his own community. Wilson Jeremiah Moses, a black historian, is right: Afrocentrism is a historiography of decline, like the mythic epic of the
South. The tragedy is that black people fail to see their "Ameri-
canization" as one of the great human triumphs of the past five
hundred years. The United States is virtually the only country
where the ex-masters and the ex-slaves try to live together as
equals, not only by consent of the ex-masters but by the demand

of the ex-slaves. Ironically, what the Afrocentrist can best hope for is precisely what multiculturalism offers: the idea that American culture is a blend of many white and nonwhite cultures. In the end, although many Afrocentrists claim they want this blending, multiculturalism will not satisfy. For if the Euro-American is reminded through this that he is not European or wholly white, the African American will surely be reminded that he is not African or wholly black. The Afrocentrist does not wish to be a mongrel. He wants, like the Southerner, to be pure.

Afrocentrism is intense now because blacks are in a special period of social development in a nation going through a period of fearsome transition. Social development, by its nature, is ambivalent, characterized by a sense of exchange, of gaining and losing. Afrocentrism, in its conservatism, is opposed to this ambivalence and to this sense of exchange. What blacks desire during these turbulent times is exactly what whites want: the security of a golden past that never existed. A significant number of both blacks and whites want, strangely, to go back to an era of segregation, a fantasy time between 1920 and 1955, when whites felt secure in a stable culture and when blacks felt unified and strong because black people were forced to live together. Afrocentrism wants social change without having to pay the psychic price for it. Perhaps many black folk feel that they have paid too much already, and who is to say they are not right.

The issue raised by Afrocentrism is the meaning and formation of identity, which is the major fixation of the American, especially the black American. In a country that relentlessly promotes the myth of self-reliance because it is unable to provide any sense of security in a cauldron of capitalistic change, identity struggle is so acute because so much is at stake. Afrocentrism may be wrong in many respects, and it certainly can be stifling and restrictive, but some of its impulses are right. In a culture where information and resources of knowledge are the main levers for social and economic advancement, psychological well-being has become increasingly important as, in the words of one scholar, "a social resource," just as "social networks of care and community support [have become] central features of a dynamic economy." Black folk know, and rightly so, that their individual identities are tied to the strength of their community. The struggle over black identity in the United States has been the struggle over the creation of a true black community here. What integration has done to the individual black mind in the United States is directly related to what it has done to the black community. This is the first lesson we must learn. The second is that perhaps many black folk cling to Afrocentrism because the black *American* experience still costs more, requires more courage, than white Americans — and black Americans — are willing to admit.

JOSEPH EPSTEIN

The Art of the Nap

FROM THE AMERICAN SCHOLAR

INTELLECTUAL SERENITY IN the United States, I have heard it said, consists in not giving a damn about Harvard. Having been in Cambridge recently, I sensed — no, actually, I knew — I had achieved it. Bopping about Harvard Square, peeping into the Yard, popping into a building or two, I felt not the least yearning. I did not wish to be the Seymour Boylston Professor at Harvard or even to give the Charles Eliot Skolnik Lectures — not now, not ever. I have no children whom I wished to be admitted to Harvard. Yes, Harvard could continue to get along nicely without me, as it seems to have done over the past 350-odd years, and I, in the time remaining to me, can get along nicely without it.

With such serene thoughts, I set myself on my back on my comfortable bed at The Inn at Harvard, the hotel where I was staying. I had on gray wool trousers, a blue shirt, and a four-in-hand knit tie, which I didn't bother to unloosen. My hands were folded together on my chest in the corpse-in-the-casket position, and I hadn't bothered to turn back the bedspread. It was three-thirty on a cold and gray February afternoon. My next appointment was at five o'clock. There was nothing, at that moment, that I was eager to read. Into the arms of Morpheus I slipped, and for the next half hour I slept, I won't say like a baby, or like a log, or like a turtle, but like what I now prefer to think myself — a man who has mastered, in all its delicate intricacy, the art of the nap.

I did not move, I did not stir. I woke, as planned, without a wrinkle in my shirt, trousers, or cheek, not a hair out of place. A most impressive, if I do say so myself — and at that moment I did say so to myself — performance. Really quite brilliant. The term "control freak" is almost never used approvingly, I know, but I felt myself at that moment a control freak entirely happy in his work — that is to say, in perfect control. I carefully slipped off the bed and walked into the bathroom, where I gazed at my clear eyes in the large mirror. Another fine nap successfully brought off. I was rested, perhaps a touch less than radiant, and ready to continue not giving a damn about Harvard.

I don't ordinarily nap on a bed or on my back. As a nap-master, I fear too much comfort and the consequent difficulty of pulling myself out of the pleasures of too deep sleep to go back into the world. I also wish to avoid rumpledness, the toll that a nap on one's back on a couch often takes. Most of my napping therefore is done sitting up, on a couch, shoes off, with my feet resting on a low footstool. Having one's feet up is important.

Most of my naps — and I usually get on the average of three or four a week — take place late in the afternoon, around five or five-thirty, with the television news playing softly in the background. As the reports of earthquakes, plagues, arson, pillaging, and general corruption hum on, I snooze away, a perfect symbol of the indifference of man in the modern age. These naps last from twenty to thirty-five minutes. ("A nap after dinner was silver," says old Price Bolkonsky in *War and Peace,* "a nap before dinner golden.") Should the telephone ring while I am in mid-nap, I answer it in an especially clear and wide-awake voice that I don't usually bother evoking when I am in fact wide awake. Some of these naps leave me a touch groggy, though this soon enough disappears. Usually, they all do the job, which is to help get me through the evening.

Taste in naps differs. I not long ago asked a friend, an Englishman, if he naps. "Whenever possible," he replied. Prone or sitting up? "Prone." On a bed or couch? "Bed." Trousers on or off? "Generally off." And for how long? "That depends," he said, "on when the cats choose to depart." Joseph Conrad wrote that his task was "by the power of the written word, to make you hear, to make you feel — it is, before all, to make you *see.*" The picture of my friend with his cats napping atop him is almost too easily seen.

I nap well on airplanes, trains, buses, and cars and with a special proficiency at concerts and lectures. I am, when pressed, able to nap standing up. In certain select company, I wish I could nap while being spoken to. I have not yet learned to nap while I myself am speaking, though I have felt the urge to do so. I had a friend named Walter B. Scott who, in his late sixties, used to nap at parties of ten or twelve people that he and his wife gave. One would look over and there Walter would be, chin on his chest, lights out, nicely zonked; he might as well have hung a Gone Fishing sign on his chest. Then, half an hour or so later, without remarking upon his recent departure, he would smoothly pick up the current of the talk, not missing a stroke, and get finely back into the flow. I saw him do this perhaps four or five times, always with immense admiration.

Certain jobs seem to carry (unspoken) napping privileges. Writing in 1931, H. L. Mencken noted that one of the tests of a good cop was the talent of "stealing three naps a night in a garage without getting caught by the rounds-man." Surely, movie projectionists get to nap to their heart's content. Cab and limousine drivers must nap. Napping on the job can scarcely be unknown to psychoanalysts and other workers in the head trades. ("Uh-huh," mumbles the dozing psychiatrist in the caption of a cartoon that shows the feet of his patient who has just jumped out the window.) The only job in which I ardently longed to nap was guard duty in army motor pools on cold nights in Missouri, Texas, and Arkansas. Ah, to have slipped into the back of a deuce and a half (as the big trucks in the army were called) and zzz'd-out for a quick half hour! But fear, that first goad to conscience, won out and, difficult though it was, I stayed awake.

At a job I held one summer in college at a phonograph needle factory, one of the maintenance men, a dwarfish man of Italian ancestry, regularly slipped up to the fourth floor for a forty-minute shot of sleep. I have seen lots of people nod off at corporate meetings and at conferences. One steamy summer day in Washington, at a meeting of the national council of the National Endowment for the Arts, held at the Old Post Office Building on Pennsylvania Avenue, I noted an entire half table of council members, heads nodding, necks jerking, eyelids drooping, effectively sedated by a slide show on city planning. I envied them, and doubtless should have joined them but for the fact that I had myself only recently awoken from a delightfully soporific lecture on the meaning of the avant-garde.

I have always slept reasonably well during lectures and never better than when a lecturer is foolhardy enough to darken the room for slides. Lecture and classroom naps tend to be of the variety I call whiplash naps — the ones where your head seems always to be snapping to. At the University of Chicago, I slept through the better part of the Italian Renaissance, or at any rate through a course in the history of its art. As a teacher myself, I am now being justly repaid by having students fall asleep in my own classes. I don't say that they drift off in droves, but I have — how to put it? — relaxed a respectable number of students in my time. At first, I found myself resenting a student falling asleep in one of my classes. But I long ago ceased taking it personally. I have come to look upon it avuncularly: poor dears, they may have been up all the previous night doing I prefer not to think what. My view of students sleeping in my classes is that, what the hell, if they cannot arise from my teaching inspired, let them at least awake refreshed.

My own youthful naps were owing, as I hope are those of my students, to happy excess. My current napping, I regret to report, is all too much part of the machinery beginning to break down. Not that I long for a nap each afternoon; if I am out in the world, I do not think about napping. My condition certainly does not yet begin to approximate the eponymous hero of Goncharov's novel *Oblomov:* "Lying down was not for Oblomov a necessity, as it is for a sick man or for a man who is sleepy; or a matter of chance, as it is for a man who is tired; or a pleasure, as it is for a lazy man; it was his normal condition." Still, if an opportunity for a nap presents itself, I find I take it.

I live in an early morning household. I generally rise by 4:45 A.M. I like the early morning; it is, for me, the best part of the day. I used to joke that one met a better class of person (namely, oneself) at that hour, but, in fact, what I enjoy about it is the stillness, the absence of interruption it provides, the gradual awakening of life around me. I make coffee, I begin reading; sometimes, if what I am reading is not all-demanding, I turn on a classical music station. And life seems under control, flush with possibility, hope-filled.

I have become, no doubt about it, a morning person. I was not always thus. As a young man, I used to come in around the time I now wake up. Weekends I slept till two or three in the afternoon, resting up to return to the sweet fray. So much was I a night person

— a player in all-night card games, a dropper-off of dates at three or four in the morning — so congenial did I find the night that, one quarter at university, when all my classes met in the morning, I decided to sleep days and stay up nights.

Time has never again seemed so expansive as it did during that quarter. I would return from my classes, eat a light lunch, and sleep till six-thirty or seven. After arising, watering and feeding myself, I searched for distractions: movies, television, ball or card games. Not the least pressed for time, I schmoozed with all and sundry. Generally, I socialized till eleven or twelve and then I returned to my room with its hot plate, box of tea, small record collection, and books.

I might study for two or three hours. Then I found myself alone, no one else up in the student quarters in which I lived, at three in the morning, with nothing to do but read or listen to music, or both, till roughly eight in the morning. I went to a school where only great books were taught, so these free hours allowed me time to read some merely good books, for which I was hungry. I read, as I recall, chiefly novels: Christopher Isherwood and John O'Hara and Truman Capote and Evelyn Waugh; also lots of Edmund Wilson's literary criticism, which I had just discovered. I drank dark tea till my nerves achieved a fine jangle; I greeted the rising sun with a slight palsy of the hands: wired, happy, ready for class.

After my classes, I returned to bed and began the entire cycle again. This period of time lasted ten weeks and, from my present perspective, is something of a blur, but it was, it seems to me, time deliciously well spent. It also gave me the first evidence of my taste, and even minor talent, for solitude.

Something there is about being awake for sunrise that gives pleasure. The only exception to this that I can recall are those times, also at college, when I decided to stay up all night to cram for an examination. My junior year at school I discovered, through a friend, the stimulating effects of the pill known as Dexamyl (or was it Dexedrine?). These little pellets allowed me to stay up round the clock while mastering narratives of English history. They also, toward sunrise, set my heart pounding at a furious clip. I can recall my heart clanging away in my chest as I sat in a classroom giving three significant effects of enclosure on British politics and five reasons for the bloodlessness of the 1688 revolution. By the time

I got back to my room, my heart was playing a very up-tempo version of "Take the A Train." I used to think of it as studying English history with only a slight threat of death behind it. Nothing, though, that twelve or fourteen hours of sleep couldn't cure, and always did. I have been fortunate in my sleep life. For one thing, the night, from as far back as I can recall, never held any terror for me. Not even as a small child did I imagine monsters in the corner, snakes under the bed, spiders on the spread, or anything else that might go bump in the night. The chief reason for this, I suspect, was that when I was a child my family lived in fairly small urban apartments and my parents were always nearby, so the element of fear was largely removed, as it wasn't for children who lived in large two- and three-story houses. I have no memories of nightmares. I had the reverse of nightmares — sweetmares, night-delights? I remember often dreaming of being in possession of marvelous things — elaborate electric trains, entirely realistic metal cap pistols, vast quantities of bubble gum — that weren't available to children during World War II. Toward morning, I regretted having to wake and, alas, give them up.

So well do I generally sleep that, when I roll round in bed for more than fifteen minutes or so before falling off, I consider it a troublous night. Occasionally, and at no set intervals I can make out, I will hit a dread night of insomnia. Usually, this comes about less from anxiety than from the condition I think of as a racing mind. Too much is flying loose in my skull: words and phrases for things I am writing, obligations, trivial yet nagging memories, and (the last step, the nail in the mattress) fear that, owing to not being able to sleep, I shall be tired and blow the next day. I roll, I turn, I mutter, finally I surrender and get up. Less than an hour's bleary reading or listening to the idiot chatter of a late-night television talk show generally does the trick, and I slog back to my bed, where Somnus almost always agrees to treat me more hospitably.

True insomnia of the relentless night-after-night kind must be absolute hell. Such a torture is it that I don't for a moment believe Bertrand Russell, who said: "Men who are unhappy, like men who sleep badly, are always proud of the fact." I have a number of friends who have suffered from insomnia. One walked about with the dark-rimmed eyes of a raccoon to prove it. Another friend suffered insomnia and (nonclinical) paranoia, which allowed him to stay up most of the night and think about his enemies. Once, in Florence, I suffered an extended — that is, roughly two-week — bout of insomnia, not at all helped by a too soft bed and an almost continuous flow of motor-scooter traffic vrooming past my hotel window. I tried to concentrate on pleasant things: small animals I have loved, tennis courts in the rain, giraffes cantering off into the distance. None of it worked. All I was finally left to think about was the longing for sleep itself — a topic always guaranteed to keep one awake.

Insomnia has its own small place in literature. Ernest Hemingway deals with the subject in his story "Now I Lay Me," which is about a wounded soldier in World War I who is recovering in a military hospital but unable to sleep. He is afraid that, should he fall asleep, "my soul would go out of my body." The soldier, who tells the story — and it seems a very autobiographical story — remembers every trout stream he fished as a boy and invents others, he says prayers for all the people he has known, he imagines what kind of wives the various girls he has met would make. He allows that some nights he must have "slept without knowing it — but I never slept knowing it," which is exactly what the sleep of insomnia often feels like.

F. Scott Fitzgerald cites Hemingway's story at the outset of "Sleeping and Waking," his essay of 1934. Fitzgerald himself suffered insomnia, beginning in his late thirties, and became something of a connoisseur of the illness, if that is what it is. He tells of a friend, awakened one night by a mouse nibbling on his finger, who never slept peacefully again without a dog or cat in the room. Fitzgerald's own insomnia began with a battle with a mosquito, which he won, though only in a Pyrrhic sense, for ever afterward he was haunted by what he called "sleep-consciousness," which meant he worried in advance whether he would be able to fall asleep. With an imagination for disaster, he prepared for sleeplessness, setting by his bedside "the books, the glass of water, the extra pyjamas lest I wake in rivulets of sweat, the luminol pills in the little round tube, the notebook and pencil in case of a night though worth recording."

Fitzgerald's insomnia took the not uncommon form of dividing his sleep into two parts. He slept, that is, until roughly two-thirty, then woke for a cruel ninety-minute or so intermission during which pleasant fantasies (of playing football at Princeton, of wartime heroics) availed him nothing. He was left, awake against his own desires, to think of the horror and waste of his life: "what I might have been and done that is lost, spent, gone, dissipated, unrecapturable. I could have acted thus, refrained from this, been bold where I was timid, cautious where I was rash." And so he tortured himself, until, like a reverse mugger, sleep beautifully snuck up on him, and his dreams, "after the catharsis of the dark hours, are of young and lovely people doing young and lovely things, the girls I knew once, with big brown eyes, real yellow hair."

Vladimir Nabokov was another insomniac, though he referred to himself instead as "a poor go-to-sleeper." (That *iac* suffix has something sad or reprehensible about it: hemophiliac, hypochondriac, paranoiac, kleptomaniac, none of them jolly conditions.) Easy sleep was a matter of amazement to him, so much so that he found something vulgar about people who slept easily: "People in trains, who lay their newspapers aside, fold their silly arms, and immediately, with an offensive familiarity of demeanor, start snoring, amaze me as much as the uninhibited chap who cozily defecates in the presence of a chatty tubber, or participates in huge demonstrations, or joins some union in order to dissolve in it." The fact is, Nabokov not only didn't like but rather resented sleep, which put his endlessly inventive mind temporarily out of commission. He calls sleepers, in *Speak, Memory,* "the most moronic fraternity in the world, with the heaviest dues and crudest rituals."

Perhaps if one had a mind as richly stocked, as assailed by perception, as happily imaginative as Vladimir Nabokov's, one wouldn't wish to turn it off either. But enough writers have suffered from insomnia to make it seem almost an occupational disease. De Quincey, Nietzsche, Jorge Luis Borges, who once referred to the "atrocious lucidity of insomnia," all knew its horrors. Borges is the only one to write his way to a cure — specifically, through "Funes the Memorious," his wonderful story about a young man who dies from what one can only call a memory overload.

Does insomnia inflame the imagination? Or is an inflamed imagination the cause of insomnia? But then, too, life can deal out punishment of a kind that allows no easing even in sleep. After his wife's death, Raymond Chandler reported: "I sit up half the night playing records when I have the blues and can't get drunk enough to get sleepy. My nights are pretty awful." Sufficiently awful, it turned out, for Chandler, during this period, to attempt suicide.

Even as a middle-aged adult I have known the condition of not wishing to turn off my mental machinery and retire to sleep; and I have also known the pleasure of awakening eager to turn it back on. Most nights, though, I am ready to close up shop, pack it in, send up the white flag, not of surrender, but of cease-fire. Sleep on such occasions seems a marvelously sensible arrangement. But on other nights sleep seems an inconvenience, a drag, even something of a bore.

What removes some of the boredom is that one can never be sure what awaits one in sleep. "But she slept lightly and impatiently," writes Robert Musil in his story "The Temptation of Quiet Veronica," "as someone for whom the next day there is something extraordinary in store." Sometimes it seems there are quite as many states of sleep as of wakefulness: light sleep, troubled sleep, restless sleep, wakeful sleep, deep sleep, well-earned sleep. People talk, walk, snore, and emit semen in their sleep. They may be more receptive of the truth when asleep than when awake. "To sleep:" as the man with the notably receding hairline said, "perchance to dream. . . ." Not much perchance about it.

Envy has long ago begun to desert me, but I admit to feeling it for people who seem not to require much sleep. Those who can get by, indefinitely, on four or five hours of sleep a night have a small jump on the rest of us. I myself require six or seven hours of sleep, which beats by a bit the line from the old song that runs: "I work eight hours, I sleep eight hours, that leaves eight hours for fun." Still, the prospect of sleeping roughly a third of one's life away is more than a little dismaying.

But then who among us would like to be presented with a careful accounting of how he has spent his time on earth? My own might look something like this: sleep — slightly less than one third of total; watching men hit, chase, kick, and throw various-sized balls — eleven years, seven months; reading — thirteen years, four months; following the news — three years, six months; eating and activities connected with digestion — four years, eleven months; daydreaming and hopeless fantasizing — five years and seven months; gossiping, sulking, talking on the telephone, and miscellaneous time wasting — undeterminable but substantial . . .

As a fellow mindful of time, I tremendously dislike the notion of losing any of this valuable substance. Worry about the loss of time must kick in at a certain age. I know that it has been more than two decades since I have been able to stay abed later than seven in the morning with a good conscience. When I have, I feel as if the day has quite escaped me. Yet I recall reading with admiration, in *Howards End,* about the character Mrs. Wilcox, who spends entire days in bed, paying bills, answering letters, taking care of the small but necessary details in her life as well as recharging her batteries. I have also heard, as doubtless we all have, about people who in defeat, or more often in depression, repair to their beds and do not emerge for days, sometimes weeks. Not getting out of bed for weeks at a time — there's something, I find, rather enticing about that. My guess, though, is that I could not last more than an eight-hour stretch, and then I would lose to guilt whatever I gained in rest.

Sleeping in some beds, of course, is more pleasurable than sleeping in others. From childhood memories, doubtless by now nicely coated with nostalgia, I recall the comfort of sleeping on trains, with the clickety-clack of the tracks beneath, the stars above, the occasional lights from towns passing by. I have only read about sleepers on airplanes, which were in service, I gather, during World War II; or at least I recall A. J. Liebling remarking that, trying to sleep in a bed on a military transport, he heard his watch and pen, in a bedside table, rattling around "like dice in a crap-shooter's hand." It would have been nice, I imagine, to have watched the sky pass as one awaited sleep. As a boy, I would have been delighted to have slept in a bunk bed; I only did so later in the army. I have never slept in a hammock. The idea of camping out-of-doors, which I also had a taste of in the army, could only be made tolerable to me today if I could find a campsite where room service was included. Sleeping in the cramped quarters of a submarine wouldn't be easy for me. Sleeping alone in a hotel in a king-size bed, on the other hand, gives me the willies.

I often go to sleep with music playing. My bedside clock radio has a sleeper function, which allows the radio to play for a specified amount of time before it clicks off automatically. Usually I go to

sleep listening to classical music. Cello music is perhaps most
soporific. Opera music, with only rare exceptions, doesn't work:
too much blatant emotion. Most modern music is hopeless for
sleeping. (Glenn Gould also slept with his radio on and said that
sometimes the news got into his dreams.) But nothing puts me out
faster than Chicago Cub games broadcast from the West Coast.
When heard late at night from a prone position, the droning of
the announcers, who with their impressive assemblage of clichés
are describing a game in which there is nothing whatsoever at stake
— a Mickey Finn could not be more effective.

It is 4:15 in the afternoon, and, owing to my having had less
sleep than usual the night before, I am beginning to grow a bit
tired. So I walk out to mail a few letters, and on the way back I
stop at the public library a block or so away to pick up a copy of
Freud's *Interpretation of Dreams*. The brief walk in the fresh air has
put me in the perfect mood for a little nap.

I betake myself to the couch on which I do my serious napping.
I remove my glasses, loosen the belt on my trousers, slip out of my
shoes, rest my feet on a small black leather-covered footstool, and
set my head against the back of the couch. I call out to my cat,
who chooses not to join me (she is napping elsewhere in the
apartment). I am, for the next thirty minutes, history — sleeping
with my head back and, I believe, my mouth open. I am now nicely
fortified for the longish drive I have to make out to the western
suburbs to meet with cousins for dinner. A bit of water over the
eyes, a rinse of mouthwash, and, yo! I'm on my way.

I do not recall having had any dreams, but if I did they must
not have been worth remembering. I tend not to dream, at any
rate not very vividly, when napping. My dreaming during the night
seems to me, if I may say so, rather commonplace, even a little
drab. By setting us to the task of interpreting our dreams, Sigmund
Freud put us all on the road to being both novelist and critic of
our own sleep life. Beginning well before Freud, though, there
exists a lengthy literature on the meaning and function of dreams.
To what extent one's dreams provide the key to one's unconscious
and subconscious still seems to me very much, after all these years,
in the flux of controversy. From time to time — less often than I
would like — people I love who are dead show up in my dreams;
I long for them not to leave, but, like the electric trains, cap pistols,

and bubble gum of my childhood, they, too, inevitably depart. Many of my own dreams are sheer whimsy. The other night, for example, I dreamt about a bespoke suit that cost only $150. When I asked the woman in whose shop I saw it how she was able to produce such a suit at so low a price, she authoritatively answered: "Simple — low-quality material and poor workmanship." When I have nightmares, I find I am able, after only a brief spell, to turn them off, rather as if I am changing television channels. In fact, sometimes I will gain semiconsciousness during such nightmares and quite lucidly announce to myself, Who needs this? and then turn over and await another dream. In sleep, if not in actual life, I seem to have something akin to a satellite dish with almost endless channels available to me.

Along with the whimsy channel, I seem fairly often to find myself on the anxiety channel. My dentist informs me that I am a man who grinds his teeth at night, a sufferer from the dental problem known as bruxism, which these anxiety dreams must help along. One of these dreams, in fact, which comes up perhaps once a year, is about losing my teeth, or at least a few key teeth. Occasionally, I have a mugging dream, in which I find myself in a hallway or on a deserted street confronting two or three young guys, one of whom has a knife, who want my money. Usually I am able to change channels, or I simply awake, before any violence is done.

My more common anxiety dreams, though, have to do with my making a great fool of myself in public. The setting here is invariably pedagogic. I have agreed to give a lecture or to teach a course on a subject about which I know absolutely nothing: Persian literature, say, or astrophysics. Screwup follows hard upon screwup. I cannot find the room; I have lost my notes; I need frightfully to make water. "Persian literature," I begin, before a large crowd well stocked with Iranian faces, "is extremely rich." And then I realize that I do not know the names of any Persian writers apart from Omar Khayyám. I hem. I haw. I wonder what extraordinary hubris propelled me into agreeing to deliver this lecture in the first place. "Persian literature," I continue, "is more than extremely rich — it is highly varied. Take the case of Omar Khayyám . . ."

When young, I had a student variant of these anxiety dreams in which I walk into a final exam of a course I have not attended all quarter long. The course is inevitably on a subject that is abstract yet also specific — Boolean algebra, say, or eighteenth-century musicology — something, in other words, that I cannot bluff my way through with stylish writing. Particular knowledge is needed, and, in these dreams, particular knowledge is exactly what I never have. Now, thirty years later, as a teacher rather than a student, in my dreams I still don't have it.

I occasionally have more ordinary nightmares: squirrels or possums or other animals with sharp claws are crowding in on me. A thief is at the window, but I cannot muster the energy to shut it as he begins to crawl in. I am traveling to Europe by plane, and I cannot locate my luggage, my tickets, my wife. Time is running out. I am never going to make it. As I say, all these seem to me fairly commonplace dreams. I have had only a single dream in which the Nazis figured, and it was connected, as I remember noting, to no recent book or movie or discussion of the subject I had encountered. It just came up arbitrarily — out of the dark, one might say. I am just not much of a world-historical dreamer.

Unlike Graham Greene, who kept a dream diary that has recently been published under the title *A World of My Own,* and whose dreams had a richness that make my own scarcely worth changing into pajamas for. Greene regularly dreamed of popes and heads of state and dictators. He dreamed of spying; in one dream, he helped capture Hitler. His dreams have a political line — they are reliably anti-American. Living and dead writers drop in with some frequency. Kim Philby recruits Ernest Hemingway to work for the Communists in Hong Kong. Evelyn Waugh, in another dream, shoots W. H. Auden. Henry James joins Greene on a river trip to Bogotá. T. S. Eliot queries a line of a poem he has written and turns out to be wearing a mustache. Greene's nightmares have to do with birds and spiders and urinating *crevettes* and *langoustines.* But in a darker, a true writer's, nightmare, his publisher cannot be talked out of praising the novels of C. P. Snow.

Graham Greene refers, in this book, to his dreamworld as "My Own World," in contradistinction to "the world I share," which is his designation for the real world. Impressively rich though the world Greene shared was — filled with mistresses, politics, intrigue, literary success, religious crises, and the rest of it — his Own World is even richer. With dreams of the kind he records, I should imagine he could hardly wait to get to sleep at night.

But then artists have always been dreamers. Maurice Ravel felt that because they do spend so much time dreaming, even when awake, it wasn't fair for artists to marry. In my own case, though much of the material of my youthful fantasies — world fame, sexual conquest, appalling riches, enemies nicely discouraged — has lost its allure, I still manage to spend a goodly portion of my waking hours in a semi–dream state. I wish I could tell you more precisely than I can what it is I daydream about, but so vague, not to say misty, are these little sallies on which I float off that they are quite unmemorable and insubstantial. I am in a gentle clime; I drive along a blue coast in a convertible with a grandchild seated next to me; I have written something immemorially beautiful.

Many years ago, I read in a biography of Hannah Arendt that Miss Arendt set aside an hour every afternoon during which she lay on a couch in her Manhattan apartment and did nothing but think. I kitchen- or rather couch-tested this procedure and found I was unable to concentrate that long when on my back; in fact, engaged in concentrated thinking, I soon dozed off. Most of my thinking, if thinking it really is, comes in inconvenient spurts while daydreaming: in the shower, at the wheel of my car, with a book in my hand, while napping, just before falling off to sleep at night. For me, stray — and occasionally useful — thoughts, if not responsibilities, begin in dreams.

I was of that generation of children who said their prayers before going to sleep. I cannot recall whether doing so was my parents' or my own idea. But the prologue to the prayer I said was the standard one that ran:

> Now I lay me down to sleep;
> I pray the Lord my soul to keep.
> If I should die before I wake,
> I pray the Lord my soul to take.
> God bless my mother, my father . . .

Looking at these words in cold type, this little prayer seems quite terrifying — at least for a small child — holding out as it does the distinct prospect of imminent death coming in one's sleep. Beyond a certain age — nowadays I suppose it is eighty — it is thought extremely good luck to be allowed to die in one's sleep. She just slept, and slipped, away, one reports of some deaths, usually with a suggestion in one's voice of the mercifulness of the arrangement. Departing thus does deprive one of the drama of possibly uttering profound last words — "More light!" "What is the question?" "Trade Kingman!" "Is it a little hot in here, or do I imagine it?" — but most people, I suspect, would be willing to forgo those last words for a calmer because unconscious departure.

Shelley refers, in the opening lines of *Queen Mab,* to "Death and his brother Sleep!" Sleep itself has been called "little death." It's not a bad description of the phenomenon of sleep. To fall asleep, after all, entails a letting go, a giving up of consciousness, a journey to one knows not where. As with death, so with sleep, no one knows with certainty what awaits on the other side: nightmares, sweetmares, brief (one hopes) oblivion.

I have described my prowess at napping, or the art of napping in action. What I have not gone into is the secret behind the attainment of this prowess. In no small part, it has to do with wanting a time-out — with wanting out of life, not deeply, not permanently, but at least for a while. The English writer A. Alvarez, in a book titled *Night,* allows that he has become addicted to sleep — that he finds it no less than, in his own word, "sensual." He remarks that in his adolescence and twenties he chiefly thought about sex; once he married and that department of his life was in order, in his thirties "the obsession with sex was replaced by an obsession with food"; and now, in his sixties, this has been "usurped by a new obsession: sleep."

I wonder if the larger meaning of the obsession with sleep isn't a slow, albeit unconscious, preparation for closing up shop. I wonder, too, if this is such a bad thing. I know many people will despise this notion, arguing that one must never give in, give out, give up. They will claim, with much right on their side, that life is too precious a gift for one to permit it to slip away of one's own volition — in effect, for one to welcome death. Stay in the game, turn up the music, keep fighting, they will argue, plenty of time for napping in the grave. And they are, again, right.

Yet there is something marvelously seductive about sleep, and especially about a nap, which might best be viewed as a lovely and harmless touch of cheating, comparable, if one wishes to talk about sleep in terms usually reserved for sex instead of for death, to an afternoon tryst. As an artful napper, a nap remains, in my mind, one of life's fine things just so long as, when napping, one doesn't dream that one has been made some fantastic, some really quite impossible to refuse, offer by Harvard.

JAMES FENTON

A Lesson from Michelangelo

FROM THE NEW YORK REVIEW OF BOOKS

IN OLD AGE, Giambologna used to tell his friends the story of
how, as a young man, a Flemish sculptor newly arrived in Rome,
he made a model to his own original design, finished it *coll'alito*,
"with his breath" — that is to say, with the utmost care, bringing
it to the very peak of finish — and went to show it to the great
Michelangelo. And Michelangelo took the model in his hands and
completely destroyed it, and then remodeled it according to his
way of thinking, and did so with marvelous skill, so that the
outcome was quite the opposite of what the young man had done.
And then Michelangelo said to Giambologna: Now go and learn
the art of modeling before you learn the art of finishing.

One supposes from this terrible story that the model must have
been made of wax. One supposes that, even on a hot summer's
afternoon in Rome, it would have needed a certain amount of
working before wax became malleable enough for Michelangelo
to shape according to his own wishes. Who knows, perhaps several
minutes were involved. They must have seemed like hours, as the
young sculptor watched, and the wrathful old genius, biting his
lower lip, squeezed and squashed and pounded away at the model
that had been so lovingly finished. And well before the new model
began to emerge, and with it the ostensive reason for the exercise
— learn to model before you learn to finish — another point was
being made: See how I crush all your ambitions and aspirations,
see how feeble your work is in comparison with mine, see how
presumptuous you were even to dare to cross the threshold — *Thus
I destroy you!*

There were compensations, of course, for the young Giambologna. He had walked in with an example of his juvenilia, and he left carrying a vibrant little Michelangelo. You might say that he was lucky the master had thought him worthy of the lesson, even if the lesson had to be delivered in such a devastating way. You might say this. Or you might argue that the ostensive lesson was only a pretext for the destruction of the young man's work.

There is no such thing as the artistic personality — not in poetry, not in the visual arts. Michelangelo's personality was just one of the colorful range on offer. He was paranoid about his productions, keeping his drawings secret not only from his contemporaries who might include potential plagiarists, but also from posterity itself. As his days drew to a close he made two large bonfires, and not a drawing or cartoon was found in his studio after his death. And this paranoia extended to his relations with other artists. He did not "bring on young talent." He appears to have surrounded himself deliberately with no-hopers, and it is easy to imagine that it was the skill, not the shortcomings, of Giambologna that drove him into such a rage.

But you don't have to be like that in order to be a great artist, or a great poet. If Michelangelo was both, so, apparently, was Leonardo, of whom Vasari tells us that, in addition to his gifts as a musician, he was the most talented improviser in verse of his time. We are told by one scholar that while "Michelangelo jealously guarded his artistic property against other artists, it was not in keeping with Leonardo's nature to trouble himself to preserve the authorship of the wealth of ideas which poured out of him," that he was

> amiable by nature, communicative and ready to be of help . . . when he turned to the greater themes of painting or sculpture, he was interested above everything else in the solution of some fundamental problem; when he had succeeded to his own satisfaction, perhaps only theoretically, he liked to leave its execution to others; and what happened further to his work of art seems to have troubled him but little, much less did it occur to him to sign it. He was so independent and had so little vanity that in the execution of his work the identity of the patron had not the slightest influence with him.

And yet there were, as Vasari makes clear, limits to Leonardo's lack of vanity: he did not tolerate insulting behavior, he could not stand a foolish, ignorant patron, and he couldn't bear to remain in the same city as Michelangelo. Nor Michelangelo with him. So one went off to Rome, and the other to the court of the king of France, and thereby they put between themselves about as great a distance as they possibly could, without falling off the edge of what they deemed the civilized world.

But it does not follow from this that genius always repels genius. Verrocchio presents a further type, a teacher who was happy to surround himself with talent, who trained Lorenzo di Credi and loved him above all others. Verrocchio it was who took on the young Leonardo and who famously decided to renounce painting when he recognized that Leonardo's angel in the *Baptism* outshone his own work. He was ashamed to have been outpainted by a mere boy. But if this renunciation seems hysterical, I would say that it is less so in Verrocchio's case than it would have been in others'. Verrocchio had plenty of other fish to fry. He had begun life as a goldsmith. In Rome, he

saw the high value that was put on the many statues and other antiques being discovered there, and the way the Pope had the bronze horse set up in St. John Lateran, as well as the attention given even to the bits and pieces, let alone the complete works of sculpture, that were being discovered every day.

So he decided to give up being a goldsmith and be a sculptor instead. And when he had won honor as a sculptor so that "there was nothing left for him to achieve," he turned his hand to painting.

I take these stories about artists, from Baldinucci and Vasari, because they date from a period when it appears that one could acknowledge straightforwardly motives of which we would today be obscurely ashamed. Verrocchio observes that there is much honor to be gained in the field of sculpture, so he becomes a sculptor, and when he feels he has won the honor that is going, he turns to painting with the same motive, but when he sees his way blocked by Leonardo he turns back to sculpture again. There is something equable about this temperament and something generous about the recognition of which it was capable. But this generosity was far from typical of its time and place. It was noteworthy. It was a cause célèbre.

Otherwise one feels that the Italy these artists worked in was a place of the most vicious rivalry and backbiting, maneuverings for commissions, anglings for patronage, plots, triumphs, and disappointments. You had to wait literally for years to be paid. If your work was deemed ugly, you soon learnt about it from lampoons or pasquinades. You got stabbed in the back. Anonymous denunciations for sodomy would arrive, as regular as parking tickets.

Since your work, standing, and honor were all bound together, the award of a grand commission to a friend or rival would be a devastating blow. It would make you rethink your life, as — and this is the last of the Vasarian exempla — Brunelleschi and Donatello were forced to do when Ghiberti won the famous competition for the Florence Baptistry doors. The contest had taken a year. When the entries were exhibited, it was clear to the two friends that Ghiberti's work was better than theirs, and so they went to the consuls and argued that Ghiberti should get the commission. And for this, Vasari says, "they deserved more praise than if they had done the work perfectly themselves. What happy men they were! They helped each other and found pleasure in praising the work of others. What a deplorable contrast is presented by our modern artists who are not content with injuring one another, but who viciously and enviously rend others as well!"

So Vasari praises the two artists, and he is not sentimental either, for he goes on to relate how the consuls asked Brunelleschi, who had clearly come a very good second, whether he would cooperate with Ghiberti on the doors, but Brunelleschi said no, since "he was determined to be supreme in some other art rather than merely be a partner or take second place. . . ." Nor was this a passing fit of pique, although both artists eventually did return to Florence and did help Ghiberti. Perhaps the strength of their sense of failure may be gauged from the fact that Donatello, who had not done so well, took a year away from Florence, whereas Brunelleschi, the honorable runner-up, took at least five, and when he did return, he did so principally as an architect.

It's not enough to fail. You have to come to feel your failure, to live it through, to turn it over in your hand, like a stone with strange markings. You have to wake up in the middle of the night and hear it whistling around the roof, or chomping in the field

below, like some loyal horse — My failure, my very own failure, I
thought I'd left it behind in Florence, but look, it's followed me
here to Rome. And the horse looks up at you in the moonlight
and you feel its melancholy reproach. This is after all the failure
for which you were responsible. Why are you neglecting your
failure?

Many people live in such a horror of failure that they can never
embark on any great enterprise. And this inability to get going in
the first place is the worst kind of failure because there truly is no
way out. You can cover up. You can hide behind a mask of exquisite
sensibility. You can congratulate yourself on the fact that your
standards are so high that no human effort could possibly match
up to them. You can make yourself unpleasant to your contemporaries by becoming expert on their shortcomings. In the end,
nothing is achieved by this timidity.

Or you can permit yourself one failure in life, and devote your
remaining days to mourning. "Alas, alas, the critics panned my
play." "When did this happen, friend?" "In 1894!" This failure, it
would seem, has been kept like a trophy, lovingly polished and
always on display. But for a productive life, and a happy one, each
failure must be felt and worked through. It must form part of the
dynamic of your creativity.

The judgment on Donatello's competition entry was: good design, poor execution. Donatello could decipher from that a message saying: You are not yet fully formed as an artist; you must
study. But the message received by Brunelleschi was: You will never
be as good as Ghiberti. This was a hard blow. Brunelleschi did what
he felt necessary — sold a small farm and, with Donatello, walked
down to Rome. And there something happened to them that I
hope will happen to any poet reading this. Failure rewarded them
a thousandfold.

For they came to a place, a sort of Land of Green Ginger, where
every answer to every urgent inquiry lay literally at their feet. This,
for a poet, would be like discovering voice, technique, and infinite
subject matter, fresh and unused, and finding them all in a flash.
The ruins of Rome were fresh and unused. You pulled back a caper
bush and there lay an architrave. You peered behind the pigpen
and there was a sarcophagus. You dug a little and there was a bust,
a capital, a herm.

And so they dug and drew and made measurements of the astonishing buildings all around them, and they went without food, and they got filthy, and people decided they must be geomancers in search of treasure. Which wasn't far wrong. For the secrets of the classical orders were revealing themselves, and the lost technology of the ancient world. But all this time Brunelleschi never revealed to Donatello — especially not to Donatello — the scope of his ambition to revive the classical art of architecture and make that his bid for fame. They were friends. They were rivals. For the project to be worthwhile, it had to be the means whereby Brunelleschi would defeat not only Ghiberti, but also Donatello, his best friend from the Salon des Refusés.

Why should artistic ambition be like that? Why should a sculptor, a poet, feel the need to be the unique object of admiration, to create around himself an illusion of being quite the only pebble, the only boulder on the beach? Why should uniqueness itself be so closely involved with our definition of a work of art, so that we expect every performance to be unique, every hand, every voice, every gesture?

Without looking too far for an answer, we might say that our efforts in the direction of art have something to do with a moment, or a period, in which we felt or knew ourselves to be unique. Feeding at the breast we were unique. (I mean, normally speaking. We are not piglets. We weren't born in a litter.) Dandled on the lap we were unique, when our parents taught us all the new things we could do with our lips and our limbs. And this was a time of pure inventiveness. Everything we did was hailed as superb. We leapt up and down and our innards went wild with surprise. And the palms of our hands were beaten together. We learnt about rhythm and we learnt new ways of making a noise, and every noise we made was praised. And we learnt how to walk, and all eyes were upon us, the way they never would be again.

Because there follows the primal erasure, when we forget all those early experiences, and it is rather as if there is some mercy in this, since if we could remember the intensity of such pleasure it might spoil us for anything else. We forget what happened exactly, but we know that there was something, something to do with music and praise and everyone talking, something to do with flying through the air, something to do with dance.

And during this period of forgetting we have been forced to take a realistic view of the world, and to admit that there are other people in it besides ourselves and our adoring audience. And in our various ways of coping with this fact we form the basis of our personality. And one will say through his art: There can be only me — the rest being counterfeits. And another will say: There is me, and my best friend, and we are the best. And a third version would be: There is me and my best friend, who (but don't tell him) isn't as good as me.

Auden wrote a wonderful thing to Stephen Spender in 1942 — it is quoted in Auden's *Juvenilia* — when he said: "You (at least I fancy so) can be jealous of someone else writing a good poem because it seems a rival strength. I'm not, because every good poem, of yours say, is a strength, which is put at my disposal." And he said that this arose because Spender was strong and he, Auden, was weak, but his was a fertile weakness.

And it would indeed be a source of fertility to be blessed with that attitude both to the living and to the dead, so that everybody's good poem is a source of strength to you, and the corpus of published poetry lies before you as the ruins of Rome appeared to Brunelleschi. One associated Auden's luck in this regard with his abiding conviction that in any gathering he was always the youngest person in the room.

An extreme case of the opposite attitude would be that of Wordsworth in old age, at least the attitude that Carlyle claimed to detect:

I got him upon the subject of great poets, who I thought might be admirable equally to us both; but was rather mistaken, as I gradually found. Pope's partial failure I was prepared for; less for the narrowish limits visible in Milton and others. I tried him with Burns, of whom he had sung tender recognition; but Burns also turned out to be a limited inferior creature, any genius he had a theme for one's pathos rather; even Shakespeare himself had his blind sides, his limitations: — gradually it became apparent to me that of transcendent unlimited there was, to this Critic, probably but one specimen known, Wordsworth himself! He by no means said so, or hinted so, in words; but on the whole it was all I gathered from him in this considerable *tête-à-tête* of ours; and it was not an agreeable conquest. New notion as to Poetry or Poet I had not in the smallest degree got; but my insight into the depths of Wordsworth's pride in himself had considerably augmented; — and it did not increase my love of him; though I did [not] in the least hate it either, so quiet was it, so fixed, *un*appealing, like a dim old lichened crag on the wayside, the private meaning of which, in contrast with any public meaning it had, you recognized with a kind of not wholly melancholy *grin.*

You notice how far we have come from the candid psychology of ambition as perceived by Vasari to the uncandid, sly, deceitful self-love as perceived by Carlyle, whose meaning, unpacked, was — there is only me, *and there only ever has been me.*

Nor was this simply something that Wordsworth came to believe at the end of his life. There was a period when his "intolerance of others," as Gittings tells us, "was reported to have reached alarming lengths." And it happened that this was the period in which Keats, who admired Wordsworth to distraction, was ushered into his presence. He had sent a copy of his 1817 poems to Wordsworth, who, if he had read them, had done so without cutting all the pages. But all went well initially, and Wordsworth kindly asked what Keats had been writing recently. And from this point I shall follow Haydon's account, even though the detail has been disputed. What seems not in dispute is that Keats did a bit of a Giambologna. Haydon says:

> *I* said he has just finished an exquisite ode to Pan — and as he had not a copy I begged Keats to repeat it — which he did in his usual half chant, (most touchingly) walking up & down the room — when he had done I felt really, as if I had heard a young Apollo — Wordsworth drily said "a Very pretty piece of Paganism" — This was unfeeling, & unworthy of his high Genius to a young worshiper like Keats — & Keats felt it *deeply* — so that if Keats has said any thing severe about our Friend; it was because he was wounded — and though he dined with Wordsworth after at my table — he never forgave him.

If it did not happen quite like this, something quite like this appears nevertheless to have happened, and Keats became aware of that quiet, fixed, unappealing, dim old lichened crag, and got a whiff of its meaning. Because his attitude does change, and it is not so long after this encounter that Keats writes his celebrated letter to Reynolds of February 3, 1818. Nothing from the surviving letters gives Keats's side of the encounter, unless we take this passage as a record of a man recovering from an insult.

It may be said that we ought to read our Contemporaries, that Wordsworth &c should have their due from us, but for the sake of a few fine
imaginative or domestic passages, are we to be bullied into a certain
Philosophy engendered in the whims of an Egotist — Every man has
his speculations, but every man does not brood and peacock over them
till he makes a false coinage and deceives himself.

And a few lines later:

We hate poetry that has a palpable design upon us — and if we do not
agree, seems to put its hand in its breeches pocket. Poetry should be
great & unobtrusive, a thing which enters into one's soul, and does not
startle it or amaze it with itself but with its subject. — How beautiful are
the retired flowers! how they would lose their beauty were they to
throng into the highway crying out, "admire me I am a violet! dote
upon me I am a primrose!"

Well, we hate an insult both for the evidence it gives us of
another's malice and for the way it finds us out, the way it gets at
our self-esteem, or worse, if the insult thinks it can get at us, even
though we feel passionately that we are not as base-minded as that.
If Keats came from his encounter with Wordsworth insulted and
disillusioned, it is not surprising that he should have refrained
from saying so directly, for it is humiliating to admit that some
trivial remark has cut us to the quick, humiliating further to give
any evidence that the jibe has lodged with us, that it has arrived
with all its luggage and intends to stay for a long time. Keats looked
into Wordsworth's soul and saw something unexpectedly petty:

Modern poets differ from the Elizabethans in this. Each of the moderns
like an Elector of Hanover governs his petty state, & knows how many
straws are swept daily from the Causeways in all his dominions & has a
continual itching that all the Housewives should have their coppers well
scoured: the ancients were Emperors of vast Provinces, they had only
heard of the remote ones and scarcely cared to visit them — I will cut
all this — I will have no more of Wordsworth or Hunt . . .

It may be that there was something about Keats that created
alarm in his contemporaries. Byron seems hysterical in his attack
on Keats's "piss-a-bed" poetry: "No more *Keats* I entreat — flay him
alive — if some of you don't I must skin him myself[:] there is no

bearing the drivelling idiotism of the Mankin. — — " And "Mr. Keats whose poetry you enquire after — appears to me what I have already said; — such writing is a sort of mental masturbation — he is always f — gg — g his *Imagination*. — I don't mean that he is *indecent* but viciously soliciting his own ideas into a state which is neither poetry nor any thing else but a Bedlam vision produced by raw pork and opium." Then he becomes a "dirty little black-guard," simply for having been praised in the *Edinburgh Review*. And then, in death, he is assumed to be a person of "such inordinate self-love he would probably not have been very happy." Byron assumes it to be true, and becomes obsessed by the idea that Keats was killed off by a burst blood vessel after receiving a savage review in the *Quarterly*. He affects a kind of regret, but cannot conceal an illicit excitement at the story. It is hard not to conclude that Keats was seen as a threat by Byron, and that this was his greatest sin. As for Wordsworth, going through his impossible phase, Gittings says: "From 1815 to 1820, the difficult second half of a man's forties, Wordsworth showed at his worst, and his emergence at fifty to something like his normal self was greeted by all with relief. It is an irony that his malaise coincided precisely with the whole of Keats's writing life."

Irony doesn't seem quite strong enough a word to cover the implication of this passage: that one of the supremely gifted poets of his time should be driven into something that looked like a kind of mental illness by the mere fact of another poet's existence; that Wordsworth could not be at ease with himself until he knew that Keats was dead.

But if it *were* true, and if it were true that Byron suffered something like the same disease, then one would suppose that what identified Keats as a threat was his aspiration for greatness rather than the greatness itself. It is not that either of the older poets had been put into a pother after reading the odes. It's the *Poems* of 1817, stuff that might strike us, for the most part, as not exactly threatening — and anyway Wordsworth hadn't even read all of it, and there's no guarantee that Byron had either.

It seems unfair, excepting in this sense, that Keats's encounter with opposition, with envy perhaps on Wordsworth's part, and his disenchantment, seems to have benefited him, to have made him stronger, whereas it was nothing unless debilitating to Wordsworth.

Keats had a strong and just sense of his own development, and he didn't mind taking a nose dive:

> The Genius of Poetry must work its own salvation in a man: It cannot be matured by law & precept, but by sensation & watchfulness in itself — That which is creative must create itself — In Endymion, I leaped headlong into the Sea, and thereby have become better acquainted with the Soundings, the quicksands, & the rocks, than if I had stayed upon the green shore, and piped a silly pipe, and took tea & comfortable advice. — I was never afraid of failure; for I would sooner fail than not be among the greatest.

So it might have been the aspiration that was the problem, as it is indeed a problem for anyone setting out in poetry. If I aspire to musicianship, I am at once set on a journey through a series of immensely complicated disciplines. It is extremely improbable that I will get anywhere without training. And it therefore does not happen that even a precocious musician seems pretentious. We feel, however much we envy the success, that it must have been earned. But it is far from clear how we are supposed to *earn* success in poetry. Poetry often seems unearned.

Nor is it all clear how we could be delayed, held back from achieving our aim, if we looked like a bit of a threat. Verrocchio can always hold Leonardo back, keeping him grinding colors or preparing panels or busy at any number of prentice tasks. Or he could affect to bring him on, keeping him sketching from dawn till dusk, but always delaying the dread moment when he picks up the paintbrush. But in poetry there is really no equivalent for these in intermediate disciplines. The way to learn to write poetry is: to write poetry. So we pass directly from the aspiration to the activity itself, and that leaves us at first vulnerable, because, looked at in a certain way, we have no *right* to be writing poems at this stage. But unfortunately we have no option *but* to give it a whirl. The old joke — Do you play the violin? I don't know, I've never tried — describes our predicament. We are in the position of someone who takes up a violin for the first time and has a go at giving a concert.

But you might object: surely there are things one can do, like writing parodies, like trying out the traditional forms, like studying other people's poetry, like going in for competitions.

I would certainly say that people who have no interest at all in

studying other people's poetry are unlikely to produce it themselves, although it is not at all uncommon for them to attempt to
do so. As for parodies and the trying out of forms, these are things
that some people do and find useful. In the case of parody, its chief
usefulness is in getting people to write poetry who are too shy or
sly to admit that that is what they want to do.

As far as the trying out of traditional forms is concerned, I have
this to say: that there seems to me to be a fundamental difference
between trying out a traditional form as an exercise and writing a
poem in a traditional form. It is true that, in the context of a
workshop, structure may be given to a group's work by the trying
out of certain famous forms, and it is true that such things can be
fun as competitions or games among friends. But I do not think
that the trying out of forms is an exercise that points in the
direction of the writing of poems. Trying out the sonnet — taking
a sonnet for a spin, putting the little filly through her paces —
seems a rather different activity from the writing of poetry. The
great questions of form go deeper than that, and the commitment
implied is much more profound than the respectful nod in the
direction of form-as-exercise would imply. Don't try out a sonnet.
Try to *write* a sonnet. Try to write a *real* sonnet. But that's the whole
aim. That's not an exercise.

Auden tried everything there was going, but his attitude was different. It was much more like Brunelleschi and Donatello going
crazy among the ruins of Rome, digging things up, finding how
they worked, imitating them. And imitating for Auden meant
much more than the banal copying of metrical pattern and rhyme
scheme. It meant a recapturing and reinterpretation of the quality
of a thing — a madrigal, a calypso, whatever it was.

There is another form of activity, though, besides reading other
people's work and trying perhaps to imitate it, and this is showing
your work to other people. And this activity is of the essence. And
of course it can be most devastating, usually because what one has
written turns out to be a complete turkey, and we only realize this
at the moment we hand the thing to our friends. We should all
take heart though from the case of Flaubert, who put a phenome-
nal effort into the composition of the first version of his *Temptation
of Saint Anthony* (one single episode involved him in the reading
of sixty ancient texts, histories, and scholarly commentaries) and

finally read it aloud to his friends Louis Bouilhet and Maxime DuCamp, who recalled later that

> the hours that Bouilhet and I spent listening to Flaubert chant his lines — we sitting there silent, occasionally exchanging a glance — remain very painful in my memory. We kept straining our ears, always hoping that the action would begin, and always disappointed, for the situation remains the same from beginning to end. St. Anthony, bewildered, a little simple, really quite a blockhead if I dare say so, sees the various forms of temptation pass before him and responds with nothing but exclamations: "Ah! Ah! Oh! Mon dieu! Mon dieu!" . . . Flaubert grew heated as he read, and we tried to grow warm with him, but remained frozen. . . . After the last reading [and the whole thing had taken thirty-two hours] Flaubert pounded the table: "Now; tell me frankly what you think."
>
> Bouilhet was a shy man, but no one was firmer than he once he decided to express his opinion; and he said: "We think you should throw it into the fire and never speak of it again."
>
> Flaubert leapt up and uttered a cry of horror. . . . He repeated certain lines to us, saying "But that is beautiful!"
>
> "Yes, it is beautiful. . . . There are excellent passages, some exquisite evocations of antiquity, but it is all lost in the bombast of the language. You wanted to make music and you have made only noise."

I think we can assume that there was justice in what the two friends said, rather than envy, which is what Flaubert's mother thought. But there remains the problem first of daring to show the work to your friends, next of bearing to listen to what they say about it, but finally, finally and most importantly, there is the whole matter of interpreting what your friends say, deciding whether to accept or reject their judgment, and figuring out where you are going to go from there. And this is where the delicate matter of the relations between poets comes in.

Why should it be, for instance, that Coleridge wrote "Kubla Khan" in the late 1790s, say October or November 1797; that the Wordsworths definitely knew it in 1798 because Dorothy says in her Hamburgh journal that she "carried Kubla to a fountain," meaning, we believe, that she carried her drinking can, which she called Kubla; but that Coleridge is not recorded as reciting the poem till 1811–1812, and that it was not published until 1816.

If we had written the poem, would we be so reticent?

I believe the answer is that Coleridge wrote the poem, much as one writes any poem, with a great deal of excitement, and that he put it in his pocket and went over to see the Wordsworths. Now the state of mind one is in after writing a poem is rather like the state of mind that continues in a waking person after a particularly vivid dream, but with this difference: that we are under the illusion, after such a dream, that it will be of interest to others. But very few dreams are. They might interest our lovers, and they are meat and drink to our analysts, but not to anyone else. But we don't know this, because the state of mind that produced the dream is still with us. Nor do we know, after we have written the poem, whether it will be of interest to others. Put it away for a while, and you can possibly tell, but at the moment of completion you merely hope that the thrill is not an illusion.

Coleridge came bounding over to see the Wordsworths, as he had often done, to read his latest work. And they sat in a rather damp parlor, and Coleridge launched into his reading, and while he was at it, full tilt, Dorothy was watching William, as she always did, for his reaction. And there was a little gesture that she knew well, which meant that his nose had been put out of joint. Keats noticed it too, and it survived in one of the passages I quoted. Wordsworth put his hand in his breeches pocket. And Dorothy knew that all was not well. Coleridge was in the process of committing an utter Giambologna.

The reading was over. Silence fell. And Coleridge, who was on a natural high not caused by anything remotely resembling substance abuse, thought, Great, they're impressed. And he waited for a compliment or two. And nothing happened, and finally he too began to suspect that something was up. And then Dorothy said, in a bright voice, "Well, at least I shall know what to call my drinking *can* now. Come along, Kubla, we're going to the well." And Wordsworth suddenly burst out laughing in a rather horrible, forced way, and said, "I say, Dorothy, that's awfully good — Kubla Can — do you get it, Coleridge?" And Dorothy left the room, and silence fell again, punctuated occasionally by Wordsworth's chuckling over Dorothy's joke.

Finally it was Coleridge's turn to say something, to cover up the dreadful Giambologna he appeared to have committed. And he began telling a story about how he had been taking opium and gone into a trance, and something about a person from Porlock, all of it made up. And Wordsworth turned to him and said: "I think you should throw that poem in the fire, Coleridge, and never speak of it again."

Now if Coleridge had been Keats, he would have fallen out of love with Wordsworth on the spot. But Coleridge was not Keats. He was absolutely convinced, and puzzled by the fact, that he had made a faux pas of the worst kind, because he could not recognize that thing that Keats and Carlyle recognized when they looked into Wordsworth's soul — that unappealing, lichen-covered thing.

It was not that he was not sly — in his own way he was incredibly sly. He affected to like Southey's poetry, of which he had a low opinion. Same with Byron. He thought he was the greatest of Wordsworth's admirers, but he once went to great lengths to write a two-volume book, the *Biographia Literaria,* merely in order to be able to print a whole chapter on the defects of Wordsworth's poetry, which he knew would be enough to send Wordsworth *up the wall.* A whole chapter on Wordsworth's defects! And Byron read that chapter with particular interest. And Coleridge never knew what he, Coleridge, was up to.

If he'd been a character out of Vasari, he could have understood that Wordsworth had to be the only one in his field, and he might even have done a better job of going off to Rome, or going to work at the court of the king of France, or whatever the equivalent would have been. But he couldn't manage to fall out of love with him. He couldn't leave him alone.

But "Kubla Khan" wouldn't go away. Coleridge had improvised the story whereby he turned it into a curiosity, and it was as a curiosity that he would recite it to his friends. One day in early April 1816 he did so in the company of Byron — Byron who, despite his views on the Lake Poets, always had time for Coleridge (his letters show this), always admired poems such as "Christabel," and had even put work in Coleridge's way.

Byron was impressed, and immediately asked why Coleridge had not published such a fine work. Coleridge shrugged and said that Wordsworth hadn't liked it. Thereupon my suggestion is that Byron set Coleridge right upon the character of his friend. When the poem saw print, it was with an acknowledgment of Byron's encouragement.

The following fragment is here published at the request of a poet of great and deserved celebrity, and, as far as the Author's own opinions are concerned, rather as a psychological curiosity, than on grounds of any supposed *poetic* merits.

But Coleridge did not think Byron's celebrity as a poet was deserved. As Henry Nelson Coleridge reported in his *Table Talk* (June 2, 1824),

Nothing of Lord Byron's would live, nor much of the poetry of the day. The *art* was so neglected; the verses would not scan.

This then is the essence of a true Giambologna. It is based on a gross misunderstanding of the actual state of affairs. Giambologna takes a statuette to show to Michelangelo, and he thinks he's just a poor Flemish nobody, wanting a pat on the head. But Michelangelo takes one look at Giambologna and what he sees is a threat. In fact Michelangelo hallucinates. What he sees is a gleaming, nude bronze warrior, a sort of glistening David, striding into the studio with some kind of weapon in his hands, and he thinks: Oh, so I'm supposed to be Goliath, am I? And he seizes the weapon and crushes it with all his might. And the hallucination passes, and he sees that it's just that Flemish twerp who keeps pestering . . .

Giambologna emerges from his meeting with Michelangelo, with the wax model still warm from the worker's hand. He can't believe that Michelangelo, whom he had worshiped as a god, could have been so perfectly foul to him. He feels sorry for himself as a foreigner. He thinks: He wouldn't have behaved like that if I'd been a Florentine; the bastard just said to himself, Who does this Flemish twerp think he is? And so he walks on through a Rome with which he is now distinctly out of love, the Rome that had once seemed to him like the Land of Green Ginger, until he comes to the small tavern where he and several of his countrymen live. And it's evening, and his friends are at table and they call out to him: Hey, Jean, how did it go? And then they say: Oh, like that, was it? And Giambologna takes a taper and goes up to his room, lights a lamp and places the little model on the table, the model that he had made to his own design and finished so beautifully.

And he thinks: It's so banal, that advice — first learn to model before you learn to finish. It's like saying learn to walk before you learn to run. Who needs it? What's the point? Why set yourself up as a genius if that's the best that you can do?

And then he thinks: Who's he to talk about modeling, anyway? The *Bacchus* looks as if it's going to fall over. The *David*'s got one leg longer than the other. Who's he to talk about modeling? And the thought of the injustice of it makes him throw his shoes across the room with such force that one of his countrymen comes up to see what's wrong.

And Giambologna says: "Michelangelo's idea of modeling, I mean, *his idea of modeling*, is sticking a couple of breasts on a bloke to make a woman. That's his idea of modeling!"

And the friend says: "Yes, Jean, yes, come and have a drink."

But Giambologna says: "He talks about learning to model before you learn to finish. I mean — what does he know about finishing? When was the last time he ever finished anything? Tell me! When?"

"Sistine Chapel?" says the friend, but Giambologna doesn't hear.

"The façade of San Lorenzo is a disgrace. The tomb of Julius is just a fragment. He doesn't even bother anymore, he thinks he's so clever he can leave half the block untouched."

"You're right," says the friend, "he's a complete tosser. Now come on down." But Giambologna stays upstairs, calmer now that he has fallen out of love with Rome and out of love with Michelangelo, now that the scales have fallen from his eyes. And from time to time he goes over to the table and examines the little *bozzetto*, and really it's not entirely bad, it's just that it's full of all the things that Giambologna now can't stand about Michelangelo.

And soon, without knowing it, he is biting his lower lip and working away at the red wax till it becomes malleable again. And now he begins to revise the figure according to his way of thinking, reducing the gigantism of the muscles, giving the features an elegance and brio, working away with his finest tools until every centimeter of surface is brought to the most beautiful finish he has ever achieved.

Dawn comes. He can hear the shepherds making their way up the Janiculum, singing their peasant songs to their clanking flocks. And now all the bells of Rome begin to ring. It sounds like the introduction to the last act of *Tosca*. It *is* the introduction to the last act of *Tosca*. Giambologna feels a surge of hope once again. He thinks he will be able to excel anyone in his art.

And he is right to think so, for his mental apprenticeship to that angry genius has come to an end. Giambologna will become sculptor to the Medici. His works will be like a sort of diplomatic currency, given only to princes, distributed the length and breadth of Europe. He has taken Michelangelo's advice, but he has rejected the spirit of that advice. His works will be known, yes, for the bravura of their modeling, but they will be known above all for the brilliance of their finish.

IAN FRAZIER

Take the F

FROM THE NEW YORKER

BROOKLYN, NEW YORK, has the undefined, hard-to-remember shape of a stain. I never know what to tell people when they ask me where in it I live. It sits at the western tip of Long Island at a diagonal that does not conform neatly to the points of the compass. People in Brooklyn do not describe where they live in terms of north or west or south. They refer instead to their neighborhoods, and to the nearest subway lines. I live on the edge of Park Slope, a neighborhood by the crest of a low ridge that runs through the borough. Prospect Park is across the street. Airplanes in the landing pattern for La Guardia Airport sometimes fly right over my building; every few minutes, on certain sunny days, perfectly detailed airplane shadows slide down my building and up the building opposite in a blink. You can see my building from the plane — it's on the left-hand side of Prospect Park, the longer patch of green you cross after the expanse of Green-Wood Cemetery.

We moved to a co-op apartment in a four-story building a week before our daughter was born. She is now six. I grew up in the country and would not have expected ever to live in Brooklyn. My daughter is a city kid, with less sympathy for certain other parts of the country. When we visited Montana, she was disappointed by the scarcity of pizza places. I overheard her explaining — she was three or four then — to a Montana kid about Brooklyn. She said, "In Brooklyn, there is a lot of broken glass, so you have to wear shoes. And, there is good pizza." She is stern in her judgment of pizza. At the very low end of the pizza-ranking scale is some pizza she once had in New Hampshire, a category now called New Hampshire pizza. In the middle is some OK pizza she once had at the Bronx Zoo, which she calls zoo pizza. At the very top is the pizza at the pizza place where the big kids go, about two blocks from our house.

Our subway is the F train. It runs under our building and shakes the floor. The F is generally a reliable train, but one spring as I walked in the park I saw emergency vehicles gathered by a concrete-sheathed hole in the lawn. Firemen lifted a metal lid from the hole and descended into it. After a while, they reappeared, followed by a few people, then dozens of people, then a whole lot of people — passengers from a disabled F train, climbing one at a time out an exit shaft. On the F, I sometimes see large women in straw hats reading a newspaper called the *Caribbean Sunrise,* and Orthodox Jews bent over Talmudic texts in which the footnotes have footnotes, and groups of teenagers wearing identical red bandannas with identical red plastic baby pacifiers in the corners of their mouths, and female couples in porkpie hats, and young men with the silhouettes of the Manhattan skyline razored into their short side hair from one temple around to the other, and Russian-speaking men with thick wrists and big wristwatches, and a hefty, tall woman with long, straight blond hair who hums and closes her eyes and absently practices cello fingerings on the metal subway pole. As I watched the F-train passengers emerge among the grass and trees of Prospect Park, the faces were as varied as usual, but the expressions of indignant surprise were all about the same.

Just past my stop, Seventh Avenue, Manhattan-bound F trains rise from underground to cross the Gowanus Canal. The train sounds different — lighter, quieter — in the open air. From the elevated tracks, you can see the roofs of many houses stretching back up the hill to Park Slope, and a bumper crop of rooftop graffiti, and neon signs for Eagle Clothes and Kentile Floors, and flat expanses of factory roofs where seagulls stand on one leg around puddles in the sagging spots. There are fuel-storage tanks surrounded by earthen barriers, and slag piles, and conveyor belts leading down to the oil-slicked waters of the canal. On certain days, the sludge at the bottom of the canal causes it to bubble. Two men fleeing the police jumped in the canal a while ago; one made it across, the other quickly died. When the subway doors open at the Smith–Ninth Street stop, you can see the bay, and sometimes smell the ocean breeze. This stretch of elevated is the highest point of the New York subway system. To the south you can see the Verrazano-Narrows Bridge, to the north the World Trade towers. For just a few moments, the Statue of Liberty appears between passing buildings. Pieces of a neighborhood — laundry on clotheslines, a standup swimming pool, a plaster saint, a satellite dish, a rectangle of lawn — slide by like quickly dealt cards. Then the train descends again; growing over the wall just before the tunnel is a wisteria bush, which blooms pale blue every May.

I have spent days, weeks on the F train. The trip from Seventh Avenue to midtown Manhattan is long enough so that every ride can produce its own minisociety of riders, its own forty-minute Ship of Fools. Once a woman an arm's length from me on a crowded train pulled a knife on a man who threatened her. I remember the argument and the principals, but mostly I remember the knife — its flat, curved wood-grain handle inlaid with brass fittings at each end, its long, tapered blade. Once a man sang the words of the Lord's Prayer to a mournful, syncopated tune, and he fitted the mood of the morning so exactly that when he asked for money at the end the riders reached for their wallets and purses as if he'd pulled a gun. Once a big white kid with some friends was teasing a small old Hispanic lady, and when he got off the train I looked at him through the window and he slugged it hard next to my face. Once a thin woman and a fat woman sitting side by side had a long and loud conversation about someone they intended to slap silly: "Her butt be in the *hospital!*" "Bring out the ar-*tillery!*" The terminus of the F in Brooklyn is at Coney Island, not far from the beach. At an off hour, I boarded the train and found two or three passengers and, walking around on the floor, a crab. The passengers were looking at the crab. Its legs clicked on the floor like varnished fingernails. It moved in this direction, then that, trying to get comfortable. It backed itself under a seat, against the wall. Then it scooted out just after some new passengers had sat down there, and they really screamed. Passengers at the next stop saw it and laughed. When a boy lifted his foot as if to stomp it, everybody cried, "Noooh!" By the time we reached Jay Street–Borough Hall, there were maybe a dozen of us in the car, all absorbed in watching the crab. The car doors opened and a heavyset woman with good posture entered. She looked at the crab; then, sternly, at all of us. She let a moment pass. Then she demanded, "*Whose* is *that?*" A few stops later, a short man with a mustache took a manila envelope, bent down, scooped the crab into it, closed it, and put it in his coat pocket.

The smells in Brooklyn: coffee, fingernail polish, eucalyptus, the breath from laundry rooms, pot roast, Tater Tots. A woman I know who grew up here says she moved away because she could not stand the smell of cooking food in the hallway of her parents' building. I feel just the opposite. I used to live in a converted factory above an army-navy store, and I like being in a place that smells like people live there. In the mornings, I sometimes wake to the smell of toast, and I still don't know exactly whose toast it is. And I prefer living in a borough of two and a half million inhabitants, the most of any borough in the city. I think of all the rural places, the pine-timbered canyons and within-commuting-distance farmland, that we are preserving by not living there. I like the immensities of the borough, the unrolling miles of Eastern Parkway and Ocean Parkway and Linden Boulevard, and the disheveled outlying parks strewn with tree limbs and with shards of glass held together by liquor-bottle labels, and the tough bridges — the Williamsburg and the Manhattan — and the gentle Brooklyn Bridge. And I like the way the people talk; some really do have Brooklyn accents, really do say "dese" and "dose." A week or two ago, a group of neighbors stood on a street corner watching a peregrine falcon on a building cornice contentedly eating a pigeon it had caught, and the sunlight came through its tail feathers, and a woman said to a man, "Look at the tail, it's so ah-range," and the man replied, "Yeah, I soar it." Like many Americans, I fear living in a no-where, in a place that is no-place; in Brooklyn, that doesn't trouble me at all.

Everybody, it seems, is here. At Grand Army Plaza, I have seen traffic tie-ups caused by Haitians and others rallying in support of President Aristide, and by St. Patrick's Day parades, and by Jews of the Lubavitcher sect celebrating the birthday of their Grand Rebbe with a slow procession of ninety-three motor homes — one for each year of his life. Local taxis have bumper stickers that say

"Allah Is Great"; one of the men who made the bomb that blew
up the World Trade Center used an apartment just a few blocks
from me. When an election is held in Russia, crowds line up to
cast ballots at a Russian polling place in Brighton Beach. A while
ago, I volunteer-taught reading at a public elementary school
across the park. One of my students, a girl, was part Puerto Rican,
part Greek, and part Welsh. Her looks were a lively combination,
set off by sea-green eyes. I went to a map store in Manhattan and
bought maps of Puerto Rico, Greece, and Wales to read with her,
but they didn't interest her. A teacher at the school was directing
a group of students to set up chairs for a program in the auditorium, and she said to me, "We have a problem here — each of
these kids speaks a different language." She asked the kids to tell
me where they were from. One was from Korea, one from Brazil,
one from Poland, one from Guyana, one from Taiwan. In the
program that followed, a chorus of fourth and fifth graders sang
"God Bless America," "You're a Grand Old Flag," and "I'm a
Yankee-Doodle Dandy."

People in my neighborhood are mostly white, and middle class
or above. People in neighborhoods nearby are mostly not white,
and mostly middle class or below. Everybody uses Prospect Park.
On summer days, the park teems with sound — the high note is
kids screaming in the water sprinklers at the playground, the mid-
range is radios and tape players, and the bass is idling or speeding cars. People bring lawn furniture and badminton nets and
coolers, and then they barbecue. Charcoal smoke drifts into the
neighborhood. Last year, local residents upset about the noise
and litter and smoke began a campaign to outlaw barbecuing in
the park. There was much unfavorable comment about "the barbecuers." Since most of the barbecuers, as it happens, are black
or Hispanic, the phrase "Barbecuers Go Home," which someone
spray-painted on the asphalt at the Ninth Street entrance to the
park, took on a pointed, unkind meaning. But then park officials
set up special areas for barbecuing, and the barbecuers complied,
and the controversy died down.

Right nearby is a shelter for homeless people. Sometimes people
sleep on the benches along the park, sometimes they sleep in the
foyer of our building. Once I went downstairs, my heart pounding,
to evict a homeless person who I had been told was there. The

immediate, unquestioning way she left made me feel bad; later I always said "Hi" to her and gave her a dollar when I ran into her. One night, late, I saw her on the street, and I asked her her last name (by then I already knew her first name) and for a moment she couldn't recall it. At this, she shook her head in mild disbelief.

There's a guy I see on a bench along Prospect Park West all the time. Once I walked by carrying my year-old son, and the man said, "Someday he be carrying you." At the local copy shop one afternoon, a crowd was waiting for copies and faxes when a man in a houndstooth fedora came in seeking signatures for a petition to have the homeless shelter shut down. To my surprise, and his, the people in the copy shop instantly turned on him. "I suppose because they're poor they shouldn't even have a place to sleep at night," a woman said as he backed out the door. On the park wall across the street from my building, someone has written in black marker:

COPS PROTECT CITIZENS
WHO PROTECT US FROM COPS.

Sometimes I walk from my building downhill and north, along the Brooklyn waterfront, where cargo ships with scuffed sides and prognathous bows lean overhead. Sometimes I walk by the Brooklyn Navy Yard, its docks now too dormant to attract saboteurs, its long expanses of chain-link fence tangled here and there with the branches of ailanthus trees growing through. Sometimes I head southwest, keeping more or less to the high ground — Bay Ridge — along Fifth Avenue, through Hispanic neighborhoods that stretch in either direction as far as you can see, and then through block after block of Irish. I follow the ridge to its steep descent to the water at the Verrazano-Narrows; Fort Hamilton, an army post dating from 1814, is there, and a small Episcopal church called the Church of the Generals. Robert E. Lee once served as a vestryman of this church, and Stonewall Jackson was baptized here. Today the church is in the shade of a forest of high concrete columns supporting an access ramp to the Verrazano-Narrows Bridge.

Sometimes I walk due south, all the way out Coney Island Avenue. In that direction, as you approach the ocean, the sky gets bigger and brighter, and the buildings seem to flatten beneath it.

Dry cleaners advertise "Tallis Cleaned Free with Every Purchase Over Fifteen Dollars." Then you start to see occasional lines of graffiti written in Cyrillic. Just past a Cropsey Avenue billboard welcoming visitors to Coney Island is a bridge over a creek filled nearly to the surface with metal shopping carts that people have tossed there over the years. A little farther on, the streets open onto the beach. On a winter afternoon, bundled-up women sit on the boardwalk on folding chairs around a portable record player outside a restaurant called Gastronom Moscow. The acres of trash-dotted sand are almost empty. A bottle of Peter the Great vodka lies on its side, drops of water from its mouth making a small depression in the sand. A man with trousers rolled up to his shins moves along the beach, chopping at driftwood with an ax. Another passerby says, "He's vorking hard, that guy!" The sunset unrolls light along the storefronts like tape. From the far distance, little holes in the sand at the water's edge mark the approach of a short man wearing hip boots and earphones and carrying a long-handled metal detector. Treasure hunters dream of the jewelry that people must have lost here over the years. Some say that this is the richest treasure beach in the Northeast. The man stops, runs the metal detector again over a spot, digs with a clamming shovel, lifts some sand, brushes through it with a gloved thumb, discards it. He goes on, leaving a trail of holes behind him.

I like to find things myself, and I always try to keep one eye on the ground as I walk. So far I have found seven dollars (a five and two ones), an earring in the shape of a strawberry, several personal notes, a matchbook with a 900 number to call to hear "prison sex fantasies," and two spent .25-caliber shells. Once on Carroll Street, I saw a page of text on the sidewalk, and I bent over to read it. It was page 191 from a copy of *Anna Karenina*. I read the whole page. It described Vronsky leaving a gathering and riding off in a carriage. In a great book, the least fragment is great. I looked up and saw a woman regarding me closely from a few feet away. "You're reading," she said wonderingly. "From a distance, I t'ought you were watchin' ants."

My favorite place to walk is the Brooklyn Botanic Garden, not more than fifteen minutes away. It's the first place I take out-of-towners, who may not associate Brooklyn with flowers. In the winter, the

garden is drab as pocket lint, and you can practically see all the
way through from Flatbush Avenue to Washington Avenue. But
then in February or March a few flowerings begin, the snowdrops
and the crocuses, and then the yellow of the daffodils climbs
Daffodil Hill, and then the magnolias — star magnolias, umbrella
magnolias, saucer magnolias — go off all at once, and walking
among them is like flying through cumulus clouds. Then the
cherry trees blossom, some a soft and glossy red like makeup,
others pink as a dessert, and crowds fill the paths on weekends and
stand in front of the blossoms in their best clothes and have their
pictures taken. Security guards tell people, "No eating, no sitting
on the grass — this is a garden, not a park." There are traffic jams
of strollers, and kids running loose. One security guard jokes into
his radio, "There's a pterodactyl on the overlook!" In the pond in
the Japanese Garden, ducks lobby for pieces of bread. A duck
quacks, in Brooklynese, "Yeah, yeah, yeah," having heard it all
before.

Then the cherry blossoms fall, they turn some paths completely
pink next to the grass's green, and the petals dry, and people tread
them into a fine pink powder. Kids visit on end-of-school-year field
trips, and teachers yell "Shawon, get back on line!" and boys with
long T-shirts printed from neck to knee with an image of Martin
Luther King's face run by laughing and swatting at one another.
The yellow boxes that photographic film comes in fall on the
ground, and here and there an empty bag of Crazy Calypso potato
chips. The lilacs bloom, each bush with a scent slightly different
from the next, and yellow tulips fill big round planters with color
so bright it ascends in a column, like a searchlight beam. The roses
open on the trellises in the Rose Garden and attract a lively air
traffic of bees, and June wedding parties, brides and grooms and
their subsidiaries, adjust themselves minutely for photographers
there. A rose called the Royal Gold smells like a new bathing suit,
and is as yellow.

In our building of nine apartments, two people have died and
six have been born since we moved in. I like our neighbors — a
guy who works for Off-Track Betting, a guy who works for the
Department of Correction, a woman who works for Dean Witter,
an in-flight steward, a salesperson of subsidiary rights at a publishing house, a restaurant manager, two lawyers, a retired machinist,

a Lebanese-born woman of ninety-five — as well as any I've ever had. We keep track of the bigger events in the building with the help of Chris, our downstairs neighbor. Chris lives on the ground floor and often has conversations in the hall while her foot props her door open. When our kids are sick, she brings them her kids' videos to watch, and when it rains she gives us rides to school. One year, Chris became pregnant and had to take a blood-thinning medicine and was in and out of the hospital. Finally, she had a healthy baby and came home, but then began to bleed and didn't stop. Her husband brought the baby to us about midnight and took Chris to the nearest emergency room. Early the next morning, the grandmother came and took the baby. Then for two days nobody heard anything. When we knocked on Chris's door we got no answer, and when we called we got an answering machine. The whole building was expectant, spooky, quiet. The next morning I left the house and there in the foyer was Chris. She held her husband's arm, and she looked pale, but she was returning from the hospital under her own steam. I hugged her at the door, and it was the whole building hugging her. I walked to the garden seeing glory everywhere. I went to the Rose Garden and took a big Betsy McCall rose to my face and breathed into it as if it were an oxygen mask.

AMITAV GHOSH

The Ghosts of Mrs. Gandhi

FROM THE NEW YORKER

NOWHERE ELSE IN the world did the year 1984 fulfill its apocalyptic portents as it did in India. Separatist violence in the Punjab;
the military attack on the great Sikh temple of Amritsar; the
assassination of the prime minister, Mrs. Indira Gandhi; riots in
several cities; the gas disaster in Bhopal — the events followed
relentlessly on each other. There were days in 1984 when it took
courage to open the New Delhi papers in the morning.

Of the year's many catastrophes, the sectarian violence following
Mrs. Gandhi's death had the greatest effect on my life. Looking
back, I see that the experiences of that period were profoundly
important to my development as a writer; so much so that I have
never attempted to write about them until now.

At the time, I was living in a part of New Delhi called Defence
Colony — a neighborhood of large, labyrinthine houses, with little
self-contained warrens of servants' rooms tucked away on rooftops
and above garages. When I lived there, those rooms had come to
house a floating population of the young and straitened — journalists, copywriters, minor executives, and university people like
myself. We battened upon this wealthy enclave like mites in a
honeycomb, spreading from rooftop to rooftop, our ramshackle
lives curtained from our landlords by chiffon-draped washing lines
and thickets of TV aerials.

I was twenty-eight. The city I considered home was Calcutta, but
New Delhi was where I had spent all my adult life except for a few
years away in England and Egypt. I had returned to India two years
before, upon completing a doctorate at Oxford, and recently

found a teaching job at Delhi University. But it was in the privacy
of my baking rooftop hutch that my real life was lived. I was writing
my first novel, in the classic fashion, perched in a garret.

On the morning of October 31, the day of Mrs. Gandhi's death,
I caught a bus to Delhi University, as usual, at about half past nine.
From where I lived, it took an hour and a half: a long commute,
but not an exceptional one for New Delhi. The assassination had
occurred shortly before, just a few miles away, but I had no knowledge of this when I boarded the bus. Nor did I notice anything
untoward at any point during the ninety-minute journey. But the
news, traveling by word of mouth, raced my bus to the university.

When I walked into the grounds, I saw not the usual boisterous,
Frisbee-throwing crowd of students but small groups of people
standing intently around transistor radios. A young man detached
himself from one of the huddles and approached me, his mouth
twisted into the tight-lipped, knowing smile that seems always to
accompany the gambit "Have you heard . . . ?"

The campus was humming, he said. No one knew for sure, but
it was being said that Mrs. Gandhi had been shot. The word was
that she had been assassinated by two Sikh bodyguards, in revenge
for her having sent troops to raid the Sikhs' Golden Temple of
Amritsar earlier that year.

Just before stepping into the lecture room, I heard a report on
All India Radio, the national network: Mrs. Gandhi had been
rushed to hospital after an attempted assassination.

Nothing stopped: the momentum of the daily routine carried
things forward. I went into a classroom and began my lecture, but
not many students had shown up and those who had were distracted and distant; there was a lot of fidgeting.

Halfway through the class, I looked out through the room's
single, slit-like window. The sunlight lay bright on the lawn below
and on the trees beyond. It was the time of year when Delhi was
at its best, crisp and cool, its abundant greenery freshly watered
by the recently retreated monsoons, its skies washed sparkling
clean. By the time I turned back, I had forgotten what I was saying
and had to reach for my notes.

My unsteadiness surprised me. I was not an uncritical admirer
of Mrs. Gandhi. Her brief period of semi-dictatorial rule in the
mid-seventies was still alive in my memory. But the ghastliness of

her murder was a sudden reminder of the very real qualities that had been taken for granted: her fortitude, her dignity, her physical courage, her endurance.

Yet it was not just grief I felt at that moment. Rather, it was a sense of something slipping loose, of a mooring coming untied somewhere within.

The first reliable report of Mrs. Gandhi's death was broadcast from Karachi, by Pakistan's official radio network, at around 1:30 P.M. On All India Radio, regular broadcasts had been replaced by music.

I left the university in the late afternoon with a friend, Hari Sen, who lived at the other end of the city. I needed to make a long-distance phone call, and he had offered to let me use his family's telephone.

To get to Hari's house, we had to change buses at Connaught Place, the elegant circular arcade that lies at the geographical heart of Delhi, linking the old city with the new. As the bus swung around the periphery of the arcade, I noticed that the shops, stalls, and eateries were beginning to shut down, even though it was still afternoon.

Our next bus was not quite full, which was unusual. Just as it was pulling out, a man ran out of an office and jumped on. He was middle-aged and dressed in shirt and trousers, evidently an employee in one of the nearby government buildings. He was a Sikh, but I scarcely noticed this at the time.

He probably jumped on without giving the matter any thought, this being his regular, daily bus. But, as it happened, on this day no choice could have been more unfortunate, for the route of the bus went past the hospital where Indira Gandhi's body then lay. Certain loyalists in her party had begun inciting the crowds gathered there to seek revenge. The motorcade of Giani Zail Singh, the president of the republic, a Sikh, had already been attacked by a mob.

None of this was known to us then, and we would never have suspected it: violence had never been directed at the Sikhs in Delhi.

As the bus made its way down New Delhi's broad, tree-lined avenues, official-looking cars, with outriders and escorts, overtook us, speeding toward the hospital. As we drew nearer, it became evident that a large number of people had gathered there. But this was no ordinary crowd: it seemed to consist mostly of red-eyed young men in half-unbuttoned shirts. It was now that I noticed that my Sikh fellow passenger was showing signs of increasing anxiety, sometimes standing up to look out, sometimes glancing out the door. It was too late to get off the bus; thugs were everywhere. The bands of young men grew more and more menacing as we approached the hospital. There was a watchfulness about them; some were armed with steel rods and bicycle chains; others had fanned out across the busy road and were stopping cars and buses.

A stout woman in a sari sitting across the aisle from me was the first to understand what was going on. Rising to her feet, she gestured urgently at the Sikh, who was sitting hunched in his seat. She hissed at him in Hindi, telling him to get down and keep out of sight.

The man started in surprise and squeezed himself into the narrow footspace between the seats. Minutes later, our bus was intercepted by a group of young men dressed in bright, sharp synthetics. Several had bicycle chains wrapped around their wrists. They ran along beside the bus as it slowed to a halt. We heard them call out to the driver through the open door, asking if there were any Sikhs on the bus.

The driver shook his head. No, he said, there were no Sikhs on the bus.

A few rows ahead of me, the crouching, turbaned figure had gone completely still.

Outside, some of the young men were jumping up to look through the windows, asking if there were any Sikhs on the bus. There was no anger in their voices; that was the most chilling thing of all.

No, someone said, and immediately other voices picked up the refrain. Soon all the passengers were shaking their heads and saying, No, no, let us go now, we have to get home.

Eventually, the thugs stepped back and waved us through.

Nobody said a word as we sped away down Ring Road.

Hari Sen lived in one of New Delhi's recently developed residential colonies. It was called Safdarjang Enclave, and it was neatly and solidly middle class, a neighborhood of aspirations rather than opulence. Like most such New Delhi suburbs, the area had a mixed population: Sikhs were well represented.

A long street ran from end to end of the neighborhood, like the spine of a comb, with parallel side streets running off it. Hari lived at the end of one of those streets, in a fairly typical, big, one-story bungalow. The house next door, however, was much grander and uncharacteristically daring in design. An angular structure, it was perched rakishly on stilts. Mr. Bawa, the owner, was an elderly Sikh who had spent a long time abroad, working with various international organizations. For several years, he had resided in Southeast Asia; thus the stilts.

Hari lived with his family in a household so large and eccentric that it had come to be known among his friends as Macondo, after Gabriel García Márquez's magical village. On this occasion, however, only his mother and teenage sister were at home. I decided to stay over.

It was a very bright morning. When I stepped into the sunshine, I came upon a sight that I could never have imagined. In every direction, columns of smoke rose slowly into a limpid sky. Sikh houses and businesses were burning. The fires were so carefully targeted that they created an effect quite different from that of a general conflagration: it was like looking upward into the vault of some vast pillared hall.

The columns of smoke increased in number even as I stood outside watching. Some fires were burning a short distance away. I spoke to a passerby and learned that several nearby Sikh houses had been looted and set on fire that morning. The mob had started at the far end of the colony and was working its way in our direction. Hindus and Muslims who had sheltered or defended Sikhs were also being attacked; their houses, too, were being looted and burned.

It was still and quiet, eerily so. The usual sounds of rush-hour traffic were absent. But every so often we heard a speeding car or a motorcycle on the main street. Later, we discovered that these mysterious speeding vehicles were instrumental in directing the carnage that was taking place. Protected by certain politicians, "organizers" were zooming around the city, assembling "mobs" and transporting them to Sikh-owned houses and shops.

Apparently, the transportation was provided free. A civil rights report published shortly afterward stated that this phase of the violence "began with the arrival of groups of armed young people in tempo vans, scooters, motorcycles or trucks," and went on to say, "With cans of petrol they went around the localities and systematically set fire to Sikh houses, shops and gurdwaras. . . . The targets were primarily young Sikhs. They were dragged out, beaten up and then burnt alive. . . . In all the affected spots, a calculated attempt to terrorize the people was evident in the common tendency among the assailants to burn alive the Sikhs on public roads."

Fire was everywhere; it was the day's motif. Throughout the city, Sikh houses were being looted and then set on fire, often with their occupants still inside.

A survivor — a woman who lost her husband and three sons — offered the following account to Veena Das, a Delhi sociologist: "Some people, the neighbours, one of my relatives, said it would be better if we hid in an abandoned house nearby. So my husband took our three sons and hid there. We locked the house from outside, but there was treachery in people's hearts. Someone must have told the crowd. They baited him to come out. Then they poured kerosene on that house. They burnt them alive. When I went there that night, the bodies of my sons were on the loft — huddled together."

Over the next few days, some twenty-five hundred people died in Delhi alone. Thousands more died in other cities. The total death toll will never be known. The dead were overwhelmingly Sikh men. Entire neighborhoods were gutted; tens of thousands of people were left homeless.

Like many other members of my generation, I grew up believing that mass slaughter of the kind that accompanied the partition of India and Pakistan, in 1947, could never happen again. But that morning, in the city of Delhi, the violence had reached the same level of intensity.

As Hari and I stood staring into the smoke-streaked sky, Mrs. Sen, Hari's mother, was thinking of matters closer at hand. She was about fifty, a tall, graceful woman with a gentle, soft-spoken manner. In an understated way, she was also deeply religious, a devout Hindu. When she heard what was happening, she picked up the phone and called Mr. and Mrs. Bawa, the elderly Sikh couple next door, to let them know that they were welcome to come over. She met with an unexpected response: an awkward silence. Mrs. Bawa thought she was joking, and wasn't sure whether to be amused or not.

Toward midday, Mrs. Sen received a phone call: the mob was now in the immediate neighborhood, advancing systematically from street to street. Hari decided that it was time to go over and have a talk with the Bawas. I went along.

Mr. Bawa proved to be a small, slight man. Although he was casually dressed, his turban was neatly tied and his beard was carefully combed and bound. He was puzzled by our visit. After a polite greeting, he asked what he could do for us. It fell to Hari to explain.

Mr. Bawa had heard about Indira Gandhi's assassination, of course, and he knew that there had been some trouble. But he could not understand why these "disturbances" should impinge on him or his wife. He had no more sympathy for the Sikh terrorists than we did; his revulsion at the assassination was, if anything, even greater than ours. Not only was his commitment to India and the Indian state absolute, but it was evident from his bearing that he belonged to the country's ruling elite.

How do you explain to someone who has spent a lifetime co-cooned in privilege that a potentially terminal rent has appeared in the wrappings? We found ourselves faltering. Mr. Bawa could not bring himself to believe that a mob might attack him.

By the time we left, it was Mr. Bawa who was mouthing reassurances. He sent us off with jovial pats on our backs. He did not actually say "Buck up," but his manner said it for him.

We were confident that the government would soon act to stop the violence. In India, there is a drill associated with civil disturbances: a curfew is declared; paramilitary units are deployed; in extreme cases, the army marches to the stricken areas. No city in India is better equipped to perform this drill than New Delhi, with its huge security apparatus. We later learned that in some cities — Calcutta, for example — the state authorities did act promptly to prevent violence. But in New Delhi — and in much of northern India — hour followed hour without a response. Every few minutes, we turned to the radio, hoping to hear that the army had been ordered out. All we heard was mournful music and descriptions of Mrs. Gandhi's lying in state; of the comings and goings of dignitaries, foreign and national. The bulletins could have been messages from another planet.

As the afternoon progressed, we continued to hear reports of the mob's steady advance. Before long, it had reached the next alley: we could hear the voices; the smoke was everywhere. There was still no sign of the army or the police.

Hari again called Mr. Bawa, and now, with the flames visible from his windows, he was more receptive. He agreed to come over with his wife, just for a short while. But there was a problem: How? The two properties were separated by a shoulder-high wall, so it was impossible to walk from one house to the other except along the street.

I spotted a few of the thugs already at the end of the street. We could hear the occasional motorcycle, cruising slowly up and down. The Bawas could not risk stepping out into the street. They would be seen: the sun had dipped low in the sky, but it was still light. Mr. Bawa balked at the thought of climbing over the wall: it seemed an insuperable obstacle at his age. But eventually Hari persuaded him to try.

We went to wait for them at the back of the Sens' house — in a spot that was well sheltered from the street. The mob seemed terrifyingly close, the Bawas reckless in their tardiness. A long time passed before the elderly couple finally appeared, hurrying toward us.

Mr. Bawa had changed before leaving the house: he was neatly dressed, dapper even — in blazer and cravat. Mrs. Bawa, a small, matronly woman, was dressed in a *salwar* and *kameez*. Their cook was with them, and it was with his assistance that they made it over the wall. The cook, who was Hindu, then returned to the house to stand guard.

Hari led the Bawas into the drawing room, where Mrs. Sen was waiting, dressed in a chiffon sari. The room was large and well appointed, its walls hung with a rare and beautiful set of miniatures. With the curtains now drawn and the lamps lit, it was warm and welcoming. But all that lay between us and the mob in the street was a row of curtained French windows and a garden wall.

Mrs. Sen greeted the elderly couple with folded hands as they came in. The three seated themselves in an intimate circle, and soon a silver tea tray appeared. Instantly, all constraint evaporated, and, to the tinkling of porcelain, the conversation turned to the staples of New Delhi drawing room chatter.

I could not bring myself to sit down. I stood in the corridor, distracted, looking outside through the front entrance.

A couple of scouts on motorcycles had drawn up next door. They had dismounted and were inspecting the house, walking in among the concrete stilts, looking up into the house. Somehow, they got wind of the cook's presence and called him out.

The cook was very frightened. He was surrounded by thugs thrusting knives in his face and shouting questions. It was dark, and some were carrying kerosene torches. Wasn't it true, they shouted, that his employers were Sikhs? Where were they? Were they hiding inside? Who owned the house — Hindus or Sikhs?

Hari and I hid behind the wall between the two houses and listened to the interrogation. Our fates depended on this lone, frightened man. We had no idea what he would do: of how secure the Bawas were of his loyalties, or whether he might seek revenge for some past slight by revealing their whereabouts. If he did, both houses would burn.

Although stuttering in terror, the cook held his own. Yes, he said, yes, his employers were Sikhs, but they'd left town; there was no one in the house. No, the house didn't belong to them; they were renting from a Hindu.

He succeeded in persuading most of the thugs, but a few eyed the surrounding houses suspiciously. Some appeared at the steel gates in front of us, rattling the bars.

We went up and positioned ourselves at the gates. I remember a strange sense of disconnection as I walked down the driveway, as though I were watching myself from somewhere very distant.

We took hold of the gates and shouted back: Get away! You have no business here! There's no one inside! The house is empty!

To our surprise, they began to drift away, one by one.

Just before this, I had stepped into the house to see how Mrs. Sen and the Bawas were faring. The thugs were clearly audible in the lamplit drawing room; only a thin curtain shielded the interior from their view.

My memory of what I saw in the drawing room is uncannily vivid.

Mrs. Sen had a slight smile on her face as she poured a cup of tea for Mr. Bawa. Beside her, Mrs. Bawa, in a firm, unwavering voice, was comparing the domestic-help situations in New Delhi and Manila.

I was awed by their courage.

The next morning, I heard about a protest that was being organized at the large compound of a relief agency. When I arrived, a meeting was already under way, a gathering of seventy or eighty people.

The mood was somber. Some of the people spoke of neighborhoods that had been taken over by vengeful mobs. They described countless murders — mainly by setting the victims alight — as well as terrible destruction: the burning of Sikh temples, the looting of Sikh schools, the razing of Sikh homes and shops. The violence was worse than I had imagined. It was decided that the most effective initial tactic would be to march into one of the badly affected neighborhoods and confront the rioters directly.

The group had grown to about 150 men and women, among them Swami Agnivesh, a Hindu ascetic; Ravi Chopra, a scientist and environmentalist; and a handful of opposition politicians, including Chandra Shekhar, who became prime minister for a brief period several years later.

The group was pitifully small by the standards of a city where crowds of several hundred thousand were routinely mustered for political rallies. Nevertheless, the members rose to their feet and began to march.

Years before, I had read a passage by V. S. Naipaul that has stayed with me ever since. I have never been able to find it again, so this account is from memory. In his incomparable prose Naipaul describes a demonstration. He is in a hotel room, somewhere in Africa or South America; he looks down and sees people marching past. To his surprise, the sight fills him with an obscure longing, a kind of melancholy; he is aware of a wish to go out, to join, to merge his concerns with theirs. Yet he knows he never will; it is simply not in his nature to join crowds.

For many years, I read everything of Naipaul's I could lay my hands on; I couldn't have enough of him. I read him with the intimate, appalled attention that one reserves for one's most skillful interlocutors. It was he who first made it possible for me to think of myself as a writer, working in English.

I remembered that passage because I believed that I, too, was not a joiner, and in Naipaul's pitiless mirror I thought I had seen an aspect of myself rendered visible. Yet as this forlorn little group marched out of the shelter of the compound I did not hesitate for a moment: without a second thought, I joined.

The march headed first for Lajpat Nagar, a busy commercial area a mile or so away. I knew the area. Though it was in New Delhi, its streets resembled the older parts of the city, where small, cramped shops tended to spill out onto the footpaths.

We were shouting slogans as we marched: hoary Gandhian staples of peace and brotherhood from half a century before. Then, suddenly, we were confronted with a starkly familiar spectacle, an image of twentieth-century urban horror: burned-out cars, their ransacked interiors visible through smashed windows; debris and rubble everywhere. Blackened pots had been strewn along the street. A cinema had been gutted, and the charred faces of film stars stared out at us from half-burned posters.

As I think back to that march, my memory breaks down, details dissolve. I recently telephoned some friends who had been there. Their memories are similar to mine in only one respect: they, too, clung to one scene while successfully ridding their minds of the rest.

The scene my memory preserved is of a moment when it seemed inevitable that we would be attacked.

Rounding a corner, we found ourselves facing a crowd that was larger and more determined-looking than any other crowds we had encountered. On each previous occasion, we had prevailed by marching at the thugs and engaging them directly, in dialogues that turned quickly into extended shouting matches. In every instance, we had succeeded in facing them down. But this particular mob was intent on confrontation. As its members advanced on us, brandishing knives and steel rods, we stopped. Our voices grew louder as they came toward us; a kind of rapture descended on us, exhilaration in anticipation of a climax. We braced for the attack, leaning forward as though into a wind.

And then something happened that I have never completely understood. Nothing was said; there was no signal, nor was there any break in the rhythm of our chanting. But suddenly all the women in our group — and the women made up more than half of the group's numbers — stepped out and surrounded the men; their saris and *kameezes* became a thin, fluttering barrier, a wall around us. They turned to face the approaching men, challenging them, daring them to attack. The thugs took a few more steps toward us and then faltered, confused. A moment later, they were gone.

The march ended at the walled compound where it had started. In the next couple of hours, an organization was created, the Nagarik Ekta Manch, or Citizens' Unity Front, and its work — to bring relief to the injured and the bereft, to shelter the homeless — began the next morning. Food and clothing were needed, and camps had to be established to accommodate the thousands of people with nowhere to sleep. And by the next day we were overwhelmed — literally. The large compound was crowded with vanloads of blankets, secondhand clothing, shoes, and sacks of flour, sugar, and tea. Previously hard-nosed, unsentimental businessmen sent cars and trucks. There was barely room to move.

My own role in the Front was slight. For a few weeks, I worked with a team from Delhi University, distributing supplies in the slums and working-class neighborhoods that had been worst hit by the rioting. Then I returned to my desk.

In time, inevitably, most of the Front's volunteers returned to their everyday lives. But some members — most notably the women involved in the running of refugee camps — continued to work for years afterward with Sikh women and children who had been rendered homeless. Jaya Jaitley, Lalita Ramdas, Veena Das, Mita Bose, Radha Kumar: these women, each one an accomplished professional, gave up years of their time to repair the enormous damage that had been done in a matter of two or three days.

The Front also formed a team to investigate the riots. I briefly considered joining, but then decided that an investigation would be a waste of time because the politicians capable of inciting violence were unlikely to heed a tiny group of concerned citizens.

I was wrong. A document eventually produced by this team — a slim pamphlet entitled "Who Are the Guilty?" — has become a classic, a searing indictment of the politicians who encouraged the riots and the police who allowed the rioters to have their way.

Over the years the Indian government has compensated some

of the survivors of the 1984 violence and resettled some of the homeless. One gap remains: to this day, no instigator of the riots has been charged. But the pressure on the government has never gone away, and it continues to grow: every year, the nails hammered in by that slim document dig just a little deeper.

That pamphlet and others that followed are testaments to the only humane possibility available to people who live in multiethnic, multireligious societies like those of the Indian subcontinent. Human rights documents such as "Who Are the Guilty?" are essential to the process of broadening civil institutions: they are the weapons with which society asserts itself against a state that runs criminally amok, as this one did in Delhi in November of 1984.

It is heartening that sanity prevails today in the Punjab. But not elsewhere. In Bombay, local government officials want to stop any public buildings from being painted green — a color associated with the Muslim religion. And hundreds of Muslims have been deported from the city's slums — in at least one case for committing an offense no graver than reading a Bengali newspaper. It is imperative that governments ensure that those who instigate mass violence do not go unpunished.

The Bosnian writer Dzevad Karahasan, in a remarkable essay called "Literature and War" (published last year in his collection *Sarajevo, Exodus of a City*), makes a startling connection between modern literary aestheticism and the contemporary world's indifference to violence: "The decision to perceive literally everything as an aesthetic phenomenon — completely sidestepping questions about goodness and truth — is an artistic decision. That decision started in the realm of art, and went on to become characteristic of the contemporary world."

When I went back to my desk in November of 1984, I found myself confronting decisions about writing that I had never faced before. How was I to write about what I had seen without reducing it to mere spectacle? My next novel was bound to be influenced by my experiences, but I could see no way of writing directly about those events without recreating them as a panorama of violence — "an aesthetic phenomenon," as Karahasan was to call it. At the time, the idea seemed obscene and futile; of much greater importance were factual reports of the testimony of the victims. But these were already being done by people who were, I knew, more competent than I could be.

Within a few months, I started my novel, which I eventually called *The Shadow Lines* — a book that led me backward in time, to earlier memories of riots, ones witnessed in childhood. It became a book not about any one event but about the meaning of such events and their effects on the individuals who live through them.

And until now I have never really written about what I saw in November of 1984. I am not alone: several others who took part in that march went on to publish books, yet nobody, so far as I know, has ever written about it except in passing.

There are good reasons for this, not least the politics of the situation, which leave so little room for the writer. The riots were generated by a cycle of violence, involving the terrorists in the Punjab, on the one hand, and the Indian government, on the other. To write carelessly, in such a way as to appear to endorse terrorism or repression, can add easily to the problem: in such incendiary circumstances, words cost lives, and it is only appropriate that those who deal in words should pay scrupulous attention to what they say. It is only appropriate that they should find themselves inhibited.

But there is also a simpler explanation. Before I could set down a word, I had to resolve a dilemma, between being a writer and being a citizen. As a writer, I had only one obvious subject: the violence. From the news report, or the latest film or novel, we have come to expect the bloody detail or the elegantly staged conflagration that closes a chapter or effects a climax. But it is worth asking if the very obviousness of this subject arises out of our modern conventions of representation; within the dominant aesthetic of our time — the aesthetic of what Karahasan calls "indifference" — it is all too easy to present violence as an apocalyptic spectacle, while the resistance to it can as easily figure as mere sentimentality, or, worse, as pathetic or absurd.

Writers don't join crowds — Naipaul and so many others teach us that. But what do you do when the constitutional authority fails to act? You join, and in joining bear all the responsibilities and obligations and guilt that joining represents. My experience of the violence was overwhelmingly and memorably of the resistance to it. When I think of the women staring down the mob, I am not filled with a writerly wonder. I am reminded of my gratitude for being saved from injury. What I saw at first hand — and not merely on that march but on the bus, in Hari's house, in the huge compound that filled with essential goods — was not the horror of violence but the affirmation of humanity: in each case, I witnessed the risks that perfectly ordinary people were willing to take for one another.

When I now read descriptions of troubled parts of the world, in which violence appears primordial and inevitable, a fate to which masses of people are largely resigned, I find myself asking, Is that all there was to it? Or is it possible that the authors of these descriptions failed to find a form — or a style or a voice or a plot — that could accommodate both violence *and* the civilized, willed response to it?

The truth is that the commonest response to violence is one of repugnance, and that a significant number of people everywhere try to oppose it in whatever ways they can. That these efforts so rarely appear in accounts of violence is not surprising: they are too undramatic. For those who participate in them, they are often hard to write about for the very reasons that so long delayed my own account of 1984.

"Let us not fool ourselves," Karahasan writes. "The world is written first — the holy books say that it was created in words — and all that happens in it, happens in language first."

It is when we think of the world the aesthetic of indifference might bring into being that we recognize the urgency of remembering the stories we have not written.

ADAM GOPNIK

Wonderland

FROM THE NEW YORKER

CONTEMPORARY PEOPLE, it seems, like split personalities just as much as their Romantic predecessors did, though for a different reason. The old cult of the divided self was, at its secret heart, optimistic and expansive, implying that every quality included its opposite, and that anyone could be anything: a tender aesthete might lead the Arabs in revolt; a novelist by day might be a rake by night. We like double people, too (all those stockbroker psychos, all those gender-busting heroines), but our cult of them is pessimistic and is based on the idea that none of us can ever say just what we mean, or be quite what we seem to be. Even the cross-dressers who are now presented as heroes of our time seem less self-expanding than self-exploding, resigning their identities to their nylons.

Of all these double people, none looks more divided than the Reverend Charles Dodgson of Christ Church, Oxford. The *Alice* books he wrote as Lewis Carroll remain, more than a century after their publication, one of the few common repositories of reference; at a time when nobody knows who Damon and Pythias were, everybody still knows where the Walrus and the Carpenter went walking. But Dodgson's supposedly split personality continues to overtake his books as a subject. Soon Robert Wilson will launch his multimedia theater piece *Alice* at the Brooklyn Academy of Music; according to the press release, it will investigate the "curious mind" of a man who "seemed the perfect Victorian Englishman as a clergyman and a well-known mathematician, but was also a compulsive photographer with a strong preference for young girls." Wilson's Dodgson seems likely to repeat the traits of the Dodgson of Dennis Potter's uncharacteristically leering 1985 movie *DreamChild,* in which Dodgson appeared as a pathologically timid and isolated Oxford don, rabbit-shy and stammering, who came alive only in the company of little girls — and was just this side of being a child molester.

The trouble with this emphasis on Dodgson's neurosis is that it obscures the essential sanity of his writing. It also revives the older, sentimental notion that the two *Alice* books really belong to the literature of subversive protest. Only in the guise of children's literature, the homily went, could Carroll attack the horrors of Victorian respectability, and introduce his dream child, and himself, to the stranger, stronger world of irrational forces. (In recent decades, this idea has informed both André Gregory's Grotowskian production of *Alice* and Jonathan Miller's Freudian one.) Wilson's piece threatens to be an updated compendium of all these clichés. "The White Knight, on the one hand, and the Photographer beneath the black cloth, on the other, are two sides of the same person," Wilson says. "Who is to say where the line is drawn that divides protection from harm, or help from exploitation?" A divided Dodgson, these days, seems to demand a broken *Alice.*

The best thing about Morton Cohen's *Lewis Carroll: A Biography* is that it patiently disassembles most of these myths. The real Dodgson, it turns out, was about as happily engaged in the world around him as any of us can hope to be. If he had some of the Victorian vices, he had almost all the Victorian virtues: energy, drive, moral seriousness, and a limitless self-confidence. He was the leading amateur photographer of the day, at a time when photography, with its heavyweight equipment and endless delays, involved dogged and thick-skinned persistence. Dodgson was also one of the great Victorian correspondents. He kept a register of every personal letter he received and wrote, and by the end of his life was working toward a hundred thousand. These weren't notes, either, but long and inventive letters, full of a stirring Victorian intensity and earnest italics. His regular correspondents included Tennyson and Christina Rossetti; Dodgson wrote familiarly to Lord Salisbury when he was prime minister, giving him worldly counsel on the Irish question. People were inclined to take Dodgson seriously on any subject, since he had been a success in practically every enterprise he touched. He got the equivalent of tenure at Christ Church when he was only twenty, at a time when it was the most glamorous of Oxbridge colleges. (Queen Victoria sent two of her sons there.) Those rooms where he received little girls for dinner, which you may have imagined as a furtive donnish hideaway, were among the largest apartments in the entire university. He published the *Alice* books as an entrepreneurial gamble, keeping all the details of production and distribution under his steely control, and made them one of the big publishing successes of the day. He was even a whiz at merchandizing — arranging for his *Alice* characters to be turned into cookie tins and postage-stamp cases. He could be shy, but his shyness didn't prevent him from preaching, lecturing, and going out into the world; he was a devoted theatergoer at a time when, as Max Beerbohm wrote of the theater, "Ministers of even the Church of England were very dubious about it and never attended it." His nephew, who knew him well, believed that the great romantic disappointment of his life might not have been Alice Liddell but, rather, Ellen Terry, one of the stars of the London stage. He was, above all, a public character, of the kind the British enjoy — one of these eccentrics, like J. R. Ackerley or John Betjeman, whose oddities are all out in the open. Even his infatuation with little girls was a public matter, a little like Ackerley's infatuation with his dogs. People wrote to tell him that they thought his behavior was bizarre, and he wrote back to tell them that they were wrong.

Dodgson, it turns out, was a man with two preoccupations — logic and little girls. He spent most of his life trying to build a bridge between them, and finally succeeded.

Charles Dodgson inhabited an Oxford landscape even before he arrived at Christ Church. He was born in 1832, the eldest son of a man who bore the same name, as well as the wonderfully Carrollian title of Perpetual Curate of Daresbury. The Oxford Movement — John Henry Newman's attempt, beginning in the 1820s, to restore quasi-Roman ritual and a sense of supernatural authority to the prosaic Church of England — had colored the elder Dodgson's life. Unwilling to go all the way over to Rome, Charles Senior took up the discouraging compromise called "ritualism," in which the ceremonies of the Church were made much of, without going over to the Romish belief that they actually meant something. On the whole, Charles Junior had a marvelously happy childhood as the oldest and superintending brother of a large, jubilant family; he published the first stanza of "Jabberwocky" in a "newspaper" he used to put out for his brothers and sisters.

He arrived at Christ Church in 1850, and stayed there for nearly fifty years. A little to his own surprise, he turned out to have a brilliant head for logic and mathematics, and though he eventually took divine orders, he found his calling as a lecturer in math. After five years, he was made a don — an extraordinary achievement even in that less regimented academic time — and he remained a formidable figure at Oxford throughout his life. From the beginning, though, he had a sense of the absurdity of academic ritual. Soon after becoming a lecturer, he wrote to his siblings, back home, an *Alice*-like version of Oxford pedagogy:

> My one pupil has begun his work with me, and I will give you a description how the lecture is conducted. It is the most important point, you know, that the tutor should be *dignified,* and at a distance from the pupil, and that the pupil should be as much as possible *degraded* — otherwise you know, they are not humble enough. So I sit at the further end of the room; outside the door *(which is shut)* sits the scout; outside the outer door *(also shut)* sits the sub-scout; halfway down stairs sits the sub-sub-scout; and down in the yard sits the *pupil.*

Christ Church may have been a glamorous place, but, like every other Victorian institution, it was thought, in some vague way, to be in need of reform. When the old presiding dean of the college died in 1855, a reformer was brought in from outside not just the college (which would have been unusual enough) but the university itself. This was Henry George Liddell, the author of a famous Greek lexicon, and his idea of reform involved turning the college from a genteel clergymen's retreat into something more along the lines of a modern, German-style university.

So the great private event of Dodgson's life — the arrival of Dean Liddell and his family — was also its great public event. Dodgson disapproved of the new regimentation of Christ Church life that Liddell ushered in (he particularly hated the new system of competitive examinations), and for the next thirty years he opposed the dean's innovations with a series of comic pamphlets. Once, for instance, Dean Liddell allowed a new, meekly geometric belfry to go up on the cathedral at Christ Church. Two chapters of Dodgson's pamphlet ran, in their entirety, as follows:

4. *On the chief architectural merit of the new Belfry, Ch. Ch.*
Its chief merit is its simplicity — a simplicity so pure, so profound, in a word, so *simple,* that no other word will fitly describe it. The meagre outline, and baldness of detail, of the present Chapter, are adopted in humble imitation of this great feature.

5. *On the other architectural merits of the new Belfry, Ch. Ch.*
The Belfry has no other architectural merits.

But he couldn't resist the dean's family. He spent years opposing the dean and pursuing his daughters. At the time, the dean had three: Lorina, Alice, and the baby, Edith. When Dodgson first met Alice, she was a week shy of four, and for a long time he seemed to divide his attention equally among the girls. It was not until six years later, when Alice was turning ten, that he became exclusively infatuated with her. Dodgson began pursuing her through a long series of summer afternoon engagements (croquet games, boating parties, picnics in Christ Church meadow) attended by all three girls, which climaxed with the famous expedition on July 4, 1862, when he told them the story of the little girl who fell down the rabbit hole, and Alice asked him to write it down. He did, though it took him almost a year to start, and in the spring of 1863 he began a manuscript entitled "Alice's Adventures Under Ground." It was a love offering, which he had no plans to publish.

Then, almost immediately after he began writing his book for her, Dodgson was banned from the Liddells' house. It is hard to be sure what happened: after his death, his niece cut out his diary pages for the days just before he was excluded from the deanery. The first certain thing that emerges from the record, seen whole, is that the eleven-year-old Alice Liddell was not an improbable object of even a thoroughly unneurotic man's attentions. Everyone assumes, in writing about Alice and Charles, that the emphasis should be on his neuroses, projections, and so forth. On the evidence, there was nothing particularly odd about it. Alice Liddell seems to have been a kind of pint-size Zuleika Dobson: a girl *everyone* in Oxford fell in love with sooner or later. She was no ordinary little girl — as Dodgson's unforgettable picture of her as "The Beggar Maid" shows. In the photograph, she is a young girl of precocious wisdom and a Lulu-like coldness — a disdainful arrogance that is still shocking to see in a Victorian child. (Dodgson's photographs of Alice Liddell, in fact, are among the most moving examples of that Victorian preoccupation *la belle dame sans merci*.) Ruskin, a lifelong friend of the Liddells', was so overwhelmed by young Alice that he wrote longingly about her in his autobiography. When the queen sent her fourth son, Leopold, up to Christ Church, *he* fell desperately in love with Alice Liddell, too, and was prevented from marrying her only by the queen's intercession. Dodgson, who was in his early thirties, may simply have had the bad luck to fall in love with an amazing woman who happened to be eleven. The Alice we know is not a neurotic's projection onto a passive object but an artist's tribute to a remarkable woman, albeit a very small one.

That he was in love with her no one disputes, and that she was intrinsically lovable no one should dispute. But what, exactly, did that mean? "If this is taken to mean that he wanted to marry her or make love to her, there is not the slightest evidence for it," Martin Gardner (whose *The Annotated Alice* is still the best commentary on the books) wrote a generation ago. Cohen thinks that he wanted to do both. With a dogged but useful pedantry, Cohen has tabulated Dodgson's references in his private diaries to himself as a man consumed by sin, and points out that they cluster around the time of his most frequent visits with the Liddell girls. Three weeks after the famous July 4 expedition, in fact, he actually put off preaching a sermon because "till I can rule myself better, preaching is but a solemn mockery — 'thou that teachest another, teachest thou not thyself?' God grant this may be the last such entry I may have to make! that so I may not, when I have preached to others, be myself a castaway."

Victorian standards of sin were different from ours — Cardinal Manning's diary used to record the same kind of breast-beating when he had eaten too much cake — but Cohen says that "it is naïve to insist that Charles's troubled conscience stemmed solely from professional shortcomings or indolence." This clearly wasn't just conventional piety but real pain, and with a point. Further evidence that Dodgson wanted Alice, and knew it, is a poem he wrote, around the time of his infatuation with her, in which a sub-Tennysonian youth has sex with a quasi-Tennysonian maiden, who then turns into a withered old hag.

But it's likely that Dodgson declared his passion as openly as he could, and that his hope that he might be able to make that love legitimate was not nearly so unrealistic in its day as it may seem now. For, as Cohen reveals, there were *two* Dodgsons in love with little girls named Alice during the 1860s. Charles's brother Wilfred was in love with a fourteen-year-old named Alice Donkin — and that romance, on the surface only a little more plausible than Charles's, ended happily. Wilfred waited a few years and then married her. The brothers exchanged confidences about their loves; three years after his contretemps with the Liddells, Charles dined twice with his uncle Skeffington Lutwidge, and noted in his diary, "On each occasion we had a good deal of conversation about Wilfred, and about A.L. It is a very anxious subject."

Eleven is not fourteen, of course, but then Charles could simply have waited for A.L. a little longer. (Victorian mores accepted such marriages easily: the future Archbishop of Canterbury, E. W. Benson, proposed to *his* love when she was only twelve.) Cohen imagines that Alice might at some point have playfully said, "I'm going to marry Mr. Dodgson," and that this casual remark may have led the dean and his wife to throw Dodgson out. But one wonders if Cohen isn't underestimating the strength of Dodgson's passion, and his moral seriousness. Given what was apparently his advice to Wilfred — propose, and then propose to wait — it seems much likelier that Dodgson suggested a similar Elvis-and-Priscilla arrangement to the Liddells. Mrs. Liddell's outrage may say less about her virtues as a mother than about her calculations as a marriage broker. She was an appalling snob, who wanted a more aristocratic suitor for her daughter. Dodgson, though a rising don, was still only a don. That something like this — something open rather than covert — happened seems confirmed by a letter that Lord Salisbury wrote to his wife years later: "They say that Dodgson has half gone out of his mind in consequence of having been refused by the real Alice. It looks like it."

Two things about these events matter for lovers of the *Alice* books. The first is that the peculiar strength of Alice's character in the books — and she is one of the few completely sane, self-assertive, and undamaged female characters in English fiction created between Jane Austen and Virginia Woolf — comes out of the strength of a particular person. Alice is a portrait, not a projection. The other is that the curious melancholy and beautiful pathos of the books reflect the fact that by the time Dodgson had written them that forceful person had passed out of his life for good. The *Alice* books weren't really written for her; they were written about her.

Dodgson's unhappy love for Alice Liddell unleashed in him a taste for prepubescent girls. It was only after that, for instance, that he began to take nudes of other little girls. (He seems never to have photographed Alice nude.) Soon, though, his desire to take nudes of little girls came to verge on the obsessive; and his letters directed in this pursuit are not, for those of us who love his work, very nice to read. They go a long way toward explaining his reputation as a dirty old man, if an incautious, recklessly extroverted one.

On one occasion, he wrote to the father of a trio of girls — Ethel Mayhew, who was six or seven, Janet, who was around eleven, and Ruth, who was already in her teens — whom he wanted to photograph nude. "The permission to go as far as bathing-drawers is very charming, as I presume it includes *Ethel* as well as Janet," Dodgson wrote, with cajoling aplomb, and he continues:

> I can make some charming groups of Ethel and Janet in bathing-drawers, though I cannot exaggerate how much better they would look without. Also the bathing-drawers would enable me to do a full front view of Ethel, which of course could not be done without them: but why should you object to my doing a *back* view of her without them? It would be a *perfectly* presentable picture, and far more artistic than with them.

He goes on to say that he had already asked two of the girls about doing nude photography and that "both Ruth and Ethel seemed quite sure that *Janet* wouldn't object in the least to being done naked, and Ethel, when I asked her if *she* would object, said in the most simple and natural way, that she wouldn't object at all." He concludes, "If the worst comes to the worst, and you won't concede any nudities at all, I think you ought to allow *all three* to be done in bathing-drawers, to make up for my disappointment!" Then, in a postscript, he writes that he would much rather that Mrs. Mayhew not come along for the session.

This must have been — in its breathlessness and slightly unhinged detail (all those bathing-drawers!), and even in its inevitable reference to "artistic" needs — a creepy letter for a parent to get. Surprisingly, the Mayhews reacted mildly, granting Dodgson permission to do the pictures on condition that Mrs. Mayhew come along, though Dodgson — overreacting from guilt? — wrote back a desperately painful, hurt, and humiliated letter: "I should have no pleasure in doing any such pictures, now that I know I am not thought fit for such a privilege except on condition of being under chaperonage."

Nowadays, of course, a photographer with Dodgson's tastes would be in jail, or else doing a Calvin Klein campaign. Yet the mothers, or most of them, continued to send him little girls, and Dodgson continued to take their pictures, and nobody seems to have suffered at all. For almost a century, Dodgson's nudes were thought to have been lost; Dodgson had most of the negatives destroyed. Cohen has found four of them, and they are reprinted in his book. Hand colored by professional artists, with Pre-Raphaelite landscapes brushed in, they are less intensely realized than one had hoped they would be — though, at least in the case of Dodgson's "full frontal" of Evelyn Hatch, explicit enough to get one kicked off America Online. For all their immersion in the properties and stage scenery of what we have been taught to call Victorian sentimentality, the girls emerge as something more than exploited objects. Alice Liddell had seemed scarily older than her years; Dodgson's eye, trained on his first love, saw the Alice in all her successors, but he saw their innocence, too. They are granted their sexuality without being deprived of their childhood. These days, we assume that to grant sexuality is to end childhood: the real scandal about Calvin Klein's kids is not how young they look but how *old*.

In a curious way, the sentimentality of the Victorians, for which they are still maligned, allowed Dodgson to express his passion without ruining his life. He came up with a public explanation for his private obsession — that it was the little girls' "innocent unconsciousness" that he loved, and that his was a chaste passion — and the interesting thing is that his claim to innocence was true, or became true. He *didn't* molest his child friends, and they universally remembered him with affection. From the social point of view — which is to say, from the point of view of the little girls — Dodgson's passion *was* innocent.

Today, we would insist that any college don who wanted to take pictures of naked little girls was just a pervert, and we would drive him out of the school and into the tabloid press ("OXFORD DON IN KIDDIE-PORN RING"). We know, or think we do, that there is no such thing as an innocent passion for the bodies of young children. Yet, reflecting on Dodgson's life (and photographs), one can't help feeling that the Victorian tendency to compartmentalize the passions had its humane side, too. The Victorians genuinely believed that a passion could be snipped off at its roots and then, so to speak, brought indoors and placed in a glass of water, like a cut flower. They recognized a low passion for little girls' bodies, but they also believed that there was an innocent passion for little girls' bodies, where we would insist that the innocent passion was just the evil passion in bathing-drawers. The Victorians' tastes may have been a little unreal, but in some ways they were much more tolerant than we are. The Victorians may have been hypocrites, but they were not hysterics. Dodgson's appetite could at least still be acknowledged to exist, if only in some unreal, free-floating form — like the Cheshire Cat.

Dodgson's conviction of his own essential rectitude also allowed him to see his subjects as something more than a reflection of his obsessions. One of the virtues of his photographs of little girls is that they are not too pious. What makes most of the new, sexually charged pictures of children so depressing isn't that they are erotic but that they are so impersonal: coarsely dehumanized in the case of the Calvin Klein–Steven Meisel variety; pointedly abstract in the case of the Sally Mann art version. If we compare Dodgson with Mann, for instance, the odd thing is that it is the Victorian moralist who seems able to look at his subjects for their own sake, while in the postmodern pictures we are conscious that a point is always being sought. Dodgson turned a sin into a sentiment, and then turned a sentiment into a portrait; Sally Mann turns the breaking of a taboo into another kind of piety, and does it over and over again. The new pictures and books want to argue that the child's real sexuality is being ignored, denied, repressed, and that the photographer or writer is merely the therapeutic enabler. So what emerges is just that prefab "sexuality," a pinched and forlorn self-consciousness. Though we are obsessed with the sexuality of children, we are no longer able to do credit, as Dodgson could, to the real libidinal energy of children, as opposed to their mimicry of the grown-up kind. Looking even at a fully clothed photograph of Dodgson's, like that of the recumbent, smoldering Irene Mac-Donald, one feels that the picture is as much hers as his. She reminds us that sexiness at least resides in people, even small ones, while "sexuality" resides in categories.

After the drama of the Alice incidents, accounts of Dodgson's life grow a bit becalmed. By the 1870s, Dodgson had become a tycoon of whimsy. He published the first *Alice* book — *Alice's Adventures in Wonderland,* an elaborated version of his love offering — in 1865, when the real Alice was a teenager. *Through the Looking-Glass and What Alice Found There* was published in 1871; Alice Liddell saw it only after it appeared in the bookstores.

The Alice of the John Tenniel woodcuts looks nothing like her original. We have become so accustomed to Tenniel's illustrations as dry counterpoint to Carroll's genius that it is hard to remember that Tenniel was incomparably the more famous of the two men when they first collaborated. Tenniel, in fact, was the most fashionable and formidable political cartoonist of the day, and the idea of his illustrating a children's book — much less one by an Oxford don famous only in Oxford — was as improbable as the idea of Garry Trudeau's illustrating a kids' book by an unknown professor now. But Dodgson recognized that he needed Tenniel's sharpness of vision to illustrate his fantasy, and it was a sign of his extraordinary doggedness that he pursued a reluctant Tenniel again to illustrate *Through the Looking-Glass,* until the cartoonist at last agreed to cooperate, and wearily ensured his own immortality.

From the first, everyone saw that the *Alice* books were perfect. "A glorious artistic treasure," one early reviewer declared. The books had sold 120,000 copies by 1885, and, since Dodgson had decided to publish them himself, using all his own capital, this meant — in a looking-glass reversal that will be dear to the heart

of any author — that he kept 90 percent of the money and gave
his publisher 10 percent. He used the money to support his family,
and to take long vacations by the shore at Eastbourne, where he
could troll for little girls.

The conventional reading of the *Alice* books, which Cohen continues, depicts them as quest stories. They are about the achievement of maturity: Alice undergoes ordeals and so achieves a new
wisdom. But in fact Alice's is not a growing-up story. She learns
nothing: she's already the most mature person in Wonderland
when she arrives. She just experiences it all, and, at the end, she
doesn't say "There's no place like home" but just "I can't stand
this any longer!"

The details that Cohen marshals allow us to find in Dodgson's
life a context of events that helps illuminate his art. For there's a
straightforward sense in which the two processes that Cohen describes — the transformation of Oxford life and the nature of
Dodgson's love for little girls — help throw at least a slanting light
on what makes the books so good.

One process, which Cohen describes but whose significance he
doesn't elaborate on, is the growth of the university and, with it,
the birth of modern intellectual life. Dodgson's forty-eight years
at Christ Church saw the transformation of Oxford from what was
essentially a theological seminary with a finishing school for the
wealthy attached into something like a modern university — a
place where people go to talk about ideas. Dodgson not only witnessed this change but, for all his contentious ambivalence, was
part of it. At the beginning of his career, he is still a learned parson,
a figure from the world of Sydney Smith. By its end, in the 1890s,
he is writing his books about logic and corresponding with the
Cambridge circle, and we are in the world of Bertrand Russell.
Dodgson began as a mathematician, repeating axioms to undergraduates; he ended as a formal logician, publishing in *Mind*
paradoxes that showed, in ways that anticipate Gödel and Wittgen-
stein, how easily rational argument tends to rebound on itself.

Dodgson hated the most obvious signs of modernization — the
new architecture of Christ Church, the cult of competitive exams,
the secularization of learning. Yet he helped lead a revolt of the
younger faculty to reform the Constitution of Christ Church. And
when it came to the new ideas themselves he was, especially for a

clergyman, remarkably open-minded. After Darwin published *The Expression of Emotions in Man and Animals,* Dodgson wrote to him offering to collaborate on a new volume, to which he would contribute photographs.

More important, Dodgson discovered a new comic subject: people who were trying to find out about the world just by thinking about it. The folly of the supposed wise was an ancient subject, of course, but Carroll's characters — the White Knight, Humpty Dumpty, the White Queen, the Mad Hatter, and the March Hare — are intellectuals in what was then a new sense: people who like to come up with chains of abstract logical reasoning for their own sake, just to see where they will lead. Even the White Knight, the inventor, is engaged — as you find in his discussion of the pudding he invented during the meat course (made of blotting paper, sealing wax, and gunpowder) — in pure research. "In fact," the Knight says, "I don't believe that pudding ever *was* cooked! In fact, I don't believe that pudding ever *will* be cooked! And yet it was a very clever pudding to invent." Or there is the less familiar Professor in Carroll's later *Sylvie and Bruno,* who designs boots the tops of which are open umbrellas. "In *ordinary* rain," the Professor admits, "they would *not* be of much use. But if ever it rained *horizontally,* you know, they would be invaluable — simply invaluable!" Throughout *Sylvie and Bruno,* the source of the humor is made explicit: *all* the comic figures are professors, explicitly identified as such, and the maddest of all is a German professor called Mein Herr. It was, in particular, the influence of German philosophical idealism, which had exactly the same kind of prestige then that French post-structuralism has now, that Dodgson thought was absurd. In one of his anti-Liddell pamphlets he has a professor say, "For now-a-days all that is good comes from the German. . . . No learned man doth now talk, or even so much as cough, save only in German. The time has been, I doubt not, when an honest English 'Hem!' was held enough, both to clear the voice and rouse the attention of the company, but now-a-days no man of Science, that setteth any store by his good name, will cough otherwise than thus, *Ach! Euch! Auch!"* *Alice in Wonderland* and *Through the Looking-Glass* are descriptions of the new world in which people are trying to make ideas do the work of experience.

In fact, Carroll never really wrote "nonsense" — save "Jabberwocky," and even that gets explained by Humpty Dumpty. Everyone's ideas in the Looking-Glass world are not only sensible but strictly logical: the White King's remark about using hay as a palliative for fainting ("I didn't say there was nothing *better,*" he says. "I said there was nothing *like* it"); Humpty Dumpty's insistence on the literalness of conversations; the Hatter's riddle with no answer. Just by casting these lines of pure reasoning, Dodgson anticipated not just the shape but many of the sounds of intellectual fashions yet to come.

The flow of imagination and free-form logic is irresistible, but Carroll also sees its limits. "We're all mad here," the Cheshire Cat says, and they are. The *Alice* books are about what happens when you let thinking do away with sense. What Dodgson saw as the corrective to the folly of trying to live by thought wasn't beautiful intuition or irrational passion; it was the common sense of a well-brought-up little girl who sees things as they are. The books are written from the point of view of the dysfunctional intellectual — Dodgson was one himself — but with an understanding that it is better to have a little bit of real life than any amount of pure reason. What makes the books so cheering is that Alice's common sense keeps winning out; what makes them touching is that Dodgson understood that any well-brought-up little girl was more deeply *dans le vrai* than he would ever be. Alice is that honest English "Hem!"

This, I think, helps to explain the popularity of the *Alice* books, long after many of their references and jokes have become antiquated. (Booksellers say they are still among the strongest-selling children's books.) The abstract jokes don't appeal to children, but Alice does. They don't identify with her confusion; they identify with her confidence. Even if you don't see the object of the satire, the purpose is plain. Grown-ups, who appreciate the paradoxes, think they are getting the point; children, who appreciate Alice's impatience with them, get the point.

Dodgson had — unusually for a writer — good last years instead of sad ones. Cohen views him as a heroic rather than a neurotic figure, and, to the extent that a heroic figure is just a neurotic who fights it, he was. He spent several years, and an enormous amount of even his unquenchable energy, as the curator of the Christ

Church Common Room — a job that was essentially that of head caterer. He devoted the same intelligence to the fine points of champagne and port that he had devoted to photography and logic. His pamphlet, "Twelve Months in a Curatorship by One Who Has Tried It," is still funny: "The consumption of Madeira (B) has been, during the past year, zero. . . . After careful calculation, I estimate that, if this rate of consumption be steadily maintained, our present stock will last us an infinite number of years." He spent most of his later years working on two long, strange novels, *Sylvie and Bruno* and *Sylvie and Bruno Concluded*. They were commercial failures, and it is hard even now to master their mixture of piety and brilliant satire. The real failure of the *Sylvie and Bruno* books is that Sylvie is so much less interesting than Alice. She is a simpering fairy princess, where Alice had been a real girl.

Dodgson died in 1898. In the end, his split personality seems earned. If he was a double man, it was for the best of reasons: he saw twice as much as other people did. The Looking-Glass people convince us that abstract thought need not be tedious; Alice convinces us that common sense need not be charmless. It has become commonplace to see Dodgson as the crucial influence on the fantastic and anti-natural strains in twentieth-century writing. Yet surely the figure of Alice herself has affected the novel as much as the satirical parts of the *Alice* books have affected the anti-novel. Mrs. Dalloway, in her open-eyed, polite registering of a world gone mad, is unthinkable without the example of Alice, and so are the knowing heroines of Stevie Smith and, more recently, Cathleen Schine's polite, ironic observers. It sometimes seems as if all literary-minded women see themselves, sooner or later, as Alice, just as literary-minded men have always seen themselves as Hamlet. (Men choose Hamlet because every man sees himself as a disinherited monarch; women choose Alice because every woman sees herself as the only reasonable creature among crazy people who think that they are disinherited monarchs.) Mark Twain once called Dodgson his "dream-brother," and it is surely the case that Huck and Alice, the hero and heroine of the two best children's books of the nineteenth century, have become models for heroes and heroines of grown-up books in the twentieth century. The modern novel, with a stream of consciousness as its only order, needed an idea of the wise, reflecting innocent who experiences things without being transformed by them. Huck just moves on. Alice just wakes up.

Dodgson's last work was an elegant, incomplete logical proof of the impossibility of the doctrine of hell. At the end of one of those long, absurd sequences of logic there might be laughter, but beyond that, it seemed, there might be Truth — or even God. The religious doubts of his time all turned on the question of how you could have faith in an absurd universe, a world without order. If chance was built into the nature of things, as Darwin had proved, and if an attempt to renew order could lead only to anachronism and absurdity (as the Oxford Movement had proved), what was left? Gaiety and good manners, the *Alice* books suggest: turning your toes out while you walk; looking squarely at a slant world. Dodgson died regretting that he hadn't been able to finish a book that would "treat some of the religious difficulties of the day from a logical point of view." But he didn't have to worry. He had already written it, twice.

GORDON GRICE

The Black Widow

FROM HIGH PLAINS LITERARY REVIEW

I HUNT BLACK WIDOW. When I find one, I capture it. I have found them in discarded wheels and tires and under railroad ties. I have found them in house foundations and cellars, in automotive shops and toolsheds, in water meters and rock gardens, against fences and in cinderblock walls. I have found them in a hospital and in the den of a rattlesnake, and once on the bottom of the chair I was sitting in.

Sometimes I raise a generation or two in captivity. The egg sacs produce a hundred or more pinpoint cannibals, each leaving a trail of gleaming light in the air, the group of them eventually producing a glimmering tangle in which most of them die, eaten by stronger sibs. Finally I separate the three or four survivors and feed them bigger game.

Once I let several egg sacs hatch out in a container about eighteen inches on a side, a tight wooden box with a sliding glass top. As I tried to move the box one day, the lid slid off and I fell, hands first, into the mass of young widows. Most were still translucent newborns, their bodies a swirl of brown and cream. A few of the females had eaten enough to molt; they had the beginnings of their blackness. Their tangle of broken web clung to my forearms. They felt like trickling water in my arm hairs.

I walked out into the open air and raised my arms into the stiff wind. The widows answered the wind with new strands of web and drifted away, their bodies gold in the late sun. In about ten minutes my arms carried nothing but old web and the husks of spiderlings eaten by their sibs.

I have never been bitten.

*

The black widow has the ugliest web of any spider. The orb weavers make those seemingly delicate nets that poets have traditionally used as symbols of imagination, order, and perfection. The sheet-web spiders weave crisp linens on the grass. But the widow makes messy-looking tangles in the corners and bends of things and under logs and debris. Often the web is littered with leaves. Beneath it lie the husks of insect prey, their antennae still as gargoyle horns, cut loose and dropped; on them and the surrounding ground are splashes of the spider's white urine, which looks like bird guano and smells of ammonia even at a distance of several feet. This fetid material draws scavengers — ants, sow bugs, crickets, roaches, and so on — which become tangled in vertical strands of silk reaching from the ground up into the web. The widow comes down and, with a bicycling of the hind pair of legs, throws gummy silk onto this new prey.

When the prey is seriously tangled but still struggling, the widow cautiously descends and bites the creature, usually on a leg joint. This is a killing bite; it pumps neurotoxin into the victim. The widow will deliver a series of bites as the creature dies, injecting substances that liquefy the organs. Finally it will settle down to suck the liquefied innards out of the prey, changing position two or three times to get it all.

Before the eating begins, and sometimes before the victim dies from the slow venom, the widow usually moves it higher into the web. It attaches some line to the prey with a leg-bicycling toss, moves up the vertical web strand that originally snagged the prey, crosses a diagonal strand upward to a higher point on a different vertical strand, and here secures the line. It has thus dragged the prey's body up off the ground. The whole operation is like that of a person moving a load with block and tackle. It occurs in three dimensions — as opposed to the essentially two-dimensional operations of orb weavers and sheet weavers.

You can't watch the widow in this activity very long without realizing that its web is not a mess at all but an efficient machine. It allows complicated uses of leverage and also, because of its complexity of connections, lets the spider feel a disturbance anywhere in the web — usually with enough accuracy to tell the difference at a distance between a raindrop or leaf and viable prey.

The web is also constructed in a certain relationship to movements of air so that flying insects are drawn into it. This fact partly explains why widow webs are so often found in the face-down side of discarded car wheels — the wheel is essentially a vault of still air that protects the web, but the central hole at the top allows air-borne insects to fall in. An insect that is clumsy and flies in random hops, such as a June beetle, is especially vulnerable to this trap. The widow often seems to choose her building sites according to indigenous smells rather than creating her own stinking waste pile from scratch. The webs turn up, for example, in piles of trash and rotting wood. A few decades ago, the widow was notorious for building its home inside the works of outdoor toilets. Scraping around with a stick before using the toilet was a common practice.

The architectural complexities of the widow web do not particularly impress the widows. They move around in these webs almost blind, yet they never misstep or get lost. In fact, a widow forcibly removed from its web and put back at a different point does not seem confused; it will quickly return to its habitual resting place. Furthermore, widows never snare themselves, even though every strand of the web is a potential trap. A widow will spend a few minutes every day coating the clawed tips of its legs with the oil that lets it walk the sticky strands. It secretes the oil from its mouth, coating its legs like a cat cleaning its paws.

The human mind cannot grasp the complex functions of the web but must infer them. The widow constructs it by instinct. A brain smaller than a pinhead contains the blueprints, precognitive memories the widow unfolds out of itself into actuality. I have never dissected with enough precision or delicacy to get a good specimen of the black widow brain, but I did glimpse one once. A widow was struggling to wrap a praying mantis when the insect's forelegs, like scalpels mounted on lightning, sliced away the spider's carapace and left exposed the clear droplet of bloody brain.

Widows reportedly eat mice, toads, tarantulas — anything that wanders into that remarkable web. I have never witnessed a widow performing a gustatory act of that magnitude, but I have seen them eat scarab beetles heavy as pecans; carabid beetles strong enough to prey on wolf spiders; cockroaches more than an inch long; and hundreds of other arthropods of various sizes. Widows begin life by eating their siblings. An adult female will fight any other female; the winner often eats the loser. A popular game among Mexican children is to stage such fights and bet on the outcome. The children put the widows on a stick and pass it around so that everyone can see. Sometimes one female ties another up and leaves without killing her. I have come across such black pearls wrapped in silk and, upon peeling off the skin, seen the pearls unfold their legs and rush away.

The widow gets her name by eating her lover, though this does not always happen. He distinguishes himself from ordinary prey by playing her web like a lyre. Sometimes she eats him without first copulating; sometimes she snags him as he withdraws his palp from her genital pore. Sometimes he leaves unharmed after mating; in this case, he soon withers and dies on his own. I have witnessed male and female living in platonic relationships in one web. The males' palps, still swollen with sperm, proved that these relationships had not been sexual.

Many widows will eat as much as opportunity gives. One aggressive female had an abdomen a little bigger than an English pea. She snared a huge cockroach and spent several hours subduing it, then three days consuming it. Her abdomen swelled to the size of a largish marble, its glossy black stretching to a tight red-brown. With a different widow, I decided to see whether that appetite was really insatiable. I collected dozens of large crickets and grasshoppers and began to drop them into her web at a rate of one every three or four hours. After catching and consuming her tenth victim, this bloated widow fell from her web, landing on her back. She remained in this position for hours, making only feeble attempts to move. Then she died.

The first thing people ask when they hear about my fascination with the widow is why I am not afraid. The truth is that my fascination is rooted in fear.

I have childhood memories that partly account for my fear. When I was six my mother took my sister and me to the cellar of our farmhouse and told us to watch as she killed a widow. With great ceremony she produced a long stick (I am tempted to say a ten-foot pole) and, narrating her technique in exactly the hushed voice she used for discussing religion or sex, went to work. Her flashlight beam found a point halfway up the cement wall where two marbles hung together — one crisp white, the other a glossy black. My mother ran her stick through the dirty silver web around them, and as it tore it sounded like the crackling of paper in fire. This sound is unique to the widow's powerful web — anybody with a little experience can tell a widow's work from another spider's by ear. The black marble rose on thin legs to fight off the intruder. As the plump abdomen wobbled across the wall, it seemed to be constantly throwing those legs out of its path. The impression it gave was of speed and frantic anger, but actually a widow's movements outside the web are slow and inefficient. My mother smashed the widow onto the stick and carried it up into the light. It was still kicking its remaining legs. Mom scraped it against the sidewalk, grinding it to a paste. Then she returned for the white marble — the widow's egg sac. This, too, came to an abrasive end.

My mother's stated purpose was to teach us how to recognize and deal with a dangerous creature we would probably encounter on the farm. But of course we also took the understanding that widows were actively malevolent, that they waited in dark places to ambush us, that they were worthy of ritual disposition, like an enemy whose death is not sufficient but must be followed with the murder of his children and the salting of his land and whose unclean remains must not touch our hands.

The odd thing is that so many people, some of whom presumably did not first encounter the widow in such an atmosphere of mystic reverence, hold the widow in awe. Various friends have told me that the widow always devours her mate, or that her bite is always fatal to humans — in fact, it almost never is. I have heard told for truth that goods imported from the Orient are likely infested with widows and that women with bouffant hairdos have died of widow infestation. Any contradiction of such tales is received as if it were a proclamation of atheism.

The most startling contribution to the widow's mythical status I have ever encountered was *Black Widow: America's Most Poisonous Spider,* a book that appeared in 1945. Between genuine scientific observations, the authors present the widow as a lurking menace with a taste for human flesh. They describe the experiments of other investigators; one involved inducing a widow to bite a laboratory rat on the penis, after which event the rat "appeared to become dejected and depressed." Perhaps the most psychologically revealing passage is the authors' quotation from another writer, who said the "deadliest Communists are like the black widow spider; they conceal their *red* underneath."

We project our archetypal terrors onto the widow. It is black; it avoids the light; it is a voracious carnivore. Its red markings suggest blood. Its name, its sleek, rounded form invite a strangely sexual discomfort; the widow becomes an emblem for a man's fear of extending himself into the blood and darkness of a woman, something like the legendary Eskimo vampire that takes the form of a fanged vagina.

The widow's venom is, of course, a soundly pragmatic reason for fear. The venom contains a neurotoxin that can produce sweats, vomiting, swelling, convulsions, and dozens of other symptoms. The variation in symptoms from one person to the next is remarkable. The constant is pain. A useful question for a doctor trying to diagnose an uncertain case: "Is this the worst pain you've ever felt?" A "yes" suggests a diagnosis of black widow bite. Occasionally people die from widow bites. The very young and the very old are especially vulnerable. Some people seem to die not from the venom but from the infection that may follow; because of its habitat, the widow carries dangerous microbes.

Some researchers hypothesized that the virulence of the venom was necessary for killing beetles of the scarab family. This family contains thousands of species, including the June beetle and the famous dung beetle the Egyptians thought immortal. All the scarabs have thick, strong bodies and unusually tough exoskeletons, and many of them are common prey for the widow. The tough hide was supposed to require a particularly nasty venom. As it turns out, the venom is thousands of times more virulent than necessary for this purpose. The whole idea is full of the widow's glamour: an emblem of eternal life killed by a creature whose most distinctive blood-colored markings people invariably describe as an hourglass.

No one has ever offered a sufficient explanation for the dangerous venom. It provides no evolutionary advantages: all of the widow's prey items would find lesser toxins fatal, and there is no particular benefit in killing or harming larger animals. A widow that bites a human being or other large animal is likely to be killed.

Evolution does sometimes produce such flowers of natural evil — traits that are neither functional nor vestigial but utterly pointless. Natural selection favors the inheritance of useful characteristics that arise from random mutation and tends to extinguish disadvantageous traits. All other characteristics, the ones that neither help nor hinder survival, are preserved or extinguished at random as mutation links them with useful or harmful traits. Many people — even many scientists — assume that every animal is elegantly engineered for its ecological niche, that every bit of an animal's anatomy and behavior has a functional explanation. This assumption is false. Nothing in evolutionary theory sanctions it; fact refutes it.

We want the world to be an ordered room, but in a corner of that room there hangs an untidy web. Here the analytical minds find an irreducible mystery, a motiveless evil in nature, and the scientist's vision of evil comes to match the vision of a God-fearing country woman with a ten-foot pole. No idea of the cosmos as elegant design accounts for the widow. No idea of a benevolent God is comfortable in a world with the widow. She hangs in her web, that marvel of design, and defies teleology.

EDWARD HOAGLAND

Brightness Visible

FROM HARPER'S MAGAZINE

A BRISTLY, LOVELY, although hot and fearsome recklessness invigorates God in the Old Testament when he loses patience. *Behold now behemoth, which I made with thee,* he says to Job, who has been complaining of his unjust sufferings. But justice is not what the majesty of Creation is all about. Consider, for instance, the hippopotamus. *He moveth his tail like a cedar . . . his bones are like bars of iron . . .*

For me too religion needs to wear a mask of jubilation. Yet unmixed glee is beyond my capacities. I begin to flag if I am required to be upbeat for many hours at a stretch — though I have in fact had just the sort of biblical experience that warrants a lifelong commitment to the happy tangents of faith. It happened during my late fifties, when two eye operations restored my sight after two or three years of legal blindness. My vision had shrunk to the point where I couldn't see faces, birds, or trees. Through my telescope I studied the rising moon or the way that branches interlaced, but even the lenses of such an instrument could barely recapitulate what my eyes with ordinary eyeglasses had formerly seen.

Quite suddenly, however, within a period of half a dozen weeks, the miracle of the streaming clouds, the blowing grass, the leaping birds, the upspread trees, and the variety of expressions on my friends' faces was given back to me. For possibly an entire year, in the exalting aftermath of regaining my eyesight, I was incapable of being depressed — I simply needed to glance out the window. I couldn't believe how golden the sunshine was, how softly green each leaf, or how radiant the city night could be, with its great arc-like sparkling bridges and hooded mobs of apartment houses, each of the thousands of lives packed inside signified by a small yellow light. If I was in the city, the slant of lion-skinned building stone on a skyscraper's face was breathtaking. In the country, I was lifted to rapture by the prismatic pointillism of the wildflowers, or a sea of seed heads shimmering underneath the black outcrops on a mountainside, the puce and pink of a slow dawn, the white slats of birch bark under a purple rainstorm medallioned by a rainbow or slashed by a crimson shaft of half-set sun, a sky big enough to fall right into forever and ever if I lay on my back and didn't grip the grass.

And, of course, I didn't neglect to look up Christ's miracle-working episodes, impromptu as they were. Set against the scale of eternal redemption, the temporary plight of the blind and sick whom he encountered accidentally was not his preoccupation. But pity for their anguish mixed with his practicality when he asked whether they "believed." Presumably, since God had created heaven and earth, God could cure blindness, leprosy, or whatnot with or without "belief," but Christ's own powers, swift and serene though they seem, may have needed that extra catalyst. Indeed, in Mark 8, the act requires two applications of Christ's hands: the first only restores the blind man of Bethsaida's sight to the extent that people look to him *like trees . . . walking about.* So *Jesus laid his hands on his eyes again.* Rather like my surgeon.

I was truly, sadly startled, though, in the midst of my exuberance, to notice how many of my friends' faces had changed during my blind years. They looked battered, bruised, disheartened, bereft of illusion, apprehensive, or knocked a bit awry by the very campaigns and thickets of life that I was giddy with delight to have regained. I was seeing the forest, I decided, while they were engrossed by the trees. Like a prisoner sprung from a dungeon, I didn't care about minor harassments, frictions, frettings, inconveniences. The sky, the clouds, the colors and movement, and my sudden freedom were plenty for me. I could be irascible, impatient, and hard to get on with, but never unhappy; that's not what life was for. Instead I was charged up, alight, Lazarus-like, and I realized that such a marked alteration in my friends' faces and the cast of strangers' expressions could not be the result of my having just been "away" for a while, but that everything was clearer. The fox-red coat of a deer in June; the glow of a checkered, fat garter snake, its white skin shining between its black scales; a goldfinch's trampoline bounce on the wing; the fire-engine pace of a chimney swift tearing around; leaf shadows running on a tree trunk like a crowd of squirrels as the wind blew. Such a lovely, vivid, vibrant world — what does it matter if your marriage is going rancid? "Cheer up, for heaven's sake!" I wanted to say when the shaft of a stranger's glance on the street told me a tale of misery. Funky neon at midnight in the city, or raindrops zigging down a windowpane, a sky of feather blue, a sky of sleety pewter, a lady's dachshund walking like a leashed salamander down the sidewalk — and the piercing pleasure of a toddler seeing it — old bricks on a town-house or a church front.

In Manhattan I went to services at the church where I'd been christened more than fifty years before, and both before and after my crucial operations I seemed so otherworldly or beamish to the vicars and the vergers that they assumed I was one of the homeless, fiftyish men who were mingling with the well-heeled parishioners for the sake of the sandwiches served afterward. There was no end to how glad I was at any hour to wake up, step outside, or simply pour and stir a cup of coffee and stretch my feet into the spill of zebra-patterned sunlight that the venetian slats threw on the rug so marvelously.

Behold now behemoth, God says. . . . *He lieth under the shady trees, in the covert of the reed . . . the willows of the brook compass him about. Behold, he drinketh up a river, and hasteth not; he trusteth that he can draw up Jordan into his mouth.* Or, God continues angrily to Job, *Canst thou draw out leviathan with an hook. . . . Canst thou put an hook into his nose? . . . Will he make many supplications unto thee? . . . Wilt thou play with him as with a bird?*

I use the King James translation, and "leviathan" may be either a whale or a crocodile, though this spiky, vivid description goes on to resemble in its particulars a scaly, toothy crocodile, who, like the often dangerous hippo, could make the Jordan River terrifying. The biblical Hebrews were an inland people, not seafarers like the Phoenicians; but on the other hand, the author of the Book of Job is considered to have been a later, more traveled and worldly individual than some of the other writers. The Revised English Bible of 1989 splits this chapter, 41, into two entries divided by Chapter 40, so that "leviathan" can represent both of these wondrous and unconquerable creatures. And the whole glorious dithyramb to the animal kingdom — peacocks; lions; wild, gleeful goats; formidable wild oxen; wild, nifty asses; dashing ostriches; soaring cliff-eagles — recited by God pridefully to the much abused Job out of a "whirlwind," is in marked contrast to that earlier, more famous God whose injunction to Adam and Eve at the beginning of Genesis is that they and humankind should *subdue . . . and have dominion over the fish of the sea, and over the fowl of the air, and over every living thing that moveth upon the earth.*

The Hebrew God is whimsical, jealous, inconsistent: mad, of course, very soon after that first chapter of Genesis, at Eve and Adam, with somewhat the same tone of thunderous petulance he later directs at poor Job for rather less reason. (Job's long sufferings have been the result of a sort of a sporting bet between God and a manipulative, teasing Satan, not an impulsive act of disobedience at the behest of some newly fledged Serpent.) Even in the single book of Deuteronomy, where Moses transmits, at God's instruction in Chapter 5, the Ten Commandments (plus at different points a considerable amount of merciful detail as to how bondservants, widows, orphans, and destitute wayfarers shall be treated), God also decrees, in Chapters 2 and 3, the genocide of the tribes of Heshbon — *the men, and the women, and the little ones* — and also of Og — *utterly destroying the men, women, and children, of every city.* And again, in Chapter 20, God ordains a further holocaust: *Thou shalt save alive nothing that breatheth. But thou shalt utterly destroy them; namely, the Hittites, and the Amorites, the Canaanites, and the Perizzites, the Hivites, and the Jebusites; as the Lord thy God hath commanded thee.* Deuteronomy does contain the brief, winsomely generous admonition in Chapter 25 that *thou shalt not muzzle the ox when he treadeth out the corn* (in other words, not let him feel hunger), but it also includes, in Chapter 28, the dire warning that if God's established "holy people," the Jews, don't follow his commandments they will become cannibals from famine, conquest, siege, and plague, eating their own children. And in Exodus 20 and 34 the vindictive threat is floated that a father's sins will be visited upon his son even to the fourth generation — although, in fairness, Deuteronomy 24, Jeremiah 30, and Ezekiel 18 contradict this. *I wound, and I heal,* he says in Deuteronomy 32.

He seems a berserk and hideous deity in some of the more perfervid remarks that Moses and others record or attribute to him. He is an angry caliph who might better suit the Serbs or Hutus of 1994 or the Hitlerian Catholics of World War II, and he did not have much appeal for me as a boy, though the Old Testament stories we heard in church and Sunday school were riveting — the drama of baby Isaac almost being sacrificed by his father, Abraham; of Judith cutting off the head of Holofernes; of Joseph sold into slavery by his brothers; of little Moses in the bulrushes; of Job's faith and loss of faith; of David fighting Goliath with a slingshot; of Samson rendered powerless when the treacherous Delilah cut off his hair (Judith a heroine but Delilah a villainess). The sheer, gala accretion of these tales, extending over a good number of centuries, had more narrative weight than did the thirty-year story of Jesus, from Bethlehem to Calvary.

But Jesus spoke for a God whose teachings I could better swallow. His, too, in its abbreviated way, is a matchless tale. Born in a manger, although he was the Son of God, because there was no room at the inn, yet visited in his infancy by wise men and shepherds drawn by a radiant star; healing blind men and lepers, raising the dead, and throwing the money changers out of the Temple, accompanied by a small band of "fishers of men"; betrayed by Judas for thirty pieces of silver and crucified between two criminals, dying in agony and thirst after several hours but forgiving his captors, "for they know not what they do," and on the third day rising from the dead to sit at the right hand of God himself. A most direct parable — just lengthy enough, yet coherent and confirmed by four testimonials. You can't beat it for what it is, and the interpretations within our own language and time have ranged from "Onward Christian Soldiers" to Martin Luther King. You see on TV the pomp of the Pope versus Mother Teresa. And whatever these elaborations have become, the central addenda of Christianity seem as essential to me as the Bill of Rights added on to a basic Constitution. Judaism without the Sermon on the Mount seems a religion incomplete, *lex talionis* — an eye for an eye — without the Golden Rule: *Whatsoever ye would that men should do to you, do ye even so to them* (Matthew 7).

Jesus added to the undercarriage of Judaism not to destroy *but to fulfill,* he says. And like Moses before him, he went into the wilderness on a walkabout, up to a mountaintop for revelation — which I take to be more evidence of biblical ambivalence about the idea that the wilderness ought to be bridled and ruled, that the snake and crocodile, the elephant and hippo, the whale and lion should have no untrammeled territory left in which to strut their stuff and play their fateful, antique roles. Still, as against the legend of Christ, shimmering and imperishable as it is (and, indeed, priests and ministers wear desert dress), you have Judaism beginning not with a baby's birth but with the very universe's. You have the theater of Eve and her Serpent; then Noah's brave Ark; wise Solomon; the visions of Isaiah; Jeremiah and Zechariah; Daniel in the Lions' Den; Jonah in the Whale; the Song of Songs; and zestfully on. No wonder so many Jews have regarded themselves as a people chosen by God.

My own bias is against a monotheism so people-centered, and thus the Old Testament God who most appeals to me is least "Hebrew." ("There is no certainty that the author was an Israelite," says Marvin Pope, a leading scholar on the Book of Job.) God's magnificently hair-raising answer to Job from out of the whirlwind outguns anything of the sort in the New Testament, which after all is more fit for the advent of Saint Francis, lover of tiny birds, or the pacifism of Martin Luther King than for the preservation of old values. *Where wast thou when I laid the foundations of the earth?* God declares (a lover of carnivorous tigers as well as small birds) *. . . when the morning stars sang together? . . . Hast thou commanded the morning since thy days? . . . Hast thou entered into the springs of the sea? . . . Have the gates of death been opened unto thee? . . . Hast thou perceived the breadth of the earth? . . . Where is the way where light dwelleth? and as for darkness, where is the place thereof? . . . Hath the rain a father? or who hath begotten the drops of dew? Out of whose womb came the ice? and the hoary frost of heaven? . . . Knowest thou the ordinances of heaven? . . . Canst thou lift up thy voice to the clouds? . . . Canst thou send lightnings? . . . Wilt thou hunt the prey for the lion? or . . . provideth for the raven his food?*

For me, that's plenty good enough as an underlying Constitution, an underpinning for my American Transcendentalism, as well as a basic link to other world religions and beyond them to the grandfather, or "pagan," spiritual impulses that occasionally well up in so many of us at the ocean, in the woods, or during slam-crash thunderstorms or the extraordinary hallucinations that afflict us when someone we love dies. Genesis's intolerance of wilderness was tailor made for the Industrial Revolution. It covered the clergy on every lame excuse given for ducking their heads as the skies and fields and rivers turned sooty black, and breathing space and sunny light and a whole panoply of flashing creatures disappeared. Just as on other issues such as slavery, child labor, racial prejudice, and colonial genocide, the church was rarely in the vanguard to intervene, but, rather, brought up the rear of the mainstream, snubbing the earnest mavericks while the situation rapidly grew worse. In my lifetime alone, perhaps half the species that were alive on earth when I was born will have been snuffed out.

Christianity displays these contradictions in Saint George slaying the dragon while Saint Francis plays with birds, in Androcles plucking a thorn from the lion's paw while Saint Patrick drives the snakes out of Ireland. And Judaism has faced its own immiscibility in the task of peacemaking in Israel, where rabbits and religious folk have not seemed to play an adequate part in whatever reconciliation has been accomplished with the Palestinians. Instead, it's been mostly the work of military men and secular idealists, as if the Jewish religion itself is incomplete, a religion of resistance, of "silence, exile, and cunning" (in James Joyce's analogous definition of how art should be engendered), but not yet a religion brought to closure, not yet a savior's religion here on earth.

No stretch of grief or the imagination, no precedent in science or logic can get a handle on this catastrophe — half of Creation extinguished in a single life span. Noah did not materialize again to save God's handiwork, or even a Mother Teresa. Flying beings, swimming things, creeping, crawling, running existences, long-legged or short-winged, brought to life over many, many millennia, had no escape and simply blinked out. People, says a friend of mine who is a Congregational minister, "are born in solidarity with Creation but live in brokenness with Creation," or, as he adds, "in sin."

The author of the Song of Songs, another extravaganza, might testify to that. You may recall some of his imagery: *Your eyes are*

*doves behind your veil, your hair like a flock of goats streaming down
Mount Gilead. Your teeth are like a flock of ewes newly shorn . . . your
parted lips . . . like a pomegranate cut open. . . . Your two breasts are like
two fawns, twin fawns of a gazelle grazing among the lilies.* (This from
the Revised English Bible, which is more lyric here.) *Come with me,*
the speaker adds to his new bride, *from the summit of Amana, from
the top of Senir and Hermon, from the lions' lairs, and the leopard-haunted
hills,* to civilization. The duality of nature in the Bible is like that
in other ancient epics, such as *Gilgamesh,* the *Odyssey,* or *Beowulf,*
and our own literary figures, Melville, Hardy, and Conrad. Psalm
104 boasts affectionate references to wild goats and rock badgers,
storks, whales that sport in the sea, wild donkeys, and young lions
seeking their food from God. But in Psalm 102, *I am stricken, withered
like grass. . . . I am like a desert owl in the wilderness, like an owl that
lives among ruins,* the writer says. The King James Version uses the
intriguing translation "pelican," but wild places are not habitats
where you'd want to be.

And in Isaiah, Chapter 34, after the Lord has sated his bloody
wrath upon the residents of Edom, *horned owl and bustard will make
it their home; it will be the haunt of screech-owl and raven. . . . It will be
the lair of wolves. . . . Marmots will live alongside jackals. . . . There too
the nightjar will return to rest and . . . there the sand-partridge will make
her nest, lay her eggs and hatch them, and gather her brood under her
wings; there will the kites gather, each with its mate . . . they will occupy
it for all time, and each succeeding generation will dwell there.* (The King
James substitutes unicorns and cormorants, bitterns, dragons, sat-
yrs, and vultures for some of these; and the American Revised
Standard Version, porcupines, ostriches, and hyenas.) Likewise,
when Babylon is overthrown in Isaiah 13, *marmots will have their
lairs in her, and porcupines will overrun her houses; desert-owls will dwell
there, and there he-goats will gambol; jackals will occupy her mansions,
and wolves her luxurious palaces.* Sounds like the epitome of desola-
tion but also like a bit of fun. The desert fathers lived closer to
nature than we do.

Here, as in Job, the wilderness is presented as an alternative to
cities and to agriculture, certainly not one that man wishes for, yet
one that, for God's superbly diverse purposes, continues to celebrate the glory of earth. Though God had been mean to the
Snake, back in Genesis, for tempting Eve *(upon thy belly shalt thou*

*go, and dust shalt thou eat all the days of thy life: And I will put enmity
between thee and the woman, and between thy seed and her seed . . .),* wild
animals are generally God's children, too. What he envisions for
them at the end of time is summed up in Isaiah 11. *Then the wolf
will live with the lamb, and the leopard lie down with the kid; the calf and
the young lion will feed together, with a little child to tend them. The cow
and the bear will be friends . . . and the lion will eat straw like cattle. The
infant will play over the cobra's hole, and the young child dance over the
viper's nest. There will be neither hurt nor harm in all my holy mountain;
for the land will be filled with the knowledge of the Lord as the waters cover
the sea.*

No permission is given in Isaiah, Job, or Genesis for the holocaust mankind has visited upon the natural world, whereby the
rhinoceros may soon be as scarce as the unicorn. Behemoths,
crocodiles, and the soaring eagles and fearsome lions that en-
riched, mythologized, and demonized the banks of the Jordan as
manifestations of God's majesty are long gone, with their like being
pursued to the edge of the planet. The blackened woods, the sooty
skies, "leviathan" more than decimated: God is not just. He is
cryptic, elliptical, even countenancing your death, *my* death. Like
sand in a wasp-waisted egg timer, we tumble through the slot
before we're quite ready to, and the tumbling process does not
ensure fairness even in priority. You and I, born the same year,
may die thirty years apart. Justice is not God's department; justice
is a man-made concept, except in the somewhat different sense
that character is often fate, as, in fact, Job's is, finally winning him
back God's favor, or, to be exact, *fourteen thousand sheep, and six
thousand camels, a thousand yoke of oxen, and as many she-asses,* so that
he's exactly twice as rich as before God allowed Satan to toy so
cruelly with him. In life we don't necessarily see people receiving
their just deserts, but over a couple of decades we do notice their
muddied faces and bitten nails if, although rich as Croesus, they
have lived nastily. Time wounds all heels.

The Old Testament God seemed as primitive as a tribal sheik,
being too much constructed in the splintered, banal image of man.
Thus the New Testament, although less dramatically embellished
with centuries' worth of narrative, convinced me more as a boy. I
was a Tolstoyan then, and from that teenage base of idealism I
discovered jubilee "shout" singing in the black Pentecostal church

I used to go to in San Francisco in the late 1950s. I later discovered Saint Francis's hymn of adoration called "The Canticle of the Creatures": "Most high and most holy, most powerful Lord. . . . To Thee and Thy creatures we proffer our praise: / To our brother the sun in the heavens ashine, / Who brings us the beauty and joy of our days, / Thine emblem and sign. / We praise Thee, O Lord, for our sister the moon, . . . / For our brother the wind, for the bright of the noon, / For all of Thy weather. / For our sister the water, so humble and chaste, / For beautiful fire, with his perilous powers, / For our mother the earth, who holds us embraced, / Who delights us with flowers . . ."

Transcendentalism naturally followed, and I stopped describing myself as a Christian. Nevertheless, Psalm 148 does say it all: *Praise the Lord from the earth, you sea monsters and ocean depths; fire and hail, snow and ice, gales of wind that obey his voice; all mountains and hills; all fruit trees and cedars; wild animals and all cattle, creeping creatures and winged birds. . . . Praise the Lord.* And Psalm 150, the famous one: *Praise the Lord. Praise God in his holy place, praise him in the mighty vault of heaven. . . . Praise him with fanfares on the trumpet, praise him on harp and lyre; praise him with tambourines and dancing, praise him with flute and strings; praise him with the clash of cymbals; with triumphant cymbals praise him . . .*

Behold now behemoth, which I made with thee! An electrifying injunction, and for practically a lifetime I've been doing just that — observing zebras, and genuine behemoths like elephants, hippos, giraffes, whales, jaguars, and grizzlies. I have believed that they were indeed "made with me," and by the age of eighteen I was already thrusting my hand down a circus hippo's mouth to scratch the back of her tongue and the inside of her cheeks, much in the way that tick birds or "ox-peckers" do in Africa, searching out leeches. I also communed with Siberian and Sumatran tigers, both now almost extinct, and black-maned lions and Indian elephants, and I rubbed a rhino's itchy lips on sweltering afternoons, not in a trivializing manner but single-mindedly, with a passion that had begun with turtles when I was five or six — like that of city kids for dinosaurs nowadays. Leopard seals and eponymous leopards, killer whales in the Arctic and Antarctic, and Nile River crocodiles: I've traveled far and wide since then to glimpse these stirring beings.

Canst thou draw out leviathan with an hook? . . . Will he make many supplications unto thee? Can you *make a banquet of him* or *part him among the merchants?* God asks Job jeeringly, and, alas, it's come to pass that we can, with religion frequently a handmaiden to the merchants.

On the street, with my rejuvenated sight — $15,000 plastic implants — I seemed to see right back into the exhaustion and poignant anxiety in the recesses of other people's eyes, the thwarted potential for love and fun and dedication, the foiled altruism, now in abeyance, and the exasperation. And yet I could also see the imp that lived in them, the child that hadn't died. So often the variables that exist in somebody's face, from mirth to aggravation, add up to the wish to still believe in virtue, hope, and God.

"I have seen the elephant," the Gold Rushers and other frontiersmen used to say after they returned to town. For me, with a lifelong belief that heaven is on earth, not nebulously up in the sky, I see it every dawn and sunset and in the head-high joe-pye weed, smelling like vanilla in July (and used by the Indians in treating typhus, colds, chills, "sore womb after childbirth," diarrhea, liver and kidney ailments, "painful urination," gout, and rheumatism). I see it in the firmament at night and in a stand of spruce or a patch of moss beside a brook. And during the time when I was blind I could smell it in the scent of a blossoming basswood tree, or hear it in a toad's trill, or lay my head flat on the ground and gaze at the forest of fervent moss, inches away, a beetle or a caterpillar crawling. *Behold now behemoth.*

CHANG-RAE LEE

Coming Home Again

FROM THE NEW YORKER

WHEN MY MOTHER began using the electronic pump that fed her liquids and medication, we moved her to the family room. The bedroom she shared with my father was upstairs, and it was impossible to carry the machine up and down all day and night. The pump itself was attached to a metal stand on casters, and she pulled it along wherever she went. From anywhere in the house, you could hear the sound of the wheels clicking out a steady time over the grout lines of the slate-tiled foyer, her main thoroughfare to the bathroom and the kitchen. Sometimes you would hear her halt after only a few steps, to catch her breath or steady her balance, and whatever you were doing was instantly suspended by a pall of silence.

I was usually in the kitchen, preparing lunch or dinner, poised over the butcher block with her favorite chef's knife in my hand and her old yellow apron slung around my neck. I'd be breathless in the sudden quiet, and, having ceased my mincing and chopping, would stare blankly at the brushed sheen of the blade. Eventually, she would clear her throat or call out to say she was fine, then begin to move again, starting her rhythmic *ka-jug;* and only then could I go on with my cooking, the world of our house turning once more, wheeling through the black.

I wasn't cooking for my mother but for the rest of us. When she first moved downstairs she was still eating, though scantily, more just to taste what we were having than from any genuine desire for food. The point was simply to sit together at the kitchen table and array ourselves like a family again. My mother would gently set herself down in her customary chair near the stove. I sat across from her, my father and sister to my left and right, and crammed in the center was all the food I had made — a spicy codfish stew, say, or a casserole of gingery beef, dishes that in my youth she had prepared for us a hundred times.

It had been ten years since we'd all lived together in the house, which at fifteen I had left to attend boarding school in New Hampshire. My mother would sometimes point this out, by speaking of our present time as being "just like before Exeter," which surprised me, given how proud she always was that I was a graduate of the school.

My going to such a place was part of my mother's not so secret plan to change my character, which she worried was becoming too much like hers. I was clever and able enough, but without outside pressure I was readily given to sloth and vanity. The famous school — which none of us knew the first thing about — would prove my mettle. She was right, of course, and while I was there I would falter more than a few times, academically and otherwise. But I never thought that my leaving home then would ever be a problem for her, a private quarrel she would have even as her life waned.

Now her house was full again. My sister had just resigned from her job in New York City, and my father, who typically saw his psychiatric patients until eight or nine in the evening, was appearing in the driveway at four-thirty. I had been living at home for nearly a year and was in the final push of work on what would prove a dismal failure of a novel. When I wasn't struggling over my prose, I kept occupied with the things she usually did — the daily errands, the grocery shopping, the vacuuming and the cleaning, and, of course, all the cooking.

When I was six or seven years old, I used to watch my mother as she prepared our favorite meals. It was one of my daily pleasures. She shooed me away in the beginning, telling me that the kitchen wasn't my place, and adding, in her half-proud, half-deprecating way, that her kind of work would only serve to weaken me. "Go out and play with your friends," she'd snap in Korean, "or better yet, do your reading and homework." She knew that I had already done both, and that as the evening approached there was no place to go save her small and tidy kitchen, from which the clatter of her mixing bowls and pans would ring through the house.

I would enter the kitchen quietly and stand beside her, my chin lodging upon the point of her hip. Peering through the crook of her arm, I beheld the movements of her hands. For *kalbi*, she would take up a butchered short rib in her narrow hand, the flinty bone shaped like a section of an airplane wing and deeply embedded in gristle and flesh, and with the point of her knife cut so that the bone fell away, though not completely, leaving it connected to the meat by the barest opaque layer of tendon. Then she methodically butterflied the flesh, cutting and unfolding, repeating the action until the meat lay out on her board, glistening and ready for seasoning. She scored it diagonally, then sifted sugar into the crevices with her pinched fingers, gently rubbing in the crystals. The sugar would tenderize as well as sweeten the meat. She did this with each rib, and then set them all aside in a large shallow bowl. She minced a half-dozen cloves of garlic, a stub of ginger-root, sliced up a few scallions, and spread it all over the meat. She wiped her hands and took out a bottle of sesame oil, and, after pausing for a moment, streamed the dark oil in two swift circles around the bowl. After adding a few splashes of soy sauce, she thrust her hands in and kneaded the flesh, careful not to dislodge the bones. I asked her why it mattered that they remain connected. "The meat needs the bone nearby," she said, "to borrow its richness." She wiped her hands clean of the marinade, except for her little finger, which she would flick with her tongue from time to time, because she knew that the flavor of a good dish developed not at once but in stages.

Whenever I cook, I find myself working just as she would, readying the ingredients — a mash of garlic, a julienne of red peppers, fantails of shrimp — and piling them in little mounds about the cutting surface. My mother never left me any recipes, but this is how I learned to make her food, each dish coming not from a list or a card but from the aromatic spread of a board.

I've always thought it was particularly cruel that the cancer was in her stomach, and that for a long time at the end she couldn't eat. The last meal I made for her was on New Year's Eve, 1990. My sister suggested that instead of a rib roast or a bird, or the usual overflow of Korean food, we make all sorts of finger dishes that our mother might fancy and pick at.

We set the meal out on the glass coffee table in the family room.

I prepared a tray of smoked-salmon canapés, fried some Korean bean cakes, and made a few other dishes I thought she might enjoy. My sister supervised me, arranging the platters, and then with some pomp carried each dish in to our parents. Finally, I brought out a bottle of champagne in a bucket of ice. My mother had moved to the sofa and was sitting up, surveying the low table. "It looks pretty nice," she said. "I think I'm feeling hungry."

This made us all feel good, especially me, for I couldn't remember the last time she had felt any hunger or had eaten something I cooked. We began to eat. My mother picked up a piece of salmon toast and took a tiny corner in her mouth. She rolled it around for a moment and then pushed it out with the tip of her tongue, letting it fall back onto her plate. She swallowed hard, as if to quell a gag, then glanced up to see if we had noticed. Of course we all had. She attempted a bean cake, some cheese, and then a slice of fruit, but nothing was any use.

She nodded at me anyway, and said, "Oh, it's very good." But I was already feeling lost and I put down my plate abruptly, nearly shattering it on the thick glass. There was an ugly pause before my father asked me in a weary, gentle voice if anything was wrong, and I answered that it was nothing, it was the last night of a long year, and we were together, and I was simply relieved. At midnight, I poured out glasses of champagne, even one for my mother, who took a deep sip. Her manner grew playful and light, and I helped her shuffle to her mattress, and she lay down in the place where in a brief week she was dead.

My mother could whip up most anything, but during our first years of living in this country we ate only Korean foods. At my harangue-like behest, my mother set herself to learning how to cook exotic American dishes. Luckily, a kind neighbor, Mrs. Churchill, a tall, florid young woman with flaxen hair, taught my mother her most trusted recipes. Mrs. Churchill's two young sons, palish, weepy boys with identical crew cuts, always accompanied her, and though I liked them well enough, I would slip away from them after a few minutes, for I knew that the real action would be in the kitchen, where their mother was playing guide. Mrs. Churchill hailed from the state of Maine, where the finest Swedish meatballs and tuna casserole and angel food cake in America are made. She readily demonstrated certain techniques — how to layer wet sheets of pasta for a lasagna or whisk up a simple roux, for example. She often brought gift shoeboxes containing curious ingredients like dried oregano, instant yeast, and cream of mushroom soup. The two women, though at ease and jolly with each other, had difficulty communicating, and this was made worse by the often confusing terminology of Western cuisine ("corned beef," "deviled eggs"). Although I was just learning the language myself, I'd gladly play the interlocutor, jumping back and forth between their places at the counter, dipping my fingers into whatever sauce lay about.

I was an insistent child, and, being my mother's firstborn, much too prized. My mother could say no to me, and did often enough, but anyone who knew us — particularly my father and sister — could tell how much the denying pained her. And if I was overconscious of her indulgence even then, and suffered the rushing pangs of guilt that she could inflict upon me with the slightest wounded turn of her lip, I was too happily obtuse and venal to let her cease. She reminded me daily that I was her sole son, her reason for living, and that if she were to lose me, in either body or spirit, she wished that God would mercifully smite her, strike her down like a weak branch.

In the traditional fashion, she was the house accountant, the maid, the launderer, the disciplinarian, the driver, the secretary, and, of course, the cook. She was also my first basketball coach. In South Korea, where girls' high school basketball is a popular spectator sport, she had been a star, the point guard for the national high school team that once won the all-Asia championships. I learned this one Saturday during the summer, when I asked my father if he would go down to the schoolyard and shoot some baskets with me. I had just finished the fifth grade, and wanted desperately to make the middle school team the coming fall. He called for my mother and sister to come along. When we arrived, my sister immediately ran off to the swings, and I recall being annoyed that my mother wasn't following her. I dribbled clumsily around the key, on the verge of losing control of the ball, and flung a flat shot that caromed wildly off the rim. The ball bounced to my father, who took a few not so graceful dribbles and made an easy layup. He dribbled out and then drove to the hoop for a layup on the other side. He rebounded his shot and passed the ball to my mother, who had been watching us from the foul line. She turned from the basket and began heading the other way.

"*Um-mah,*" I cried at her, my exasperation already bubbling over, "the basket's over *here!*"

After a few steps she turned around, and from where the professional three-point line must be now, she effortlessly flipped the ball up in a two-handed set shot, its flight truer and higher than I'd witnessed from any boy or man. The ball arced cleanly into the hoop, stiffly popping the chain-link net. All afternoon, she rained in shot after shot, as my father and I scrambled after her.

When we got home from the playground, my mother showed me the photograph album of her team's championship run. For years I kept it in my room, on the same shelf that housed the scrapbooks I made of basketball stars, with magazine clippings of slick players like Bubbles Hawkins and Pistol Pete and George (the Iceman) Gervin.

It puzzled me how much she considered her own history to be immaterial, and if she never patently diminished herself, she was able to finesse a kind of self-removal by speaking of my father whenever she could. She zealously recounted his excellence as a student in medical school and reminded me, each night before I started my homework, of how hard he drove himself in his work to make a life for us. She said that because of his Asian face and imperfect English, he was "working two times the American doctors." I knew that she was building him up, buttressing him with both genuine admiration and her own brand of anxious braggadocio, and that her overarching concern was that I might fail to see him as she wished me to — in the most dawning light, his pose steadfast and solitary.

In the year before I left for Exeter, I became weary of her oft-repeated accounts of my father's success. I was a teenager, and so ever inclined to be dismissive and bitter toward anything that had to do with family and home. Often enough, my mother was the object of my derision. Suddenly, her life seemed so small to me. She was there, and sometimes, I thought, *always* there, as if she were confined to the four walls of our house. I would even complain about her cooking. Mostly, though, I was getting more and more impatient with the difficulty she encountered in doing everyday things. I was afraid for her. One day, we got into a terrible argument when she asked me to call the bank, to question a discrepancy she had discovered in the monthly statement. I asked her why she couldn't call herself. I was stupid and brutal, and I knew exactly how to wound her.

"Whom do I talk to?" she said. She would mostly speak to me in Korean, and I would answer in English.

"The bank manager, who else?"

"What do I say?"

"Whatever you want to say."

"Don't speak to me like that!" she cried.

"It's just that you should be able to do it yourself," I said.

"You know how I feel about this!"

"Well, maybe then you should consider it *practice*," I answered lightly, using the Korean word to make sure she understood.

Her face blanched, and her neck suddenly became rigid, as if I were throttling her. She nearly struck me right then, but instead she bit her lip and ran upstairs. I followed her, pleading for forgiveness at her door. But it was the one time in our life that I couldn't convince her, melt her resolve with the blandishments of a spoiled son.

When my mother was feeling strong enough, or was in particularly good spirits, she would roll her machine into the kitchen and sit at the table and watch me work. She wore pajamas day and night, mostly old pairs of mine.

She said, "I can't tell, what are you making?"

"*Mahn-doo* filling."

"You didn't salt the cabbage and squash."

"Was I supposed to?"

"Of course. Look, it's too wet. Now the skins will get soggy before you can fry them."

"What should I do?"

"It's too late. Maybe it'll be OK if you work quickly. Why didn't you ask me?"

"You were finally sleeping."

"You should have woken me."

"No way."

She sighed, as deeply as her weary lungs would allow.

"I don't know how you were going to make it without me."

"I don't know, either. I'll remember the salt next time."

"You better. And not too much."

We often talked like this, our tone decidedly matter-of-fact, chin up, just this side of being able to bear it. Once, while inspecting a potato fritter batter I was making, she asked me if she had ever done anything that I wished she hadn't done. I thought for a moment, and told her no. In the next breath, she wondered aloud if it was right of her to have let me go to Exeter, to live away from the house while I was so young. She tested the batter's thickness with her finger and called for more flour. Then she asked if, given a choice, I would go to Exeter again.

I wasn't sure what she was getting at, and I told her that I couldn't be certain, but probably yes, I would. She snorted at this and said it was my leaving home that had once so troubled our relationship. "Remember how I had so much difficulty talking to you? Remember?"

She believed back then that I had found her more and more ignorant each time I came home. She said she never blamed me, for this was the way she knew it would be with my wonderful new education. Nothing I could say seemed to quell the notion. But I knew that the problem wasn't simply the *education;* the first time I saw her again after starting school, barely six weeks later, when she and my father visited me on Parents Day, she had already grown nervous and distant. After the usual campus events, we had gone to the motel where they were staying in a nearby town and sat on the beds in our room. She seemed to sneak looks at me, as though I might discover a horrible new truth if our eyes should meet.

My own secret feeling was that I had missed my parents greatly, my mother especially, and much more than I had anticipated. I couldn't tell them that these first weeks were a mere blur to me, that I felt completely overwhelmed by all the studies and my much brighter friends and the thousand irritating details of living alone, and that I had really learned nothing, save perhaps how to put on a necktie while sprinting to class. I felt as if I had plunged too deep into the world, which, to my great horror, was much larger than I had ever imagined.

I welcomed the lull of the motel room. My father and I had nearly dozed off when my mother jumped up excitedly, murmured how stupid she was, and hurried to the closet by the door. She pulled out our old metal cooler and dragged it between the beds. She lifted the top and began unpacking plastic containers, and I thought she would never stop. One after the other they came out, each with a dish that traveled well — a salted stewed meat, rolls of Korean-style sushi. I opened a container of radish kimchi and suddenly the room bloomed with its odor, and I reveled in the very peculiar sensation (which perhaps only true kimchi lovers know) of simultaneously drooling and gagging as I breathed it all in. For the next few minutes, they watched me eat. I'm not certain that I was even hungry. But after weeks of pork parmigiana and chicken patties and wax beans, I suddenly realized that I had lost all the savor in my life. And it seemed I couldn't get enough of it back. I ate and I ate, so much and so fast that I actually went to the bathroom and vomited. I came out dizzy and sated with the phantom warmth of my binge.

And beneath the face of her worry, I thought, my mother was smiling.

From that day, my mother prepared a certain meal to welcome me home. It was always the same. Even as I rode the school's shuttle bus from Exeter to Logan airport, I could already see the exact arrangement of my mother's table.

I knew that we would eat in the kitchen, the table brimming with plates. There was the *kalbi*, of course, broiled or grilled depending on the season. Leaf lettuce, to wrap the meat with. Bowls of garlicky clam broth with miso and tofu and fresh spinach. Shavings of cod dusted in flour and then dipped in egg wash and fried. Glass noodles with onions and shiitake. Scallion-and-hot-pepper pancakes. Chilled steamed shrimp. Seasoned salads of bean sprouts, spinach, and white radish. Crispy squares of seaweed. Steamed rice with barley and red beans. Homemade kimchi. It was all there — the old flavors I knew, the beautiful salt, the sweet, the excellent taste.

After the meal, my father and I talked about school, but I could never say enough for it to make any sense. My father would often recall his high school principal, who had gone to England to study the methods and traditions of the public schools, and regaled students with stories of the great Eton man. My mother sat with us, paring fruit, not saying a word but taking everything in. When it was time to go to bed, my father said good night first. I usually watched television until the early morning. My mother would sit with me for an hour or two, perhaps until she was accustomed to me again, and only then would she kiss me and head upstairs to sleep.

During the following days, it was always the cooking that started our conversations. She'd hold an inquest over the cold leftovers we ate at lunch, discussing each dish in terms of its balance of flavors or what might have been prepared differently. But mostly I begged her to leave the dishes alone. I wish I had paid more attention. After her death, when my father and I were the only ones left in the house, drifting through the rooms like ghosts, I sometimes tried to make that meal for him. Though it was too much for two, I made each dish anyway, taking as much care as I could. But nothing turned out quite right — not the color, not the smell. At the table, neither of us said much of anything. And we had to eat the food for days.

I remember washing rice in the kitchen one day and my mother's saying in English, from her usual seat, "I made a big mistake."

"About Exeter?"

"Yes. I made a big mistake. You should be with us for that time. I should never let you go there."

"So why did you?" I said.

"Because I didn't know I was going to die."

I let her words pass. For the first time in her life, she was letting herself speak her full mind, so what else could I do?

"But you know what?" she spoke up. "It was better for you. If you stayed home, you would not like me so much now."

I suggested that maybe I would like her even more.

She shook her head. "Impossible."

Sometimes I still think about what she said, about having made a mistake. I would have left home for college, that was never in doubt, but those years I was away at boarding school grew more precious to her as her illness progressed. After many months of exhaustion and pain and the haze of the drugs, I thought that her mind was beginning to fade, for more and more it seemed that she was seeing me again as her fifteen-year-old boy, the one she had dropped off in New Hampshire on a cloudy September afternoon.

I remember the first person I met, another new student, named Zack, who walked to the welcome picnic with me. I had planned to eat with my parents — my mother had brought a coolerful of food even that first day — but I learned of the cookout and told her that I should probably go. I wanted to go, of course. I was excited, and no doubt fearful and nervous, and I must have thought I was only thinking ahead. She agreed wholeheartedly, saying I certainly should. I walked them to the car, and perhaps I hugged them, before saying goodbye. One day, after she died, my father told me what happened on the long drive home to Syracuse.

He was driving the car, looking straight ahead. Traffic was light on the Massachusetts Turnpike, and the sky was nearly dark. They had driven for more than two hours and had not yet spoken a word. He then heard a strange sound from her, a kind of muffled chewing noise, as if something inside her were grinding its way out.

"So, what's the matter?" he said, trying to keep an edge to his voice.

She looked at him with her ashen face and she burst into tears. He began to cry himself, and pulled the car over onto the narrow shoulder of the turnpike, where they stayed for the next half hour or so, the blank-faced cars droning by them in the cold, onrushing night.

Every once in a while, when I think of her, I'm driving alone somewhere on the highway. In the twilight, I see their car off to the side, a blue Olds coupe with a landau top, and as I pass them by I look back in the mirror and I see them again, the two figures huddling together in the front seat. Are they sleeping? Or kissing? Are they all right?

JAMES ALAN McPHERSON

Crabcakes

FROM DOUBLETAKE

SEVERAL WEEKS AFTER the call from Elizabeth McIntosh, and my response to it, the letter from Mr. Herbert Butler arrives.

Dear Mr. McPherson,
I am doing fine. I want to thank you for your card, letter and kindness during (my) the loss of my beloved Channie. She is with the Lord now . . .

Mr. Butler has crossed out the initial "my," his personal claim to Mrs. Channie Washington, and has instead generalized her death into a significance greater than his own loss.

His use of "the" implies acceptance.

I am glad that Mr. Butler is in this frame of mind. I am glad that he is open to acceptance of loss. I have clear fee simple in the house he now occupies. Mr. Butler was never the official tenant. Mrs. Washington was the person who sent the monthly rent. Although she never signed an agreement, there existed an essential understanding between the two of us. Mr. Butler was always in the background of our private, unwritten contract, as he was always in the background of her monthly letters to me. I have no bond with him.

I have decided to sell the house. I now intend to take the profits I have been avoiding all these years, and be rid of my last connection with Baltimore. A friend in Washington, D.C., has already put me in contact with a real estate agent in Baltimore, and this woman has already made an appointment to see me. I have already begun preparing, by the time his letter arrives, just what I will say to Mr.

Butler: For almost eighteen years, I have not made one cent of profit on this house. I have carried it, almost on my back, at great loss. You must remember that when I purchased this house back in 1976, I lowered the rent to eighty-six dollars a month. Over the years, I have raised it only enough to cover the rise in property taxes. After seventeen years, the rent is still only two hundred dollars a month. Repairs, fire insurance, ground rents — all these additional expenses I have paid for, over all these years, out of my own pocket. Now I am tired of, and can no longer afford, so many scattered responsibilities. I must cut my losses now and try to consolidate. You, Mr. Butler, will have to go. But there are homes for senior citizens, with nurses on call and with organized activities for elderly people. Meals will be regular, healthy, and free. I have already checked into them for you. There will be a private telephone by each bed, free heat and electricity, family and visitors can come and go freely at almost any hour. In such well-cared-for places, the furnaces always work in winter. Mr. Butler, you will be more comfortable, and maybe happy, in such a new home. Now, in this old place, you have nothing but memories to comfort you, or to haunt you. The change I am suggesting is probably, when you really think about it, a good thing. You should take some time and think carefully about it, Mr. Butler. I am not setting a deadline for you to go.

My plan now is to work on this speech and make it right.

It is essential that Mr. Butler understand my point of view. I am no longer affluent enough, or arrogant enough, to do for anyone else what the state could more easily afford to do. I do not plan to be ruthless. I will only disclose my intentions to Mr. Butler. The real estate agent, Ms. Gayle Wilson, will handle the hard part. As soon as she finds a buyer, she can handle the eviction. I will not have to get involved. No one could possibly blame me. I have already done more than enough for them. Their needs have become infinite, while my own surplus has shrunk. Mr. Butler will have to see the motif in my narration. It is the old story. Perhaps Mrs. Washington's death was, paradoxically, heaven-sent to bring the story to its end. Both Mr. Butler and I agree that she must be in heaven now. It may well be that the end her death brought to the story was her final letter to me.

Over close to eighteen years, I calculate, Mrs. Washington must have sent me almost 208 letters with her rent checks.

I remember some of them.

I go through the boxes of letters received this year and find several from her. I inspect them and see now, for the first time, that the very last letter, sent the first week in this month, is not even in her handwriting. I sense this, but take care to check this last letter against the handwriting in the one that arrived with the September rent. This one is in Mrs. Washington's hand. It is her uneven writing, her flow of sentences without periods. I read it carefully and notice something unfamiliar. She has written "Dear James Family" instead of her usual "Dear James and Family." Also, there is a line that is completely new, something I have never seen before in any of her monthly letters. This new line is: "I will close my letter but not our love . . ." This new language seems strange. It suggests an intimacy that has never existed between us. It also suggests a finality that frightens me.

Mrs. Washington seemed to have known, back in early September, that she was about to die.

But I dismiss this thought. Besides, her profession of unending love is inappropriate. Mrs. Washington did not know me in that way. She knew only a few facts about my life. She knew that I once lived on Barclay Street in Baltimore, two blocks away from the house in which she lived. She knew that I made my living as a teacher. She knew that I was married. She knew that I moved from Baltimore to Virginia, and she knew that after two years I moved to New Haven. She knew that I moved back to Virginia for two more years. And she knew that I moved then to Iowa. Her monthly rent checks and letters followed me to these new addresses. I never wrote back to her and offered any more details about my life. I did visit her in Baltimore from time to time, to see about her and the needs of the house. But for almost eighteen years the facts of my own life have been kept from her, while the facts of her life have been hidden from me by the standard phrases in her monthly letters. These phrases have not varied in 208 months: "Everything

is fine." "Thank the Good Lord." "May God bless you all." "May
God be with you all." "Thank the Good Lord For every thing." I
wonder what the new owner of the house would think about the
letters wrapped around her monthly rent checks, if Mrs. Washington were still alive to write them. Then I think about its future sale.
Then I begin to remember the sweating, hungry heat of the
crowd.
    I begin to remember.
    I begin to imagine and remember.

An Old Portrait in Black and White, July 1976

Two elderly black people, a man and a woman, sit on a porch in
a tarnished metal swing. It is the porch of a rundown red-brick
row house. The swing, under their weight, is straining against the
rusty chains suspending it and swaying back and forth. The two
people are sitting in the swing on the porch of 3114 Barclay Street
in Baltimore. It is a weekday, but they seem dressed in their Sunday
best. The woman wears a white necklace and matching white
earbobs. She is smiling as if it were indeed Sunday morning and
she is lost in the sermon of a church. An otherworldly serenity, or
perhaps a childish inability to appreciate finely textured reality, is
in her smile. She looks wide-eyed from behind large spectator
eyeglasses. But the man looks, from a distance, sheepish and
embarrassed. He wears a gray touring cap pulled down close to his
eyes. His belly rises up from behind his belt. There is a this-worldly
awareness in his fat brown face. Other people, white, move
through and out of the screen door of the house. They slide
behind the couple on the swing, jostling windows, knocking on the
fragile woodframes, scraping new rednesses into the worn bricks.
Others move up and down the gray concrete steps or mill about
on the sidewalk. A white auctioneer is standing on the top cement
step speaking rapidly and abstractedly to all questioning newcomers. His dead eyes always focus on a space above their heads. He
has the ritual assurance, the slow, sure movements, of a priest.
Parked and double-parked along Barclay Street, glistening in the
wet, hot morning sunlight, are tail-fin Cadillacs, wide-reared
Buicks, Oldsmobiles, Fords, and Chevrolets — the nests of middle-

class army ants. From a distance, from across Barclay Street, the entire scene, with the house at its center, seems too restless to be real life. It looks speeded up in time, like an animated cartoon. Framed as the slow-moving backdrop of such relentless restlessness, the two black people seem frozen in time. They look like stage props, brought by mistake onto the wrong movie set. An awareness of this error seems to be in the old man's face. The old woman seems to see secret amusements in the show. As the priestly auctioneer opens the bidding, time seems to flow backward, as if a hidden director now realizes his mistake in the staging of the scene. *This is not Barclay Street,* something is reminding. It is a public square in Virginia, South Carolina, Georgia. It is 1676, 1776, 1876, *not* 1976. The relentlessness of the ritual has only temporarily sucked open black holes into the flow of time, opening a portal into a finished past that has come alive again and oozed out and forward, into the future. Soon it will move back to where it was freeze-framed dead. Something in the air assures this coming correction of the scenery. This is why the two black people are so passive. This is why the white auctioneer seems so abstracted. The milling crowd, too, is restless for correction. The weight of ritual has pushed their roles too far back in time. *The portal into the past must close.* All — the crowd included — have found unholy meaning in the slipshod staging of this moment. All are looking from far back into what will be and from the here and now back on what was only *then* inevitable. The reflections in the life-linked mirror belie all notions of age and elevation and change. Time is not a circle. What was was, before *was* was? — the answer to the puzzle *should not be* "is." No matter that in Virginia, South Carolina, and Georgia such people always wore their best clothes, *someone,* at a distance from the crowd, thinks. This is not Virginia or Georgia or South Carolina. It is 1976. It is the celebration of the Bicentennial. *Someone* moves from the other side of Barclay Street and through the lines of cars and into the crowd. He moves close just as the auctioneer opens the bidding. It is anger that now makes his voice heard above all the others. It is arrogance, too, *but also something else,* that causes him to make a stand within the circling centuries on the hot morning sidewalk. *What was that thing? What became of that something else?* The white auctioneer chants his mass. It is anger, and also arrogance, that causes *someone* to match each bid and raise by five hundred dollars. The blood sport flowing through the crowd begins to slow and ebb. Its forward motion is arrested by a single collective thought: this *must* be some trick, some sly rhetoric left over from the public bluster of the past decade. Time can prove promiscuous on such hot days. *But what if there is no bluff and the price keeps rising?* The collective voice falls into weak and individualized efforts at continuing combat. The heat in their blood begins to flow backward, into the past, while time hurries forward first to apologize and then to make its correction. The white auctioneer points disinterestedly and mouths the sacred incantation: "*Sold!*" The circle breaks. The black hole closes. The mirror looking out and in from hell is cracked. Time flows like clockwork, forward, while the crowd mills. Those who are most nimble speed off first in their cars toward the next house on the list. The auctioneer holds his hand out for a cash deposit. The balance is to be secured by mortgage in three days. He keeps his hand held out, like a kindly priest reclaiming the chalice from a slow communicant. *This is my body. This is my blood.* Now someone walks up onto the porch and kisses the forehead of the old black woman on the swing. She says, *someone remembers now* that she said, "You must be from up *there!*" The woman, close up, looks even more serene and on vacation from this world. The old man seems ashamed. But the woman seems to be smiling for both of them. Someone says to her, *not to him,* "You won't have to move now. You can live here for as long as you want. No matter what you are paying now, the new rent will be eighty-six dollars a month." The view, facing Barclay Street from the old porch, is now unobstructed. The last of the wide-reared cars, the habitats of army ants, are leaving. It is a wet, hot summer morning in Baltimore, July 1976. The auctioneer, in his short-sleeved shirt, is sweating while he waits on the top cement step, away from the comfort of the porch.

I recollect now that day and that time.

It was not a public square in Virginia, South Carolina, or Georgia, in any of the other centuries. It was Baltimore, in 1976. The time moved forward then, not backward. Nor did it circle round. The only time made sacred was the three days' deadline for payment imposed under force of law by the auctioneer. The news was not about ships reaching ports with fresh slave stock. It was about inflation, gasoline shortages. It was about oil-rich Arabs buying up the Sea Islands. It was about money and the lack of it and the fear of everything that made people afraid. I do not like to remember that time.

But while I am planning my trip, I remember the good things that I liked.

I liked Baltimore in summers and in winters. I liked the old harbor, the way it was before it was gentrified with shops and lights for the benefit of tourists. I liked to watch the boats and ships out on the water. I liked the old, worn bricks in certain streets, the ancient buildings, the squares with their statues, and the abundance of seafood from Chesapeake Bay. These aspects of Baltimore remind me of Savannah, where I grew up. There is a certain little square, I think on Monument Street in Baltimore, with a metal statue and cobblestones that reminds me of Pulaski Square in Savannah. When I lived in Baltimore, I liked to walk through the neighborhoods and watch people sitting on the steps of their narrow row houses to escape the summer heat. On hot summer mornings, in both cities, people wash down the steps of their houses and let them dry in the hot sunlight. The heat in both cities, because of their proximity to water, is humid and wet. People in Baltimore, like those in Savannah, accept sweat as an unfortunate incident of summer. In both cities, the early mornings and the early evenings are the best times for walking. People in both places are most polite during those cool and special times of the day.

The soul of Baltimore, for me, is the old Lexington Market on Lexington and Eutaw streets. It is a kind of warehouse off the downtown section that is crowded with little shops and concession stands, many of them selling crabcakes and other seafood. In this almost open-air market, all sections of Baltimore meet and breathe in common the moist aromas of fresh shrimp, oysters, crabs, every possible Atlantic Ocean fish, a variety of fruits, vegetables, and fresh meats. I remember oyster bars, where people stand and eat raw oysters after spicing them with condiments. I remember the refrigerated display cases featuring, among many other choices, row after row of uncooked crabcakes. These are a very special delicacy, made Maryland style. The basic recipe is a mixture of crabmeat (fresh lump, blue, backfin, or special) and eggs, bread crumbs, Worcestershire sauce, fresh parsley, mayonnaise, baking powder, salt, and a variety of spices. This mixture, after being caked in the bread crumbs, is deep-fat fried, drained, and served while moist and hot and brown. All crabcakes are good, but Maryland crabcakes have special ingredients, or spices, not found in those crabcakes made according to the recipes of other regions.

Unlike in Savannah, in Baltimore they have soft, white, wet, clinging snow during the winter months. It seldom gets cold enough for the snow to freeze, so it remains white and clear and fluffy in the bright winter sunlight. I liked that. I liked the way the white, sun-melting snow would slide lazily and waterily off the skeletal branches of high-reaching trees and plop wetly on anything beneath the boughs. In Savannah, during the winter months, we got only cold rain. Still, I did not mind walking in it, as long as I was warm and dry and walking very quickly. I consider the number eighty-six lucky for me. It was the number of my old newspaper route, my very first job, when I was a boy in Savannah. I used to walk that route six days a week, in the sweaty summer heat and in the cold winter rains, with my papers. I used to take a personal interest in the lives and health of all my customers along that route. I used to be sympathetic to their excuses for not having the money to pay their paper bills. I tried my best to have compassion for them. I believed, then, that everything would eventually even out.

I have always considered eighty-six my lucky number.

The Natural Facts of Death and Life in Baltimore, November 1993

I fly from Iowa into New York, then rent a car at the Newark airport, in order to avoid the traffic of the city, and drive south on Interstate 95. It is late fall in the East, and all the bright, crisp, red and brown and green and gold colors have bled from the sparse stretches of trees lining the interstate. The last brown leaves are wilting and falling in the warm morning breezes, and the cars around me seem to be navigating at unnatural speeds, all heading homeward from the sadness of the fall. Then I realize that the pace of eastern interstate traffic is too fast for my driving skills, which have become settled now into the slow and easy habits of country roads. Neither do I have, any longer, personal investments in the landscape. I can no longer remember, or care about, where I was going to, or where I was returning from, when I parked at the official rest stops in New Jersey, Pennsylvania, Delaware, on my way up and down this road. My polarities have now become strictly east and west.

I am told, when I arrive at the office, that my own agent, Ms. Gayle Wilson, has been detained. While I wait for her, I listen to an elderly, extremely muscular black man who is flirting with the young receptionist at her desk. He has just retired, and is now about to close on a house, his first in a lifetime of working. He talks about the kindness of the Jewish woman who has sold it to him. He brags about the new appliances he has purchased. I think, while I listen to him talk, This is what our struggle has been about all along. That man, this late in his life, has become renewed by the ethic that exists in ownership. This has always been the certified way people show that they have moved up in life. It is what the society offers, and it is enough for most people. *What did I have against it all these years?* The man is joyous, flirting with the young black woman. He is no longer a laborer. He is now an owner. He is now her equal. He now has a house, new appliances, and is on the lookout for a companion who would want to share the castle of his dreams. *It has always been as simple as that.* I have not observed the styles of black people in many years. The kindly flirtation between the two of them reminds me of something familiar that I have almost forgotten. It seems to be something about language being secondary to the way it is used. The forgotten thing is about the nuances of sounds that only employ words as ballast for the flight of pitch and intonation. It is the pitch and the intonation that carry *meaning.* I had forgotten this.

Ms. Gayle Wilson, my agent, comes into the office. She is a very tall, very attractive black woman in formal dress. "I've just come from a funeral at my church," she tells me. "It was a close friend who died and I was an usher." We sit down and get to business. She hands me her brochure. It says she is active in the affairs of her church, her community, and in the organizations related to her business. She tells me, "I know of someone who is buying up houses out in that area. We can probably make a sale today. I'll call him up right now." She picks up her telephone, dials a number, and the ringing is answered immediately. She says, "Mr. Lee, I told you about that house coming up for sale out on Barclay? The owner is in my office right now. Good. Can you meet us over there in half an hour? Fine." She hangs up and says to me, "I think Mr. Lee will buy the house from you right away. He's a speculator. He buys up old houses and then fixes them for resale. He said he would meet us over there in half an hour."

She leaves the office to tell the receptionist where we will be.

A car crash calls my attention to the busy street outside the plate-glass window of Ms. Wilson's office. Other people, including Ms. Wilson, rush out the front door. A speeding car has sideswiped another car, and this car has been knocked off the street, across the sidewalk and the narrow lawn, and into the brown wooden fence surrounding the real estate office. The driver's side of the car has caved in. The windshield glass is broken, cracked into white webs. Some men, white passersby and store clerks, are trying to ease the passenger out of the collapsed car. The passenger is an elderly woman, white, who seems to be in a daze. She wobbles like a rubber doll as they handle her. Her thin, vanilla-white hair is scattered on her head. I cannot see any blood. But the car seems totaled.

It is only an accident on the busy suburban street. But I watch the men crowd around the old woman. More and more of them come. There seems to be among them a desperate hunger to be helpful. The men, in their numbers, seem to be trying to make up for something. Although all their efforts are not needed, more and more men come from the service station across the street to push the car away from the wooden fence. There seems to be among them almost a lust for participation in some kindly, communal action.

Ms. Gayle Wilson comes back into her office.

I tell her that I think, now, that it would be inappropriate for her and Mr. Lee to meet me at the house. I say that first I must pay my respects to Mr. Butler.

Ms. Wilson agrees that this is the proper thing. She talks about the work she does in her church, about her love for rhyming poetry, about this afternoon's funeral, about the accident outside. We watch the crowd of men pushing the caved-in car away from the wooden fence, out of our view from the office window. The old woman has already been taken away. There has not been the sound of a siren or the lights of an ambulance. I assume that the crowd of men has grabbed this opportunity, too.

Ms. Wilson writes out detailed directions for my drive back into the city and over to Barclay Street.

I promise to call her from Iowa in a few days.

Barclay is a right turn off Thirty-third Street, one block before Greenmount. You are careful to not look at the house on the corner you once rented. You drive straight to 3114, two blocks to the right of Thirty-third, and park. The street is making a resurgence. There is a new neighborhood store, and several of the houses have been refurbished and are up for sale. Careful sanding has restored old blood to their red bricks. They seem freshly painted, too, waiting confidently for occupants. This seems to you a good sign. Life here is poised for movement, when spring comes. But there is the same rusty, white-spotted swing on the porch at 3114 Barclay. It is empty, speckled with peeling paint, and seems ancient. You do not pause to look at it. You knock, and a young black man opens the door. He invites you into the overwarm living room. Mr. Butler sits in his usual place: to the right of the door, in his old armchair, against the window. He wears his gray touring cap. He looks tired and old. His voice is only a croak. You shake his hand but do not hold his hand, or look long at him. Mr. Butler says to the young man, "This is the landlord. He came here from Iowa." The young man, who has resumed his place on the sofa, answers, "Yes, sir." He is sitting in Mrs. Washington's place at the right end of the sofa, almost side by side with Mr. Butler. The television is turned to a late afternoon game show. The room is overwarm and dusty, but still retains a feeling that is familiar.

The young man's name is Eric. He seems to be about sixteen or seventeen.

You express your sympathies to Mr. Butler and to Eric. Eric keeps nodding and saying to you "Yes, sir." You do not want this formality.

You miss Mrs. Washington's otherworldly good cheer. You miss her smile. You miss her saying "The landlord come. Yes *indeed!* He come all the way from *Ioway!* Thank the Good Lord. Yes, yes in*deed!*" But her voice does not come except in memory. Eric says, "My daddy left my mama when I was born. My mama is Elizabeth McIntosh, my Aunt Channie's niece. Aunt Channie raised me while my mama worked. She was mama, daddy, aunt, uncle, parents, and grandparents to me. Yes, sir. I miss her. I come over here every evening and sit with Mr. Herbert. I don't know how he lives, sir, now that my Aunt Channie is gone."

You ask Eric if you can inspect the house. Eric asks Mr. Butler for his permission. The old man nods from his chair. Eric leads the tour. The small box of a basement contains only an old refrigerator and the ancient, red-rusted furnace. It is the old friend you have been nursing over all these years. It is so old it embarrasses you. "Why did she never mention the true condition of the furnace?" you ask Eric. He says, "My Aunt Channie didn't like to throw away nothing that could be fixed, sir. And she never liked to bother nobody. I gave her that refrigerator over there myself, because her old one was so bad." He leads you back up the loose, sagging basement steps to the dining room, where he shows you the cot where Mr. Butler sleeps. He is much too weak, Eric says, to climb the steps to the second floor. Eric leads the way up them. The top floor has three bedrooms and a bath. One of the bedrooms is obviously used by an occasional boarder. Another, Eric tells you, remains empty and ready as a place for guests. For an instant, this seems to you a very extravagant gesture for a person in poverty. Then you recollect the dusty picture of Jesus, about to knock, on the wall above the television. Here you almost laugh. Eric opens, and closes very quickly, the door to Mrs. Washington's bedroom. In the brief illumination of light, you can see her bed, made up, with its pillow in place, waiting. All of the ceilings in the rooms upstairs are cracked and peeling. You ask Eric why she never asked for repairs. He says, again, that she did not like to bother anybody with her problems. He says "sir" once more. The two of you go downstairs again, through the kitchen, and out onto the back porch. Its boards are broken and split. The wood is soft from age and weather. Eric says that Mr. Butler fell recently here. The twisted old tree still bends over the porch at an ugly angle, as if poised to grow confidently through the broken wooden porch and into the house. The bent tree, with its roots encased in concrete, seems to be nature's revenge on the illusory order of city life. You suddenly say to Eric, "Please don't keep calling me sir." He says, "But I *always* say sir to older people."

This also reminds you of something old.

Elizabeth McIntosh, Eric's mother, comes into the house then. Mrs. Washington was her mother's sister, she tells you. She talks freely about her Aunt Channie's life. Mrs. Washington had been married once, but had no children. She had come to Baltimore from a rural community in South Carolina. She had worked as a short-order cook in several restaurants around the city, until bad health caused her to retire. She was, of course, a churchwoman. "She loved you," Elizabeth says. "She considered you part of the family. She always wrote a letter to you to send with the rent check. Even when she was sick in bed, she insisted on dictating the letters to me. She kept saying, 'You *have* to write it. I *always* send a letter with my check.'"

You ask Elizabeth to send you, in Iowa, a copy of Mrs. Washington's funeral program.

You tell Mr. Butler, watching from his armchair, that everything will be fine.

You call Eric back to the back porch and tell him that the needed repairs will be made.

Eric says, "Yes, sir."

When you go back into the living room, you sit in Mrs. Washington's place on the sofa, before Eric can get to it. You sit there. You look at the game show on the television, and at the picture on the wall behind it. You ask Elizabeth whether Mrs. Washington ever prayed.

"Almost every hour of every day," Elizabeth answers.

You still sit there. You watch a few minutes of television with Mr. Butler. Then, for some reason, you ask the three of them to pray for you.

Then you want to see again, as quickly as possible, the brown stubble left, after fall harvest, in the rolling, open fields of Iowa.

But you still drive around the area until the streets begin to connect again in your memory. You are trying hard now to remember the other things you still have to do. You will have to find a short way back to the interstate, heading north. While driving, you look for your favorite bookstore on Greenmount. It is gone. So is the movie theater that was once several doors away. So is the Chinese restaurant. But the Ennoch Pratt Library branch on Thirty-third and Barclay is still there. You decide that you do not have time to drive past the stadium. You will have to hurry, to better negotiate the early evening traffic collecting near Interstate 95, heading north. But you do stop, impulsively, at the liquor store on Greenmount, not for any purchase but just to see another familiar place. Old memories are returning now. But the yelling Jewish owners are gone. The new owners seem to be Koreans. Black clerks still do the busywork.

Now the connection you have been waiting for is suddenly made. You can now remember the route from here to the Lexington Market. You can remember the names of streets from here to there. Your plan now is to get some crabcakes and find some way to keep them fresh enough to survive the trip back to Iowa. You will need ice and a plastic cooler. And you will need luck in shipping the plastic cooler on two different flights. There is an element of madness in this plan, but it also contains a certain boldness that you have not felt in many years. You determine to do it.

To get to the Lexington Market from Greenmount Avenue, you must turn left onto Thirty-third Street and head south. At the point where Thirty-third intersects St. Paul, you should take another left. The buildings and campuslands of Johns Hopkins should be in the distance as you turn left onto St. Paul. You should follow St. Paul Street south all the way downtown, pass the more stately row houses on both left and right, pass the shops and bars and restaurants near North Avenue, the mostly black section of St. Paul, pass Penn Station, and go all the way to the traffic circle on Monument Street, the old street with cobblestones and a bronze statue of Washington at the center of the circle, like those they have in the squares in Savannah. The other landmark here is the Walters Gallery. You should pass Monument Street and keep going down St. Paul. You are now approaching the downtown section of Baltimore. Here the buildings become taller and newer. The traffic becomes much more concentrated and the people walk with much greater purpose. On your left, just off the corner of Charles Street, should be the old building where your painter friend has a loft. Just beyond Charles, the buildings become mostly commercial. The lights of the harbor should be invisible in the distance, farther down St. Paul. On Franklin Street, you should take a right. Several blocks down, the main branch of the Ennoch Pratt Library should appear on your left. Go several blocks beyond the Ennoch Pratt, then turn left onto Eutaw. This is near the street of the Lexington Market. Find parking wherever you can.

The Threat of Downsizing at the Soul of the City

We find that the market has not changed that much after all these years. There are now some upscale boutiques and displays, and Korean families now run some of the produce stands and shops. But the old oyster bars are still there, as are the high, narrow tables where people add condiments to their oysters and stand while eating them raw. We breathe in the same familiar smells of fresh fish, flowers, fruits, vegetables, and raw meats. We see the same familiar mixture of people from all segments of the city, blending one accord of accents into the commercial mass.

All of the seafood stands display crabcakes. Rather than waste time, we decide on those displayed in the showcase of just one stand. The most appealing, and the most expensive, are the lump crabcakes, made up in round, crumb-coated balls. They swell up out of their trays like overfed bellies. The other crabcakes on display — backfin, special, regular — are less expensive and therefore less attractive. The black woman standing beside us is also deciding. She is partial to the lumps. "Them's the best ones," she says. "They taste best just out the pan. But all these other crabcakes is just as good." We decide on two lump crabcakes, to be eaten now, and a dozen regulars packed in ice to go.

Behind the counter of the stand, three black teenage boys in white aprons and white paper hats are filling orders. Behind them, at the stove, an elderly black woman lowers and raises webbed metal trays of crabcakes and French fries into deep frying pits of hot bubbling oil. Around the counter people lean, as if at communion, waiting for their hot orders to come. The woman and the boys seem to us essential to the operation. They set the standard of taste. The owner, or the manager, a white man, hovers near the cash register, giving orders in an unfamiliar accent. Then we remember that this is Baltimore, where the musical pitch of the South meets and smothers the gruffness of Germanic habits. We are savvy enough to say that we are a tourist from out in Iowa, have heard good things about Maryland crabcakes, and want to take a dozen of them back home. We will need a dozen of the regulars, uncooked and packed in ice, to go, and two of the lump, cooked to eat now. The boy who takes our order communicates the problem to the owner. He comes up to the counter and says, "There ain't no way you can keep them fresh, even in ice, if you're drivin' such a distance." We respond that we are flying out of New York tomorrow afternoon, and that only enough ice is needed to keep the crabcakes fresh long enough, this evening, to drive into New York. There they can be frozen in the apartment of a friend. From New York, tomorrow, it will only be a four-hour flight to Iowa. Much like the mail. As an incentive, we add that people in Iowa seldom taste fresh Maryland crabcakes and that a desire to share a delicacy is at the basis of this gift. But in order to remain a gift, we say, it is essential that the crabcakes keep moving. If they lose refrigeration before New York, they will have to be eaten there. They will then become a simple meal. But if they should survive the trip into the city, and are frozen quickly, and then, tomorrow, survive again the two separate flights into Iowa — if the gift keeps moving at the same speed as it thaws — then, with luck, it can be shared with friends in Iowa tomorrow evening. Our plan, we say, is to ensure that some good part of Maryland will take up residence in the memories of friends in Iowa. We say again: It is essential that the gift keep moving. If it stops moving at any point before it can be given, the crabcakes will thaw quickly and lose the basic intention of their identity. They *must*, therefore, be shared with Iowa friends to remain essentially what they are. But to ensure this, they must be kept moving. Once they stop moving, short of their goal, they will become just another meal. The action of the original intention will have then been defeated. To avoid this fate for them, we *must* have lots of ice. Fresh ice, if it is needed, might be found along the interstate heading back to Newark. We want now to risk this chance.

The manager becomes suspicious that we are mad. But we also

sense that it is his bottom-line business to sell. Our request, or our outlandish demand, upsets the Teutonic order of his scale of values. To him, and to his black workers, the calculation of air time is as distant from the imagination as the lonely status of the "I" in uppercase. Perhaps he sees unrelenting cornfields in his imagination, or a bleak world of perpetual pork. Perhaps it is this that arouses his sympathy, and his skills. He gives orders to the black boy waiting at the counter. The boy nods politely but cautiously while he listens, his slow-moving eyes seeing the details of a radical plan. We enlist him deeper into our designs by ordering two lump crabcakes, deep-fat fried, to be eaten now, while we wait. This is the familiar thing. He passes the order to the black woman, the short-order cook, frying at the stove.

We are satisfied now that something that can be shown will be brought back from Baltimore into Iowa. We have been, and *are*, of both places. The balance between them that was disrupted has now been temporarily restored. But, while waiting, we become bothered by our lack of decisiveness, by the steady weakening of our initial strong resolve. A muscular "I" in the uppercase drove into Baltimore, but a fragmented self, crowded now into the lowercase, will be driving out. We worry over this problem when our steaming crabcakes come and we eat them at the counter. They are delicious. This is the body and blood that had been lost. This is the content of the cup that was long quested for. *It restoreth our soul.* We eat them, though, without the ketchup from the counter. The red would only spoil the delicate browns of their color. We savor what is already there in them. The taste and texture and wetness take us back many years, back to our original appetite for crabcakes. *This* is the body. *That* is the blood. "I bring you news of one who died and has returned. If winter comes, can spring be far behind?"

We think that this is the hidden basis of all belief.

But as we now consume the remaining crabcake, the missing part of us begins to reclaim its old, accustomed place. It says to us we have become sentimental about Mrs. Washington and her scant facts. She died. We had carried her above and beyond all expectation before she died. We have taken losses. We are reminded, now, that we should follow through on our original plan to sell the house immediately. Earlier today, we recollect, we almost became responsible again for its taxes and repairs. The two hundred dollars each month that will come now from Mr. Butler will barely cover the taxes. We should have come *here first*, to the Lexington Market, to satisfy our renewed appetite for Maryland crabcakes. We have done that now, even though in the wrong order of visits. But we can take comfort in the fact that Ms. Gayle Wilson, the real estate agent, is still available. She will maintain the business sense we need to rely on now. Our house can still be sold. Repairs will only enhance its value on the market, we are reminded. In the end, the house will have much more curbside appeal. It has never before had this, except during impersonal auctions. We are remembering now that it has been sentimentality, and that alone, that has undermined our purpose. The entire day has been a series of impersonal assaults on the muscularity of our self-standing "I." *I resent this.* It has taken us many, many years to move upward from the lowercase, and it has taken only one day for our *I* to be undermined into a wilderness of scattered, self-defeating selves. We sense that Eric has had something to do with this development. *I* should not have allowed him to continue saying *"Yes, sir. Yes, sir."* His subtle plea implied elderliness, and therefore liens of loyalty. We recollect now that these were snares, set to pull us down into the confusions of the lowercase. We recollect Eric's voice now, with no hint of a muscular "I" in it, chanting its leveling litany: *My Aunt Channie was like daddy, mama, grandmother, grandfather, aunt, and uncle to me. "Yes, sir. Yes, sir." Now that my Aunt Channie is dead, I come over every evening and sit with Mr. Herbert.* Eric has an "I" that is employed for only limited purposes. It would not know what to do if it became dislodged from the clutch of fealty. We follow this thread, and re-collect into it the new language in Mrs. Washington's last letter. *Dear James Family.* Another subtle assault against the self-standing of our uppercase. Even Mr. Butler had been uncomfortable in claiming the autonomy of personal loss for himself. He generalized his pain. Those were the traps, we are reminded now, that pulled our purposeful "I" down into the lowercase. This is why we are now who we are *now.* This is the source of our present mood of indecision. We decide, now finished with our crabcakes, that the only solution is to say the final goodbye that was originally intended.

Our dozen regular crabcakes are ready. The manager puts them proudly on display. They have been wrapped tightly in foil. The foil package has been wrapped inside layers of plastic bags. There is a layer of ice in each plastic bag. There are three plastic bags, each containing a layer of crushed ice, cooling the crabcakes. We pay our bill. The owner says, "Now we ain't go'n guarantee the ice will last till New York. But we done our best to get you there." Then he whispers to the black boy who is making change. The young man goes away, then returns with a large soft drink, ice cold, in a plastic cup. "One for the road. A gift," the manager says. Both of them take a mysterious pleasure in offering the liquid to us.

It is the impulse beneath the boosterism that contains the mystery.

Our drive to Interstate 95, heading north, is easier from the Lexington Market area. We drive much more comfortably now, inside the flow of early evening traffic. We plan ahead to the bus from Newark into the city, and the short cab ride from Port Authority to the friend's apartment on Riverside Drive. This friend is Japanese, and we think we should offer some of the crabcakes as a gift. The crabcakes will be cool by then, and a few might benefit from the changed intention. They might reach a much more healthy end as a commodity, or as a souvenir brought back from travel. The Japanese are great lovers of souvenirs. The presentation of one is considered a prologue to each meeting. It is not the quality of the gift, they say, but the purity of the intention behind it that is considered sacred. But then the apostate "I" of the scattered self reminds us that we are still stuck in lowercase, moving now from one small village-sense into another. We had thought *they* would be left behind us now, in the city. But even here, speeding purposefully through the evening traffic of Walt Whitman's south New Jersey, we find ourselves still de-selfing. We are still stuck in the village mode of mind.

We pull ourselves into full registration and *vote* with unanimity.

It is determined, once again, that our plan should remain the original one. All twelve crabcakes will be left overnight in the friend's freezer. After ten or so hours there, they should be frozen solid. By tomorrow afternoon, when we begin our flight, the crabcakes should still be fresh. They will fly next to us on the airplane, like express-mailed letters. All baggage will arrive together, *re-collected,* from the separation caused by the two flights. When the brown, harvested cornfields are seen, we will know that we are *home.* All of us, the friends included, will have a feast. Once the gift is put into motion again, around the dinner table, the lure of de-selfing will have abated, and the other parts of us that have been scattered can be reclaimed.

Our "I" will be at home again, and can make its best decisions unfettered by the chains of ancient memories, is the thought that is kept fixed as we drive north.

But once at home again, beyond the welcome of the brown, harvested Iowa cornfields, there is a sudden decision to refreeze the crabcakes.

The Rescue of a Self from the Snares of the Past

There is hard work involved in relocating a respectable batch of the letters. They must be looked for in boxes of old letters, papers, magazines, bills that have been stored over the years in various corners of the basement. They must be put into a pile on the dining room table and reread. It is here that an initial intuition proves to be the correct one. The letters report few facts. They never vary in their language and in their focus. Nor do they ever mention the rent checks that accompany them. I find enough of the letters to pinpoint the dates of several repairs on the old furnace, one replacement of electric wiring, one occasion of work on leaking water pipes. These have been the only emergencies. The costs of the smaller repairs are always deducted from the rent. The receipts are always enclosed. These occasions are the only ones for news about reality. All other letters say almost the same ritual things: "Everything is fine," "God bless you and the family," "Thank the Good Lord," "By By." I realize now how accustomed *I* have become to these monthly reports on the nonfacts of life. Still, over the years they have become a respite of some kind. They have been monthly reminders of the insubstantial elements comprising even the most permanent of things.

But as I continue reading through the letters, my mature instincts keep reminding me that no human being is this simple. No human being could be *only* the repetition of the same old assertions from one month to the next. I do not expect a secret life in Mrs. Washington, but I find myself needing something more to mourn. It may be that the years have taught me to be untrusting of what once seemed simple, uncomplicated, pure. My mind has grown used to being vigilant. I have learned that things that seem to be *are not* what they seem to be. The thing that seems most like itself has, most likely, been calculated to seem to be that way. There is always something hidden. There is always that extra fact. I continue reading through the letters, all that I can find, for the clue that will lead to the private intuition, which in turn, in time, will merge with a larger and expanding reality, and give rise to the experience of truth. This is the metaphysic of detectives during times of universalized corruption. It is also the refuge of cynics. I cannot truly move against Mr. Butler until the self-interested action can be rationalized in terms of some hidden fact. This is, after all, the way of the world. It is the art of self-interested, savage discovery.

The funeral program, sent from Baltimore by Elizabeth McIntosh, arrives at my home a week after me. I let the letter sit unopened for several days before reviewing the folded sheet. It is called a Homegoing Service for Channie Washington. A faded picture of her is below this title. She looks the way I first saw her on the porch. She looks dressed for church on Sunday morning. Her funeral had taken place on October 26, at the Second Antioch Baptist Church, 3123 Barclay Street, in Baltimore. Her church, like her family, was only a few doors away. The obituary recites the basic facts of her life.

> Channie Washington, daughter of the late Cornelius and Annie Gibson, was born on January 29, 1915, in Hartsville, South Carolina. She departed this life on October 21, 1993, after a brief illness.
>
> She received her education in the Darlington County Public Schools, in South Carolina.
>
> Channie was married to the late Isaac Washington.
>
> At a young age, she moved to Baltimore, Maryland.
>
> Later, she became a member of the Second Antioch Baptist Church. She served faithfully as a Missionary.

She worked at several restaurants, as a Short Order Cook, until she retired.

She loved to cook and enjoyed having her family and friends on Sundays, for her big meals.

Channie was a loveable and well-liked person. She loved her family and could never say no to anyone in need. She will be greatly missed.

She leaves to cherish her memory: her long-time beloved companion, Herbert Butler; two sisters, Mrs. Olivia Allen and Mrs. Rebecca Hankins of Norfolk, Virginia; eleven nieces; twelve nephews; fifteen great nieces; sixteen great nephews; fifteen great great nieces and nephews; and a host of other relatives and friends.

> God saw the road was getting rough
>   The hills were hard to climb;
> He gently closed her loving eyes
>   And whispered, "Peace Be Thine."
> Her weary nights are passed
> Her ever patient, worn out frame
>   Has found sweet rest at last.
>   Humbly Submitted,
>   The Family

The opening hymn was "What a Friend We Have in Jesus."

There were remarks, a solo, a reading of the obituary, by the various sisters and brothers of Mrs. Washington's church.

It comes to me now that Mrs. Washington had never been alone on that porch when I first saw her. For all her life, she had been an intimate part of something much larger than herself. She had not really needed my help. My old friend, the teacher, had been right all along. I might have passed by the scene, and nothing tragic would have happened to her. She might have been allowed by the new owner to remain in the house. She might have moved in with one of her two sisters, or with one of her many nieces or nephews. Her church might have found another place for her. The welfare people, if all else had failed, might have moved both her and Mr. Butler into a state-supported retirement home, where their lives might have been much more protected and pleasant during these last eighteen years. My old mentor had been right all along. I had taken upon myself, in a publicly arrogant way, a responsibility that was not my own. Now the needed fact begins to emerge in outline.

I had grown drunk on an infatuation with my own sense of "goodness" and had employed Mrs. Washington, and also Mr. Butler, as a prop for the background of the self-display I had wanted, then, to dramatize. I had challenged the white men in the crowd, inspired by motives I had rationalized into a higher sense of things, when I had, all along, been an actual member of the crowd. "Father, I am not like these other men. I pray ten times a day, I give tithes in the synagogue, I minister to widows and orphans, I . . ."

The fact comes clearly to me then: a value is not a value as long as it depends for its existence on a comparison with something else.

Then I remember a something else. It is a something else recollected from a time much longer ago than Baltimore. This memory merges with Mr. Herbert Butler and Elizabeth McIntosh and with the young man named Eric. He was just a baby, two or three porches away on Barclay Street, when I first bought the house. I think to myself, What if she had been forced to move away and had not been available to Eric during those years, after his father abandoned him and his mother went to work? How different would Eric's life be now if Mrs. Washington had not been there?

I think about this additional fact.

I think, again, that time *must* be a cycle, because this fact brings me back, back, back to my *self*.

I *re-collect* what there was in Eric that had made me so uncomfortable.

Now I remember. Now I remember it all.

Eric Abstracted and Recombined

When running away, you always found that first pit stop. Your plans have been fueled by fear, by aloneness, by questions the answers to which no one seems to know because no one is *really* there. You are far past fantasy now, young adolescent, pushing with passion against all that does not push back. Nothing does. No one is there who has time to care. You are feeling the freedom to test yourself against something larger than yourself, something familiar at first, something gentle that will still push back. This becomes the place of the pit stop in your plans for running away. You always go there first, to the environs of the familiar, to gather strength for this first solo flight out into the world. This familiar foreign place is always on the outskirts of this woman's voice. She is a few doors down the block, a few blocks distant, the other side of town. Her house is a safe place to stop during the first part of your flight. She stands over you, looking down. She says things like "Come in, boy. Take a load off your mind." She says, "Come on in and rest your feets." The renegotiation usually began in this ritual way. She is too old to be a bitch and much too far removed from this world to be a ho'. She is not the mammy of folklore. In the distant past of her life she has made the same mistakes you are inviting. You are not "black male" to her, but blood. She cares about the special ways it flows. She knew your father before he was your father, and your mother before the girlish dreams in her died. It is not her fault they have been taken from you by life. Unlike you, she long ago learned to expect not much good from it. She knows that you must learn to do the same. Her life has been a preparation for the worst, and her small joys derive from anything less. It is life's hard lesson, this special peace that is past all understanding, and she will take her time in teaching it. But just now she protects you from the central mystery she has learned to master. She does not yet want to instruct in the quiet joy she has located on the ebb of unrelieving pain. This will be life's lesson, not her own. She cooks. She seems always to be at home. Her place is where you pause to get your bearings for the road. Her familiar name, the name you call her, always has two sounds, preceded by "Aunt." They represent her as solid and without pretension. "Chi-na." "Beu-lah." "Gus-sie." "Ma-ry." "Chan-nie." She is the eternal aunt of archetype, not the mammy. Hers is the first outside model of finished woman you explore. She has lost all belief in even the most pedestrian possibilities of the self-standing "I" and has learned to live carefully inside a populated "we." She is the fountainhead, the base at the whisk of the broom that keeps the "we," the "us," collected. You are one of the straws about to stray. You feel safe running away as far as her house, for a pause at this pit stop, because you know there is fellow feeling kept in unlimited supply for you there. But she still makes you feel uncomfortable. She has no material proof for her belief in God, but believes anyway. This increases her mystery. She has learned to see miracles in small, comic things: it is not too hot or too cold, a cool breeze comes through the window, the old furnace still operates all through winter. She also irritates you by giving all credit to "The Man Upstairs," to "The Good Lord," even when she can clearly see the causal physics involved. You want to teach her what you are learning in the streets, from radio, from television. But you also take secret comfort in the fact that her higher world, the one above your frustrations in this one, is viewed by her as under the strict control of a good *Man*. You would not want to be as burdened as *He* is, but at the same time you are glad that He is there. He is the only Man, as far as you can see, to whom she defers. She talks always of His will. Because she is on such intimate terms with Him, you never consider that this man is white, or female. Her manner assures you that the world where He lives is beyond all such concerns. This man has to do only with things that are ultimate. He lists lies. He watches sparrows. He knows all secrets. There are no private plans that will not come to light. This man already knows why you are running. While she talks and looks at you, you begin to believe that she knows, too. Coming here always seems to cause a reconstruction. Maybe today, after all, you will not leave the comfort of her house. But tomorrow, or the next time, you will not come here first. You will just continue down the road. When she sees you again, years from now, you will be worldly, a grown man, with all the things you worry about not having now. You will pay her back for the meal she is giving you. You will bring back solid, seeable proofs that The Man Upstairs is much too busy with the flights of sparrows to see into the hidden corners you have found. The proofs you will bring back will be from fairyland, from Jacksonville, from the New York she has never seen. They might come, much more quickly, from the crack house just several blocks away, where other boys your age are already making money. Boys much younger than yourself have already made their own miracle. They have abstracted the assembly line from McDonald's and sell, with a smart efficiency that you admire, small plastic bags of crack to white people from the sub-urbs who drive by. One, some boy you know personally and admire, Bro' or Dupe or Home, takes the orders; one, farther on, collects money; and the third boy, at the end of the block, just by the corner, delivers the plastic sandwich bags, the very ones that used to hold your lunch at school, to the eager white hand reaching out the window of the car. You have been invited to become part of this process, to stand at one end of the McDonald's line or at the other. It looks easy. Sometimes, in your bed at night, in the quiet and the darkness, you can imagine such an assembly line stretching *down* southward from Savannah, into Jacksonville, Miami, Tampa, or *up* from Baltimore, north, like in the old stories, to Dover, Philly, Newark, New York, New Haven, Hartford, and Boston. *Phillymeyork.* With yourself at either end of the line, taking McDonald's orders or delivering white dust. *Phillymeyork. Cowboys and silver dollars.* Meanwhile, now, she is talking at the child who is leaving you, in a language that no longer fits the way things are. Maybe tomorrow, or sometime soon, you will be going all the way. But for now, with the food and considering the time of day . . . and considering her sparrows and the ever-watching eyes she apparently looks into, and sees through . . . *In later years,* close friends will tell you that in moments of frustration you tend to say "*Oh Lord!*" You will think back on the source of this, trying to remember. It is somehow connected, you recollect, with firm intentions that have come unglued. It will be connected with memories that are embarrassing. This Lord you petition will somehow have to do with the old dream of money, and with memories of fellow feeling and food, and also with the natural flow of sympathy. But you are a man now and no longer think much about childhood. Still, you will begin to *recollect* a tired black woman who stood in her doorway between the lures of the streets and you. She was one of your first loves. Inside her door you always felt a degree of safety, the sense of which has now been lost. But these recollections of dependency now threaten to intrude upon your present self-possession. You are self-made, in the terms of, and in the view of, the principalities and powers of *this* world. You know no other Lord beyond yourself. Besides, you say to those who heard your voice reaching, it would be crazy to call into the empty air for help. The voice that was heard was not your own. It possibly slipped out from the locked travel trunks of another time. It was a simple error in articulation . . . *But for now, here inside this house, in this beforetime,* all appeals to the other world belong to her. You confess to her, while eating, your fear that the holes in your world cannot be fixed. You do not expect her to understand. She does not understand. But at the same time she is there, has always been there, just to listen. It is enough while she feeds you, while she talks in her private language. She cooks the things she likes best that you do not like. You eat them anyway. She talks, selectively, about her own early life, in her own Old Country. She tells stories about the old-fashioned time in the old-fashioned place. She says things like "Take the bitter with the sweet." She says things like "Catch more flies with honey than with vinegar." But her language does not enter into the sore spots of *your* problems. It is only a meaningless counterthrust of words that obscures *your own specifics*. She always finds ways to turn you away from yourself, away from the life-and-death issues that first stalled you at her door. You had come to her for just a hint of understanding. You wait long for this, but it never comes. You eat the meal and decide to not come back again. But you always do come back, each time you make fresh steps toward that better world beyond her door. Her home is the secret pit stop you visit first, for food, for fuel, before continuing on up the road. You know that you could get there much more quickly if she were not there. But she is always there, like the police squad cars, like the ticket agent in the toll booth at the entrance to the interstate, who has already memorized the exact price of travel up or down the road. She warns you to be careful and to watch your speed. She inspires you to slow down. She becomes the counterthrust to your full-forward. Sometimes she seems to be the bitch your older friends have learned to moan about. You think she will always be in your path, like a stoplight frozen forever on blood red. But one day, quite suddenly, she is not. You grieve some, but soon find the loss is less important than the life ahead of you. She can be forgotten. You still retain a mother and a growing lease on life. At her funeral you take comfort in reciting, in line with her beliefs, that the two of you will meet again. You *move on* in your own life, not really remembering much, until one day it happens. *You see her.* The armies of the world have massed to remove her from her house. The crowd does not know the importance of the place to her, *or to you*. They see only something that is free-floating above the ground, obsolete, old. They see a rundown row house. You see a temple. It is the place where she *must be* for those times when you run away. The crowd does not understand this house's history. It cannot contemplate that something larger is involved. *"My Aunt*

Chan-nie-Chi-na-Beu-lah-Gus-sie-Ma-ry must *be there for me.*" Her house is your one refuge from the world. In that place your "I" is a less troubled "we." She has always lived a few doors down the street, a few blocks away, a rapid run across the backdirt lanes of town. You have grown used to dropping in and sitting. She has always been your rock of ages, who lifted you *up* above all undertows. You do not worry as long as she is there. But the crowd cannot see this always unfinished business. It threatens the unseeable self that has always lived between the two of you. It is cutting a connection that cannot be encased in reason. You cannot tell it that you have come to pause here and eat your meal before continuing down or up the road. Perhaps you can say that you *must* sit evenings with Mr. Herbert. Tell the crowd *anything* that will *make it go away . . . !*

I understand now why I claimed Eric's place on the sofa: the source of the bond we share was in that special seat.

I had sensed this *something,* almost eighteen years ago, during my walk that sweaty July morning.

After exploring up and down both coasts, *I* had circled back *home.*

Now I search again for the *nonfacts* in Mrs. Washington's last letter, the one sent in September, with the meaning of its new language suddenly clarified.

"Dear James Family": She was drawing me closer in, *claiming.*

"Only a few lines to let you hear from us": *De-selfing.*

"I am doing much better now": *De-selfing.*

"Mr. Butler is fine": *Beloved.*

"Give the family our love": *Consideration, same monthly basis.*

"I will close my letter but not our love": *"My" ends, "Our" lives on. Offer.*

"May God Bless you all with much love and Happiness": *Source of future surplus, to back offer.*

"By By": *Extra understanding concealed in formulaic signature.*

"Channie Washington and Herbert": *Lifelong tenants.*

In the new ways I am now sensing beyond thinking thoughts, this last letter is Mrs. Channie Washington's last will and testament.

*

I can read the nonfacts now. She has drawn me into her family. She has affirmed the stability of the present *status quo*. The declaration of her family's love stretching far into the future is her offer of consideration for something. It seems to be the kiting of the present circumstance against the surplus of some future time. There is a promise of abundant giving to balance something given of my own.

That is the way it has been for almost eighteen years.

Now I read back from the nonfacts and reconstruct the facts. Because she knew she was dying, Mrs. Washington was looking out for her family. She was intent on sheltering her beloved. She was deeply skilled in the uses of the intimate nonlanguage of black people, the language that only employed words as ballast and sound. Because the money rent she paid had never been sufficient, she had grown used to sending what compensation she could. Now she was offering, from the surplus she expected, the same rate of extra compensation far into the future. Mrs. Washington was stationed in future time, looking back on the now, making her usual spiritual adjustment in her monthly rent.

This nonlanguage was her offer to lock me in, as the landlord of her home, at the usual rate of payment, for many years to come. Mrs. Washington was offering a renewal of our old spiritual contract, locating future rent adjustments in the only source of surplus she knew. She had touched the most ultimate expression of kiting.

There was no will in the world sufficient to compete with the power of this offer. Mrs. Washington had always *known better.*

It is only now that I unfreeze my crabcakes and begin to eat them. Now I do not worry about their freshness, or about how they taste. Now they represent only a secret signature, the symbolic acceptance of an offer.

JOYCE CAROL OATES

They All Just Went Away

FROM THE NEW YORKER

I MUST HAVE been a lonely child. Until the age of twelve or thirteen, my most intense, happiest hours were spent tramping desolate fields, woods, and creek banks near my family's farmhouse in Millersport, New York. No one knew where I went. My father, working most of the day at Harrison's, a division of General Motors in Lockport, and at other times preoccupied, would not have asked; if my mother asked, I might have answered in a way that would deflect curiosity. I was an articulate, verbal child. Yet I could not have explained what drew me to the abandoned houses, barns, silos, corncribs. A hike of miles through fields of spiky grass, across outcroppings of shale as steeply angled as stairs, was a lark if the reward was an empty house.

Some of these houses had been inhabited as "homes" fairly recently — they had not yet reverted to the wild. Others, abandoned during the Depression, had long since begun to rot and collapse, engulfed by vegetation (trumpet vine, wisteria, rose of Sharon, willow) that elsewhere, on our property for instance, was kept neatly trimmed. I was drawn to both kinds of houses, though the more recently inhabited were more forbidding and therefore more inviting.

To push open a door into such silence: the absolute emptiness of a house whose occupants have departed. Often, the crack of broken glass underfoot. A startled buzzing of flies, hornets. The slithering, ticklish sensation of a garter snake crawling across floorboards.

Left behind, as if in haste, were remnants of a lost household.

A broken toy on the floor, a baby's bottle. A rain-soaked sofa, looking as if it has been gutted with a hunter's skilled knife. Strips of wallpaper like shredded skin. Smashed crockery, piles of tin cans; soda, beer, whiskey bottles. An icebox, its door yawning open. Once, on a counter, a dirt-stiffened rag that, unfolded like precious cloth, revealed itself to be a woman's cheaply glamorous "see-through" blouse, threaded with glitter-strips of gold.

This was a long time ago, yet it is more vivid to me than anything now.

This was when I was too young to think the house is the mother's body, you have been expelled and are forbidden now to reenter.

Always, I was prepared to see a face at a high, empty window. A woman's hand uplifted in greeting, or in warning. *Hello! Come in! Stay away! Run! Who are you?* A movement in the corner of my eye: the blurred motion of a person passing through a doorway, or glimpsed through a window. There might be a single shriek of laughter from a barn — piercing as a bird's cry. Murmurous, teasing voices confused with wind rippling through tall, coarse, gone-to-seed grass. Voices that, when you pause to listen, fade immediately and are gone.

The sky in such places of abandonment was always of the hue and brightness of tin, as if the melancholy rural poverty of tin roofs reflected upward.

A house: a structural arrangement of space, geometrically laid out to provide what are called rooms, these divided from one another by verticals and horizontals called walls, ceilings, floors. The house contains the home but is not identical with it. The house anticipates the home and will very likely survive it, reverting again simply to house when home (that is, life) departs. For only where there is life can there be home.

I have never found the visual equivalent of these abandoned farmhouses of upstate New York, of northern Erie County, in the area of the long, meandering Tonawanda Creek and the Barge Canal. You think most immediately of the canvases of Edward Hopper: those dreamily stylized visions of a lost America, houses never depicted as homes, and human beings, if you look closer, never depicted as other than mannequins. For Hopper is not a realist but a surrealist. His dreams are of the ordinary, as if, even in imagination, the artist were trapped in an unyielding day-light consciousness. There seems almost a kind of rage, a revenge against such restraints, in Hopper's studied, endlessly repeated *simplicity*. By contrast, Charles Burchfield, with his numerous oils and watercolors — frequently of upstate New York landscapes, houses, and farms — rendered the real as visionary and luminous, suffused with a Blakean rapture and a kind of radical simplicity, too. Then there are the shimmering New England barns, fields, and skies of our contemporary Wolf Kahn — images evoked by memory, almost on the verge of dissolution. But the "real" — what assaults the eye before the eye begins its work of selection — is never on the verge of dissolution, still less of appropriation. The real is raw, jarring, unexpected, sometimes trashy, sometimes lumi-nous. Above all, the real is arbitrary. For to be a realist (in art or in life) is to acknowledge that all things might be other than they are. That there is no design, no intention, no aesthetic or moral or teleological imprimatur but, rather, the equivalent of Darwin's great vision of a blind, purposeless, ceaseless evolutionary process that yields no "products" — only temporary strategies against ex-tinction.

Yet, being human, we think, To what purpose these broken-off things, if not to be gathered up, at last, in a single ecstatic vision?

There is a strange and profound and unknowable reality to these abandoned houses where jealously guarded, even prized posses-sions have become mere trash: windowpanes long ago smashed, and the spaces where they had been festooned with cobwebs, and cobwebs brushing against your face, catching in your hair like caresses. The peculiar, dank smell of wood rot and mildew, in one of the houses I most recall that had partly burned down, the smell of smoke and scorch, in early summer pervading even the lyric smell of honeysuckle — these haunting smells, never, at the time of experiencing, given specific sources, names.

Where a house has been abandoned — unworthy of being sold to new tenants, very likely seized by the county for default on taxes and the property held in escrow — you can be sure there has been a sad story. There have been devastated lives. Lives to be spoken of pityingly. How they went wrong. Why did she marry him, why did she stay with him? Just desperate people. Ignorant. Poor white trash. Runs in the family. A wrong turn.

Shall I say for the record that ours was a happy, close-knit, and unextraordinary family for our time, place, and economic status? Yet what was vividly real in the solid-built old farmhouse that contained my home (my family consisted of my father, mother, younger brother, grandfather, and grandmother, who owned the property — a slow-failing farm whose principal crop had become Bartlett pears by the time I was a girl) was of far less significance to me than what was real elsewhere. A gone-to-seed landscape had an authority that seemed to me incontestable: the powerful authority of silence in houses from which the human voice had vanished. For the abandoned house contained the future of any house — the lilac tree pushing through the rotted veranda, hornets' nests beneath eaves, windows smashed by vandals, human excrement left to dry on a parlor floor once scrubbed on hands and knees.

The abandoned, the devastated, was the profound experience, whereas involvement in family life — the fever, the bliss, the abrasions, the infinite distractions of human love — was so clearly temporary. Like a television screen upon which antic images (at this time, in the fifties, minimally varying gradations of gray) appear fleetingly and are gone.

I have seemed to suggest that the abandoned houses were all distant from our house, but in fact the one that had been partly gutted by fire — which I will call the Weidel house — was perhaps a half mile away. If you drove, turning right off Transit Road, which was our road, onto the old Creek Road, it would have been a distance of a mile or more, but if you crossed through our back potato field and through the marshy woods which no one seemed to own, it was a quick walk.

The Weidels' dog, Slossie, a mixed breed with a stumpy, energetic tail and a sweet disposition, sand-colored, rheumy-eyed, as hungry for affection as for the scraps we sometimes fed her, trotted over frequently to play with my brother and me. Though, strictly speaking, Slossie was not wanted at our house. None of the Weidels were wanted.

The "Weidel house," it would be called for years. The "Weidel property." As if the very land — which the family had not owned

in any case, but only rented, partly with county-welfare support —
were somehow imprinted with that name, a man's identity. Or
infamy.

For tales were told of the father who drank, beat and terrorized
his family, "did things to" his daughters, and finally set the house
on fire and fled and was arrested, disappearing forever from the
proper, decent life of our community. There was no romance in
Mr. Weidel, whom my father knew only slightly and despised as a
drinker, and as a wife- and child-beater. Mr. Weidel was a railway worker in Lockport, or perhaps an ex–railway worker, for he
seemed to work only sporadically, though he always wore a railway-
man's cap. He and his elder sons were hunters, owning a shotgun
among them and one or two deer rifles. His face was broad, fair,
vein-swollen, with a look of flushed, alcoholic reproach. He was
tall and heavyset, with graying black whiskers that sprouted like
quills. His eyes had a way of swerving in their sockets, seeking you
out when you could not slip away quickly enough. *H'lo there, little
Joyce! Joycie! Joycie Oates, h'lo!* He wore rubber boots that flapped,
unbuckled, about his feet.

Mrs. Weidel was a faded-pretty, apologetic woman with a body
that seemed to have become bloated, as with a perpetual pregnancy. Her bosom had sunk to her waist. Her legs were encased,
sausagelike, in flesh-colored support hose. *How can that woman live
with him? That pig.* There was disdain, disgust, in this frequent
refrain. *Why doesn't she leave him? Did you see that black eye? Did you
hear them the other night? Take the girls away, at least.* It was thought
that she could, for Mrs. Weidel was the only one in the family who
seemed to work at all regularly. She was hired for seasonal canning
in a tomato factory in lower Lockport and may have done house-
cleaning in the city.

A shifting household of relatives and rumored "boarders" lived
in the Weidel house. There were six Weidel children, four sons
and two daughters. Ruth was a year older than I, and Dorothy two
years younger. There was an older brother of Mr. Weidel's, who
walked with a cane and was said to be an ex-convict, from Attica.
The eldest Weidel son, Roy, owned a motorcycle, and friends of
his often visited, fellow bikers. There were loud parties, frequent
disputes, and tales of Mr. Weidel's chasing his wife with a butcher
knife, a claw hammer, the shotgun, threatening to "blow her head

off." Mrs. Weidel and the younger children fled outdoors in terror and hid in the hayloft. Sheriff's deputies drove out to the house, but no charges were ever pressed against Mr. Weidel. Until the fire, which was so public that it couldn't be denied.

There was the summer day — I was eleven years old — that Mr. Weidel shot Slossie. We heard the poor creature yelping and whimpering for what seemed like hours. When my father came home from work, he went to speak to Mr. Weidel, though my mother begged him not to. By this time, the dog had dragged herself beneath the Weidels' house to die. Mr. Weidel was furious at the intrusion, drunk, defensive — Slossie was his goddam dog, he said, she'd been getting in the way, she was "old." But my father convinced him to put the poor dog out of her misery. So Mr. Weidel made one of his sons drag Slossie out from beneath the house, and he straddled her and shot her a second time, and a third, at close range. My father, who'd never hunted, who'd never owned a gun, backed off, a hand over his eyes.

Afterward, my father would say of that day that walking away from that drunken son of a bitch with a rifle in his hands was about the hardest thing he'd ever done. He'd expected a shot between his shoulders.

The fire was the following year, around Thanksgiving.

After the Weidels were gone from Millersport and the house stood empty, I discovered Slossie's grave. I'm sure it was Slossie's grave. It was beyond the dog hutch, in the weedy back yard, a sunken patch of earth measuring about three feet by four with one of Mrs. Weidel's big whitewashed rocks at the head.

Morning glories grew in clusters on the posts of the front porch. Mrs. Weidel had planted hollyhocks, sunflowers, and trumpet vine in the yard. Tough, weedlike flowers that would survive for years.

It had been said of Ruth and her sister Dorothy that they were "slow." Yet Ruth was never slow to fly into a rage when she was teased by neighborhood boys or by her older brothers. She waved her fists and stammered obscenities, words that stung like hail. Her face darkened with blood, and her full, thick lips quivered with a strange sort of pleasure. How you loved to see Ruth Weidel fly into one of her rages; it was like holding a lighted match to flammable material.

The Weidel house was like any other rundown woodframe

house, said by my grandfather to have been "thrown up" in the 1920s. It had no cellar, only a concrete-block foundation — an emptiness that gradually filled with debris. It had an upstairs with several small bedrooms. There was no attic. No insulation. Steep, almost vertical stairs. The previous tenant had started to construct a front porch of raw planks, never completed or painted. (Though Mrs. Weidel added "touches" to the porch — chairs, a woven-rush rug, geraniums in flowerpots.) The roof of the house was made of sheets of tin, scarred and scabbed like skin, and the front was covered in simulated-brick asphalt siding pieced together from lumberyard scraps. All year round, a number of the windows were covered in transparent duct tape and never opened. From a distance, the house was the fading dun color of a deer's winter coat.

Our house had an attic and a cellar and a deep well and a solid cement foundation. My father did all the carpentry on our house, most of the shingling, the painting, the masonry. I would not know until I was an adult that he'd come from what's called a "broken home" himself — what an image, luridly visual, of a house literally broken, split in two, its secrets spilled out onto the ground for all to see, like entrails.

My mother, unlike Mrs. Weidel, had time to houseclean. It was a continuous task, a mother's responsibility. My mother planted vegetables, strawberries, beds of flowers. Petunias and pansies and zinnias. Crimson peonies that flowered for my birthday, in mid-June.

I remember the night of the fire vividly, as if it had been a festive affair to which I'd been invited.

There was the sound of a siren on the Creek Road. There were shouts, and an astonishing burst of flame in the night, in the direction of the Weidel house. The air was moist, and reflected and magnified the fire, surrounding it like a nimbus. My grandparents would claim there had never been such excitement in Millersport, and perhaps that was true. My father dressed hurriedly and went to help the firefighters, and my mother and the rest of us watched from upstairs windows. The fire began at about 1 A.M., and it would be past 4 A.M. before my seven-year-old brother and I got back to bed.

Yet what was so exciting an event was, in fact, an ending, with nothing to follow. Immediately afterward, the Weidels disappeared from Millersport and from our lives. It was said that Mr. Weidel fled "as a fugitive" but was captured and arrested the next day, in Buffalo. The family was broken up, scattered, the younger children placed in foster homes. That quickly, the Weidels were gone.

For a long time, the smell of wood smoke, scorch, pervaded the air of Millersport, the fresh, damp smell of earth sullied by its presence. Neighbors complained that the Weidel house should be razed at the county's expense, bulldozed over, and the property sold. But nothing was done for years. Who knows why? When I went away to college, the old falling-down house was still there.

How swiftly, in a single season, a human habitation can turn wild. The bumpy cinder driveway over which the eldest Weidel son had ridden his motorcycle was soon stippled with tall weeds.

What had happened to Roy Weidel? It was said he'd joined the navy. No, he had a police record and could not have joined the navy. He'd disappeared. Asked by the police to give a sworn statement about the night of his father's "arson," he'd panicked and fled.

Signs were posted — NO TRESPASSING, THIS PROPERTY CONDEMNED BY ERIE CO. — and they, too, over a period of months, became shabby and faded. My parents warned me never to wander onto the Weidel property. There was a well with a loose-fitting cover, among other dangers. As if *I* would fall into a well! I smiled to think how little my parents knew me. How little anyone knew me.

Have I said that my father never struck his children, as Mr. Weidel struck his? And did worse things to them, to the girls sometimes, it was whispered? Yes, and Mrs. Weidel, who seemed so soft and apologetic and sad, she too had beaten the younger children when she'd been drinking. County social workers came around to question neighbors, and spread the story of what they learned along the way.

In fact, I may have been disciplined, spanked, a few times. Like most children, I don't remember. I remember Mr. Weidel spanking his children until they screamed (though I wasn't a witness, was I?), but I don't remember being spanked by my parents, and in any case, if I was, it was no more than I deserved.

I'd seen Mr. Weidel urinating once at the roadside. The loose-flying skein of the kerosene he'd flung around the house before setting the fire must have resembled the stream of his urine, transparent and glittering. But they laughed, saying Mr. Weidel had been too drunk, or too careless, to have done an adequate job of sprinkling kerosene through the downstairs of the house. Wasn't it like him, such a slovenly job. Only part of the house had burned, a wall of the kitchen and an adjoining woodshed.

Had Mr. Weidel wanted to burn his family alive in their beds? Mrs. Weidel testified no, they'd all been awake, they'd run out into the yard before the fire began. They'd never been in any danger, she swore. But Mr. Weidel was indicted on several counts of attempted murder, along with other changes.

For so many years the Weidel house remained standing. There was something defiant about it, like someone who has been mortally wounded but will not die. In the weedy front yard, Mrs. Weidel's display of whitewashed rocks and plaster-of-Paris gnomes and the clay pedestal with the shiny blue glass ball disappeared from view within a year or so. Brambles grew everywhere. I forced myself to taste a small bitter red berry but spat it out, it made my mouth pucker so.

What did it mean that Erie County had "condemned" the Weidel property? The downstairs windows were carelessly boarded over, and both the front and rear doors were unlocked, collapsing on their hinges. Broken glass underfoot and a sickish stench of burn, mildew, decay. Yet there were "touches" — on what remained of a kitchen wall, a Holstein calendar from a local feed store, a child's crayon drawing. Upstairs, children's clothes, socks and old shoes heaped on the floor. I recognized with a thrill of repugnance an old red sweater of Ruth's, angora-fuzzy. There were broken Christmas tree ornaments, a naked pink plastic doll. Toppled bedsprings, filthy mattresses streaked with yellow and rust-colored stains. The mattresses looked as if they'd been gutted, their stuffing strewn about. The most terrible punishment, I thought, would be to be forced to lie down on such a mattress.

I thought of Mrs. Weidel, her swollen, blackened eyes, her bruised face. Shouts and sirens in the night, the sheriff's patrol car. But no charges filed. The social worker told my mother how Mrs. Weidel had screamed at the county people, insisting her husband hadn't done anything wrong and shouldn't go to jail. The names she'd called them! Unrepeatable.

She was the wife of that man, they'd had babies together. The

law had no right to interfere. The law had nothing to do with
them.

As a woman and as a writer, I have long wondered at the well-
springs of female masochism. Or what, in despair of a more subtle,
less reductive phrase, we can call the congeries of predilections
toward self-hurt, self-erasure, self-repudiation in women. These
predilections are presumably "learned" — "acquired" — but perhaps also imprinted in our genes, of biological necessity, neuro-
physiological fate, predilections that predate culture. Indeed, may
shape culture. Do not say, "Yes, but these are isolated, peripheral
examples. These are marginal Americans, uneducated. They tell
us nothing about ourselves." They tell us everything about ourselves, and even the telling, the exposure, is a kind of cutting, an
inscription in the flesh.

Yet what could possibly be the evolutionary advantage of self-
hurt in the female? Abnegation in the face of another's cruelty?
Acquiescence to another's will? This loathsome secret that women
do not care to speak of, or even acknowledge.

Two or three years later, in high school, twelve miles away in a
consolidated district school to which, as a sophomore, I went
by school bus, Ruth Weidel appeared. She was living now with
relatives in Lockport. She looked, at sixteen, like a woman in
her twenties; big-breasted, with full, strong thighs and burnished-
brown hair inexpertly bleached. Ruth's homeroom was "special
education," but she took some classes with the rest of us. If she
recognized me, in our home economics class, she was careful to
give no sign.

There was a tacit understanding that "something had happened"
to Ruth Weidel, and her teachers treated her guardedly. Ruth was
special, the way a handicapped person is special. She was with-
drawn, quiet; if still prone to violent outbursts of rage, she might
have been on medication to control it. Her eyes, like her father's,
seemed always about to swerve in their sockets. Her face was
round, fleshy, like a pudding, her nose oily-pored. Yet she wore
lipstick, she was "glamorous" — almost. In gym class, Ruth's large
breasts straining against her T-shirt and the shining rippled muscles and fatty flesh of her thighs were amazing to us; we were so
much thinner and less female, so much younger.

I believed that I should protect Ruth Weidel, so I told none of the other students about her family. Even to Ruth, for a long time I pretended not to know who she was. I can't explain how Ruth could have possibly believed me, yet this seems to have been so. Quite purposefully, I befriended Ruth. I thought her face would lose its sallow hardness if she could be made to smile, and so it became a kind of challenge to me to induce Ruth Weidel to smile. She was lonely and miserable at school, and flattered by my attention. For so few "normal" girls sought out "specialed" girls. At first she may have been suspicious, but by degrees she became trusting. I thought of Slossie: trust shows in the eyes.

I sat with Ruth at lunch in the school cafeteria and eventually I asked her about the house on the old Creek Road, and she lied bluntly, to my face, insisting that an uncle of hers had owned that house. She'd only visited a few times. She and her family. I asked, "How did the fire start?" and Ruth said, slowly, each word sucked like a pebble in the mouth, "Lightning. Lightning hit it. One night in a storm." I asked, "Are you living with your mother now, Ruth?" and Ruth shrugged, and made a face, and said, "She's OK. I see her sometimes." I asked about Dorothy. I asked where Mrs. Weidel was. I said that my mother had always liked her mother, and missed her when she went away. But Ruth seemed not to hear. Her gaze had drifted. I said, "Why did you all move away?" Ruth did not reply, though I could hear her breathing hard. "Why did you abandon your house? It could have been fixed. It's still there. Your mom's hollyhocks are still there. You should come out and see it sometime. You could visit me." Ruth shrugged, and laughed. She gave me a sidelong glance, almost flirtatiously. It was startling to see how good-looking she could be, how sullen-sexy; to know how men would stare at her who would never so much as glance at a girl like me. Ruth said slowly, as if she'd come to a final, adamant conclusion to a problem that had long vexed her, "They all just went away."

Another time, after lunch with Ruth, I left a plastic change purse with a few coins in it on the ledge in one of the girls' lavatories, where Ruth was washing her hands. I don't recall whether I left it on purpose or not. But when I returned, after waiting for Ruth to leave the lavatory, the change purse was gone.

Once or twice, I invited Ruth Weidel to come home with me on the school bus some afternoon, to Millersport, to have supper with my family and stay the night. I must not have truly believed she might accept, for my mother would have been horrified and would have forced me to rescind the invitation. Ruth had hesitated, as if she wanted to say yes, wanted very badly to say yes, but finally she said, "No. I guess I better not."

MARY OLIVER

Owls

FROM ORION

UPON THE DUNES and in the shaggy woodlands of the Provincelands, I have seen plenty of owls. Heard them at twilight and
in the dark, and near dawn. Watched them, flying over Great Pond,
flying over Rose Tasha's noisy barnyard, flying out of the open
fretwork of the spire of the old Methodist church on Commercial Street, where the pigeons sleep, and disappear one by one. I
have seen them in every part of the woods, favoring this or that
acreage until the rabbits are scarce and they move to new hunting
grounds, and then, in a few seasons, move back.

In January and February I walk in the woods and look for a large
nest in a tall tree. In my mind's eye I see the great horned, the
early nester, sitting upon her bulk of sticks, like an old woman on
a raft.

I look in every part of the Provincelands that is within my walking range. I look by Clapps Pond and Bennett Pond and Round
Pond and Oak-Head Pond. I look along the riding trail that bor-
ders the landfill — in the old days a likely hunting ground and not
one disdained by the owls or much else. I look in the woods close
to the airport, so often have I flushed an owl from the pine trees
there.

And I look in the woods around Pasture Pond, where, over a
century ago, Mr. George Washington Ready, once the Province-
town town crier, saw the six-eyed sea serpent. He witnessed it, he
said, emerging from the ocean and slithering across the dunes.
Into Pasture Pond it descended, and sank from sight. Every winter
I stare into the ice of the pond and think of it — still asleep, I

suppose, in the clasp of the lily roots, for no one has ever seen it again.

And I search in the deeper woods, past fire roads and the bike trail, among the black oaks and the taller pines, in the silent blue afternoons, when the sand is still frozen and the snow falls slowly and aimlessly, and the whole world smells like water in an iron cup. And I see, on my way to the owl's nest, many marvelous things — the gray hives of the paper wasps, hidden in summer by the leaves but now apparent on the boughs; nests, including one of the Baltimore oriole, with fish line woven into it, so that it has in the wind a comet's tail of rippling white threads; and pheasants, birds that were released into fall's russet fields but find themselves still alive at the far end of winter, and are glad of it, storming upward from the fields on their bright wings; and great blue herons thin and melancholy; and deer, in their gray winter coats, bounding through the cold bogs; an owl in a tree with an unexpected face — a barred owl, seen once and once only.

Finally the earth grows softer, and the buds on the trees swell, and the afternoon becomes a wider room to roam in, as the sun moves back from the south and the light grows stronger. The bluebirds come back, and the robins, and the song sparrows, and great robust flocks of blackbirds, and in the fields blackberry hoops put on a soft plum color, a restitution; the ice on the ponds begins to thunder, and between the slices is seen the strokes of its breaking up, a stutter of dark lightning. And then the winter is over, and again I have not found the great horned owl's nest.

But the owls themselves are not hard to find, silent and on the wing, with their ear tufts flat against their heads as they fly and their huge wings alternately gliding and flapping as they maneuver through the trees. Athena's owl of wisdom, and Merlin's companion, Archimedes, were screech owls surely, not this bird with the glassy gaze, restless on the bough, nothing but blood on its mind.

When the great horned is in the trees its razor-tipped toes rasp the limb, flakes of bark fall through the air and land on my shoulders while I look up at it and listen to the heavy, crisp, breathy snapping of its hooked beak. The screech owl I can imagine on my wrist, also the delicate saw-whet that flies like a big soft moth down by Great Pond. And I can imagine sitting quietly before that luminous wanderer the snowy owl, and learning, from the white gleam of its feathers, something about the Arctic. But the great horned I can't imagine in any such proximity — if one of those should touch me, it would be to the center of my life, and I must fall. They are the pure wild hunters of our world. They are swift and merciless upon the backs of rabbits, mice, voles, snakes, even skunks, even cats sitting in dusky yards, thinking peaceful thoughts. I have found the headless bodies of rabbits and bluejays, and known it was the great horned owl that did them in, taking the head only, for the owl has an insatiable craving for the taste of brains. I have walked with prudent caution down paths at twilight when the dogs were puppies. I know this bird. If it could, it would eat the whole world.

In the night, when the owl is less than exquisitely swift and perfect, the scream of the rabbit is terrible. But the scream of the owl, which is not of pain and hopelessness, and the fear of being plucked out of the world, but of the sheer rollicking glory of the death-bringer, is more terrible still. When I hear it resounding through the woods, and then the five black pellets of its song dropping like stones into the air, I know I am standing at the edge of the mystery, in which terror is naturally and abundantly part of life, part of even the most becalmed, intelligent, sunny life — as, for example, my own. The world where the owl is endlessly hungry and endlessly on the hunt is the world in which I live too. There is only one world.

Sometimes, while I have stood listening to the owl's auguring song drifting through the trees, when it is ten degrees above nothing and life for any small creature is hard enough without *that,* I have found myself thinking of summer fields. Fields full of flowers — poppies or lupines. Or, here, fields where the roses hook into the dunes, and their increase is manyfold. All summer they are red and pink and white tents of softness and nectar, which wafts and hangs everywhere — a sweetness so palpable and excessive that, before it, I'm struck, I'm taken, I'm conquered, I'm washed into it, as though it was a river, full of dreaming and idleness — I drop to the sand, I can't move; I am restless no more; I am replete, supine, finished, filled to the last edges with an immobilizing happiness. And is this not also terrible? Is this not also frightening?

Are the roses not also — even as the owl is — excessive? Each flower is small and lovely, but in their sheer and silent abundance the roses become an immutable force, as though the work of the wild roses was to make sure that all of us who come wandering over the sand may be, for a while, struck to the heart and saturated with a simple happiness. Let the mind be teased by such *stretches* of the imagination, by such balance. Now I am cringing at the very sound of the owl's dark wings opening over my head — not long ago I could do nothing but lounge on the sand and stare into the cities of the roses.

I have two feathers from the big owl. One I found near Round Pond; the other, on another day, fell as I watched the bird rise from one tree and flap into another. As it rose, some crows caught sight of it, and so began another scrimmage in their long battle. The owl wants to sleep but the crows pursue it, and when it settles a second time the crows — now a dozen — gather around and above it, and scream into its face with open beaks and wagging tongues. They come dangerously close to its feet, which are huge and quick. The caught crow is a dead crow. But it is not in the nature of crows to hide or cower — it is in their nature to gather and to screech and to gamble, in the very tree where death stares at them with molten eyes. What fun to aggravate the old bomber! What joy to swipe at the tawny feathers even as the bird puffs and hulks and hisses.

But finally the owl rises from the trees altogether and climbs and floats away, over two or three hills, and the crows go off to some other merriment.

And I walk on, over the shoulder of summer and down across the red-dappled fall; and, when it's late winter again, out through the far woodlands of the Provincelands, maybe another few hundred miles, looking for the owl's nest, yes, of course, and looking at everything else along the way.

DARRYL PINCKNEY

Slouching Toward Washington

FROM THE NEW YORK REVIEW OF BOOKS

1

PEOPLE, black and white, say that the throngs of upstanding black
men at the Million Man March showed a picture of the Black Man
different from what the nation is accustomed to. Because this has
always been my primary image of the Black Man — the men in
my family, my father, his friends, my friends, total strangers at
traffic lights, and sometimes even myself — what struck me was not
the vast crowd's proud demeanor or the insult that the crowd's
peacefulness was a pleasant surprise to most whites and to some
blacks, but that the black men deserved a message more worthy
of their journey than the numerology and self-election of Louis
Farrakhan.

It was not a civil rights march or even a march, though one
Nation of Islam spokesman said on television that it was a march
in Washington rather than a march on Washington. As more than
one of the day's speechmakers insisted, they had come neither to
demand nor to ask anything of government and whites. They had
come for themselves and to ask something of themselves. It was
billed as a day of atonement and reconciliation. It was a mass rally,
a religious convocation, a camp revival meeting on a grand scale,
with some competition among the speechmakers to see who could
blow the emotional lid off the patient multitudes. Perhaps those
black men and the women mingling among them — 1.5 million,
2 million, 400,000, 870,000? — came to experience just what it
felt like to be in command of that place where history had been

made a few times before. A lot of those present on October 16, 1995, had not been born in 1963.

"Thank God it's not a million white men marching on Washington," a white Englishman had said to me. The mean country South of the song "I'm coming with my razor and my gun" was all that had been radiating from Capitol Hill for months. On the shuttle on Sunday, the day before the March, a black youth dressed in immaculate baggy white, including a white knit cap, did not address a word to me across the empty seat, nor I to him, as if in the commuter privacy of laptops and phone calls made from the air we had succumbed, as usual, to the inhibition of being outnumbered. Then, too, I worried that he would think it presumptuous of me to assume that just because he was young, chic, and black he was on his way to the March.

Washington, D.C., is a predominantly black city, and a large percentage of its population lives below the poverty line. After the emancipated slaves came to town, Congress periodically addressed poverty's look. Jacob Riis was brought in at the turn of the century, legislators were taken on tours of alleys, told that those were the same flies that landed on their sandwiches back at the club, and during World War I the first of a few redevelopment schemes was passed. In the 1950s the worst area near the Capitol was razed, its residents relocated. Blocks have been boarded up at other times, because of the riots in the 1960s, because of "gentrification." Black doormen perhaps had been coming back downtown without their uniforms even before Marion Barry's first and second acts, but a part of the excitement surrounding the Million Man March was that a precinct of official marble was about to be taken over.

That Sunday afternoon, along the broad street of leaves that had not yet turned, a vanguard of black entrepreneurs had set up tables of commemorative T-shirts, caps, buttons, and sweatshirts of slogans and rhymes. Go-go music thumped from the rear of a parked truck. On the Mall itself, that expanse of green between the Capitol and the Washington Monument, people ambled and reconnoitered, many of them middle-aged black men. Perhaps for them the Mall had been the site of earlier pilgrimages. The black men, the father-and-son-like pairs, the lawn, and the red of the Smithsonian Castle in the distance took me back to 1967, to the centenary celebrations of Morehouse College in Atlanta, when my father tried to show me around and to show off his uncomprehending offspring to President Mays. I dimly recall their chuckling over the night Martin Luther King Jr.'s classmates short-sheeted his bed. Before the Million Man March was over I would feel very sad for King. Farrakhan had no qualms about extracting blessings from black leaders made cooperative by being dead.

Everything was ready — the long banks of portable single toilets, the giant television screens, the attitudes. Everyone seemed in a prescriptive frame of mind, willing to go on record about what black men and therefore black people needed to do. "It's time that we as black men get together. We need this unification to start being in front," one black vendor said. We needed to throw off that European indoctrination, I heard. We needed to trust each other, I was told. We needed to start someplace. We needed to unite like the Koreans, the first groups of whom, someone informed me, were brought over like the Cubans by the CIA and set up in business. They, whites, needed to stop stereotyping, a father of two concluded.

"We need to teach our young men," two middle-aged black women sitting on a park bench agreed. One, who planned to accept the men-only vibe by staying home with her television, said she didn't want to see a blade of grass when the men came. When I mentioned the objections of some black women to the premise of the March, they said, "Angela Davis needs to decide." Other black leaders also needed to decide. "We have all these ministers. Can't be a minister and a politician. Preaching over and over. It's very redundant." It was obvious what was happening to black people, and it was obvious who was doing it to them. "Look at what they had to do to try to bring O.J. back down."

I saw a group of young black men photographing and filming one another. Some of them wore the bow ties and dark suits of the Nation of Islam. New recruits from Portland, Oregon, they gave their names as Gary X, William X . . . The X marks the spot where the slave master's name has been crossed out. We lacked self-knowledge, one of the recruits decided. We lacked self-love. "You cannot love what you do not know." I thought of the remote men in bow ties and dark suits who had been on the streets of my childhood, before suburbs, when most blacks, in the North at least, grew up in neighborhoods that Black Muslims either visited or lived in themselves.

I see them, in memory, passing the barber's window. Sometimes they stepped inside, and if the shop owner was in the right mood, he'd let them try to sell the newspaper *Muhammad Speaks,* a source of new Creation myths and science fiction for the Jim Crow audience. *Muhammad Speaks's* cartoon illustrations caused some heads in the barbershop to shake in a perplexed way. The Black Muslims rang doorbells, but were less persistent than Jehovah's Witnesses. They were regarded as members of a cult, which, in the days before Charles Manson, meant merely that some troubled souls had found a refuge, a place where they could deliver themselves up for safekeeping. However, Black Muslims were also different from the other groups of the saved, like the women who renounced lipstick and served fried chicken in Father Divine's faded restaurants, because the face of the Black Muslim was that of a black man armed with a grudge.

The cult was known to attract ex-convicts. The men seemed contained and unafraid, as if all that hustler and jailbird knowledge had been packed down tight. They were clean and quiet, unlike the thugs hanging out on the corner, people the Black Muslims may have been like before they joined up and stopped drinking. They were left alone, because black people used to have a great deal of tolerance for how people got by and also because Black Muslims were considered a little off, being reformed, single-minded, and secretive.

If anything made the barbershop customers wary of Black Muslims as possibly unbalanced behind their display of superior stability, it was their separatism. Black Muslims were scornful of the civil rights movement and especially of civil rights leaders. At a time when black people were braving dogs and rednecks to integrate schools and get to the polls, the rejection of white institutions, the call for a separate nation, seemed unhelpful to the struggle, or helpful only to Elijah Muhammad and the John Birch Society. The cult was said to own farms in Alabama. How the Nation of Islam was financed was murky, but the barbershop's regulars understood that Black Muslims thought of Negroes as the dupes of white society; and they, in turn, provoked by the thought that another black man considered them Uncle Toms, called Black Muslims the tools of segregationists.

James Baldwin, in *The Fire Next Time*, recalled a visit in 1962 to the Chicago mansion headquarters of Elijah Muhammad, Supreme Head of the Nation of Islam, during which the Messenger of Allah told him that the white man's time was actually up in 1913, but Allah was waiting for the lost black nation, "the so-called Negro" in the United States, to be freed from white masters and returned to the true faith. Baldwin, as a former child preacher and Harlem street rat, had no trouble understanding the appeal the Black Muslims held for a soapbox constituency: the police seemed afraid of them, and since the white God had failed, maybe the black God wouldn't. But having heard prophecies of divine justice from many quarters every day of his youth, Baldwin wondered how someone went home on a given night, looked around, and decided to believe. The need to hear that whites were sinners, devils, inferior, and doomed assured that the market for doctrines of black salvation or black supremacy would never dry up.

My Indianapolis barbershop was psychologically far from the mosques and bean pies of Chicago or Harlem. The "men among men" were distant from us, "the Lost-Founds," the still-Negro. Muhammad Ali was more famous than Malcolm X as a symbol of the kind of defiant brotherhood that whites seemed to find so threatening and that was therefore so gratifying to blacks. Ali's name change in 1964 made a more favorable impression than Malcolm X's calling the 1963 March on Washington a "circus" or the Civil Rights Act of 1964 a "con game." Malcolm X's notoriety was derived from his appearances on the evening news as the gifted aphorist of racial apocalypse. Not until his assassination in 1965, the publication of his autobiography that same year, and the shock of the slogan "Black Power" to the country's psyche did blacks in general feel that Malcolm X had been with them all along and that they had been in sympathy with him all that time, too.

They say that Malcolm X liked to quote a line from Aesop: "Even when you are dead, you can get even with an enemy." He can certainly worry some whites from the grave, as evidenced by the anxiety surrounding the making and release three years ago of

Spike Lee's *Malcolm X,* a film as harmless as *Gandhi.* But the momentary fashion for "X" caps and "By Any Means Necessary" T-shirts, the possibility that young black men might be influenced by Malcolm X's inspired belligerence, set off a delirium of alarm, even though *The Autobiography of Malcolm X* has never been out of print.

Malcolm X died estranged from the Nation of Islam, the cult his charisma had done so much to broaden into a movement. Among those who expressed an unsavory satisfaction in the heretic's punishment was Louis Farrakhan. As Malcolm X's protégé, the suspicion goes, Farrakhan had to reassure the jealous Elijah Muhammad.

The Nation of Islam first permitted its members to vote in 1966, around the time that the civil rights movement left the red roads of the South and came up north to falter among the concrete towers. The National Guard was called in to put out fires, more whites left town, plenty of businesses and some blacks followed them. While the Vietnam War spread the mystique of revolution, racial solidarity and group autonomy, supported by rediscovered episodes of U.S. history such as Marcus Garvey's Back to Africa movement, seemed like alternative faiths or secret passageways to power. The exasperated pointed to Muhammad as the most successful disciple of Booker T. Washington's program of economic self-sufficiency, but blacks on campuses were busy arguing over the validity of armed self-defense and the legacy of Malcolm X.

In his lifetime Malcolm X brought large numbers of young people into what had been an organization composed mostly of the middle-aged. In death he introduced the children of the black middle class and the students everyone expected to become middle class to what had been, historically, black working-class sentiments about race redemption. Garveyism had been most attractive to the laboring masses who migrated from the South around World War I. Garvey's movement fell apart in the 1920s, but it left behind in its urban settings a deep feeling about the ancestral destiny of blacks. The founder of Harlem's largest sect of black Jews had been Garvey's director of music. Elijah Muhammad, born Elijah Poole in Sandersville, Georgia, in 1897, moved to Detroit in 1923 and became a corporal in the local Garvey group. During the Depression he met W. D. Fard, founder of the Temple of Islam, whose ideas were a mixture of millenarianism and Garveyism. When Fard inexplicably vanished from the scene, Poole, now Muhammad, claimed that Fard was the Messiah, the Mahdi, and eventually he left Detroit to spread the Messiah's truth. Perhaps this tradition of making converts to racial mysticism among those who had left the South explains why separatists, in the late 1960s and early 1970s, always sounded like city slickers trying to wise up countrified cousins just off the bus.

Muhammad had once predicted that Armageddon would come in 1970, but it was difficult to connect him with the Black Muslims who perished the following year in Attica. He trusted in God's solution, but in 1973 rumors began to circulate that the Nation of Islam's financial empire was crumbling. The Nation of Islam chain of clothing stores and bakeries may have been overvalued in the public mind to begin with. A $3 million loan was said to have been obtained from Libya, and there was some talk that financial difficulties had brought about a shift in the policy of no contact with white devils and that this pragmatism had led to internal strife. Some weakness at the center was suggested by what looked like a collapse in discipline at the outposts. Stories appeared about sectarian murders of Muslims in Washington, D.C., in New Jersey, about Muslim involvement in murder cases in Baton Rouge in 1972 and in San Francisco in 1973. Muhammad countered that they were not affiliated with his temples. In those days everything made sense as an FBI conspiracy once it had been denounced as such. The Nation of Islam had had run-ins with the FBI since the 1930s.

The Dear Holy Apostle was reportedly ailing, and Farrakhan became increasingly visible as press spokesman for the Nation of Islam, much as Malcolm X had been before him. He addressed the Black Solidarity Rally in Harlem in 1971 and attended the National Black Convention in Gary, Indiana, in 1972. Later that year a violent police confrontation at the Harlem mosque resulted in allegations of police misconduct and in a Muslim campaign to have only black policemen deployed in Harlem. Malcolm X, too, had first come to the attention of the New York press during a militant standoff with police in 1957. An observer of those days told me that Muhammad was probably contemptuous of Farrakhan for such claims. As with Malcolm X, he really didn't like his people making themselves conspicuous, because that brought him to the attention of the IRS.

When Muhammad died in 1975, Farrakhan did not succeed him. One of his sons, Wallace Deen Muhammad, was affirmed as leader. He wanted to bring the group closer to conventional Islamic teachings, and within a year of his father's death he had repudiated the doctrine about white devils and had even invited whites to join. *Muhammad Speaks* became *Bilalian News*. In 1977 Farrakhan, who had been transferred from Harlem's Mosque #7 to Chicago headquarters, broke with the younger Muhammad over his conciliatory policies. Some of Farrakhan's children had married some of Elijah Muhammad's grandchildren. Muhammad's illegitimate children sued for their portion. It looked like a corporate family soap opera along the lines of *Dynasty*. The Nation of Islam split into various factions. Wallace Deen Muhammad eventually renamed his group the American Muslim Mission and moved to California.

The son was free of the father, but his rival still had need of the father's imprimatur. Farrakhan revived Elijah Muhammad's litany. In 1981 he declared that Muhammad had been resurrected. By bringing the Messenger back from the dead, he could revise the act of succession and make himself heir. In 1983 he said that a hurricane that had swept through Texas was Muhammad's revenge for the execution of a Black Muslim in that state. That Muhammad's presence was immanent removed an obstruction for Farrakhan. Unburdened of Muhammad's watchful dollarism, Farrakhan could then insinuate himself where Malcolm X had not been allowed to. He endorsed Harold Washington's candidacy for mayor of Chicago in 1983, but it was through his fraternal association with Jesse Jackson's presidential bid in 1984 that he perfected a talent for outrage and became an American celebrity.

In the task of remaking and expanding his constituency it helped Farrakhan that Reagan was in office, that deregulation of capital made every day look like White Collar Crime Day to the poor, that conservative judicial appointments seemed to most blacks like the determination of whites to take up the drawbridge, because, as

Baldwin had explained years before in *Nobody Knows My Name*, though one could not accept the Muslims' conclusions, it was "quite impossible to argue with a Muslim concerning the actual state of Negroes in this country." It also helped that Farrakhan was so richly despised, because that more than anything gave him the aura of a true black leader. His defenders boasted that King had also been reviled by many whites in his day. The loathing Farrakhan conjured up was all the persuasion he needed with young black men who believed he spoke for them, the outcast, the demonized, and the very image of the black man we were about to be asked to chastise ourselves for at the Million Man March.

In 1985, gauntlets of security guards — the Fruit of Islam — had rapidly frisked each of the men who were part of that October night's huge audience waiting to enter New York's Madison Square Garden to hear Farrakhan speak. The formality said that we were being transferred to another jurisdiction, removed from the sidewalks, where policemen gave the orders, to the arena, where authority belonged to Farrakhan. *Power at Last*, his cassette and videotape were titled. Ten years later the Fruit of Islam are famously on offer as bodyguards. There are reports that the Nation of Islam has been awarded security contracts at housing projects, television stations, and cultural festivals in various cities. Whereas in the old days the Black Muslims had rehabilitated individuals by urging them to surrender to their collective identity, the community service the Nation of Islam is now praised for is that of reclaiming neighborhoods through the sheer force of its reputation. Having tamed themselves, they hold out the promise to tame others.

I heard more than once on the Mall that Sunday afternoon that the Nation of Islam deserved credit for chasing drug dealers from black neighborhoods, such as a part of northwest Washington the police wouldn't go into. Most whites and the middle class in general live emotionally and visually isolated from people who feel their neighborhoods are abandoned and under siege. Back up Pennsylvania Avenue, on Freedom Plaza, I watched a group of nine teenagers, all male, riding skateboards in the five o'clock sun. Their shirttails and the flags high above them answered the breeze. They were white, black, and Asian, but what made them seem so upper class was that they were clearly there together.

2

That evening the hall of display tables and people in African cos-
tume at the Washington Convention Center's pre-March "Prayer
and Praise" rally resembled Black Expos, those trade fairs that have
become an annual event on the civic calendar of most U.S. cities.
Inside the large auditorium itself, the delegate-like section seating
reminded me of NAACP conventions. When we stood for "Lift
Ev'ry Voice and Sing," the black national anthem, I half expected
to hear my mother's alto at my shoulder.

Services in black churches turn easily into protest meetings, and
civil rights meetings have long been conducted as prayer services,
but this was a fundamentalist crusade. One speechmaker after
another swore that "the devil must be mad, because he'd lost the
souls he thought he had," or proclaimed that when black men said
they shall not be moved, the whole black nation stood still "in a
divine way." We saluted upper bleachers of male figures dressed in
white, the Turn Germantown Around group that had walked all
the way from Philadelphia. Marion Barry welcomed us. "He's a
black man and not afraid to be one," the MC bellowed. We were
going to march for the living, the dead, and the unborn, for the
grieving families of gunned-down black youth, for the black children born out of wedlock, for the "millions" of black boys and girls
on drugs. "Somebody needs to march for Kunta Kinte." "If they
kill you, just rise again." Former congressman Walter Fauntroy, in
his guise as a pastor, began to croon one of those old favorites with
many verses.

Something almost deliberately foreboding in tone was to stick
out in the long night of Baptist choreography. Dr. Abdul Alif
Muhammad speaks like a future rival to Farrakhan. I'd seen him
on local television earlier. Head of Washington's Mosque #4 and
president of its Abundant Life Clinic, he was articulate, telegenic,
and he'd dominated the talk-show panel with the conviction of a
man on the rise. He told us that there were men who said it could
not be done, that black, white, blue, green, and other colors of
misunderstanding had said that we would not stand, but we were
"a free, liberated people in the eyes of God." Other speechmakers
told us that for "the African nation" here in America religious
barriers were coming down, that "Christians and Muslims and

Catholics" were forming bonds, that political and economic power was riding and resting on our spiritual power. Never again would they divide us. Satan was trying to keep God's children apart. One of Elijah Muhammad's sons and two of Farrakhan's children were introduced. The promotional style of that family firm, the Nation of Islam, began to assert itself.

Some people had insisted that the message could be separated from the messenger, that black people ought to get behind any effort dedicated to unity. But others had argued that no one had come up with the idea except Farrakhan, that no one else could get them to Washington in such numbers, and several of the speechmakers at the rally were adamant that the messenger could not be removed from the message, that to do so would be for black people to let others tell them once again who their leaders were. Though the leadership of the National Baptist Convention had declined to endorse the March, the banner of the Union Temple Baptist Church stretched over the stage. Small stockholders were being sold on a merger, persuaded of a takeover the board opposed — the leveraged buyout of Jesus & Co.

We were told that the March was "totally" funded by our own community. We applauded donations. Rock Newman, the boxing manager, gave $10,000. He broke the O.J. taboo and brought people to their feet. "You can live in a big white house, with a lot of white women, and it still doesn't make you a man." Some stopped applauding because that sounded like a criticism. The MC reminded us that raising dollars was as much a part of the program as the spoken word and the choir, but people were leaving. Outside in the confusion of traffic, vendors called: history for sale, up for grabs, open to manipulation. The souvenir edition of *African American Consumer and Business* magazine featured on the cover a photograph of King's face superimposed on a crowd, and another of Farrakhan's superimposed on the same scene.

Early Monday morning we moved in the dark through the trees toward the lit-up dome of the Capitol. Black men were everywhere, atop ledges, perched on branches. Whenever someone in a bow tie and suit led forward a file of men, hand on shoulder, we squeezed aside to let them through. When the push became too great, we passed the word for everyone to take a step back. We

stepped on toes behind, on heels ahead. "Excuse me, brother."
Though the March changed somewhat in character from hour to
hour, depending on where and with whom I stood, this solemn
courtesy never went away. "Excuse me, black man."

Stage lights at the steps of the Capitol were aimed directly at us.
I could look up at the hierarchy of illumination in the sky — stars,
quarter moon, and helicopters — or behind, at the faces that
multiplied away. There was little talk, because of the sense of
occasion, because of the relentless drumming. Sometimes the long
blast of a ram's horn or the sound of a ululating woman came
from the direction of a group that had set up an encampment.
The drumming went on for an hour, until a loudspeaker crackled
and released a piercing burst of township jive. Marvin Gaye's
"What's Going On," the music of the Vietnam veteran, made the
men cheer, but they weren't in the mood for Earth, Wind, and
Fire. "This ain't no party," they chanted. "Turn the music off." The
music stopped, the men cheered, the drumming began again.
"This is all right," a man said. "This is deep." Assembled at the
steps of Pharaoh and waiting. After another hour I followed the
path made by a wheelchair and came to a lawn. The smells of
incense, barbecue, and pot wafted through the cold air.

A clear morning was coming up fast on the standing, the stroll-
ing, the reclining. A man noted ruefully that we had let the Muslim dawn go by. In the developing light I could see banners,
signs, sandwich boards, sweatshirts. First Baptist Church of Crown
Heights; the Durham, NC, Posse; Bowie State Football Team; Local
420. Duke, Georgetown, Howard, NC State, the caps said. A white
man held up a handwritten message on cardboard: "The Howard
Stern Show Salutes You." The marchers themselves carried so
many cameras and camcorders that one paranoid remark I heard
— "They're taking pictures to see who's who" — became something of a joke. However, there were times when I was glad of my
sunglasses, fierce-looking shades that went some way toward reassuring those who became suspicious of my notepad and pen, as if
jotting down what became a matter of public record as soon as it
boomed down the Mall offended the spirit of unity.

"Assalamu alaykam." A Baptist preacher introduced the muezzin,
who sang and translated the Adon. Everything in U.S. history can
seem like a turning point, but after King's martyrdom the feeling

ran high that blacks had done more for Christianity than Christianity had done for them. Islam was increasingly perceived as being Afrocentric and a declaration of one's Otherness in a thrilling way. *Time* magazine reported a year after King's death that there were 350,000 black Jews in the United States, although two years later *The Negro Almanac* put the figure at 44,000. Moreover, those who have identified themselves as Muslim are not necessarily allied with the Nation of Islam. Figures about its membership have always varied widely. But at the west front of the Capitol, facing east, the stillness, the bowed heads, the American flag, the policemen on the steps, in the dome's balcony, signaled a competing godliness in a nation getting narrower in its culture the more broadly religious it becomes. "And I bear witness that Muhammad is the Messenger of Allah." A style brochure distributed by the American Muslim Council taught us how to spell *shahadah*, the declaration of faith.

One man's unity is another man's — or woman's — repression. Dr. Muhammad castigated the "agnostics and atheists" who said it couldn't be done, but Allah had given Louis Farrakhan a vision, and the call for the March had come from God Almighty through him. Ben Chavis, executive director of the Million Man March, said that as a Christian minister he intended to stand with Farrakhan all the days of his life. A baritone was mumbling, "Before I'll be a slave, I'll be buried in my grave."

There was an almost complete absence of rap, of Public Enemy, the boom-box sound that had done so much to proselytize for Farrakhan and that was also so identified with renegade black youth. We had gotten to the "Sankofa" part of the program, where we were supposed to "go back and fetch it," go back to the glory of Africa, "the creators of technology and science." As the African Heritage Drummers and Dancers pounded, I ducked under the yellow police tape that marked lanes on the Capitol grounds and headed into what everyone was calling an ocean of black men.

Everywhere I looked, the people were upstaging the speechmakers. And everywhere somebody was hawking something, mostly newspapers: Farrakhan's *The Final Call,* John Muhammad's *Muhammad Speaks, The Anointed News Journal, Streetwise,* or *The Five Percenter,* the newspaper of a Muslim group devoted to land acquisition. There were self-help manuals, coloring books, and someone was autographing his reproductions of an all-black Last Supper. Constitution Avenue had become an immense street fair. Women and children appeared, giving the day a carnival openness. Stalls of Bob Marley posters, jewelry, incense, chicken, flags, art-works, and cassettes stretched as far as the eye could see. "That's right. I love you." There were Million Man March candy bars with Farrakhan's picture on the wrapper and Million Man March official bottled spring water. Million Man March watches were also available by order. There were brochures from African Americans Uniting for Life, a marrow donor group, from employment agen-cies, leaflets from video stores, and the Information Superhighway for Black Membership Organizations. One could have one's pic-ture inserted instantly into a souvenir frame with a Million Man March poem on the cover, and the ground was littered with order forms from the African American Archives.

We heard from international representatives, radio personali-ties, CEOs, figures from the black revolutionary nationalist past, and preachers, preachers. Poor Betty Shabazz, Malcolm X's widow, perhaps under an obligation to Farrakhan after he came to her daughter's defense when she became a victim of entrapment last summer, stuck to the safe subject of self-determination. Two cute children recited, and Maya Angelou, who will play any venue, moved herself to tears. A great accolade went up to Rosa Parks, heroine of the Montgomery bus boycott. Miss Parks was mugged not long ago in Detroit. When her neighbors found the culprits, they beat them up before handing them over.

Nobody invented the statistics about single-parent households, about who the victims of black criminals are, about which segment of the population is most likely to die of gunshot wounds, but there was a troubling capitulation in the exhortations that black men accept responsibility for their families, swear as black men not to beat their wives, promise as black men not to abuse their children, vow as black men to give up guns, drugs, and violence — as if in order to project the news of the decent Black Man, the assembled had first to humble themselves before an indictment, as if domestic violence and poverty were not also white problems. But we were supposed to concentrate on ourselves. We were made to hold up our hands if we had ever done wrong. We were told that most black children had never seen a black man at a computer, when the question should have been, What kind of equipment do these children have at the sorts of schools they attend?

Moral imperatives fell over us like tuna nets. The language about black religion and black pride was similar to that of twelve-step programs: we have surrendered to a power greater than ourselves. It is easy to abstain on Monday and backsliding usually follows rebirth, but the speechmakers were preaching to the converted.

Gang leaders stepped up to pledge themselves to a truce, but how different the day would have been had it been made to say "We are not criminals" rather than "We will be good from now on," because no one is more self-righteous than a drug dealer, white or black.

Most of the speechmakers offered lofty theology and therapy, but Al Sharpton's hope was explicit: if the political story of 1994 was that of the angry white man, then get ready for the story of 1996, when the enlightened black man votes in a new Congress. No one was more eloquent in his concreteness than Jesse Jackson, who perhaps has been set free by Colin Powell's visibility. Jails were the number-one growth industry in America, Jackson claimed. The budget for them had risen from $4 billion to $32 billion. For possession of five grams of crack, an offender could get five years. Young black men comprised 94 percent of that category. For possession of five grams of cocaine powder, an offender usually received probation. Eighty percent of such offenders were white males. To get five years for possession of marijuana, one had to have been caught with $45,000 worth; to get five years for possession of cocaine in powder form, $8,000 worth; to get five years for possession of crack, $29 worth. There are 800,000 black men in jail and 500,000 in college, Jackson reminded us. Prison labor produces $9 billion in goods. "If it's wrong in China, it's wrong in Alabama." He said that among the investors in new jails were American Express and General Electric, and that maybe the next march should be about them. "Clarence Thomas and Gingrich organized this march," he finished to a storm of applause.

"Jesse turned it out," the men around me were saying. Think of the number of black men who insisted when Clarence Thomas was nominated that we had to support him because he was black.

Before Jackson spoke, the sentiment around me was that he was past his sell-by date. By the time he walked off, he'd come back a ways in Mall credibility. His short lesson had resonance with the crowd, as Stevie Wonder's voice had moved them earlier in the day, but they were really just opening acts for the main event. By four o'clock people chanting "Farrakhan, Farrakhan" were being praised for their patience. His son, a militaristic figure, assistant supreme captain of the Fruit of Islam, was drowned out by the tumult when he finally introduced him a few speechmakers later.

Three years ago Farrakhan drew a larger crowd in Atlanta than the World Series, but that same year Wallace Deen Muhammad spoke at the Pentagon and then addressed the U.S. Senate. In 1993 Farrakhan tried very hard to get on the roster of speechmakers for the thirtieth-anniversary observances of the March on Washington, attended by more than had gone to the original march, but he was refused. The Million Man March was his one-upmanship for having been excluded, as well as the fulfillment of his dream. After all, the Mall is where the coronation is held, even if King had been down at the Lincoln Memorial end. Audiences segregated by gender used to be common at Nation of Islam happenings. But the former calypso singer, the narcissist who launched a line of skin-care products in 1986, has been selling wolf tickets for so long that he was ill prepared to play the benevolent patriarch. His debut in the sun was an anticlimax, like a tedious riverboat ride tourists regret after they've made such an effort to get to a place they've heard was so spectacular.

Farrakhan struck the pose of a history decoder and decipherer, the one who would break it all down for us. He added up 16 and 3, because this had to do with the date slaves landed at Jamestown, the height of the Lincoln Memorial, and the fact that Jefferson was the third president. It added up to the height of the Washington Monument — that obelisk shape, he interrupted pedagogically, lifted from black Egypt. Washington, a grand master of the Masonic order, and Jefferson both owned slaves; Lincoln had been ambivalent about emancipation. Hardly Masonic secrets. "What is so deep about number 19? When you have a 9, you have a woman that is pregnant. One means something secret that has to be unfolded." That we were looking where he told us to look and listening to what he was telling us revealed only that we were less confident as citizens than he was as a self-promoter.

Elijah Muhammad's *Message to the Blackman* has been retired to the cultural vaults, rather like certain founding Mormon texts that have become an inconvenience, and we don't hear much these days about Yacub, the mad scientist back in time who was expelled from Mecca and then invented white people. Farrakhan's address contained little straight Nation of Islam doctrine and not much orthodox Muslim belief either, apart from some liturgical phrases suitably provocative because they came from him. His knowing smile as he went on about Nebuchadnezzar and Josephus, and master builders getting hit on the head, reminded me of a story a friend told me about Farrakhan showing up at the *Washington Post*, where he talked a great deal about spaceships. The spaceships were left out of the published interview. Thomas Jefferson believed in the existence of extraterrestrials, but that's not what concerns us about him, not what he's famous for. We tend to listen to Farrakhan from a predisposition, either a determination or a refusal to find the lunatic riches, ready to engage in a war of contexts. But Farrakhan was convinced by the sheer presence of so many that he was adored, and this provided all the context for his words that anyone needed to understand him.

Farrakhan's scarcely unusual rhetorical strategy is to declare himself the outsider persecuted for his outspoken truthfulness. Believing in him proves the bravery of his audience. In the end, only what works to his advantage reflects credit on his audience. This may come from habit, from the experience of having navigated the higher echelons of the Nation of Islam. Much is made of his shrewdness as a publicist, but what he has most clearly demonstrated is an ability to wait, to outlast everyone in the field. The reason he is under threat, his strategy goes, is that he has something important to tell his audience, something his enemies don't want them to hear.

Farrakhan pretended to quote from a letter written in 1612 by one Willie Lynch, a slave master. "In my bag I have a foolproof method for controlling the slaves." The words Farrakhan attributed to Lynch were not in the style of the seventeenth century. No doubt he assumed that everyone understood the letter was apocryphal, a parable about fear, envy, and distrust, the means by which blacks are kept disunited. Lynch was made to say that he pitted older males against younger males, men against women, and so on. "I take these differences and I make them bigger." "The black after receiving this indoctrination shall carry this on." That, Farrakhan explained, is why black pastors and educators remained under the "control mechanism of former slave masters and their children." In other words, the black leaders most likely to oppose him have a heritage of being brainwashed. However, in spite of all the divisiveness, he said, black people had survived, as if the sacred purpose of the sons of Garvey had been to endure and one day make a pilgrimage to Washington, where he, Farrakhan, would expose his light.

There is often just enough historical truth in Farrakhan's uses of history. Slaves were separated from other slaves who spoke the same language; educated blacks were trained up to bourgeois ways. But the import of the history lesson was in its application to himself. The Lynch letter served Farrakhan by dignifying his warnings about division. By locating disunity in the historical conspiracy of whites against blacks, he showed that acclaiming him was not a personal but a collective triumph over those who did not want to see blacks united. "We are a wounded people, but we are being healed."

The elaborate process by which blacks could heal themselves involved coming into "a state of recognition that you are in the wrong." The aim of confession, forgiveness, and atonement was a more perfect union with God. But his prophecy, his healing, turned out to be a rehash of personal reform — black pride as inner peace, black pride as the foundation of domestic order — mixed with black capitalism, as if he were addressing a population of small retailers rather than low-wage earners. Once again, everything referred immediately back to him. "When you're sick, you want the doctor to make the correct diagnosis. You don't smack the doctor." However, the person who points out what is wrong with us as social beings is hated and misunderstood, especially by those who have become "entrenched in evil" and been made arrogant by power. He has been mistreated for our sake. The difference between his message and the same message from others in the past was that he was not a false prophet.

The atmosphere was like those concerts whose nostalgic fans, waiting to embrace the electrified Greatest Hits, concede the new, wobbly acoustical tunes. The crowd relished the showmanship in Farrakhan's asking each of us to take out a dollar bill, hold it up, wave it in the air — a display of our potential economic power — and keep it there until his officials arrived with slitted cartons for us to jam the money into. But some two hours later, when he was searching for yet another way to tell us why we were afflicted and why we were ready to come out of the furnace, I noticed men packing up their coolers and walking away.

Farrakhan directed to the appropriate sign-up booth those who were willing to adopt some of the thousands of black children in the United States who needed homes. He announced his voter registration drive, as if such drives had not been the main activity of black groups for the past thirty years. But he was the seer who could also get things done. He promised to get an outside accounting firm to scrutinize every dollar he'd collected, saying that he wanted to "open the coat," to show he did not have a hidden agenda. In the distance I saw people leaving in droves, rather like the rush for the parking lot at a sports event when the outcome is assured before the end of play. Farrakhan's voice followed us down to the sidewalk. It ambushed us from car radios, from hotel televisions.

3

On a day supposedly devoted to self-criticism, Farrakhan did not offer much of an apology for his uses of anti-Semitism. He claimed that he pointed out the evil in black people as no other black leader did and that black people didn't call him anti-black or "a purveyor of malice" for it. "They know I must love them." He left out that he tends to paint those blacks who don't acknowledge his leadership as anti-black. He was trying to imply that he was no harder on Jews than he was on blacks. He expressed gratitude for Moses and the Torah among "the servants of Allah," and said he did not want to "squabble" with Jewish leaders anymore. Farrakhan's olive branch was so tentative because, having set up a refusal to back down as the litmus test, he couldn't be seen to be doing so.

A key to unity these days is a group's perception of itself as being disliked and surrounded. Fear is a part of fund-raising for Jewish groups and Jewish charities. Exploiting that fear has been a part of Farrakhan's career. It was clear, for instance, that the Anti-Defamation League would not let his baiting remarks over the years go unchallenged, but had Farrakhan gone on about white people in general all this time, he would not have gotten half the attention. He wanted a way to inject himself into public consciousness. He could then advertise the reactions as evidence of his dynamism.

Most white men find it hard to imagine that a black man could think of himself as using them, just as few black people can admit that a black man who comes on as so rebellious could be using them. Because of historical pieties and griefs, many people assume that a black man is telling the truth if he sounds harsh enough, just as many assume that someone willing to express anti-Semitism in public is being honest. There are, of course, black anti-Semites, Jewish anti-Semites, and white anti-Semites, just as there are blacks, Jews, and whites who don't like blacks. Some familiar anti-Semitic conspiracy theories have been circulated by whites prominent in the Christian right, which has put Jewish neoconservatives in an awkward position.

But the liberal coalition of blacks and Jews in electoral politics has suffered most. Maybe the coalition was falling apart anyway, but Farrakhan has never wrecked a Jewish politician. He has caused problems for a few black ones. James Forman, executive director of SNCC in the 1960s and now president of the Unemployment and Poverty Action Committee in Washington, pointed out that three days before the last mayoral election in New York City, Farrakhan applied for a permit to hold a rally that he later called off. David Dinkins was thus embroiled in a dispute over Farrakhan's right to the permit. If it didn't cost him votes, Forman said, it diverted some of his energies. Farrakhan has touched several bases and tainted them all in the process.

Farrakhan's leadership seems fresh because it is untried. He seems like a truth teller because he can pretend to candor. As Murray Kempton once said, there must be a little of Malcolm X in every black, and that is what Farrakhan finds and goads. He can appear to let go and let loose in a manner that many who come to hear him can't when on the job or in the street. Other black figures seem ineffectual because they are circumspect in public or bogged down in consensus politics while not much changes for the majority of blacks. Farrakhan can remain as unapologetic as Jesse Helms. But the troops toward whom Farrakhan behaved as though he were pacifying them may find him no different as a spokesman in the wider world than other blacks already there. In a way, Farrakhan is in a position similar to that of Malcolm X when he left the Nation of Islam and complained that his followers wouldn't let him turn a corner.

James Baldwin once said that the protest novel, far from being upsetting, was a comfort to American society, and something of the same applies to Farrakhan: adversarial, menacing in tone, as if in telepathic communication with a black rage that he can harness or unleash as easily as turning on a faucet. Whites like to think there is someone in control of the taps of emotion, but Farrakhan also confirms the image of the black as separate, not a part of things, not to be trusted. The moment when a civil rights figure could be elected to high office has perhaps passed. Colin Powell's military career would have solved a problem almost without bringing it up. His institutional background was reassuring, a promise that he represented something larger than the special interests of blacks, as if civil rights or economic aid were not concerns for whites.

Malcolm X once said to Coretta Scott King that he was so militant because he wanted the government to think the only alternative to him was dealing with a moderate-seeming man like King. But Farrakhan has no intention of sacrificing himself so that someone else can be influential. He was quick to put Clinton's speech on race relations earlier that afternoon in Texas into his Million Man March address. He treated Clinton's remarks as an attempt to negotiate with him in some way, a sign of the weakness of the civil rights movement that he is able to exploit. When Ben Chavis was executive director of the NAACP, having defeated Jackson for the post, he was criticized when he invited Farrakhan to a symposium of black leaders. Perhaps Chavis included Farrakhan because of his popularity among the young. When a sex scandal later forced Chavis to resign, he landed in Farrakhan's camp. James Forman doubted that Farrakhan could have organized the Million Man March without Chavis's connections. The logistics would have been beyond his expertise. Now Farrakhan can do himself what the big civil rights groups used to do.

The most disturbing thing Farrakhan said all day came at the end of his speech, disguised as a benevolent idea. He said the mainstream groups hadn't supported him. "So what?" He said he didn't need to be in any mainstream. The mainstream was sitting in boardrooms, out of touch with reality, he said, even though most black groups are grassroots in structure. "I don't need you to validate me. My people have validated me." He proposed setting up an economic development fund with the money raised from the March and from future marches. Maybe its board, he said, would be composed of the leadership on stage with him. One of the things the fund could do would be to "free" the Urban League and the NAACP. He could imagine, he said, going to Myrlie Evers Williams, president of the board of the NAACP, and asking what the NAACP's budget was for that year. "Thirteen million? Fifteen million? Write her a check." Then, he said, the NAACP would be accountable to the board of his economic development fund.

Farrakhan was suggesting that he buy out and buy off the black organization that has been most prominent in the history of desegregation, an organization that, because of its prestige, however battered lately, has blocked his way by remaining critical, opposed, unconvinced. Blocked his way to what? So much of what Farrakhan has to say is not only about black America's plight but about his status in the mainstream he affects to despise and to find so irrelevant. He comes from that old-fashioned world where race politics represented one of the few career opportunities open to blacks. But his is also a generation that still thinks there can be only one hand at the faucets of emotion. Blacks used to have a nickname for Booker T. Washington, who very much saw himself, and was seen by whites, as the mediator between North and South, black and white, the one who went to the White House and reported back: HNIC, Head Nigger in Charge. Perhaps that was why, when Farrakhan repeated that he — and God — deserved credit for the March, he was expressing an insecurity as much as he was gloating.

In every issue Farrakhan sees a Farrakhan-shaped hole. He said he hadn't come to Washington to tear the country down. The country was tearing itself down. Derrick Bell, who attended the March but was not among the speechmakers, said he disagreed with those who objected to the March because it seemed like little more than an imitation of the conservative ideology called family values. He said he hoped that the Christian right did not have a monopoly on such things. Blacks are not necessarily society's natural liberals, contrary to stubborn fears and even more persistent expectations, but Farrakhan's ambition to create yet another religious political force also draws attention away from the secular civil rights movement. Farrakhan and black conservatives agree on what they see as the corruption to black souls in looking to government solutions to their problems. That the atonement Farrakhan offered turned out to be along the guidelines of moral choice and community responsibility is very agreeable to whites in a political climate hostile to affirmative action and the like. Thurgood Marshall as a litigator was more of a threat to the status quo than Farrakhan will ever be, because Marshall could win in the courts. Perhaps that was why Marshall dismissed one of Clarence Thomas's heroes, Malcolm X, as little more than talk.

The morning after the March I went back to the Capitol. There were a few men here and there taking last photographs of themselves at the monuments that had been coated with people the day before. Traces of straws, gum wrappers, cigarette butts, and plastic rings from bottles glinted in the grass. People had collected the garbage into heaps, but the wind had blown it around during the night. A fifty-nine-year-old black groundskeeper said he thought the March was uplifting, but he was reluctant to say too much because he worked for those people "up on the Hill." He went back to his rake. All through the thirteen-hour shower of sweeping phrases about self-reliance, I'd kept thinking that there has never been a time in America's history when blacks did not depend on self-help. As Du Bois once said to Booker T., blacks have had self-help for ages and what he wanted to know was what had it done for them so far. Between the Natural History Museum and the Smithsonian Castle, seagulls scavenged where all those men had stood.

JONATHAN RABAN

Last Call of the Wild

FROM ESQUIRE

I FIRST NOTICED that something odd was happening to fishing — the passion of my boyhood and an occasional pleasure in my adult life — on a visit to New York in 1988. The Ralph Lauren store on Madison Avenue had become a museum of old fishing tackle, and I pored affectionately over the displays of greenheart and split-cane rods, wicker creels, fly boxes, brass-bound wooden reels, and deerstalker caps stuck about with flies. Though I hadn't fished in a dozen years, I could still name the flies — Greenwell's Glory, Coch-y-bonddhu, Silver Doctor, Tup's Indispensable.

For me, the stuff was pungent with memories of the geezerly world of English brooks and chalk streams: it summoned a crew of aged gentry folk smelling of damp tweed and pipe tobacco. Liver spots. Bifocal specs. Whiskey and soda ("Chin-chin!") in the snug bar of the Dog and Duck. That these characters had somehow become the cynosure of New York fashion in the eighties, or at least that their discarded paraphernalia was being cast as a lure to hook the affluent young on shirts and pants and blousons, was so bizarre that I began to suspect Ralph Lauren of having a ribald and anarchic wit. What would he go for next? Stamp collecting? Amateur chemistry? Toy trains?

Then came Robert Redford's movie version of Norman Maclean's *A River Runs Through It* — a feature-length Ralph Lauren window display. In a rinsed sepia light, men in period leisure wear did pretty things with varnished antique fly rods. The wristy craft of casting put them in touch with the historic past, and it made them at home in nature — at home in their own natures. The grace of the line unrolling from the rod tip, the fly kissing the surface of the water as a trout rose to meet it, was pure fashion plate. Then, with the rod bent into a hoop, one could feel in the musculature of one's own forearm the burrowing shudder of the fish at the other end. In an as yet unspoiled Eden, we were joined to wild nature by a thread of oiled silk.

That image now has a poignancy that would have seemed incomprehensible a few years ago. Within the last decade, we've come to live with the idea that nature is in its fifth act. The corpses are piling up onstage — the dying species, razored forests, wrecked habitats. Wilderness, once thought of as inexhaustible, has been reduced to posted wilderness trails, with park rangers issuing permits to overnight campers. Like any other commodity, nature, by growing scarce, has shot up in value, and access to the wild has become a luxury and an emblem of social status.

But what do you do when you get there? Hugging trees palls after the first splinter or two. Hiking is too tame and objectless for people bred to displays of competitive prowess. Rock climbing is dangerous. Hunting lands one in moral difficulties in mixed company. A *River Runs Through It* offered a solution in the form of an equipage of covetable goods and garments, the attainable landscape of the Northwest, a showoff skill, and the promise of a direct line to the wild.

So the Sage graphite six-weight, encased in a monogrammed leather cylinder, slides into the BMW, its butt nudging the car phone. Even in the underground garage on the Upper East Side, the rod is capable of some remarkable distance casting, tangibly connecting its owner to a purling, snow-fed river nine states away. The line soars, loops over Wisconsin, unfolds past the Dakotas, and falls weightlessly across the current of the Clark Fork. There's an answering tug, like a small electric shock, and you're in touch.

When I moved from London to Seattle in 1990, my self-esteem was dented by the discovery that I was part of a mass movement of city people piling into the Northwest because they wanted to rub up against whatever was left of nature. We brought bird books, tree books, and Japanese microbinoculars that you can flip out of your coat pocket to zoom in on a passing bald eagle when the car's stalled in a jam on the morning commute.

Seattle is a city fixated on the countryside. Bright scraps of sea and lake show at the ends of streets, and an upward glance finds snowcapped mountains moored between the high-rises. Downtown is crowded with stores that cater to the nature industry — Patagonia, REI, Eddie Bauer. A river runs through Eddie Bauer; a makeshift mountain stream that tinkles over slate falls slap through the middle of the split-level store. The fishing department is sited on its east bank. There are no trout in the Bauer River, so far as I could see, and the rocky bottom is littered with small change instead of pebbles, but it makes the point that in Seattle, swift water is always at the heart of things. The city is bisected by the Lake Washington Ship Canal, at whose entrance by the sea locks there's an underground bunker with aquarium windows, where one can watch Pacific salmon climb the ladder on their way from the ocean to the inland rivers. In their seasons, coho and king salmon pack into the ladder as tightly as sardines in a can. Jostling one another, fin to fin, they struggle up against the current — huge, brilliant, battle-scarred creatures in a blind rage to spawn and die.

I had never seen a city with so many shops devoted to fly-fishing, each with its fly-tying classes, casting clinics, and a chalkboard for the news of the day — as that the Royal Coachman Bucktail is fishing well on the Stillaguamish. Several million dollars are spent every year in Seattle on fly rods, reels, lines, leaders, and flies — and that is only the beginning of a river of money that fills motel rooms and restaurant tables, funds the state Department of Fish and Wildlife through license fees, keeps Barbour jackets on the racks of the outdoor-clothing stores, and pays the wages of professional guides. The hankering to be purposefully alone in nature has major commercial ramifications.

Seattle and Portland, Oregon, are the twin capitals of a particularly dramatic and intense form of fly-fishing: the ritual persecution of the steelhead trout. The steelhead is a queer fish, as big as a salmon, weighing anywhere up to thirty-five pounds. It's usually described as a sea-run rainbow trout, which is like describing a Roman Catholic as a Southern Baptist with a taste for incense. It spends most of its life at sea, in the ocean south of the Aleutians, and unlike the Pacific salmon, it returns to sea after spawning in freshwater, which saves it from the helpless fatalism of its salmon cousins. Whereas salmon go up the rivers in gangs and to a strict timetable, steelhead move in ones and twos, and, though there are distinct summer runs and winter runs, they enter the rivers during every month of the year.

Wild steelhead (serious fly fishers despise hatchery-bred "plastic fish") are now rare enough to make them prized. Since they do not ordinarily feed in freshwater but live off the accumulated fat of two or three years' gluttony at sea, they are satisfyingly hard to tempt with an artificial fly, and steelheading has the quixotic glamour of a unicorn hunt. The first fly fisher I met was a man I found wading ashore from a white-water riffle on the Snoqualmie River, a half hour's drive from downtown Seattle. I hadn't yet bought any fishing gear and wanted hints and tips. I asked the man if he'd made contact with a fish.

"Yes," he said, and took on a visible glow as he described making a long cast across the current and how, after a moment's pause, the cast kept on going and going while the reel yammered like a stuck doorbell. "He was only on for a few seconds — but it's the few seconds that you remember on all the fishless days. . . . It stays with you."

"And that was just down here, this morning?"

I got a *dim bunny* look.

"That," he said, "was three months ago. Ninth of October," making it sound like a date for marching bands and fireworks displays.

East of Seattle, off Highway 405, lies the cutting edge of sub-suburbia, where new housing developments sprout from patches of freshly cut-down woodland. Here, in the foothills of the Cascades, the rivers flatten out after their headlong tumblings from the mountains. Here, the newcoming nature bibbers settle, cheek by jowl with the woods and the water. Wherever you look, the fir trees part to admit another brand-new community of identical houses. Timber with brick trimmings, they're half Olde English–gentleman's residence, half overgrown log cabin. They are painted in pastel shades of buff, pink, ocher — the colors of western Washington rain clouds. COME LIVE WITH US! implore the banners strung out over the unfinished streets, and the names of these settlements promise the house buyer that here is the perfect $140,000 rural idyll — Cottage Crest, Aspenwood, Cedar Park, Lake of the Woods (More Home and More Privacy).

This is horse-farm and software country. Small computer outfits

— satellite moons of Microsoft — dot the landscape, while the
humans in sight seem all of a piece: lightly built, thirtyish, bespec-
tacled, and brainy-looking, they drive VW Golfs with infant seats
in the back. The men would as soon admit to owning a gun as they
would to sexually harassing their personal assistants. But they go
steelheading.

In a cloud-colored house with coach lamps, in a development
called Chestnut Glen, lives the publisher, editor, and cover star of
a new folio-size slick, *Wild Steelhead and Atlantic Salmon.* I'd read
Tom Pero before I met him and enjoyed the lacquered angling
prose of his editorial credo:

> We believe in the heart-stopping swirl of a sixteen-pounder under your
> dry fly; in the twenty-four-hour Norwegian summer light; in the brilliant
> red of an October maple reflected in the Margaree; in a scratched
> Wheatley fly box filled with tiny feather-wing doubles; in a dropping
> river the color of jade; in blue campfire smoke; in the first-day music
> of wilderness steelhead water slapping rhythmically against the bot-
> tom of your loaded raft; in hundred-year-old salmon-fishing books; in
> leather rod cases; in the smell of spruce after a hard rain. . . .

Driving into Chestnut Glen, I saw how a similar nostalgia pow-
ered both Pero's writing style and the street of pale repro boxes
on which he lived: both were homesick for the genteel European
past, for nature, for old craftsmanly artifacts. It was a rainy February morning when I visited Pero, and his house was full of the
smell of wet spruce (at least wet Douglas fir), leather rod cases,
and hundred-year-old fishing books.

Eyeglassed, mustached, and weather-tanned, Pero was a few
years older than his standard-issue neighbors, but like them he
was a newcomer. His life was defined by his fishing. He grew up
in Massachusetts, but the East Coast was barren of the Atlantic
salmon that used to swim up its rivers — they had disappeared in
the eighteenth century, victims of absentee English millowners
whose dams had blocked their way upstream. "Steelhead are why
I moved to the West Coast," he said. In 1977, he began editing
Trout magazine, moving it, in 1984, to Bend, Oregon. At the
beginning of 1993, he moved up the coast to Seattle to start *Wild
Steelhead.*

With its full-page watercolors and line drawings, its edible landscape photography and ten-dollar cover price, "The Best Fishing Magazine Ever Published" is another sign of the social ascent of fly-fishing.

"Steelheading used to be a working-class sport," Pero said. Its masculine nomenclature had been given to it by loggers, Boeing engineers, construction workers. Whereas favored lies on Scottish salmon rivers had soft-spoken, drawing-room names like Home Pool, the Willows, the Birches, comparable reaches of steelhead water were called Car-Body Hole, Shit-House Run, Powerline Hole. Steelhead flies were "short, fat, bulky — real chunks of meat," with names like the Boss, Green Butt Skunk, Brad's Brat, Moose Turd, Killer, Juicy Bug. "When the runs collapsed," said Pero, "the old working-class fishermen quit."

For the new generations of anglers, the rarity of the wild steelhead was its point. To connect with one was to experience an epiphany. That a season might go by without a touch only intensified the purity of the quest. The new generation used flies tied on barbless hooks, and on the rare days when they beached a fish, they carefully wet their hands, raised the fish to have its picture taken, and let it swim free. You do not club an epiphany to death.

The class distinction between the old and new fishermen was mirrored by the distinction between the increasingly small and select runs of wild steelhead and the common mob of fish born in Department of Fish and Wildlife hatcheries. When Pero spoke of hatchery fish, he talked in a language of class metaphor. The hatchery types, conceived in buckets of pink caviar squirted with milt, were of "questionable origins," "foreign stock." They were raised in "concrete jails," and when they came back from their years at sea, they did not, like wild fish, enter the rivers like gentlemen, one by one, but came "in slugs, like motorcycle gangs." They "destroyed the character of the wild steelhead."

The politics of nature in the Northwest are fought along hard ideological lines, and when Pero blazed away about genuine and counterfeit fish, he was taking a political stand on a subject that goes far beyond the question of steelhead genetics. The diminishing runs of "wild native" fish, like the diminishing stands of old-growth forest, represent the remains of a great inheritance, now inflated and devalued by an influx of forged currency manufactured by the timber industry or the Department of Fish and

Wildlife. "Nature" here is deceiving, as the newcomer to the region quickly learns. In your innocence, you see a tract of green forest reaching up a mountainside: *wrong*. It is (you are informed) a tree farm, a plantation of firs, all exactly the same age and size, with none of the complex characteristics, the canopies and understories, that make a true forest into a suitable habitat for, say, the spotted owl, that disheveled, cross-eyed bird whose housing requirements have been at the center of so much acrimonious debate. You see a steelhead wearily finning-and-tailing its way upstream from the ocean to the creek where it was born: *wrong*. It's a hatchery mutant, a mass-produced, proletarian creature with the perverted instincts of a born-and-bred gang member.

Soon you find yourself tilting every landscape that you see this way and that against the light, like an art dealer searching a painting for signs of inauthenticity. "It's not right" is art-dealer parlance for *fake*, and a dam on a river, a planted tree, a farmed fish, a clay slide, a dusting of silt on the gravel bottom of a stream, the distant skirl of a buzz saw, are giveaway signs that the landscape is *not right*. These are severe tests. If they were applied to England, the whole country would be shown up as a gigantic fake, the product of some nine hundred years of intensive agriculture and technology, with no real nature left in it at all.

I see the point in the special case of the Pacific Northwest, where odd patches of irreplaceable habitat still survive and might yet be saved. But there's a nasty streak of consumerist connoisseurship in the way these tests are conducted. It is the newcomers themselves who are the fiercest judges of the landscape, the couple fresh from Brooklyn or New Haven who raise their voices loudest against the loggers, fish biologists, developers, and all the other despoilers of the wilderness, and they do so in the aggrieved tones of people who fear they're not getting their money's worth.

Like the spotted owl, the wild steelhead has become a touchstone species. If you can find one, you are looking at real, *natural* nature. It comes with a convenient built-in guarantee of authenticity, in the form of an intact adipose fin. (Hatchery fish have theirs chopped off before the prison gates are opened, and so carry the stigma of their industrial origins for the rest of their lives, like branded slaves.)

This obsession with locating the genuine in nature is part and parcel of the larger quest to find the genuine in our own natures. After all, we came out here to slough off our superficial urban selves (those counterfeit industrial products) and be, well, more *real* than we were back in our eastern cities. Going fishing has entered the therapy culture.

I bought a nine-weight rod and practiced casting from our third-floor deck onto the roof of the neighbors' house. I was rusty and inept, but after half an hour of tossing aerial spaghetti, my wrist began to recover its memory, and I was laying a more or less straight line just upstream of the chimney pot. I made a date to spend a day on the Skagit River with Dec Hogan, a guide known as a steelhead magician.

We'd arranged to meet at the crack of a late-February dawn, at a gas station outside the town of Concrete, Washington, where I checked into a motel and went barhopping along Main Street. Concrete was barely a hundred miles to the northeast of Seattle, but the two-hour drive seemed longer: it took one back to the middle of the 1970s, to an enviably guiltless and robust attitude toward nature.

Concrete people were still smokers. In the bars, drifts of pungent violet fog threw the pool players into soft focus. The Saturday-night crowd of broad-beamed folk put one in mind of corn dogs, jo-jos, and tubs of chocolate-chip-cookie-dough ice cream. The bars were monuments to local sport and industry. Their walls were hung with rusty two-man saws, with mirrors advertising the Winchester Repeating Arms Company alongside Michelob and Budweiser, with antlers, stags' heads, and the pinned-out skins of wild cats. No bar in Concrete was properly a bar without a stuffed lynx or bobcat, its back arched, its right-hand foreclaws raised against the viewer, jaws wide open for the kill.

The taxidermist (the half-dozen examples of the genre that I saw all looked as if they were by the same hand) had gone to a lot of trouble to represent these creatures as the embodiment of primal ferocity. An inartistically stuffed lynx might easily look like the bartender's pet mouser; the ones in Concrete had been equipped with gleaming dentures with two-inch fangs, and their throats were painted in Day-Glo scarlet. They stood for the wilderness as man's mortal enemy, for the hunter as hero. In Concrete, people knew how to relate to nature: they chopped it down, shot it, trapped it, killed it, ate it.

I liked Concrete a lot. It was a welcome escape from the goody-goody atmosphere of Seattle. I dined on chicken-fried steak, lit up a Swisher Sweet, called for a Christian Brothers brandy, and felt pleasantly red in tooth and claw for the first time in ages.

Next morning, there was a dusting of frost on the ground outside the motel and a lumpy skin of ice on the car windshield. Dec Hogan was waiting at the gas station, his boat in tow behind a mud-slathered truck. He'd said over the phone that he was thirty, but his face was so eroded that he looked a good ten years older. Like Pero, he wore a mustache, for warmth, I guessed: freezing rain is thought to be ideal weather for winter-run steelhead, and Hogan's face, crevassed and windburned, might have belonged to some arctic explorer. The sight of it made me want to go home.

We drove a dozen miles up Highway 20, the road clinging to the weaving contour of the riverbank. Hogan, nodding at the water, said, "My office." The Skagit was swollen with snowmelt from the recent warm spell, and its windless surface was riddled with the crazy Arabic of deep turbulence — water in friction with water, moving in great swirls and boils. Patches of fleecy white showed where the river's course was broken by boulders the size of Ford Escorts. Two hundred yards or so from bank to bank, pouring westward at eight or nine knots, the Skagit went growling, bearishly, through the woods; a big, wild brute of a river and perfect steelhead water.

Hogan launched the Mackenzie drift boat from a clearing by a trestle bridge. The sun, a hazy wafer, had narrowly topped the scissored edge of the mountain snowfields when — in neoprene chest waders, half frogs, half men — we began to raft downstream. The river was startlingly pellucid — gin with a dash of lime. Turbulence kept on throwing the bottom out of focus, like smoke in a Concrete bar, but every few seconds an oval window of water would open on an aquarium scene of boulders ten feet down.

"Steelhead motel," Hogan said, looking in.

But every room was vacant, so far as I could see. A bright flash in the rocks was someone's lost fishing lure; a promising, torpedo-shaped dark shadow was a sunken log.

In water, life is always murky, as in the plankton-rich Puget Sound, which has the appearance of thick beef soup. Sterility is pristine; and the Skagit, empty of weeds, of minnow shoals, of almost everything except the odd caddis larva, was brilliant and lifeless. Only steelhead, on an extended Ramadan after years of oceanic self-indulgence, could live happily in this prismlike torrent of melted snow.

Hogan beached the drift boat on a patch of dew. "Do you see the seam in the water there?" A sandbar deflected the current, thrusting it from the north to the south bank of the river; the "seam" was a sharp pencil line where the fast-moving water of the mainstream rubbed against the idle water on its northern side. A string of finger-size whirlpools marked its length. The idea was to fish along, and just inside, this seam. "You're looking for walking-speed water."

Steelhead do their traveling at night and rest up by day. They hang out on the fringe of the mainstream, tucking themselves in behind boulders, saving their energy for the journey they will make when covering darkness falls. The problem is first to find their hidey-holes, then to get the fly down deep enough to interest them.

Below the sandbar, hip-deep in the freezing river, I began to cast, pitching the line across the current and trying to let the fly drift downstream. Time and again, the current seized the line, bellying it out so that the fly skittered uselessly across the top of the water. Hogan, at my elbow, made suggestions while my toes lost consciousness. I improved, slowly, under Hogan's instruction, and it wasn't long before I was fishing in earnest, probing the river with the fly as it went shimmying through the deep. "Remember," he said, "you're trying to find the needle in the haystack."

Somewhere down there lay *something*. With each cast, I tried to contact it. *Pick up the phone, steelhead!*

"Nobody at home," Hogan said.

Back in the drift boat, we floated on downstream, the swirls of current crackling like a brushfire under the hull. On both banks, leafless alders climbed from an ashen tangle of blackberry and salal. I studied the fly I had been using — a nameless creation of Hogan's and a work of violent surrealism. Part polar bear, part jungle cock, part Christmas tinsel, part tangerine chenille, it was an object one might meet in Native American mythology or a seriously bad dream.

"It's meant to be lifelike," Hogan said.

"Like what? Like a shrimp or a squid or . . . ?"

"No. Like *life*."

I dangled it in the water, where it quivered and collected pin-pricks of light.

"You see how the hackles are working — "

"Is it just supposed to annoy the hell out of the fish?"

"I think it's territorial. He sees this other creature on his patch, and *bang!* I don't think he gives it too much thought."

We fished the next pool in tandem, with me leading the way downstream and Hogan following. I tried to imagine the lifelike thing as it pirouetted in a ball of turbulence and swam on a zigzag track across the current — and the fish, half asleep in the lee of a boulder, suddenly alert to the presence of an impudent, Pierrot-costumed intruder. Hunched over the rod, forefinger crooked around a loop of line, I was all expectancy and ardor; with each fresh cast, the unseen steelhead grew more palpable, until it was so nearly *there* that I was in a state of premonitory shock at the sudden, violent wrench of the fish's assault on the fly.

Underfoot, the basalt pebbles were treacherously slick, and my toes were numb. Halfway down the pool, I clambered ashore onto the warming sand. I'd saved the stub of last night's Swisher Sweet to celebrate my first fish; now I lit it in honor of a phantom. Launching a curlicue of smoke into the mountain air, I lay on the sand and watched Hogan.

He was making enormous casts with a double-handed Spey rod. It was a depressing sight, to see seventy-five or eighty feet of line spill from his rod tip and uncoil lazily over the water, where it made a weightless landing, as true as a line of longitude. Up to his solar plexus in the river, padding confidently along its slippery bottom, jaws working slowly on a quid of chewing tobacco, casting like an angel, he was giving a humiliating demonstration of how to make oneself comfortably at home in nature.

The nasal churring of a woodpecker in a tree was overlaid, on the instant, by a cowboy yodel from Hogan. It wasn't a woodpecker; it was the ratchet on the reel, and a fish running fast and deep across the current.

"Not a lightning bolt," Hogan called, as the sound dropped in pitch to a leisurely *tirra-whirra*. The big Spey rod was bent in a half circle, its sunlit tip shivering. Hampered by waders, I stumbled along the water's edge; it was like trying to spring through glue.

By the time I reached him, Hogan was a circus ringmaster. His long whip flicked and, far away, under the trees on the far bank, the fish climbed into the air and hung there, a glowing quarter moon whose sudden brilliance made the rest of the world look flat and monochrome. Hogan's leaping fish, released from the laws of perspective, a blaze of silver, spraying the air with light, looked like the manifestation of some unearthly presence. It was too big for the river, too full of life for the sterile clarity of the water from which it sprang.

Within two or three minutes, the fish was twisting wretchedly in the shallows, directly under Hogan's rod tip. It had shrunk a lot since its moment of glory in the air: it turned out to be a hen fish, wild (it exhibited an unmutilated adipose fin as it rolled), of about six pounds — a tiddler, as steelhead go. It splashed and wallowed, shook the barbless hook from its mouth, and was gone. It left a fading wink in the water, like a sinking hubcap.

"This was a good day — now it's a great day," Hogan said. It was his first full hit in more than a week.

All afternoon, we drifted and fished, drifted and fished. An eagle riding a thermal sauntered over us; we floated past the white stumps of young trees, tidily logged by beavers. We skidded over a succession of small rapids, then inched down a long, deep, translucent pool. I hung over the bow of the drift boat, searching the checkerboard of colored rocks and gravelly holes for fish. Not a fin stirred in that beautiful, deserted underwater world.

When the sun collapsed into the Douglas firs on a hilltop not far off, the whole valley was immediately refrigerated. The chill was bitter as I began to fish the last pool. The opposite bank was a sheer cliff of greenery, fast turning black, and the braids of current in the mainstream had lost their sparkle and taken on the viscous look of poured tar. A truck, its headlamps on full beam, raked the trees fifty feet above the water. I'd quite forgotten about the roads: earlier, the sound of the river, half wind, half rockfall, had drowned the noise of traffic — but now I saw that the whole day had been spent not in a wilderness but on a roadside.

Neither this thought nor the icy cold could drag me back to the boat and the last half mile to the public ramp. I could feel the steelhead, readying themselves to stir from their daytime hideouts and begin the long night's cruise upstream. I was casting better now. My luck was in.

It was just a question of getting an extra yard farther out . . . a foot or eighteen inches deeper. . . . The fly was so nearly within reach of the fish that it seemed that one last muscular push would make the connection. I cast and cast, until I could no longer see where my leader was falling on the water. Back in the boat, as Hogan ferried us into the current, I held out two frozen white forefingers within half an inch of each other. "It was this close," I said.

BRUCE SHAPIRO

One Violent Crime

FROM THE NATION

ALONE IN MY HOME, I am staring at the television screen and
shouting. On the evening local news I have unexpectedly encountered video footage, several months old, of myself writhing on an
ambulance gurney, bright green shirt open and drenched with
blood, skin pale, knee raised, trying desperately and with utter
futility to find relief from pain.

On the evening of August 7, 1994, I was among seven people
stabbed and seriously wounded in a coffee bar a few blocks from
my house. Any televised recollection of this incident would be
upsetting. But the anger that has me shouting tonight is quite
specific, and political, in origin: my picture is being shown on the
news to illustrate why Connecticut's legislature plans to lock up
more criminals for a longer time. A picture of my body, contorted
and bleeding, has become a propaganda image in the crime war.

I had not planned to write about this assault. But for months
now the politics of the nation have in large part been the politics
of crime, from last year's federal crime bill through the fall elections through the Contract with America proposals awaiting action
by the Senate. Among a welter of reactions to the attack, one
feeling is clear: I am unwilling to be a silent poster child in this
debate.

The physical and political truth about violence and crime lies in
their specificity, so here is what happened: I had gone out for
after-dinner coffee that evening with two friends and New Haven
neighbors, Martin and Anna Broell Bresnick. At 9:45 we arrived
at a recently opened coffeehouse on Audubon Street, a block

occupied by an arts high school where Anna teaches, other community arts institutions, a few pleasant shops and upscale condos. Entering, we said hello to another friend, a former student of Anna's named Christina Koning, who the day before had started working behind the counter. We sat at a small table near the front of the café; about fifteen people were scattered around the room. Just before ten o'clock, the owner announced closing time. Martin stood up and walked a few yards to the counter for a final refill.

Suddenly there was chaos — as if a mortar shell had landed. I looked up, heard Martin call Anna's name, saw his arm raised and a flash of metal and people leaping away from a thin bearded man with a ponytail. Tables and chairs toppled. Without thinking I shouted to Anna, "Get down!" and pulled her to the floor, between our table and the café's outer wall. She clung to my shirt, I to her shoulders, and, crouching, we pulled each other toward the door.

What actually happened I was only able to tentatively reconstruct many weeks later. Apparently, as Martin headed toward the counter the thin bearded man, whose name we later learned was Daniel Silva, asked the time from a young man named Richard Colberg, who answered and turned to leave.

Without any warning, Silva pulled out a hunting knife with a six-inch blade and stabbed in the lower back a woman leaving with Colberg, a medical technician named Kerstin Braig. Then he stabbed Colberg, severing an artery in his thigh. Silva was a slight man, but he moved with demonic speed and force around the café's counter. He struck Martin in the thigh and in the arm he raised to protect his face. Our friend Chris Koning had in a moment's time pushed out the screen in a window and helped the wounded Kerstin Braig through it to safety. Chris was talking on the phone with the police when Silva lunged over the counter and stabbed her in the chest and abdomen. He stabbed Anna in the side as she and I pulled each other along the wall. He stabbed Emily Bernard, a graduate student who had been sitting quietly reading a book, in the abdomen as she tried to flee through the café's back door. All of this happened in about the time it has taken you to read this paragraph.

Meanwhile, I had made it out the café's front door onto the brick sidewalk with Anna, neither of us realizing yet that she was wounded. Seeing Martin through the window, I returned inside and we came out together. Somehow we separated, fleeing opposite ways down the street. I had gone no more than a few steps when I felt a hard punch in my back, followed instantly by the unforgettable sensation of skin and muscle tissue parting. Silva had stabbed me about six inches above my waist, just beneath my rib cage. (That single deep stroke cut my diaphragm and sliced my spleen in half.) Without thinking, I clapped my left hand over the wound even before the knife was out, and its blade caught my hand, leaving a slice across my palm and two fingers.

"Why are you doing this?" I cried out to Silva in the moment after feeling his knife punch in and yank out. As I fell to the street he leaned over my face; I vividly remember the knife's immense and glittering blade. He directed the point through my shirt into the flesh of my chest, beneath my left shoulder. I remember his brown beard, his clear blue-gray eyes looking directly into mine, the round globe of a street lamp like a halo above his head. Although I was just a few feet from a café full of people, and although Martin and Anna were only yards away, the street, the city, the world felt utterly empty except for me and this thin bearded stranger with clear eyes and a bowie knife. The space around us — well-lit, familiar Audubon Street, where for six years I had taken a child to music lessons — seemed literally to have expanded into a vast and dark canyon.

"You killed my mother," he answered. My own desperate response: "Please don't." Silva pulled the knifepoint out of my chest and disappeared. A moment later I saw him flying down the street on a battered, ungainly bicycle, back straight, vest flapping and ponytail flying.

After my assailant had gone I lay on the sidewalk, hand still over the wound on my back, screaming. Pain ran over me like an express train; it felt as though every muscle in my back were locked and contorted; breathing was excruciating. A security guard appeared across the street from me. I called out to him but he stood there frozen, or so it seemed. (A few minutes later, he would help police chase Silva down.) I shouted to Anna, who was hiding behind a car down the street. Still in shock and unaware of her own injury, she ran for help, eventually collapsing on the stairs of a nearby brownstone where a prayer group that was meeting upstairs answered her desperate ringing of the doorbell. From where

I was lying, I saw a second-floor light in the condo complex across the way. A woman's head appeared in the window. "Please help me," I implored. "He's gone. Please help me." She shouted back that she had called the police, but she did not come to the street. I was suddenly aware of a blond woman — Kerstin Braig, though I did not know her name then — in a white-and-gray-plaid dress, sitting on the curb. I asked her for help. "I'm sorry, I've done all I can," she muttered. She raised her hand, like a medieval icon; it was covered with blood. So was her dress. She sank into a kind of stupor. Up the street I saw a police car's flashing blue lights, then another's, then I saw an officer with a concerned face and a crackling radio crouched beside me. I stayed conscious as the medics arrived and I was loaded into an ambulance — being filmed for television, as it turned out, though I have no memory of the crew's presence.

Being a victim is a hard idea to accept, even while lying in a hospital bed with tubes in veins, chest, penis, and abdomen. The spirit rebels against the idea of oneself as fundamentally powerless. So I didn't think much for the first few days about the meaning of being a victim; I saw no political dimension to my experience.

As I learned in more detail what had happened, I thought, in my jumbled-up, anesthetized state, about my injured friends — although everyone survived, their wounds ranged from quite serious to critical — and about my wounds and surgery. I also thought about my assailant. A few facts about him are worth repeating. Until August 7 Daniel Silva was a self-employed junk dealer and a homeowner. He was white. He lived with his mother and several dogs. He had no arrest record. A New Haven police detective who was hospitalized across the hall from me recalled Silva as a socially marginal neighborhood character. He was not, apparently, a drug user. He had told neighbors about much violence in his family — indeed, not long before August 7 he showed one neighbor a scar on his thigh he said was from a stab wound.

A week earlier, Silva's seventy-nine-year-old mother had been hospitalized for diabetes. After a few days the hospital moved her to a new room; when Silva saw his mother's empty bed he panicked, but nurses swiftly took him to her new location. Still, something seemed to have snapped. Earlier on the day of the stabbings, police say, Silva released his beloved dogs, set fire to his house, and rode away on his bicycle as it burned. He arrived on Audubon Street with a single dog on a leash, evidently convinced his mother was dead. (She actually did die a few weeks after Silva was jailed.)

While I lay in the hospital, the big story on CNN was the Clinton administration's 1994 crime bill, then being debated in Congress. Even fogged by morphine I was aware of the irony. I was flat on my back, the result of a particularly violent assault, while Congress eventually passed the anti-crime package I had editorialized against in *The Nation* just a few weeks earlier. Night after night in the hospital, unable to sleep, I watched the crime-bill debate replayed and heard Republicans and Democrats (who had sponsored the bill in the first place) fall over each other to prove who could be the toughest on crime.

The bill passed on August 21, a few days after I returned home. In early autumn I read the entire text of the crime bill — all 412 pages. What I found was perhaps obvious, yet under the circumstances compelling: not a single one of those 412 pages would have protected me or Anna or Martin or any of the others from our assailant. Not the enhanced prison terms, not the forty-four new death-penalty offenses, not the three-strikes-you're-out requirements, not the summary deportations of criminal aliens. And the new tougher-than-tough anti-crime provisions of the Contract with America, like the proposed abolition of the Fourth Amendment's search and seizure protections, offer no more practical protection.

On the other hand, the mental-health and social-welfare safety net shredded by Reaganomics and conservatives of both parties might have made a difference in the life of someone like my assailant — and thus in the life of someone like me. My assailant's growing distress in the days before August 7 was obvious to his neighbors. He had muttered darkly about relatives planning to burn down his house. A better-funded, more comprehensive safety net might just have saved me and six others from untold pain and trouble.

From my perspective — the perspective of a crime victim — the Contract with America and its conservative Democratic analogs are really blueprints for making the streets even less safe. Want to take away that socialist income subsidy called welfare? Fine. Connecticut Governor John Rowland proposes cutting off all benefits after eighteen months. So more people in New Haven and other cities will turn to the violence-breeding economy of crack, or emotionally implode from sheer desperation. Cut funding for those soft-headed social workers? Fine; let more children be beaten without the prospect of outside intervention, more Daniel Silvas carrying their own traumatic scars into violent adulthood. Get rid of the few amenities prisoners enjoy, like sports equipment, musical instruments, and the right to get college degrees, as proposed by the congressional right? Fine; we'll make sure that those inmates are released to their own neighborhoods tormented with unchanneled rage.

One thing I could not properly appreciate in the hospital was how deeply many friends, neighbors, and acquaintances were shaken by the coffeehouse stabbings, let alone strangers who took the time to write. The reaction of most was a combination of decent horrified empathy and a clear sense that their own presumption of safety was undermined.

But some people who didn't bother to acquaint themselves with the facts used the stabbings as a sort of Rorschach test on which they projected their own preconceptions about crime, violence, and New Haven. Some present and former Yale students, for instance, were desperate to see in my stabbing evidence of the great dangers of New Haven's inner city. One student newspaper wrote about "New Haven's image as a dangerous town fraught with violence." A student reporter from another Yale paper asked if I didn't think the attack proved New Haven needs better police protection. Given the random nature of this assault — it could as easily have happened in wealthy, suburban Greenwich, where a friend of mine was held up at an ATM at the point of an assault rifle — it's tempting to dismiss such sentiments as typical products of an insular urban campus. But city-hating is central to today's political culture. Newt Gingrich excoriates cities as hopelessly pestilential, crime-ridden, and corrupt. Fear of urban crime and of the dark-skinned people who live in cities is the right's basic text, and defunding cities a central agenda item for the new congressional majority.

Yet in no small measure it was the institutions of an urban

community that saved my life last August 7. That concerned police officer who found Kerstin Braig and me on the street was joined in a moment by enough emergency workers to handle the carnage in and around the coffeehouse, and his backups arrived quickly enough to chase down my assailant three blocks away. In minutes I was taken to Yale–New Haven Hospital, less than a mile away — built in part with the kind of public funding so hated by the right. As I was wheeled into the ER, several dozen doctors and nurses descended to handle all the wounded.

By then my abdomen had swelled from internal bleeding. Dr. Gerard Burns, a trauma surgeon, told me a few weeks later that I arrived on his operating table white as a ghost; my prospects, he said, would have been poor had I not been delivered so quickly, and to an ER with the kind of trauma team available only at a large metropolitan hospital. In other words, if my stabbing had taken place in the suburbs, I would have bled to death.

"Why didn't anyone try to stop him?" That question was even more common than the reflexive city-bashing. I can't even begin to guess the number of times I had to answer it. Each time, I repeated that Silva moved too fast, that it was simply too confusing. And each time, I found the question not just foolish but offensive.

"Why didn't anyone stop him?" To understand that question is to understand, in some measure, why crime is such a potent political issue. To begin with, the question carries not empathy but an implicit burden of blame; it really asks "Why didn't *you* stop him?" It is asked because no one likes to imagine oneself a victim. It's far easier to graft onto oneself the aggressive power of the attacker, to embrace the delusion of oneself as Arnold Schwarzenegger defeating a multitude single-handedly. *If I am tough enough and strong enough, I can take out the bad guys.*

The country is at present suffering from a huge version of this same delusion. This myth is buried deep in the political culture, nurtured in the historical tales of frontier violence and vigilantism and by the action-hero fantasies of film and television. Now, bolstered by the social Darwinists of the right, who see society as an unfettered marketplace in which the strongest individuals flourish, this delusion frames the crime debate.

I also felt that the question "Why didn't anybody stop him?"

implied only two choices: Rambo-like heroism or abject victimhood. To put it another way, it suggests that the only possible responses to danger are the individual biological imperatives of fight or flight. And people don't want to think of themselves as on the side of flight. This is a notion whose political moment has arrived. In last year's debate over the crime bill, conservatives successfully portrayed themselves as those who would stand and fight; liberals were portrayed as ineffectual cowards.

"Why didn't anyone stop him?" That question and its underlying implications see both heroes and victims as lone individuals. But on the receiving end of a violent attack, the fight-or-flight dichotomy didn't apply. Nor did that radically individualized notion of survival. At the coffeehouse that night, at the moments of greatest threat, there were no Schwarzeneggers, no stand-alone heroes. (In fact, I doubt anyone could have "taken out" Silva; as with most crimes, his attack came too suddenly.) But neither were there abject victims. Instead, in the confusion and panic of life-threatening attack, *people reached out to one another.* This sounds simple, yet it suggests there is an instinct for mutual aid that poses a profound challenge to the atomized individualism of the right. Christina Koning helped the wounded Kerstin Braig to escape, and Kerstin in turn tried to bring Christina along. Anna and I, and then Martin and I, clung to each other, pulling one another toward the door. And just as Kerstin found me on the sidewalk rather than wait for help alone, so Richard and Emily, who had never met before, together sought a hiding place around the corner. Three of us even spoke with Silva either the moment before or the instant after being stabbed. My plea to Silva may or may not have been what kept him from pushing his knife all the way through my chest and into my heart; it's impossible to know what was going through his mind. But this impulse to communicate, to establish human contact across a gulf of terror and insanity, is deeper and more subtle than the simple formulation of fight or flight, courage or cowardice, would allow.

I have never been in a war, but I now think I understand a little the intense bond among war veterans who have survived awful carnage. It is not simply the common fact of survival but the way in which the presence of these others seemed to make survival itself possible. There's evidence, too, that those who try to go it alone suffer more. In her insightful study *Trauma and Recovery*, Judith Herman, a psychiatrist, writes about rape victims, Vietnam War veterans, political prisoners, and other survivors of extreme violence. "The capacity to preserve social connection . . . ," she concludes, "even in the face of extremity, seems to protect people to some degree against the later development of post-traumatic syndromes. For example, among survivors of a disaster at sea, the men who had managed to escape by cooperating with others showed relatively little evidence of post-traumatic stress afterward." On the other hand, she reports that the "highly symptomatic" ones among those survivors were "'Rambos,' men who had plunged into impulsive, isolated action and not affiliated with others."

The political point here is that the Rambo justice system proposed by the right is rooted in that dangerous myth of the individual fighting against a hostile world. Recently that myth got another boost from several Republican-controlled state legislatures, which have made it much easier to carry concealed handguns. But the myth has nothing to do with the reality of violent crime, the ways to prevent it, or the needs of survivors. Had Silva been carrying a handgun instead of a knife on August 7, there would have been a massacre.

I do understand the rage and frustration behind the crime-victim movement, and I can see how the right has harnessed it. For weeks I thought obsessively and angrily of those minutes on Audubon Street, when first the nameless woman in the window and then the security guard refused to approach me — as if I, wounded and helpless, were the dangerous one. There was also a subtle shift in my consciousness a few days after the stabbing. Up until that point, the legal process and press attention seemed clearly centered on my injuries and experience, and those of my fellow victims. But once Silva was arraigned and the formal process of prosecution began, it became *his* case, not mine. I experienced an overnight sense of marginalization, a feeling of helplessness bordering on irrelevance.

Sometimes that got channeled into outrage, fear, and panic. After arraignment, Silva's bail was set at $700,000. That sounds high, but just 10 percent of that amount in cash, perhaps obtained through some relative with home equity, would have bought his pretrial release. I was frantic at even this remote prospect of Silva walking the streets. So were the six other victims and our families. We called the prosecutor virtually hourly to request higher bail. It was eventually raised to $800,000, partly because of our complaints and partly because an arson charge was added. Silva remains in the Hartford Community Correctional Center awaiting trial.

Near the six-month anniversary of the stabbings I called the prosecutor and learned that in December Silva's lawyer filed papers indicating that he intends to claim a "mental disease or defect" defense. If successful, it would send him to a maximum-security hospital for the criminally insane for the equivalent of the maximum criminal penalty. In February the court was still awaiting a report from Silva's psychiatrist. Then the prosecution will have him examined by its own psychiatrist. "There's a backlog," I was told; the case is not likely to come to trial until the end of 1995 at the earliest. Intellectually, I understand that Silva is securely behind bars, that the court system is overburdened, that the delay makes no difference in the long-term outcome. But emotionally, viscerally, the delay is devastating.

Another of my bursts of victim consciousness involved the press. Objectively, I know that many people who took the trouble to express their sympathy to me found out only through news stories. And sensitive reporting can for the crime victim be a kind of ratification of the seriousness of an assault, a reflection of the community's concern. One reporter for the daily *New Haven Register,* Josh Kovner, did produce level-headed and insightful stories about the Audubon Street attack. But most other reporting was exploitative, intrusive, and inaccurate. I was only a few hours out of surgery, barely able to speak, when the calls from television stations and papers started coming to my hospital room. Anna and Martin, sent home to recover, were ambushed by a Hartford TV crew as they emerged from their physician's office, and later rousted from their beds by reporters from another TV station ringing their doorbell. The *Register's* editors enraged all seven victims by printing our home addresses (a company policy, for some reason) and running spectacularly distressing full-color photos of the crime scene, complete with the coffee bar's bloody windowsill.

Such press coverage inspired in all of us a rage it is impossible to convey. In a study commissioned by the British Broadcasting Standards Council, survivors of violent crimes and disasters "told story after story of the hurt they suffered through the timing of media attention, intrusion into their privacy and harassment, through inaccuracy, distortion and distasteful detail in what was reported." This suffering is not superficial. To the victim of violent crime the press may reinforce the perception that the world is an uncomprehending and dangerous place.

The very same flawed judgments about "news value" contribute significantly to a public conception of crime that is as completely divorced from the facts as a Schwarzenegger movie. One study a few years ago found that reports on crime and justice constitute 22 to 28 percent of newspaper stories, "nearly three times as much attention as the presidency or the Congress or the state of the economy." And the most spectacular crimes — the stabbing of seven people in an upscale New Haven coffee bar, for instance — are likely to be the most "newsworthy" even though they are statistically the least likely. "The image of crime presented in the media is thus a reverse image of reality," writes sociologist Mark Warr in a study commissioned by the National Academy of Sciences.

Media coverage also brings us to another crucial political moral: the "seriousness" of crime is a matter of race and real estate. This has been pointed out before, but it can't be said too often. Seven people stabbed in a relatively affluent, mostly white neighborhood near Yale University — this was big news on a slow news night. It went national over the AP wires and international over CNN's *Headline News.* It was covered by the *New York Times,* and words of sympathy came to New Haven from as far as Prague and Santiago. Because a graduate student and a professor were among those wounded, the university sent representatives to the emergency room. The morning after, New Haven Mayor John DeStefano walked the neighborhood to reassure merchants and office workers. For more than a month the regional press covered every new turn in the case.

Horrendous as it was, though, no one was killed. Four weeks later, a fifteen-year-old girl named Rashawnda Crenshaw was driving with two friends about a mile from Audubon Street. As the car in which she was a passenger turned a corner, she was shot through the window and killed. Apparently her assailants mistook her for someone else. Rashawnda Crenshaw was black, and her shooting took place in the Hill, the New Haven neighborhood with the highest poverty rate. No Yale officials showed up at the hospital to comfort Crenshaw's mother or cut through red tape. The *New York Times* did not come calling; there were certainly no bulletins flashed around the world on CNN. The local news coverage lasted just long enough for Rashawnda Crenshaw to be buried.

Anyone trying to deal with the reality of crime, as opposed to the fantasies peddled to win elections, needs to understand the complex suffering of those who are survivors of traumatic crimes, and the suffering and turmoil of their families. I have impressive physical scars: there is a broad purple line from my breastbone to the top of my pubic bone, an X-shaped cut into my side where the chest tube entered, a thick pink mark on my chest where the point of Silva's knife rested on a rib. On my back is the unevenly curving horizontal scar where Silva thrust the knife in and yanked it out, leaving what looks like a crooked smile. But the disruption of my psyche is, day in and day out, more noticeable. For weeks after leaving the hospital I awoke nightly agitated, drenched with perspiration. For two months I was unable to write; my brain simply refused to concentrate. Into any moment of mental repose would rush images from the night of August 7; or alternatively, my mind would not tune in at all. My reactions are still out of balance and disproportionate. I shut a door on my finger, not too hard, and my body is suddenly flooded with adrenaline and I nearly faint. Walking on the arm of my partner, Margaret, one evening I abruptly shove her to the side of the road; I have seen a tall, lean shadow on the block where we are headed and am alarmed out of all proportion. I get into an argument and find myself quaking with rage for an hour afterward, completely unable to restore calm. Though to all appearances normal, I feel at a long arm's remove from all the familiar sources of pleasure, comfort, and anger that shaped my daily life before August 7.

What psychologists call post-traumatic stress disorder is, among other things, a profoundly political state in which the world has gone wrong, in which you feel isolated from the broader community by the inarticulate extremity of experience. I have spent a lot of time in the past few months thinking about what the world must look like to those who have survived repeated violent attacks, whether children battered in their homes or prisoners beaten or tortured behind bars; as well as those, like rape victims, whose assaults are rarely granted public ratification.

The right owes much of its success to the anger of crime victims and the argument that government should do more for us. This appeal is epitomized by the rise of restitution laws — statutes requiring offenders to compensate their targets. On February 7 the House of Representatives passed, by a vote of 431 to 0, the Victim Restitution Act, a plank of the Contract with America that would supposedly send back to jail offenders who don't make good on their debts to their victims. In my own state, Governor Rowland recently proposed a restitution amendment to the state constitution.

On the surface it is hard to argue with the principle of reasonable restitution — particularly since it implies community recognition of the victim's suffering. But I wonder if these laws really will end up benefiting someone like me — or if they are just empty, vote-getting devices that exploit victims and could actually hurt our chances of getting speedy, substantive justice. H. Scott Wallace, former counsel to the Senate Judiciary Subcommittee on Juvenile Justice, writes in *Legal Times* that the much-touted Victim Restitution Act is "unlikely to put a single dollar into crime victims' pockets, would tie up the federal courts with waves of new damages actions, and would promote unconstitutional debtors' prisons."

I also worry that the rhetoric of restitution confuses — as does so much of the imprisonment-and-execution mania dominating the political landscape — the goals of justice and revenge. Revenge, after all, is just another version of the individualized, take-out-the-bad-guys myth. Judith Herman believes indulging fantasies of revenge worsens the psychic suffering of trauma survivors: "The desire for revenge . . . arises out of the victim's experience of complete helplessness," and forever ties the victim's fate to the perpetrator's. Real recovery from the cataclysmic isolation of trauma comes only when "the survivor comes to understand the issues of principle that transcend her personal grievance against the perpetrator . . . [a] principle of social justice that connects the fate of others to her own." The survivors and victims' families of the Long Island Rail Road massacre have banded together not to urge that Colin Ferguson be executed but to work for gun control.

*

What it all comes down to is this: What do survivors of violent crime really need? What does it mean to create a safe society? Do we need courts so overburdened by nonviolent drug offenders that Daniel Silvas go untried for eighteen months, delays that leave victims and suspects alike in limbo? Do we need to throw nonviolent drug offenders into mandatory-sentence proximity with violent sociopaths and career criminals? Do we need the illusory bravado of a Schwarzenegger film — or the real political courage of those LIRR survivors?

If the use of my picture on television unexpectedly brought me face to face with the memory of August 7, some part of the attack is relived for me daily as I watch the gruesome, voyeuristically reported details of the stabbing deaths of two people in California, Nicole Brown Simpson and Ronald Goldman. It was relived even more vividly by the televised trial of Colin Ferguson. (One night soon after watching Ferguson on the evening news, I dreamed that I was on the witness stand and Silva, like Ferguson, was representing himself and questioning me.) Throughout the trial, as Ferguson spoke of falling asleep and having someone else fire his gun, I heard neither cowardly denial nor what his first lawyer called "black rage"; I heard Daniel Silva's calm, secure voice telling me I killed his mother. And when I hear testimony by the survivors of that massacre — on a train as comfortable and familiar to them as my neighborhood coffee bar — I feel a great and incommunicable fellowship.

But the public obsession with these trials, I am convinced, has no more to do with the real experience of crime victims than does the anti-crime posturing of politicians. I do not know what made my assailant act as he did. Nor do I think crime and violence can be reduced to simple political categories. I do know that the answers will not be found in social Darwinism and atomized individualism, in racism, in dismantling cities and increasing the destitution of the poor. To the contrary: every fragment of my experience suggests that the best protections from crime and the best aid to victims are the very social institutions most derided by the right. As crime victim and citizen, what I want is the reality of a safe community — not a politician's fantasyland of restitution and revenge. That is my testimony.

WILLIAM STYRON

A Case of the Great Pox

FROM THE NEW YORKER

AMONG THE PERFORMANCES that helped make the movie *Casablanca* immortal was that of Claude Rains as the French police captain Louis Renault. Rains played the part with astringent urbanity and created a lasting model of the tough cop attractively humanized, Monsieur Nice Guy lurking behind the domineering swaggerer. I belong to the first of several generations that have fallen under the film's febrile romantic spell. By the late autumn of 1944 I had seen the film three times, and Rains seemed to me only slightly less crucial to its hypnotic unfolding than Bogart and Bergman. You may well imagine my amazement, then, when, in that wartime autumn, a veritable replica — the spitting image of Claude Rains — sat behind a desk in a doctor's office on the urological ward of the naval hospital at Parris Island, South Carolina. I stood at attention, looking down at him. A sign on the desk identified the doctor as "B. Klotz, Lieutenant Commander, Chief of Urology." I recall registering all sorts of impressions at once: the name Klotz, with its pathological overtone, and Klotz-Rains himself, duplicated — somewhat narcissistically, I thought — as he posed in prewar civvies in one of several framed photographs on the wall. The other photographs, completing a kind of triumvirate of authority, were of President Franklin D. Roosevelt and Admiral Ernest J. King, chief of naval operations. There was one notable difference between Klotz and Rains, aside from the doctor's white blouse instead of the gendarmerie kepi and tunic. It was that the actor, even when he was trying to be threatening, had a twinkly charm, a barely repressed bonhomie, while

Klotz appeared merely threatening. I knew that this was not the beginning of a beautiful friendship. That morning, Klotz sat silent for a moment, then came directly to the point. No elegant British vocables. In a flat mid-Atlantic accent, he said, "Your blood tests have been checked out, and they indicate that you have syphilis."

I remember my cheeks and the region around my mouth going numb, then beginning to tingle, as if my face had been dealt a brutal whack. Traumatic events powerfully focus the perceptions, leaving ancillary details embalmed forever in memory — in this case, the window just beyond Klotz's head, a frost-rimed pane through which I could see the vast asphalt parade ground swarming with platoon after platoon of marine recruits like me (or like me until the day before, when I was sent to the hospital), performing the rigorous choreography of close-order drill. Dawn had not yet broken, and the men moved in and out of the light that fell in bright pools from the barracks. Most of the platoons were marching with rifles, a drill instructor tramping alongside and screaming orders that I couldn't hear but that, up close, would have sounded like those of a foul-mouthed and hysterical madman. Other platoons remained still, at ease, shrouded in cigarette smoke, or exhaled breath, or both; it was a bitterly cold November. Beyond the parade ground and its clumps of marines in green field jackets were rows of wooden barracks. And beyond the barracks lay the waters of Port Royal Sound, roiled by an icy wind. All these things registered in my mind clearly, but at the same time they seemed to coalesce around a single word, uttered by the voice of Klotz: *syphilis.*

"You will remain on this ward indefinitely for further observation," Klotz continued. There was an unmistakably antagonistic tone in his voice. Most doctors in my past — the few I'd had contact with, anyway — had been chummy, avuncular, and genuinely if sometimes clumsily sweet-mannered. Klotz was of another breed, and he caused my stomach to go into spasm. I thought, What a prick. Before dismissing me, he ordered me to report to the duty pharmacist's mate, who would instruct me about the series of regulations I'd be subject to while on the ward, a regime Klotz referred to as "the venereal protocol." He then told me to return to my bed, where I would wait until further notice. I was wearing a blue hospital robe, in the pocket of which I had thrust a copy of one of the first paperback anthologies ever published, a volume that had kept me company for at least two years — *The Pocket Book of Verse*, compiled by an academic named M. Edmund Speare. My legs had an aqueous, flimsy feeling. I lurched back down the ward, still numb around the mouth, gripping the book with feverish desire, like a condemned Christian clutching a Testament.

I should say a word about the great pox, so named, in the sixteenth century, to distinguish the illness from smallpox. Although syphilis had been regarded, since the late fifteenth century, as a plague that would never in any real sense yield to the strategies of medical science, it had been dealt a sudden and mortal blow only a year or so before my diagnosis. It was one of medicine's most dramatic victories, like Jenner's discovery of a smallpox vaccine, or Pasteur's defeat of rabies. The breakthrough took place soon after American researchers — building on the work of Sir Alexander Fleming, who had discovered penicillin in the twenties, and Sir Howard Florey, who had developed a technique for producing the drug — found that a one-week course of the miraculous mold could wipe out all traces of early syphilis, and even certain late-stage manifestations of the illness. (Penicillin also had a devastating effect on the other major venereal scourge, gonorrhea, a single injection usually being sufficient to put it to rout.) Since mid-1943, the medical authorities of the American armed forces had ordered doctors in military hospitals around the globe to discontinue a syphilis treatment called arsphenamine therapy and to commence using penicillin as it became available. Arsphenamine — better known, variously, as salvarsan, 606, or the magic bullet — was an arsenic-based compound developed in 1909 by the German bacteriologist Paul Ehrlich. He discovered that his new drug (proved successful on the 606th try) could knock out syphilis without killing the patient; it was a remarkable advance after several hundred years during which the principal nostrum was mercury, a substance that worked capriciously, when it worked at all, and was for the most part as dangerous as the disease itself.

Because the disease sprang from the dark act of sex, syphilis was not a word uttered casually in the Protestant environment of my Virginia boyhood; the word raised eyebrows around America even when it was discreetly murmured in *Dr. Ehrlich's Magic Bullet,* a 1940 movie starring Edward G. Robinson, who I thought was a pretty convincing healer after his parts as a ruthless mobster. *Dr. Ehrlich's Magic Bullet* didn't make much of an impression on me; I doubtless was too young. But even if I had been older, I would probably not have realized that the movie failed to tell an essential truth. While the doctor's magic bullet was a vast improvement over the forlorn remedy of the past, his treatment was shown to be sadly insufficient; the drug rendered patients noncontagious, but it wasn't a very reliable cure, and the treatment required dozens of painful and costly injections over such a long period of time — often many months — that patients often became discouraged, and were consequently prone to relapses. So the epidemic suffered a setback but was not halted. It would take Alexander Fleming's sure-fire bactericidal fungus to produce the real magic. And I was in the vanguard of those victims upon whom this benison would descend. Or so it seemed, until, with a gradual dawning that was sickening in itself, I began to suspect that health was not so readily at hand.

As a diagnosed syphilitic, I had good cause to think passionately about penicillin during the interminable hours and days I spent in the Clap Shack, as such wards were known throughout the navy. But, from the first day following Dr. Klotz's announcement, I had the impression that I was a very special case. I was not an ordinary patient, whose treatment would follow the uneventful trajectory toward cure, but one who had been hurled into an incomprehensible purgatory where neither treatment nor even the possibility of a cure was part of my ultimate destiny. And this hunch turned out to be correct. From the outset, I was convinced not only that I had acquired the most feared of sexually transmitted diseases but that I would at some point keel over from it, probably in an unspeakable cellular mud slide or convulsion of the nervous system. As an early-blooming hypochondriac, a reader besotted with "The Merck Manual," I had a bit more medical savvy than most kids my age, and what my diagnosis actually portended made me clammy with dismay. I believed that I was beyond the reach of penicillin. I was sure that I was a goner, and that certainty never left me during the days that stretched into weeks of weirdly demoralizing confinement.

My bed was at the very end of the ward, and I had a view from two windows, at right angles to each other. From one window, I could see the sound, a shallow inlet of the Atlantic, on the edge of freezing; from the other I had a glimpse of a row of barracks not far away, and, between the barrack buildings, concrete laundry slabs, where marines bedeviled by the cold — I watched them shake and shiver — pounded at their near-frozen dungarees beneath sluiceways of water. What nasty little *Schadenfreude* I might have felt at their plight was dispelled by my own despair at having been separated from longtime buddies, whom I'd gone to college with, officer candidates like me — or like the person I had been before the onset of an illness that, because of its carnal origin and the moral shame it entailed, would prevent me from even thinking of becoming a lieutenant in the United States Marine Corps.

Winkler, the hospital corpsman who had checked me onto the ward, returned to bring me these tidings. No way, he said, that you can get a marine commission if you've had VD. He had other awful news, too, most of it bearing on my health. After escorting me to my sack and telling me where to stow my seabag, he told me — in answer to my bewildered "Why the hell am I here?" — that my Kahn test was so high it had gone off the chart. "It looks to me," he said with maddening whimsy, "like you've got a case of the great pox." When I asked him what a Kahn test was, he replied with a counter-question: Had I ever heard of a Wassermann reaction? I replied, Of course, every schoolboy knew about a Wassermann. A Kahn, Winkler explained, was almost the same as a Wassermann, only an improvement. It was a simpler blood test. And then, as I recalled the endless trips I'd made in past days to the regimental dispensary to verify the first routine test, and the vial after vial of blood extracted from my arm, I had a foreshadowing of the stern warrant that Dr. Klotz would serve up to me the following morning. I must have radiated terror, for I sensed a conscious effort by Winkler to make me feel better; his tactic was to try to cast me as one of the elite. At the moment, he told me, I was the only syphilitic on the ward. Most of the patients were

guys with the clap. And when, despondently, I asked him why
he thought victims of syphilis, as opposed to those with gonorrhea,
were such rarities, he came back with a theory that in my case
was so richly inconceivable that it caused me to laugh one of the
last spontaneous laughs I would laugh for a long time. "You can
catch the clap a lot easier than syphilis," he explained. "Syph you
really have to work at to contract." He added, with a hint of
admiration, "You must have been getting a new piece of ass every
day."

After my interview with Klotz, which had taken place very early,
before his regular morning rounds, I had a chance to sit next to
my bed and take stock of my situation while the other patients
slept. Winkler had explained the configuration of the ward. It was
a warehouse of genitourinary complaints. On one side of the ward
were a dozen beds occupied by clap patients. As a result of crowding in the clap section, I was lodged on the other side of the center
aisle, at the end of a row of patients whose maladies were not
venereal in origin. Most of these marines had kidney and bladder
disorders, primarily infections; there was a boy who had suffered
a serious blow to his kidney during one of the savage internecine
boxing matches that the drill instructors, virtually all sadists, enjoyed promoting during morning exercises. There was an unde-
scended testicle that Winkler said would never have got past the
first medical screening in the robust volunteer days, before the
draft allowed all sorts of misshapen characters into the Marine
Corps. The marine in the sack next to me, breathing softly, his face
expressionless in sleep's bland erasure, had just the day before
been circumcised by Dr. Klotz; the fellow had suffered from a
constrictive condition of the foreskin known as phimosis. Winkler's
last task the previous night had been to swaddle the guy's groin in
ice packs, lest nocturnal erections rip out the stitches — a mishap
that obviously could never happen to a Jew, said Winkler, who was
plainly New York Jewish, in a tone that was a touch self-satisfied.
As for the marines with the clap, Winkler pointed out that in most
cases this was not your standard garden-variety gonorrhea but an
intractable chronic condition that usually came about as a result
of the guys' refusing, out of shame or fear — and often out of
sheer indifference — to seek treatment, so that the invasive gono-
cocci began after time to wreak havoc in the prostate, or became

lodged in the joints as an exquisitely painful form of arthritis. Marines and sailors from up and down the Atlantic Coast came to this ward for what was possibly last-ditch therapy, since Klotz was known as the best doctor in the navy for handling such complications.

Later that first day, another hospital corpsman outlined to me the details of the venereal protocol. VD patients were in certain respects strictly segregated, both from their fellow sufferers on the ward and from the hospital population at large. Our robes were emblazoned with a large yellow V over the breast. When we went to the head, we were expected to use specially designated toilets and basins. Those of us who were ambulatory were to eat at mess hall tables reserved for our use. When we attended the twice-weekly movies at the base recreation center, we would be escorted in a separate group and then seated together in a section marked off by a yellow ribbon. I remember absorbing this information with queasiness, and then asking the corpsman why we were subject to such extraordinary precautions. While I was not unaware of the perils of VD, I had no idea that we posed such a threat. But as soon as I began to express my puzzlement, the corpsman explained that syphilis and gonorrhea were contagious as hell. True, most people got them only from sex, but one of those little microorganisms could infect through a tiny scratch. BUMED (as the Bureau of Medicine was called) was taking no chances; furthermore, he added, with a knowing look, Dr. Klotz "had a kind of personal fixation." This was an enigmatic, faintly sinister statement that became less opaque as time passed and Klotz became the dominant presence in my life.

As the only patient with syphilis, I was spared the short-arm inspection that was the centerpiece of Dr. Klotz's early rounds that morning and every morning at the stroke of six. At that hour, a bell in the ward jangled and the overhead lights came on in an explosion. The bedridden on my side of the aisle remained in their sacks. But in the interval of a minute or so between the flood of light and the appearance of Dr. Klotz, the dozen clap patients in the opposite row all scrambled to their feet and stood at ragged attention. There was usually a certain amount of wisecracking among these guys, along with self-dramatizing groans and reciprocal "Fuck you"s. Most of them were regulars, not effete college-bred recruits like me, and were five or ten years older than me. Their accents were about equally divided between Southern crack-er and Northeast working class. I soon understood that many of these die-hard cases had one thing in common: they were obses-sive. Romeos, fornicators of serene dedication whose commitment to sexual bliss was so wholehearted that they could keep up a flow of jokes even as the disease that such pleasure had cost them gnawed away at the inmost mucous membranes of the genitalia and tortured the joints of their wrists and knees.

I was amazed at this nonchalance, and also at their apparently incandescent libidos, especially since my own nineteen-year-old hormonal heat had plunged to absolute zero from the instant Dr. Klotz confirmed the nature of my problem; the word "syphilis" had made the very notion of sex nauseating, as if I were beset by some erotic anorexia. But the members of the gonorrhea faction quieted down as soon as Winkler or one of the other corpsmen shouted "Attention on deck!" and Klotz made his businesslike entrance through the swinging doors. It was important, Winkler had told me, that these bums be inspected as soon as they woke up, before heading to the urinals; from looking at the accumulated purulence called gleet, and checking the amount and consistency of the discharge, Klotz could determine how the treatment was proceed-ing. And so, accompanied by a litany — "Skin it back, squeeze it, milk it down" — intoned by the corpsman, Klotz would pass down the line of victims, making his evaluations. He didn't waste a word, and his manner was frostily judgmental, as if these rogues and whoremongers were unworthy of even so much as a casual "Good morning." Nor was his manner with me any less reproachful. As I stood stiffly at attention, I was thankful only that I didn't have to submit my dick to such a degrading scrutiny at that hour of the morning. During each tour of the ward, Klotz would glare at me briefly, ask the corpsman about my daily Kahn test — it remained at the highest (and therefore the most alarming) level, day in and day out — and then pass on to the non-venereal patients.

Early in the afternoon on that first day, however, Klotz did examine my penis. This was a procedure that I might ordinarily skip describing were it not for the monstrous effect that it had on my psychic balance, which had already been thrown badly out of whack. For it was Klotz's judgment regarding my penile history that helped crystallize my belief that I was doomed. I was summoned to his office, and, as I stood in front of him, he checked through my medical-record book and brusquely asked some routine questions. Any history of syphilis in my family? (What a question!) No, I lied. In the preceding weeks or months had I experienced any unusual rash or fever? I had not. Any swelling in the groin? No. Had I noticed any unusual growth on my penis? This would be a hard, painless ulcer, he said, called a chancre. I knew what a chancre was, everyone had heard about chancres (corpsmen were even known as "chancre mechanics"); but I had not seen one. During Klotz's interrogation, I held in view the eye-level portrait of a solemn, resolute Franklin D. Roosevelt, who kept looking back at me. I was grateful for the reassuring gaze of this surrogate father, my perennial president, the only one I had ever known, and I steadfastly stared back at him through most of Klotz's examination, which he carried out with cold, skeletal fingers.

He twisted my penis, not very gently, gave it an unnecessary squeeze or two and turned it upside down. I recall thinking that, though it had known various attitudes, it had rarely been upside down. Then he bade me to look down, saying that he had discovered, on the underside, a scar. Chancres leave scars, he murmured, and this looked like a chancre scar. I glanced down and, indeed, discerned a scar. A tiny reddish outcropping. Since the chancre had been painless, he added, it had come and gone, without my ever noticing its presence, leaving only that small scar. He seemed to have put aside, at least for the moment, his customary distaste. He said that the chance of my being infected by non-venereal contact was astronomically remote. The toilet seat was a myth. Syphilis usually created distinct symptoms, he went on — first the chancre, then, later, the fever and the rash — but quite often these symptoms never appeared, or appeared so insubstantially that they went unnoticed. Klotz surprised me by saying something that, in the midst of his dispassionate exegesis, sounded almost poetic: "Syphilis is a cruel disease." And then, after a brief silence during which I became aware that he was constructing an answer to the question that sheer fright kept me from asking, he declared, "What happens in the end is that syphilis invades the rest of the body."

He paused and concluded, before dismissing me, "We're going to have to keep you here and figure out just how far it's advanced."

I went back to my bed at the end of the ward and, in the cold midday light, lay down. You weren't supposed to lie on a bed in daytime, but I did anyway. The hospital was a venerable wooden structure, warm, even overheated, but I felt nearly frozen, listening to the windows creaking and banging in the bluster of an Atlantic gale. The sex maniacs with the clap across the aisle were noisily trading lewd adventures, and I gradually sank into a stupor of disbelief, beyond the consoling power of even *The Pocket Book of Verse*, which had saved me in many a lesser crisis but was plainly beyond the scope of this one.

Its history "is unique among great diseases," the medical historian William Allen Pusey wrote, "in that it does not gradually emerge into the records of medicine as its character becomes recognized, but appears on the stage of history with a dramatic suddenness in keeping with the tragic reputation it has made; as a great plague sweeping within a few years over the known world."

This observation, made in the early part of the century, has an all too painful resonance today, and it might be worthwhile to compare syphilis with our present pandemic. Unlike AIDS, syphilis was not invariably fatal, despite its extremely high rate of mortality. This may have been its only saving grace, depending on whether death is viewed as a blessing preferable to the terrible and irreversible damage the disease is capable of inflicting on the body and the mind. After the introduction of Dr. Ehrlich's not-so-magic bullet, and especially after penicillin's knockout blow, syphilis lost much of its capacity to evoke universal dread. Still, for various reasons, it remained a horror, aside from the fact that no one wants to be infested by millions of *Treponema pallidum,* the causative microbe, whose wriggling corkscrew can reach the bone marrow and spleen within forty-eight hours of infection, and produce a persistent malaise, rashes, ulcerous skin lesions, and other debilitating symptoms. For one thing, there was the stigma — and I mean the appalling stigma arising from anything at all suggesting misbehavior as we young people traversed the parched sexual landscape of the thirties and forties.

I've mentioned that the word itself was taboo. Among nice people, "syphilis" was uttered sotto voce, if at all, and only occasionally found its way into print. "Social disease" and "vice disease" were the usual substitutes. When I was in grade school, the only time I recall the word's catching my eye was when I happened upon it in a medical pamphlet. I asked my teacher, a maiden lady of traditional reserve, what it meant. She instantly corrected my pronunciation, but her cheeks became flushed, and she didn't answer my question. Her silence made me guess at something wicked. And wicked it was in those prim years. For most of its existence in the Anglo-Saxon world, syphilis, as AIDS has often done, stained the people who contracted it with indelible disrepute.

But there was a far graver trouble: the sheer awfulness of the malady itself. Even after medical intervention, and treatment with penicillin, there could still be dire complications. No cure was absolutely foolproof. And my obsession — that syphilis had taken possession of my system and had commenced its inroads, penetrating tissues and organs, which thus had already suffered the first effects of dissolution — grew more fixed every day as I dragged myself through Dr. Klotz's venereal protocol. I wore my yellow V stoically, and soon got used to going to the mess hall and the movies in a segregated herd. I had plenty of time to brood about my condition, since there were no organized activities for patients on the ward. I kept wondering why I was not being treated. If penicillin could work its miracle, why was it not being used? It only aggravated my distress to think that the disease, for reasons beyond my understanding, had reached a stage where treatment was useless, and was merely waiting for some fatal resolution. I had to blot out thoughts like these. Mostly, I hung around the area near my bed, sitting on a camp stool and reading books and magazines from the small hospital library. I returned hesitantly to *The Pocket Book of Verse*, to Keats and A. E. Housman and Emily Dickinson and *The Rubáiyát of Omar Khayyám*.

Except during morning rounds, I never saw Dr. Klotz. My only actual duty was to bare my arm once a day for the Kahn test, which invariably showed the same results: "Off the chart," as Winkler had said. I grew friendly with Winkler, who seemed drawn to me, most likely because I'd been to college and he'd had two years at CCNY before Pearl Harbor. One of his generosities was a loan of a little red Motorola portable radio, which I kept tuned to the Savannah station and its news about the war. The bulletins added weight to the black and anxious mood that each afternoon crept over me — a mood that I would recognize only years later as the onset of a serious depression.

Just before I entered the hospital, marines had stormed ashore on a remote Pacific island called Peleliu and had met with "heavy Japanese resistance" — a common Pentagon euphemism to describe our troops' being slaughtered. What I heard on the radio was unsettling enough, but the news chiefly reminded me of the doubtfulness of my own future. For at least three years, I had lived with the bold and heady ambition of becoming a marine lieutenant; to lead troops into combat against the Japs had been an intoxicating dream. A sexually transmitted disease was not permissible for an officer candidate, Winkler had ruefully pointed out to me — not even if he was cured, so ugly was the moral blotch — and thus I began to realize that the microorganisms seething like termites within me were destroying my vision of honor and achievement as effectively as they were laying waste to my flesh. But this regret, wrenching as it was, I could somehow deal with. What was close to intolerable — beyond the disgrace, beyond the wreckage it would make of my military ambition — was the premonition, settling around me like a fog bank, of absolute physical ruin. A death-in-life, for example, like that of my Uncle Harold, whose case was a harrowing paradigm of the malady, and of the disaster it could inflict.

He was my mother's younger brother, and at twenty-seven, during the Great War, he had gone overseas as an infantry corporal in the Rainbow Division. During the Saint-Mihiel offensive, he had suffered a bad shrapnel wound in the leg, and was mustered out in 1918 to his hometown, in western Pennsylvania, where he married, had a son, and settled down to the life of a businessman. Sometime in the late twenties, he started to display odd behavioral symptoms: he woke at night in the grip of nightmares, and began to have terrifying hallucinations. He complained of anxiety and had almost daily episodes of feverish agitation, which caused him to speak of suicide. He told anyone who would listen that he was tormented by memories of the war, the agony of men and animals, the carnage. After he disappeared for a week and was finally found in a dingy Pittsburgh hotel room, fifty miles away, his wife made him seek medical help. At a veterans' aid clinic a diagnosis was made of extreme psychosis as a result of the violence of war. The syndrome in those years was generally known as shell shock. My uncle was sent to the mental unit of the veterans' hospital in Perry Point, Maryland, and there he remained for the rest of his life.

I recall visiting Uncle Harold with my mother and father once when I was a young boy, before the war. We were going to New York, and the visit was planned as a side trip on our way from Virginia. I had never seen him, except as a figure in photographs taken years earlier: a cheery kid with prominent teeth, like my mother's, and flashing, exuberant eyes. I had been fascinated by Uncle Harold, the war hero, and he had taken on for me an almost mythic shape. My mother was devoted to him, and, as a sedulous eavesdropper, I couldn't help but absorb all the captivating details of his dramatic life: the flaming battle for Saint-Mihiel that killed more than four thousand Americans, his letters describing the savagery of combat, his painful recovery in a convalescent facility behind the front, the breakdown in Pennsylvania, his sad confinement. By the time we turned up at the veterans' hospital on a luminous June day, I was looking forward excitedly, though with a touch of squirmy disquiet, to meeting my shell-shocked uncle. I don't remember whether my parents prepared me for the encounter, but it was certainly not like anything I might have imagined, and I think that they, too, may not have been ready for such an apparition.

The male attendant who brought him outside to greet us on the lawn seemed to feel the need to urge him along, as he tottered toward us in his army-issue robe and slippers, with gentle but persistent prods to the back. This probably made him look even more helpless and disoriented than he actually was, but he was plainly a soul without a mooring. I was alarmed by his shambling gait and his empty gaze; I couldn't reconcile the old face so bony and desiccated, and the balding skull and trembling hands with the vivid boy of the pictures. Most awful to me was the moment when he mechanically embraced my mother and whispered, "Hello, Edith." It was the name of their older sister.

We remained there on the hospital lawn for perhaps no more than an hour, amid the debris of a messy picnic. Uncle Harold said almost nothing as we sat on a bench, and the monosyllables my mother coaxed from him had a softly gargled incoherence. I knew that this was a scene I couldn't continue to witness, and I turned away in misery from my uncle and his drowned, sweetly musing brown eyes, and from the sight of my mother clutching his palsied hand, squeezing it over and over in some hopeless attempt at comfort or connection.

I later learned the truth about Uncle Harold. My father did not tell me until several years after my mother died, when I was eighteen or so, and presumably old enough to absorb the dread secret that our kinsman had been suffering not from shell shock but from syphilis. My father was a candid and sophisticated man, but even he had an awkward time telling me the truth. After the shock wore off, the knowledge that my uncle was still alive — that, as was so often the case, the microbes, rather than quickly murdering their host, held him hostage while they continued their leisurely depredations — made me ache inside. The great pox could dwell in a body for decades. By the time he was sent to the veterans' hospital he was most likely afflicted by late syphilis; according to my father, the disease was acquired after his marriage and the birth of his only child. There was never a hint that either my aunt or my cousin, a boy whom I spent many summers with, had been tainted by the illness. But who knew exactly when he had got it? Somehow the plague had entered him. It had been a quiet case, but viciously malignant, beyond reach of the magic bullet or any other medical stratagem, and at the time of our visit he was succumbing to forms of neurosyphilis that devastate the brain and the spinal cord. The spirochetes had wrought a vegetative madness.

I thought a lot about Uncle Harold during my stay on the ward. Especially at night, in the dark, with Winkler's little radio pressed against my ear, trying to distract myself with the Artie Shaw or Glenn Miller tunes I could capture from the ether, I'd have a moment of sudden, heart-stopping panic and my uncle would draw ineluctably near. I could sense him in his hospital robe, silent, standing somewhere close by among the sleeping marines, a stooped figure whose presence portended a future I dared not think about.

*

While on a trip through Europe in 1760, Giovanni Casanova, that tireless gadabout, cocksman, and celebrity hound, stopped at Ferney to pay a visit to Voltaire. There seems to be no record of the two superstars talking about syphilis, but it would have been a fitting topic, given its perennial fashionableness, and if they had spoken of it their attitude, in all likelihood, would have had a mocking overtone. Voltaire never let the horrid nature of the illness obtrude upon his own lighthearted view of it — he wrote wittily about the great pox in Candide — and throughout Casanova's memoirs there are anecdotes about syphilis that the author plainly regards as excruciatingly funny. Making sport of it may have been the only way in which the offspring of the Enlightenment could come to grips with a pestilence that seemed as immutably fixed in history as war or famine. In a secular age, gags were appropriate for an inexplicable calamity that in olden times was regarded as divine retribution. Previous centuries had seen people calling on God for help, and God had not answered.

The disease first swept like a hurricane over Europe during the period of Columbus's voyages (whether Columbus and his crew were responsible for importing syphilis from the West Indies is disputed by scholars, but it seems a strong possibility), and took an exceptionally virulent form, often killing its victims in the secondary, or rash-and-fever, stage, which most people in later epochs (including me) weathered without harm. In its congenital mode, it was particularly disfiguring and malevolent, which increased the terror. No wonder that the Diet of Worms, the same assembly that condemned Martin Luther for heresy, issued a mandate declaring that the "evil pocks" was a scourge visited upon mankind for the sin of blasphemy.

But it was the doctrine of original sin, falling upon both Catholics and backslid Presbyterians like me, that made the sufferers of syphilis pay a special price in moral blame unknown to those who acquired other diseases. This was particularly true in the early Victorian era, when a return to faith, after a long time of frivolous impiety, was coupled with a return to the Pauline precept that the act of sex is an act of badness — absolute badness more often than not, exceeding all other abominations. This connection with sexuality gave syphilis, in a puritanical culture, its peculiar aura of degradation. As Susan Sontag has shown in *Illness as Metaphor*, her study of the mythology of disease, all the major illnesses have prompted a moralistic and punitive response, and have given rise to entire theoretical systems based on phony psychologizing. The bubonic plague implied widespread moral pollution; tuberculosis was the product of thwarted passion and blighted hopes, or sprang from "defective vitality, or vitality misspent"; out of emotional frustration or repression of feeling has come the curse of cancer, whose victims are also often demonically possessed. As I have discovered firsthand, mental disorders may be the worst, inviting suspicion of inborn feebleness. In such views, the disease itself expresses the character of the victim. Syphilis, however, has suffered a different stigma, one that has been of a singularly repellent sort. It has reflected neither feebleness nor misspent vitality nor repression of feeling — only moral squalor. In recent years, AIDS has been similarly stigmatized, despite extensive enlightenment. But in square, churchgoing America at the time of my diagnosis a syphilitic was regarded not as a sexual hobbyist whose pastime had got out of hand — in other words, with the ribald tolerance Voltaire would have brought to the circumstance — but as a degenerate, and a dangerously infectious one at that. Doctors are, of course, supposed to be free of such proscriptive attitudes, but there are always some who are as easily bent as anyone else by religion or ideology. Klotz was one of these, and, while I'm sure that he was only doing his duty in tracking my history, his temper was chillingly adversarial. Also, he was, in my case, guilty of an act of omission that unalterably stamped him as a doctor who hated not the disease but its victims.

As the wintry days and nights in the hospital wore on, and the Kahn tests continued to show my blood serum swarming with spirochetes, and I worried myself into a deeper and deeper feeling of hopelessness, I brooded over my past sex life, which seemed to me a paltry one, at least numerically speaking. By what improbable mischance had I sealed my doom? Even in those repressed years of the Bible Belt South, to have had at nineteen only three partners, two of whom I'd met in boozy mayfly matings already dimming in memory, scarcely made me feel like a red-hot lover, much less the randy alley cat generally associated with the disease. Still, as Winkler pointed out, even though syphilis was not as widespread as the clap, all it took was one quick poke in the wrong partner's hole and a man could be done for. Whose hole, then, and when? The actual encounters were all so recent, and together so few, that I could easily let my mind pounce on each one, trying to figure out which specific grappling had permitted the *T. pallidum* to begin its infestation.

On a bright morning, as I sat on my camp stool plunged into one of these self-lacerating reveries, Winkler came up with a mournful look to say that he was sorry but my Kahn remained "highly reactive." Then he announced that Dr. Klotz — finally, after many days — wished to see me, to take my case history. Was I religious? he asked. When I said that I wasn't but asked him why he wanted to know, the corpsman rolled his eyes, then declared, "He's got a kind of narrow-minded view of things." And he added, as he had once before, that it was all part of a "personal fixation."

As I look back on that time, I can see that Klotz, whatever the complexities of his motivation, had a need to squeeze the most out of the vindictive rage against syphilis already prevailing in the armed forces — one that mirrored the broader abhorrence in American society. While Klotz was doubtless not typical of navy doctors, or the medical profession in general, he was working well within the pious and cold-blooded restraints regarding sexually transmitted diseases that had prevailed in the navy for many years. During the First World War, President Wilson's secretary of the navy, Josephus Daniels, a godly North Carolinian if there ever was one, made history in a small way by banishing alcohol from officers' wardrooms and elsewhere on naval ships and bases, thereby bringing to an end an ancient and cherished custom. But at least this created no mortal danger. In his intolerance of carnality, Daniels ruled against a proposal that sailors and marines be given free access to condoms, and thus became responsible for unnumbered venereally related illnesses and deaths. Apart from his own belief, Klotz was obviously the inheritor of a tradition with a firm root in Southern Christian fundamentalism.

In presenting my case history to Klotz that morning, I had to describe my relations with a girl and two older women. Klotz referred to these as "exposures." While the doctor took notes, I told him that, almost exactly two years before, I had lost my virginity for two dollars in a walkup hotel room in Charlotte, North Carolina. I was a college freshman, and the woman was about thirty-five. In answer to his question whether I had used protection, I replied that I thought so but could not be sure, since I had drunk too much beer for clear memory. I then went on to the next exposure. (What I did not describe to Klotz was the interminable anxiousness of waiting in the dismal little hotel lobby while my anesthetized classmate, a raunchy dude from Mississippi who had initiated our debauch, preceded me for what seemed hours with Verna Mae, which was what she called herself. Nor did I tell the doctor that my memory of Verna Mae was of an immensely sad and washed-out towhead in a stained slip and dirty pink slippers, who raised a skinny arm and took my two dollars with such lassitude that I thought she might be ill; nor did I recount being nearly ill myself, from apprehension and a stomach-churning disbelief at the idea that what I'd awaited with anxious joy since the age of twelve was about to happen, something so unbearably momentous that I barely registered the words when, sliding the two bucks into her brassiere, she said in a countrified voice, "I sure hope you don't have to take as long as that friend of yours.")

The second exposure was a girl, age eighteen, a college sophomore I'll call Lisa Friedlaender. (It is a reflection on the aridity of sexual life in the forties — even, or I should say especially, on college campuses — that there was a gap of nearly a year and a half between Verna Mae and Lisa.) I told Klotz that I had met Lisa, who was from Kew Gardens, New York, at a college in Danville, Virginia, the previous spring. I was by then enrolled in the marine V-12 program at Duke and had traveled up to Danville for a weekend. That weekend, we had had intercourse (a word that made me writhe but that Klotz encouraged), and we had had it many times after that, both protected and unprotected, on my weekend leaves in April and May. She went home to Kew Gardens for summer vacation, and when she returned to Danville we resumed intercourse, having weekend sex until I was sent here to Parris Island. I was certain that Lisa was not the source of the disease, I went on, since I was only her second partner and she was from a proper middle-class Jewish background, where the acquiring of such an illness was unlikely. (I had often wondered how a proper middle-class Southern lad like me had come to deserve anyone as angelic as my ripe and lively Lisa, with her incontinent desires, which matched mine and were the real reason, though I didn't tell Klotz, for our frequent lack of protection: we were fucking so continuously and furiously that I ran out of condoms. My native Wasp folklore, which tended to idealize asthenic, inaccessible blondes, had not prepared me for this dark and lusty creature; we began rolling around on a moonlit golf green within two hours of our first meeting. I didn't tell this to Klotz either, though Klotz the moral inquisitor at one point tipped his hand by demanding, "Were you in love?" To this I had no reply, having a sense that such a question really implied a policy decision. What of course was impossible to make Klotz understand about love was that if you were not yet twenty, and were a marine eventually headed for the Pacific, who shared with your brothers the conviction that you would never see twenty-one, or a girl ever again, and if the delirium of joy you felt the first time Lisa Friedlaender's nipples sprang up beneath your fingertips was love, then you were probably in love.)

My last exposure was a woman named Jeanette. Age about forty. I told Klotz that I was with a fellow marine in Durham when we picked up old Jeanette and a female friend at a barbecue joint one night during the past August. They were both employees of the Liggett & Myers factory, where they worked on an assembly line making cigarettes. I had intercourse with Jeanette only once, unprotected. (The subtext in the case was largely anaphrodisiac amnesia. As with Verna Mae, the beer I had consumed made memory a slide show of incoherent instants: a wobbling ramble through the dark, collapsing together on the cold ground of a Baptist churchyard, hard by a tombstone, and inhaling the sweet raw smell of tobacco in the frizzy hair of Jeanette, who had just come off the night shift. I remembered nothing of the act itself, but for some obscure reason, as my confession spilled forth, the recollection of the carton of Chesterfields she had given me left a taste of sadness.)

When I finished, Klotz fiddled with his notes for a moment, then said, "You betrayed the girl, didn't you?"

I nodded my miserable agreement but made no reply.

"Has it occurred to you that you might have infected her?"

Again I nodded, for the possibility of having passed on the contagion had lingered in my mind for days, jabbing me with fierce self-reproach.

"You probably were infected by the prostitute in Charlotte or the woman in Durham," the doctor said. "Syphilis is prevalent among lower-class Southern white women. That's why it's dangerous to go roaming around in the wrong places if you can't practice abstinence."

I couldn't respond to this. Although I was smothered with regret, I felt no remorse and was not about to say that I was sorry.

"There's no way now of knowing which woman infected you. Suppose you now just write a letter to that girl and tell her that she may have been exposed to syphilis. You should also tell her to get tested right away and have appropriate treatment."

I recall trying to retrieve, at that moment, some serene boyhood memory, a foolish escapade, any innocent event that might let me float above this anguish, but Klotz was too quick to permit me the solace.

"Nature has a way of compensating for nearly every reckless thing we do," he said.

A day or two after my interview with Klotz, the hospital corpsmen began to place tacky Christmas ornaments up around the ward; they painted a silver "Noël" on the glass of the door and hung a hideous plastic trumpet-tooting angel from the central light fixture. The same day, I noticed that my gums were beginning to bleed. There had been some irritation before, but I had ignored the tenderness. This was serious bleeding. It was not "pink toothbrush," a symptom employed to help advertise Ipana, the hot toothpaste of the day. It was a slight but constant seepage of blood into my mouth, one that made me aware of the sweetish taste throughout the day and left a red stain on my handkerchief whenever I blotted it away. I could tell it was aggravated by smoking — but I kept steadily puffing. My gums had become raw and spongy, and that night the act of toothbrushing created a crimson cataract. I developed a feverish, cruddy feeling. I was terrified, but I kept my alarm to myself. The spirochetes were on the attack. There were countless ways the disease could make itself known, and I calculated that this was just one of them. When I told Winkler about my new trouble, he seemed puzzled, but said I should pay a visit to the hospital dentist, who might at least be able to relieve some of my distress. The dental officer was a dour man, trapped in routine, who offered neither comfort nor explanation; he did, however, swab out my mouth with a florid and repulsive lotion called gentian violet, a vial of which he gave me for daily application. It was an absurdity, a flimsy barrier against the onrushing ruin.

Days passed in a kind of suspended monotony of fear. Meanwhile, the weight of hopelessness, bearing down on my shoulders with almost tactile gravity — I thought of a yoke in the animal, burdened-down sense — had become a daily presence; I felt a suffocating discomfort in my brain. Sitting on a camp stool next to my bed, remote from the other marines, I began to withdraw into the cocoon of myself. The sex-demented clap patients, jabbering about cunt and pussy, magnified my despair. I lost my appetite. Outside my window, marines marched in the distance on the asphalt drill field, exhaling clouds of frigid breath. The glittering white inlet of the ocean rolled endlessly eastward like Arctic tundra. At night, after lights out, I began to prowl the ward, padding about in anxiety until, returning to the stool, I would sit and stare at the expanse of water, dim in the starlight and seemingly frozen solid. What a blessed relief it would be, I thought, to lie down and be encased in that overcoat of ice, motionless, without sensation and, finally, without care, gazing up at the indifferent stars.

I had kept up a busy correspondence during my early Marine Corps days. Fat envelopes, lots of them with addresses in familiar handwriting, envelopes of various colors and lengths (some with a not yet stale hint of perfume), were gifts that guys in the service awaited with greedy suspense, like children at Christmastime. I kept my seabag stuffed with reread letters, and Lisa Friedlaender had written to me often at Parris Island. In that buttoned-up age, it was probably not all that common for letter-writing lovers to express their craziness in steamy strophes, but Lisa had a gifted hand. Her remembrances to me were generously graphic and sometimes astonishing; she was way ahead of her time. But those were letters I could not read any longer; the very packet, which I kept tied up with string, was cursed with a vile pathology. Nor, despite Klotz's order, could I bring myself to write to Lisa.

Instead, I addressed myself to another problem: that of maintaining my composure in the face of a final, insupportable outrage. One morning, Winkler brought me two letters — one from Lisa (I put it away, unread) and one from my stepmother. Only two years before, my father had married, for reasons I was never able to fathom, an ungainly, humorless, pleasure-shunning middle-aged spinster, and the antipathy we felt for each other had been almost as immediate as our differences were irreconcilable. She was an observant Christian, curiously illiberal for an Episcopalian, while I had proudly begun to announce my skepticism and my fealty to Camus, whose "Le Mythe de Sisyphe" I'd read laboriously but with happiness in French at Duke, and whose principles, when I outlined them to her, she deemed "diabolical." I thought her a prig, she considered me a libertine. She was a teetotaler, I drank — a lot. Once, frankly baiting her while a little crocked, I praised masturbation as a universal delight, and she denounced me to my father as a "pervert." (I *had* gone too far.) She was educated, intelligent, and that made her bigotry the more maddening. I preserved a chill truce with the woman because of my love for my misguided father. She was a teacher of nursing, actually quite a good one — even, in a way, distinguished (onetime district president of the Graduate Nurses Association) — and therein lay another contradiction: nurses, like doctors, were supposed to be free of the moralism that drove her to write a pious letter meant to make me writhe on the rack of my dereliction.

How appalled she and my father were, she wrote, at the terrible news. (I had sent them a letter in which I was disingenuous enough to say that I had been sidelined with "a little blood problem," an evasion she immediately scented.) The only serious blood problem I could have was one of the malignant diseases like leukemia, and I plainly didn't have that, given my remarks about feeling in such good health. She went on to predict, in her chilly, professional way, that in all likelihood I could be cured by the new antibiotics, *provided* the disease had not progressed too far into the CNS (central nervous system, she explained helpfully, adding that the damage could be fearful and irreversible). Shifting into the spiritual mode, she informed me that one could only pray that the illness had not yet been invasive. She had no intention of judging me, she announced (pointing out that there was, of course, a Higher Judge), but then she asked me to look back on my recent way of life and ponder whether my self-indulgent behavior had not led to this — the words remain ineffaceable to this day — "awful moment of truth." Finally, she hoped I would be reassured that, in spite of her disapproval of the conduct that had brought me to this condition, she cared for me very, very much.

In pondering these events of fifty years ago, I've never felt seriously betrayed by memory — most of the moments I've recreated are so fresh in my mind that they have the quality of instant replay — but I know that I've been slightly tricked from time to time, and I've had to adjust my account of these events. That memory could be a clever deceiver was neatly demonstrated, when I began finishing this chronicle, by my "Medical History" — a little manual, faintly mildewed, with pages the color of a faded jonquil — that surfaced among my Marine Corps mementos while I was searching for something else. This is the standard medical record that accompanies every marine throughout his career. While my lapses were minor, the "Medical History" showed me to be quite off the mark about certain matters of chronology. I could have sworn, for example, that I was still in the hospital until a few days before Christmas, when in fact I had been returned to duty by then; the awful Yuletide decorations I recalled must have adorned not the ward but my barracks, considerably later. Also, I have written of those apparently unceasing Kahn tests, a ritual that kept me tense with fear. It seems impossible to me now that I was not bled daily — as I awaited the results, I recall, I was nearly devoured by anxiety — but the "Medical History" shows that there were only five of these procedures in the course of a month. I'm fascinated by the fact that my tendentious memory lured me into exaggerating the number of times I experienced this torture.

But Dr. Klotz and his behavior have remained mysterious. The "Medical History" reveals only his routine notations and a final, meticulously clear signature. I think Klotz has compelled my attention (slightly this side of obsession) all these years because, to put it simply, he was frightening. He represented, in his bloodless and remote way, the authority figure that most people dread encountering but so often do meet face to face: the dehumanized doctor. In later years, I would come to know many exemplary physicians, but also more than one for whom my memory of Klotz provided a creepy prototype. I never fathomed Klotz's need to chasten those whom he conceived to be sexual hoodlums among all the miserable, unwell marines who showed up for his help. I wasn't alone among these miscreants. Was it religion (as Winkler had hinted) that gave him his hangup, some narrow faith that had provided him with a view of sex that was as fastidious as it was harsh? Perhaps, as Winkler also suggested without contradiction, it wasn't religion so much as that "personal fixation." If that was true, it was a fixation animated by cruelty. Nothing else would account for his failure to tell me from the outset that there was a possibility that I didn't have syphilis at all.

Several days after I received the letter from my stepmother, I was summoned to the end of the ward by Winkler, who led me into the tiny office of Klotz's second-in-command. Everyone called him Chief. He was a chief pharmacist's mate named Moss, a sandy-haired, overweight Georgian with a smoker's hack, good-heartedness written all over him. As in the past, he put me quickly at ease. He was an old man by my standards, probably thirty-five, or older. I had come to trust and respect most of the medical corpsmen, like Moss and Winkler, who held out to sick marines a kind of spontaneous sympathy beyond the capacity of the doctors, or at least of the doctors I knew. And the feeling I had for Moss was not so tepid as mere respect; it was more like awe, for the year before he had taken part in the bloody landing at Tarawa, that slaughterhouse beyond compare, and there he had risked his big ass to save the lives of more than one marine, winning a commendation in the process. Marines and sailors were traditionally hostile to each other, but one could only regard someone like Moss with admiration, or even love, as I think I did that day. A couple of times before, he'd come by my sack to chat, always cheery and plainly eager to calm my fear, a good ol' boy from Valdosta, a bearlike, rather untidy guy who plainly conceived medicine to be a tender enterprise not entirely bound by technology. He told me that Lieutenant Commander Klotz had departed on Christmas leave but had left him instructions about my case. My case, in fact, was contained in a file on Moss's desk, and he said he wanted to talk to me about it.

First off, I didn't have syphilis.

I recall thinking, despite my apostasy, of Revelation: "He that overcometh shall inherit all things . . ."

"I had a talk on the phone with the chief dental officer," Moss said. "He told me what he told Dr. Klotz. Your Vincent's disease cleared up almost immediately. Just a couple of old-fashioned applications of gentian violet. Smile for me, boy."

I smiled widely, a big shit-eating grin, and Moss heaved with laughter. "Damned if you don't look like a Ubangi. Gentian violet. That old standby. The man who could find a way to get the violet out of gentian violet would make him some money."

"Tell me something, Chief," I said as Moss motioned me to sit down. "If I get the situation correctly, my Kahn test has gone to negative. Zero. If this is true, and I guess it is, what's the connection?"

"Let me ask you a question," said Moss. "Did you ever have this condition — it's also called trench mouth — anytime before?"

I reflected for an instant, then said, "Yes, I believe I did, come to think about it. Up at Duke. There were these marines for a while — I was one of them — complaining about this inflammation in the mouth, and bleeding. I had it badly for some time, then it seemed to go away. I didn't think about it anymore. There was talk about it being spread by the unclean water we used to wash our trays in the mess hall. So tell me, Chief, what's the connection?"

Moss patiently explained to me what appeared to be the reason for Klotz's misdiagnosis, and what in fact had been behind the entire fiasco. He said that Klotz, after receiving the dental report, had written in my record book, "Dentist discharged patient for his Vincent's." That morning, Moss, out of curiosity, had followed up on this notation, checking out various venereal-disease manuals and textbooks for further enlightenment, and had discovered that the principal causes for false serological positives in the Kahn test were leprosy and yaws. (Jesus, I thought, leprosy and yaws!) There was no chance of my having acquired either of those exotic, largely hot-climate diseases, Moss went on. Klotz must have ruled them out all along, convinced (or, I thought, wanting to be convinced) that I had syphilis in a more or less advanced form. Moss said that Vincent's disease was mentioned as a possible cause, but a rare one — so rare that Klotz must have discounted it. I learned from Moss that despite Vincent's preposterously gruesome official name — acute necrotizing ulcerative gingivitis — the inflammation of the mouth itself was relatively mild and easy to treat, often with a single application of the powerful bactericide gentian violet to the gums. One of the causative organisms in Vincent's was another busy little spirochete (Moss spelled it out, *Treponema vincentii*), and it had shown up in my blood tests. With me there had been a recurrence of symptoms. "It's a good thing you finally went to the dentist," Moss concluded, "or you might have been here forever."

As much as I felt a friend and ally in the Chief, I still hesitated to state my case against Klotz, upon whom my rage and loathing grew more grimly focused, if that was possible, at every item Moss disclosed. I didn't want to strain the rapport I had with Moss by attacking his superior — for all I knew, though only God would know why, he might hold Klotz in high esteem. At the same time, the evil suspicions that sprang to mind as Moss murmured his litany of details had actually begun to make me a little nauseated, taking the glow off my euphoria, and there was no way I could let the suspicions rest. I said, "You know, Chief, he wanted to find the worst things. I guess I was too intimidated to tell him I've had that little scar on my dick all my life." Then I said, "Anyway, what this means is that Dr. Klotz could have told me there was a possibility of a false positive. A possibility." I paused. "But he didn't do that."

"That's really right." Moss didn't wait an extra beat, uttering the words with a soft, rising inflection that had a distinct edge of contempt and carried its own conviction of wrongdoing. I knew then that he was on my side.

"He's read what you've read," I persisted. "He knew about Vincent's disease. He could have run me through that drill, couldn't he? But he didn't do that, either. He could have spared me a lot of misery. He could have given me some hope — "

"That's really right."

"What is this jerk's problem, Chief?"

Klotz was on leave. Within a few hours I would return to the barracks and the drill field, just another healthy recruit thrust back into the maw of the war machine. I would never see the Chief again. Under the circumstances, it would be safe for Moss to give voice to whatever innermost feelings he had toward Klotz. But Moss was too much the wise old salt, too professional and, doubtless, too loyal to an honorable code to go that far. Still, I sensed a comradely affinity, and it was denunciation enough, a spiritual handclasp, when he squinted at me and said, "He was punishin' you, boy, punishin' you."

As I left the hospital that day, I looked forward to the ordeal that my phantom illness had interrupted. Mean corporals with taut shiny scalps and bulging eyes would be at me again, poking their swagger sticks into my solar plexus, ramming their knees up my butt, calling me a cocksucker and a motherfucking sack of shit, terrorizing me with threats and drenching me with spittle and hatred, making my quotidian world such a miasma of fright that each night I would crawl into my bed like an invalid seeking death, praying for resurrection in another life. After that, there was the bloody Pacific, where I would murder and perhaps be murdered. But those were horrors I could deal with; in that gray ward I was nearly broken by fears that were beyond imagining.

Late that afternoon, I trudged past the drill field in the waning light, packing my seabag on my shoulder, hefting a load that seemed pounds lighter than it had a month before. At the far end of the field, a platoon of marines was tramping across the asphalt, counting in cadence, a chorus of young voices over which one voice, the drill instructor's, soared in a high maniacal wail. In some undiscoverable distance, faint yet clear, a band played "The Colonel Bogey March," that jauntily sad evocation of warfare, its brassy harmonies mingling triumph and grief. The music made me walk along with a brisk step, and I felt it hurrying me toward a future where though suffering was a certainty, it wore a recognizable face.

I had just enough time for a stop at the PX, to stock up on cigarettes and candy bars. The candy was a clandestine indulgence I felt I owed myself, and couldn't resist. Nor could I resist, along with the Baby Ruths, buying a postcard showing a photograph of marines grinning insincerely as they performed calisthenics, and the caption "Greetings from Parris Island." Toward Christmas I addressed it to my stepmother, and scribbled:

Dear Old Girl,

My frantic, obsessive copulations produced not syphilis but trench mouth. (Escaped from the Clap Shack in time to celebrate the birth of our Lord and Savior.)

Much love, Bill

Biographical Notes

JOAN ACOCELLA writes on dance, literature, and other arts for journals including *The New Yorker, The New York Review of Books,* and the *Wall Street Journal.* The author of *Mark Morris* (1993), she is currently editing the new English edition of the diary of Vaslav Nijinsky. She received a doctorate in comparative literature from Rutgers University in 1984 and was a Guggenheim Fellow in 1994–1995.

NICHOLSON BAKER has published four novels — *The Mezzanine* (1988), *Room Temperature* (1990), *Vox* (1992), and *The Fermata* (1994) — as well as an autobiographical-critical work about John Updike entitled *U and I* (1991). His most recent book is an essay collection, *The Size of Thoughts* (1996). He has written for *The New Yorker, The Atlantic Monthly, The New York Review of Books,* and *Esquire.* He is married, with two children.

JULIE BAUMGOLD, author of *Creatures of Habit* (Knopf, 1993), has just completed her second novel, *The Angelfish Club.* As "Mr. Peepers, Esq.," she writes the back page of *Esquire* magazine and longer features when life permits. For many years her articles appeared in *New York, Esquire,* and other magazines. She was born in New York around the corner from where she now lives with her husband and teenage daughter. She met Elvis Presley when he opened the International Hotel in Las Vegas. She was overcome at the time, but she thinks he may have kissed her.

JANE BROX is the author of *Here and Nowhere Else: Late Seasons of a Farm and Its Family* (Beacon Press), which received the 1996 L. L. Winship/PEN New England Award. Her essays have appeared in *The Georgia Review, The Gettysburg Review, The Ohio Review, Orion, Salamander,* and others. She is the recipient of grants from the National Endowment for the Arts and the Massachusetts Cultural Council. "Influenza 1918" is from a collection of essays-in-progress on the interweaving of industrial and agricultural life in the lower Merrimack River valley at the turn of the century. She lives on her family's farm in northeastern Massachusetts.

WILLIAM CRONON is the Frederick Jackson Turner Professor of History, Geography, and Environmental Studies at the University of Wisconsin, Madison. He is an American historian specializing in environmental history, frontier history, and the history of the American West. His books include *Changes in the Land: Indians, Colonists, and the Ecology of New England* (1983), which won the Francis Parkman Prize; *Nature's Metropolis: Chicago and the Great West* (1991), which won the Bancroft Prize and was one of three finalists for the Pulitzer Prize in American history; and, most recently, *Uncommon Ground: Toward Reinventing Nature* (1995), in which a version of this essay appears. He is a past president of the American Society for Environmental History.

STANLEY CROUCH has been an actor, playwright, jazz critic, essayist, and television commentator. He was a staff writer for the *Village Voice* from 1979 to 1988 and has published work in *Harper's Magazine*, the *New York Times*, *Vogue*, *Downbeat*, the *Amsterdam News*, and *The New Republic*, where he is a contributing editor. In 1991 he was the recipient of the Whiting Writers' Award, and in 1993 received both the Jean Stein Award from the American Academy of Arts and Letters and a MacArthur Foundation grant. Two collections of essays, *Notes of a Hanging Judge* and *The All-American Skin Game*, were nominated for awards in criticism by the National Book Critics Circle. He is currently working on a biography of Charlie Parker and a novel, *First Snow in Kokomo*.

GERALD EARLY is the Merle S. Kling Professor of Modern Letters and director of Afro-American Studies at Washington University in St. Louis. He won the 1994 National Book Critics Circle Award in criticism for *The Culture of Bruising: Essays on Prizefighting, Literature, and Modern American Culture* (Ecco Press).

JOSEPH EPSTEIN, the editor of *The American Scholar*, is the author of eleven books, the most recent of which are *Pertinent Players* (1993) and *With My Trousers Rolled* (1995). His essays and stories appear in *The Hudson Review*, *Commentary*, *The New Criterion*, and *The New Yorker*.

JAMES FENTON, a regular contributor to *The New York Review of Books*, is professor of poetry at Oxford University. His books include two collections of poetry, *Children of Exile: Poems 1968–1984* and *Out of Danger*, and a volume of reportage, *All the Wrong Places*.

IAN FRAZIER writes essays and books of nonfiction. A collection of his humor pieces, *Coyote v. Acme,* appeared in June of 1996. He now lives in Missoula, Montana.

AMITAV GHOSH is the author of three novels: *The Circle of Reason, The Shadow Lines,* and most recently *The Calcutta Chromosome.* He has also published two books of nonfiction, *In an Antique Land* and *Dancing in Cambodia.* *The Circle of Reason* was awarded the Prix Médicis Étrangère in 1990. *The Shadow Lines* won the annual award of the Indian Academy of Literature in 1991. His articles and reviews have appeared in *The New Yorker, Granta,* and *The New Republic.* He received his doctorate in anthropology from Oxford and currently teaches at Columbia University.

ADAM GOPNIK writes about pretty much everything, pretty much always for *The New Yorker,* where he has been a staff writer since 1987. Right now he writes most often about life in Paris, where he moved last fall with his wife and son, in the hope that someone there might show him how to write a book.

GORDON GRICE'S essays, poems, and short stories have appeared in *Harper's Magazine, Cimarron Review, The Chattahoochee Review,* and other magazines and journals. "The Black Widow" is part of a book-in-progress about the wildlife of the High Plains. Grice is a reporter and columnist for a newspaper.

CHANG-RAE LEE'S first novel, *Native Speaker,* was awarded the 1995 PEN/Hemingway Award. He teaches creative writing and literature at the University of Oregon, Eugene, where he lives with his wife, Michelle. He is at work on a second novel as well as a book of essays on his family.

JOYCE CAROL OATES is the author, most recently, of the story collection *Will You Always Love Me?* and the novel *We Were the Mulvaneys* (both Dutton). She is the 1996 recipient of the PEN/Malamud Award for Achievement in the Short Story.

MARY OLIVER is well known as a poet; her volume *American Primitive* received the Pulitzer Prize in poetry in 1983, and *New and Selected Poems* won the National Book Award in 1992. *Blue Pastures* (1994) was her first book of essays. A volume of her poems, *West Wind,* will be published in 1997, and she is currently working on a second book of essays, *Winter Hours.* She is a member of the faculty at Bennington College.

DARRYL PINCKNEY, a frequent contributor to *The New York Review of Books,* is the author of a novel, *High Cotton.*

JONATHAN RABAN is author of *Soft City, Arabia, Old Glory, Foreign Land, Coasting, For Love & Money, Hunting Mister Heartbreak,* and *God, Man, and Mrs. Thatcher.* He is editor of *The Oxford Book of the Sea.* His latest book, *Bad Land: An American Romance,* will be published in the fall of 1996. His essays have appeared in *Harper's Magazine, The New Republic, Granta, The New York Review of Books, Outside, Vogue, Travel-Holiday,* and *Esquire.* He is at present working on a book provisionally titled *Passage to Juneau.*

BRUCE SHAPIRO is a journalist and contributing editor of *The Nation.* He has won numerous awards for reporting and editorial writing, and was a 1995 National Magazine Award finalist in essays and criticism. He was cofounder and editor of *Haymarket,* a Chicago political monthly, and the *New Haven Independent,* a weekly newspaper noted for its innovative urban community journalism. He has taught at New York University and Yale University. He is writing a book on crime, to be published in 1997 by Basic Books. He lives in New Haven, Connecticut.

WILLIAM STYRON's autobiography, *Darkness Visible: A Memoir of Madness,* was published in 1990. He is the author of the novels *The Confessions of Nat Turner, Lie Down in Darkness, The Long March, Set This House on Fire, Sophie's Choice,* and *A Tidewater Morning,* and a book of essays, *This Quiet Dust.* He has been the recipient of the American Academy Rome Prize, Howells Medal, Pulitzer Prize, American Book Award, Cino del Duca Prize, and the National Medal of Arts. He is a member of the American Academy of Arts and Letters and the American Academy of Arts and Sciences, and is the commander of both the Order of Arts and Letters and the Legion of Honor in France.

Notable Essays of 1995

Selected by Robert Atwan

MICHAEL VENTURA
Heart of Darkness, Heart of Light.
Los Angeles Times Magazine,
January 15.

WYN WACHHORST
The Dream of Spaceflight:
Nostalgia for a Bygone Future.
The Massachusetts Review, Spring.

MCKENZIE WARK
Fresh Maimed Babies. *Transition,*
Spring.

WILLIAM W. WARNER
The Night of the Whales. *The
Wilson Quarterly,* Spring.

GEORGE WATSON
The Art of Disagreement: C. S.
Lewis (1898–1963). *The Hudson
Review,* Summer.

PAUL WEST
Rooms in College. *The Iowa Review,*
Spring/Summer.

CIA WHITE
What We Will Call Nature. *The
Kenyon Review,* Summer/Fall.

FLORENCE WILLIAMS
Polygamy in America. *The North
American Review,* March/April.

JACK WINTER
How Sweet It Wasn't. *The Atlantic
Monthly,* June.

S. L. WISENBERG
That Old-Time Religion. *Indiana
Review,* Spring.

NAOMI WOLF
Our Bodies, Our Souls. *The New
Republic,* October 16.

STEVE YARBOROUGH
Arms: A Personal Essay. *Michigan
Quarterly Review,* Summer.